*Strictly conforming to the NCERT syllabus for 2008 and guidelin...
CBSE and other Educational Boards.*

COMPOSITE MATHEMATICS

FOR MIDDLE CLASSES

CLASS VIII

(NCERT SYLLABUS)

S.K. GUPTA
Principal (Retd.)
Birla Vidya Mandir
Nainital

ANUBHUTI GANGAL
M.A. (Gold Medallist) M.Ed.
Formerly, Senior Faculty Member
The Daly College, Indore
Birla Vidya Mandir, *Nainital*

S. CHAND & COMPANY LTD.

(AN ISO 9001: 2000 COMPANY)

RAM NAGAR, NEW DELHI -110 055

S. CHAND & COMPANY LTD.

(An ISO 9001 : 2000 Company)

Head Office : 7361, RAM NAGAR, NEW DELHI - 110 055
Phones : 23672080-81-82, 9899107446, 9911310888;
Fax : 91-11-23677446

Shop at: schandgroup.com; E-mail: schand@vsnl.com

Branches :

- 1st Floor, Heritage, Near Gujarat Vidhyapeeth, Ashram Road, **Ahmedabad**-380 014. Ph. 27541965, 27542369, ahmedabad@schandgroup.com
- No. 6, Ahuja Chambers, 1st Cross, Kumara Krupa Road, **Bangalore**-560 001. Ph : 22268048, 22354008, bangalore@schandgroup.com
- 238-A M.P. Nagar, Zone 1, **Bhopal** - 462 011. Ph : 4274723. bhopal@schandgroup.com
- 152, Anna Salai, **Chennai**-600 002. Ph : 28460026, chennai@schandgroup.com
- S.C.O. 2419-20, First Floor, Sector- 22-C (Near Aroma Hotel), **Chandigarh**-160022, Ph-2725443, 2725446, chandigarh@schandgroup.com
- 1st Floor, Bhartia Tower, Badambadi, **Cuttack**-753 009, Ph-2332580; 2332581, cuttack@schandgroup.com
- 1st Floor, 52-A, Rajpur Road, **Dehradun**-248 001. Ph : 2740889, 2740861, dehradun@schandgroup.com
- Pan Bazar, **Guwahati**-781 001. Ph : 2738811, guwahati@schandgroup.com
- Sultan Bazar, **Hyderabad**-500 195. Ph : 24651135, 24744815, hyderabad@schandgroup.com
- Mai Hiran Gate, **Jalandhar** - 144008 . Ph. 2401630, 5000630, jalandhar@schandgroup.com
- A-14 Janta Store Shopping Complex, University Marg, Bapu Nagar, **Jaipur** - 302 015, Phone : 2719126, jaipur@schandgroup.com
- 613-7, M.G. Road, Ernakulam, **Kochi**-682 035. Ph : 2381740, cochin@schandgroup.com
- 285/J, Bipin Bihari Ganguli Street, **Kolkata**-700 012. Ph : 22367459, 22373914, kolkata@schandgroup.com
- Mahabeer Market, 25 Gwynne Road, Aminabad, **Lucknow**-226 018. Ph : 2626801, 2284815, lucknow@schandgroup.com
- Blackie House, 103/5, Walchand Hirachand Marg , Opp. G.P.O., **Mumbai**-400 001. Ph : 22690881, 22610885, mumbai@schandgroup.com
- Karnal Bag, Model Mill Chowk, Umrer Road, **Nagpur**-440 032 Ph : 2723901, 2777666 nagpur@schandgroup.com
- 104, Citicentre Ashok, Govind Mitra Road, **Patna**-800 004. Ph : 2300489, 2302100, patna@schandgroup.com

First Edition 1979 with subsequent Editions and Reprints.
First CBSE Edition 2006
Reprint with Corrections 2006
Reprint with Corrections 2007
Revised Edition As per New Syllabus 2008

ISBN : 81-219-2743-9

Code : 14B 521

PRINTED IN INDIA
By Rajendra Ravindra Printers (Pvt.) Ltd., 7361, Ram Nagar, New Delhi-110 055
and published by S. Chand & Company Ltd., 7361, Ram Nagar, New Delhi-110 055.

PREFACE TO THE REVISED EDITION

It gives us great satisfaction to be able to bring out this new version of our old Maths Today series for classes VI to VIII. The old series has been rehashed and redesigned incorporating the current global trends and International practices and the latest philosophy and policy of providing stress free education.

The **salient features** of this book are :

1. **It follows strictly the latest syllabus presented and released by the NCERT in 2005 and its guidelines.**

2. All the mathematical concepts have been presented in a very simple and lucid form and loading the course content with unnecessary and irrelevant details has been avoided. The approach and orientation is to lay a strong foundation for the students through adequate emphasis on the fundamentals.

3. It aims at complete involvement of the pupils in the learning process. The emphasis throughout the text is on a student-centered performance and in keeping with the sprit of the new curriculum, **activity approach** is freely used relating the mathematical concepts to real life situations.

4. Every unit is introduced by a motivating paragraph or story.

5. To facilitate easy and better understanding each unit is divided into a number of subunits with short & separate practice exercises on each subunit.

6. **An attempt has been made to expose the children more fully to the 'Why' of various operations and made abundant use of diagrams, illustrations, cartoons, tables and charts to stimulate the student's interest in the subject and to clarify difficult concepts.**

7. Colour panels are used throughout as a teaching aid to emphasize important terms and relationships and present useful tips.

8. The problems given in the book avoid tedious calculations and help in strengthening the understanding of basic principles honing the faculties of thinking and reasoning.

9. Each chapter contains a **unit summary of key points** at the end. It reviews the main points covered and helps the students in remembering them.

10. **Mental maths** exercises have been given to help the students acquire speed and sharpen their intellect.

11. **Historical Notes, Quizzes , Just For Fun, Puzzles and Enrichment Material** offer further intellectual challenge to sharp students and help them not only to maintain their interest in the subject and widen their horizon of knowledge but would also be of immense help in preparing for such competitions such as Mathematics Olympiad at various levels.

It is hoped that this book will meet more than adequately, the needs of the students they are meant for. Any suggestions for the improvement of the book would be most welcome and gratefully acknowledged.

AUTHORS

(iii)

A NOTE FOR THE TEACHERS

Dear friends,

We feel happy to be able to present for your perusal and consideration the new and thoroughly revised and updated edition of our **Composite Mathematics Series for classes VI, VII and VIII**. It has no doubt been possible as a result of the motivation and feedback received in the form of valuable comments, suggestions and criticism from the learned teachers. We strongly feel that a textbook howsoever good it may be is only a tool to help teachers to teach effectively. It is the teacher and only the teacher who is competent to decide his/her teaching strategies in the classroom and is the best judge of how to use the textbook to meet the special needs of his/her class. It is earnestly hoped that this series will be able to supplement your efforts effectively to create interest of your pupils in the subject and make the study of mathematics interesting and enjoyable and gain mastery over the subject.

Howsoever best one performs or creates there is always scope for improvement.

We would be very happy rather grateful to receive your comments, appreciation/criticism and suggestions for further improvement of the books.

With regards

Yours sincerely,
Authors

A NOTE FOR STUDENTS

Wishing you the best in life, dear students. You are the best judge to evaluate whether the book you are studying fulfills your needs and satisfies your thirst for knowledge or not. Please do not hesitate to write individually through the publishers or directly to the authors at the following address if you come across any discrepancies or if you have some suggestions to make.

S.K. Gupta
502/8, Rajendra Nagar
Dehra Dun 248001
Tel.: 2758862, 2752453
e.mail:anubhutigangal@hotmail.com.

SYLLABUS

UNIT–I NUMBER SYSTEM
(50 hrs)

(i) *Rational Numbers*
- Properties of rational numbers. (including identities). Using general form of expression to describe properties.
- Consolidation of operations on rational numbers.
- Representation of rational numbers on the number line.
- Between any two rational numbers there lies another rational number (Making children see that if we take two rational numbers then unlike for whole numbers, in this case you can keep finding more and more numbers that lie between them.
- Word problem (higher logic, two operations, including ideas like area).

(ii) *Powers*
- Integers as exponents.
- Laws of exponents with integral powers.

(iii) *Squares, Square roots, Cubes, Cube roots*
- Square and Square roots.
- Square roots using factor method and division method for numbers containing (a) no more than total 4 digits and (b) no more than 2 decimal places.
- Cubes and cubes roots (only factor method for numbers containing at most 3 digits).
- Estimating square roots and cube roots. Learning the process of moving nearer to the required number.

(iv) *Playing with numbers*
- Writing and understanding a 2 and 3 digit number *in generalized form* ($100a + 10b + c$, where a, b, c can be only digit 0-9) and engaging with various puzzles concerning this. (Like finding the missing numerals represented by alphabets in sums involving any of the four operations.) Children to solve and create problems and puzzles.
- Number puzzles and games.
- Deducing the divisibility test rules of 2, 3, 5, 9, 10 for a two or three-digit number expressed in the general form.

UNIT–II ALGEBRA
(20 hrs)

(i) *Algebraic Expressions*
- Multiplication and division of algebraic exp.(Coefficient should be integers)
- Some common errors (e.g. $2 + x \neq 2x$, $7x + y \neq 7xy$)
- Identities $(a \pm b)^2 = a^2 \pm 2ab + b^2$, $a^2 - b^2 = (a - b)(a + b)$
- Factorisation (simple cases only) as examples the following types $a(x + y)$, $(x \pm y)^2$, $a^2 - b^2$, $(x + a).(x + b)$
- Solving linear equations in one variable in contextual problems involving multiplication and division (word problems) (avoid complex coefficient in the equations).

UNIT–III RATIO AND PROPORTION
(25 hrs)

- Slightly advanced problems involving applications on percentages, profit and loss, overhead expenses, Discount, tax.
- Difference between simple and compound interest (compounded yearly up to 3 years or half-yearly up to 3 steps only), Arriving at the formula for compound interest through patterns and using it for simple problems.
- Direct variation – Simple and direct word problems
- Inverse variation – Simple and direct word problems
- Time and work problems– Simple and direct word problems

UNIT–IV GEOMETRY
(40 hrs)

(i) *Understanding shapes:*

- Properties of quadrilaterals – Sum of angles of a quadrilateral is equal to 360^0 (By verification)
- Properties of parallelogram (By verification)

(i) Opposite sides of a parallelogram are equal,

(ii) Opposite angles of a parallelogram are equal,

(iii) Diagonals of a parallelogram bisect each other. [Why (iv), (v) and (vi) follow from (ii)],

(iv) Diagonals of a rectangle are equal and bisect each other,

(v) Diagonals of a rhombus bisect each other at right angles.

(vi) Diagonals of a square are equal and bisect each other at right angles.

(ii) Representing 3-D in 2-D

- Identify and Match pictures with objects [more complicated e.g. nested, joint 2-D and 3-D shapes (not more than 2)].
- Drawing 2-D representation of 3-D objects (Continued and extended)
- Counting vertices, edges and faces and verifying Euler's relation for 3-D figures with flat faces (cubes, cuboids, tetrahedrons, prisms and pyramids)

(iii) Construction:

Construction of Quadrilaterals:

- Given four sides and one diagonal
- Three sides and two diagonals
- Three sides and two included angles
- Two adjacent sides and three angles

UNIT–V MENSURATION
(15 hrs)

(i) Area of a trapezium and a polygon.

(ii) Concept of volume, measurement of volume using a basic unit, volume of a cube, cuboid and cylinder.

(iii) Volume and capacity (measurement of capacity).

(iv) Surface area of a cube, cuboid, cylinder.

UNIT–VI DATA HANDLING
(15 hrs)

(i) Reading bar-graphs, ungrouped data, arranging it into groups, representation of grouped data through bar-graphs, constructing and interpreting bar-graphs.

(ii) Simple Pie charts with reasonable data numbers.

(iii) Consolidating and generalising the notion of chance in events like tossing coins, dice etc. Relating it to chance in life events. Visual representation of frequency outcomes of repeated throws of the same kind of coins or dice.

Throwing a large number of identical dice/coins together and aggregating the result of the throws to get large number of individual events. Observing the aggregating numbers over a large number of repeated events. Comparing with the data for a coin. Observing strings of throws, notion of randomness.

Introduction to graphs   **(15 hrs)**

PRELIMINARIES:

(i) Axes (Same units), Cartesian Plane.

(ii) Plotting points for different kind of situations (perimeter vs length for squares, area as a function of side of a square, plotting of multiples of different numbers, simple interest vs number of years etc.)

(iii) Reading off from the graphs

- Reading of linear graphs
- Reading of distance vs time graph.

CONTENTS

CONTENTS

UNIT I : NUMBER SYSTEM

1. Rational Numbers

1.1 Revision

(Whole numbers, Integers and Rational numbers)

From your study in the earlier classes, you know that as a result of our wish to find a suitable number system, we extended the number system several times. We first considered the system of **natural numbers** or **counting numbers** (positive or non-negative integers) :

$$N = \{1, 2, 3, 4, 5, ...\}$$

To this we added zero and designated the new system as the system of whole numbers :

$$W = \{0, 1, 2, 3, 4, 5, ...\}$$

Then we extended this system to include the negative of each positive integer and obtained the complete system of integers :

$$I \text{ or } Z = \{... - 3, - 2, - 1, 0, 1, 2, 3, ...\}$$

The positive integers are 1, 2, 3, ...

The negative integers are – 1, – 2, – 3, ...

Zero is neither positive nor negative.

Next fractions were considered and we developed the system of rational numbers :

$$Q = \{\text{Numbers which can be expressed in the form}$$

$$\frac{p}{q}, \text{ where } p \text{ and } q \text{ are integers and } q \neq 0\}.$$

P is called the **numerator** and q is called the **denominator.**

All these are rational numbers : $- 7, \frac{8}{4}, 0, 73\%, 3.84, \sqrt{25}, \sqrt[3]{-8}$

But a number as $\frac{5}{0}$ or $-\frac{6}{0}$ is not defined and hence is not a rational number.

> **Note : 1.** Every natural number n can be written as $\frac{n}{1}$ which is a rational number, but a rational number as $\frac{1}{n}$ need not be a natural number.
>
> **2.** Zero is a rational number, as it can be expressed as $\frac{0}{q}$ where q is any non-zero integer.
>
> **3.** Every fraction is a rational number, but a rational number need not be a fraction. A number like $\frac{5}{-6}$ is a rational number but not a fraction.

1.2 Positive and Negative Rational Numbers

1. A rational number is said to **positive** if its numerator and denominator are both positive or both negative.

For example : $\dfrac{3}{4}, \dfrac{-29}{-110}$

2. A rational number is said to be **negative** if its numerator and denominator are such that, one of them is a positive integer and the other is a negative integer.

For example : $\dfrac{-9}{43}, \dfrac{78}{-215}$

1.3 Equivalent Rational Numbers

If $\dfrac{p}{q}$ is a rational number and n is a non-zero integer, then $\dfrac{p}{q} = \dfrac{p \times n}{q \times n}$.

For example : $\dfrac{-2}{5} = \dfrac{(-2) \times 2}{5 \times 2} = \dfrac{(-2) \times 3}{5 \times 3} = \dfrac{(-2) \times 4}{5 \times 4} = ...$

i.e., $\dfrac{-2}{5} = \dfrac{-4}{10} = \dfrac{-6}{15} = \dfrac{-8}{20} = ...$

All these rational numbers are *equivalent rational numbers*.

Also,

If $\dfrac{p}{q}$ is a rational number, and n is a common divisor of p and q, then $\dfrac{p}{q} = \dfrac{p \div n}{q \div n}$.

For example : $\dfrac{-32}{48} = \dfrac{(-32) \div 2}{48 \div 2} = \dfrac{-16}{24}, \dfrac{-32}{48} = \dfrac{(-32) \div 4}{48 \div 4} = \dfrac{-8}{12},$

$\dfrac{-32}{48} = \dfrac{(-32) \div 8}{48 \div 8} = \dfrac{-4}{6}, \dfrac{-32}{48} = \dfrac{(-32) \div 16}{48 \div 16} = \dfrac{-2}{3},$

As we can see $\dfrac{-2}{3}$ is in its **lowest terms**. It is also called the *standard form*.

1.4 Standard Form of a Rational Number

A rational number is said to be in standard form if it is in its lowest terms.

To express a given rational number in standard form :

Step I. *If already not so, make the denominator of the given rational number positive.*

Step II. *Divide both the numerator and denominator by their HCF.*

For example : To express $\dfrac{45}{-70}$ in standard form, proceed as follows :

Step I. *Make denominator positive :* $\dfrac{45}{-70} = \dfrac{-45}{70}$

Step II. *Divide both numerator and denominator by the HCF. HCF of 45 and 70 is 5.*

$\therefore \qquad \dfrac{-45}{70} = \dfrac{(-45) \div 5}{70 \div 5} = \dfrac{-9}{14}.$

1.5 Comparison of Rational Numbers

> **Method I.** **1.** *Express each rational number with a positive denominator.*
> **2.** *Find the L.C.M. of the positive denominators.*
> **3.** *Express each of the given rational numbers with this LCM as common denominator.*
> **4.** *The number having greater numerator is greater.*

Ex. 1. *Compare :* $\dfrac{-8}{9}$ *and* $\dfrac{-4}{5}$.

Sol. $\dfrac{-8}{9} = \dfrac{-8}{9}$ and $\dfrac{4}{-5} = \dfrac{-4}{5}$ | Express in standard form

LCM of 9 and 5 is $9 \times 5 = 45$.

$\therefore \quad \dfrac{-8}{9} = \dfrac{-8 \times 5}{9 \times 5} = \dfrac{-40}{45}, \dfrac{-4}{5} = \dfrac{-4 \times 9}{5 \times 9} = \dfrac{-36}{45}$ | Express each rational number with LCM as denominator

Since $-40 < -36 \quad \therefore \dfrac{-40}{45} < \dfrac{-36}{45} \Rightarrow \dfrac{-8}{9} < \dfrac{-4}{5} \Rightarrow \dfrac{-8}{9} < \dfrac{4}{-5}$. | Compare the numerators

> **Method II.** *If a and b are integers and c and d are positive integers, then*
>
> $\dfrac{a}{c} > \dfrac{b}{d}$, *if and only if $ad > bc$.*
>
> $\dfrac{a}{c} < \dfrac{b}{d}$, *if and only if $ad < bc$.*
>
> $\dfrac{a}{c} = \dfrac{b}{d}$, *if and only if $ad = bc$.*
>
> $\dfrac{a}{c} \bowtie \dfrac{b}{d}$
> *a and b are any integers c and d are positive integers.*

Ex. 2. *Compare :* $\dfrac{9}{-11}$ *and* $\dfrac{5}{-17}$.

Sol. $\dfrac{9}{-11} = \dfrac{-9}{11}$ and $\dfrac{5}{-17} = \dfrac{-5}{17}$ $\dfrac{-9}{11} \bowtie \dfrac{-5}{17}$

$-9 \times 17 = -153$ and $-5 \times 11 = -55$

$\therefore \quad -153 < -55 \quad \therefore \dfrac{-9}{11} < \dfrac{-5}{17} \Rightarrow \dfrac{9}{-11} < \dfrac{5}{-17}$.

Ex. 3. *Arrange* $\dfrac{-4}{5}, \dfrac{9}{-15}, \dfrac{-2}{3}$ *in descending order.*

Sol. Writing each rational number with a positive denominator, we have $\dfrac{-4}{5}, \dfrac{-9}{15}, \dfrac{-2}{3}$.

LCM of 5, 15 and 3 is 15

$\therefore \quad \dfrac{-4}{5} = \dfrac{(-4) \times 3}{5 \times 3} = \dfrac{-12}{15}, \dfrac{-9}{15}, \dfrac{-2}{3} = \dfrac{(-2) \times 5}{3 \times 5} = \dfrac{-10}{15}$

5	5, 15, 3
3	1, 3, 3
	1, 1, 1

Since $-12 < -10 < -9 \quad \therefore \dfrac{-12}{15} < \dfrac{-10}{15} < \dfrac{-9}{15} \Rightarrow \dfrac{-4}{5} < \dfrac{-2}{3} < \dfrac{-9}{15}$

i.e., $\dfrac{-9}{15} > \dfrac{-2}{3} > \dfrac{-4}{5}$.

Hence, the rational numbers is descending order are

$$\frac{-9}{15}, \frac{-2}{3}, \frac{-4}{5}, \ i.e., \ \frac{9}{-15}, \frac{-2}{3}, \frac{-4}{5}.$$

Ex. 4. *Find the absolute value of*

    (a) $\dfrac{7}{11}$ **(b)** $\dfrac{-15}{17}$ **(c)** $\left(\dfrac{-1}{3} \times \dfrac{7}{-3}\right)$ **(d)** $\left(\dfrac{-5}{4} \div \dfrac{35}{16}\right)$ **(e)** $\left(\dfrac{1}{3} - \dfrac{5}{6}\right)$

Sol. (a) $\left|\dfrac{7}{11}\right| = \dfrac{7}{11}$ (b) $\left|\dfrac{-15}{17}\right| = \dfrac{15}{17}$ (c) $\left|\dfrac{-1}{3} \times \dfrac{7}{-3}\right| = \left|\dfrac{-1}{3} \times \dfrac{-7}{3}\right| = \left|\dfrac{7}{9}\right| = \dfrac{7}{9}$

     (d) $\left|\dfrac{-5}{4} \div \dfrac{35}{16}\right| = \left|\dfrac{-5}{4} \times \dfrac{16}{35}\right| = \left|\dfrac{-4}{7}\right| = \dfrac{4}{7}$ (e) $\left|\dfrac{1}{3} - \dfrac{5}{6}\right| = \left|\dfrac{2-5}{6}\right| = \left|\dfrac{-3}{6}\right| = \left|\dfrac{-1}{2}\right| = \dfrac{1}{2}$

Ex. 5. *Compare* $\left|\dfrac{-4}{3} + \dfrac{5}{8}\right|$ *and* $\left|\dfrac{-4}{3}\right| + \left|\dfrac{5}{8}\right|$.

Sol. $\left|\dfrac{-4}{3} + \dfrac{5}{8}\right| = \left|\dfrac{-32+15}{24}\right| = \left|\dfrac{-17}{24}\right| = \dfrac{17}{24}$, $\left|\dfrac{-4}{3}\right| + \left|\dfrac{5}{8}\right| = \dfrac{4}{3} + \dfrac{5}{8} = \dfrac{32+15}{24} = \dfrac{47}{34}$.

     Obviously, $\dfrac{47}{24} > \dfrac{17}{24}$, therefore, $\left|\dfrac{-4}{3}\right| + \left|\dfrac{5}{8}\right| > \left|\dfrac{-4}{3} + \dfrac{5}{8}\right|$.

Ex. 6. *Find two rational numbers whose absolute value is* $\dfrac{1}{3}$.

Sol. Since $\left|-\dfrac{1}{3}\right| = \dfrac{1}{3}$ and $\left|\dfrac{1}{3}\right| = \dfrac{1}{3}$, two numbers whose absolute value is $\dfrac{1}{3}$ are $\dfrac{-1}{3}$ and $\dfrac{1}{3}$. They are the two equidistant numbers on opposite sides of zero.

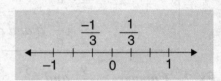

1.6 Presentation of a Rational Number on a Number Line

Every rational number has a corresponding point representing it on the number line.

We have already learnt that integers can be represented by taking positive integers to the right of the point 0 and negative integers to the left of the point 0. Let us consider the length between two successive integers to be unit length. As we know integers are also rational numbers with denominator 1.

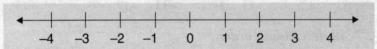

  ■ **To represent a rational number of the form** $\dfrac{p}{q}$ **where** $p < q$.

Ex. 7. *Represent* $\dfrac{2}{5}$ *and* $-\dfrac{2}{5}$ *on the number line.*

Sol.

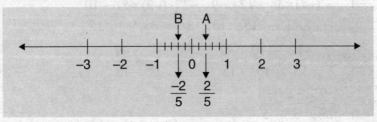

To represent $\frac{2}{5}$ on the number line we divide the unit length between 0 and 1 into 5 equal parts and take 2 out of the 5 parts. Then A represents $\frac{2}{5}$.

Similarly $-\frac{2}{5}$ can be represented by taking the unit length between 0 and -1.

■ **To represent a rational number of the form $\frac{p}{q}$ where $p > q$.**

Ex. 8. *Represent $\frac{14}{3}$ and $-\frac{14}{3}$ on the number line.*

Sol. $\frac{14}{3} = 4\frac{2}{3}$ and $-\frac{14}{3} = -\left(4\frac{2}{3}\right) - \left(4 + \frac{2}{3}\right) = -4 + \left(-\frac{2}{3}\right).$

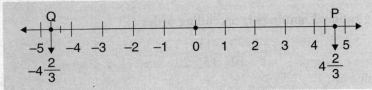

To represent $\frac{14}{3}$ or $4\frac{2}{3}$.

Start from 0 and take 4 full units. Divide the unit length between 4 and 5 into 3 equal parts. Take two out 3 parts. Then the point P represents $\frac{14}{3}$ or $\left(4 + \frac{2}{3}\right)$. Similarly point Q represents $-\frac{14}{3}$ or $-\left(4 + \frac{2}{3}\right)$ on the left side of 0.

1.7 Order Relation

1. Two equal rational numbers correspond to the same point on the number line.

2. If $\frac{p}{q}$ lies to the right of $\frac{r}{s}$, then $\frac{p}{q} > \frac{r}{s}$.

3. If $\frac{p}{q}$ lies to the left of $\frac{r}{s}$, then $\frac{p}{q} < \frac{r}{s}$.

4. All rational numbers lying to the left of 0 are negative.

5. All rational numbers lying to the right of 0 are positive.

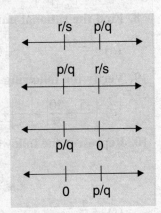

1.8 Absolute Value of a Rational Number

For a rational number x,

$$|x| = \begin{cases} x & \text{if} & x > 0 \\ 0 & \text{if} & x = 0 \\ -x & \text{if} & x < 0 \end{cases}.$$

Thus $\left|\frac{5}{7}\right| = \frac{5}{7}, \left|\frac{-12}{19}\right| = \frac{12}{19}$ and $|0| = 0.$

EXERCISE 1 (a)

1. Write four rational numbers equivalent to each of the following rational numbers :

     (a) $\dfrac{2}{5}$ (b) $\dfrac{-5}{9}$ (c) $\dfrac{8}{-11}$ (d) $\dfrac{-12}{13}$.

2. Express $\dfrac{21}{-8}$ as a rational number with denominator 24.

3. Express $\dfrac{-28}{84}$ as a rational number with numerator 4.

4. Which of the symbols <, = or > should replace the blank space ?

     (a) $\dfrac{8}{7}$ ..... $\dfrac{12}{9}$ (b) $\dfrac{-2}{3}$ ..... $\dfrac{4}{-7}$ (c) $\dfrac{10}{-11}$ ..... $\dfrac{13}{-15}$

     (d) 0 ..... $\dfrac{-3}{-8}$ (e) -1 ..... $\dfrac{-15}{7}$ (f) $\dfrac{-12}{17}$ ..... $\dfrac{-15}{19}$

5. Arrange the following rational numbers is ascending order :

     (a) $\dfrac{3}{-7}, \dfrac{-5}{14}, \dfrac{-1}{2}, \dfrac{-25}{28}$ (b) $\dfrac{-1}{5}, \dfrac{-3}{10}, \dfrac{-11}{15}, \dfrac{13}{20}$

6. Write the absolute value of :

     (a) $\dfrac{5}{8}$ (b) $\dfrac{-7}{10}$ (c) 0 (d) $\dfrac{11}{-12}$ (e) $\dfrac{-16}{19}$

     (f) $\dfrac{-5}{8} \times \dfrac{10}{-16}$ (g) $\dfrac{-8}{25} \div \dfrac{4}{100}$ (h) $\dfrac{3}{7} - \dfrac{5}{8}$ (i) $\dfrac{1}{2} - \dfrac{1}{3} \times \dfrac{1}{5}$

     (j) $-1 \div \dfrac{-1}{5} \div \dfrac{1}{-5} \div \dfrac{-1}{-5}$ (**Hint :** Operate from left to right)

7. Fill in the blanks with the correct symbol <, = ,>

     (a) $\left|\dfrac{-3}{7}\right|$ ..... $\left|\dfrac{6}{13}\right|$ (b) $\left|\dfrac{-12}{13}\right|$ ..... $\left|\dfrac{10}{-11}\right|$

8. Find the rational numbers whose absolute value is

     (a) $\dfrac{11}{13}$ (b) 7 (c) $\dfrac{23}{27}$

9. Verify the following :

     (a) $\left|\dfrac{-5}{3} \div \dfrac{20}{9}\right| = \left|\dfrac{-5}{3}\right| \div \left|\dfrac{20}{9}\right|$ (b) $\left|\dfrac{-7}{11} + \dfrac{8}{22}\right| < \left|\dfrac{-7}{11}\right| + \left|\dfrac{8}{22}\right|$

10. Represent the following points on the number line :

     (a) $\dfrac{5}{7}$ (b) $\dfrac{-8}{11}$ (c) $-3\dfrac{2}{7}$ (d) $\dfrac{15}{4}$ (e) $-2\dfrac{1}{5}$

     (f) $5\dfrac{2}{3}$ (g) $\left|\dfrac{-3}{4}\right|$ (h) $\left|\dfrac{1}{2} - \dfrac{1}{3}\right|$

11. Answer True or False :

     (a) Every whole number is a rational number.

     (b) Every rational number is a whole number.

     (c) 0 is the smallest rational number.

     (d) Every fractional number is a rational number.

     (e) Every rational number is a fractional number.

     (f) 0 is a whole number but not a rational number.

     (g) The rational number $-\dfrac{1}{3}$ lies on the left of 0 on the number line.

1.9 Operations on Rational Numbers

■ **Case I.** If $\frac{p}{q}$ and $\frac{r}{q}$ are any two rational numbers with the common denominator q, then $\frac{p}{q}+\frac{r}{q}=\frac{p+r}{q}$.

> **Note** : For addition we should covert each rational number into a rational number with positive denominator

For example : $\quad \frac{6}{13}+\frac{-2}{13} = \frac{6+(-2)}{13}=\frac{4}{13}$.

$\frac{11}{-20}+\frac{-9}{20} = \frac{-11}{20}+\frac{-9}{20}=\frac{(-11)+(-9)}{20}=\frac{-20}{20}=-1$.

■ **Case II.** For rational numbers $\frac{p}{q}$ and $\frac{r}{s}$ with different denominators, we take the LCM of the denominators and express the given rational numbers with this LCM as the common denominator. Now add as in **Case I**.

In particular, $\frac{p}{q}+\frac{r}{s}=\frac{ps+rq}{qs}$, when HCF of q and s is 1.

For example : $\quad \frac{1}{8}+\frac{3}{4} = \frac{1}{8}+\frac{3\times2}{4\times2}=\frac{1}{8}+\frac{6}{8}=\frac{1+6}{8}=\frac{7}{8}$.

> LCM of 4 and 8 is 8.

$\frac{1}{5}+\frac{-4}{7} = \frac{1\times7+5\times(-4)}{35}=\frac{7-20}{35}=\frac{-13}{35}$.

> LCM of 5 and 7 is 35

$2\frac{1}{8}+3\frac{1}{18}+\left(-2\frac{1}{24}\right) = (2+3-2)+\frac{1}{8}+\frac{1}{18}-\frac{1}{24}$

$= 3+\frac{1\times9+1\times4-1\times3}{72}=3+\frac{9+4-3}{72}$

$= 3+\frac{10}{72}=3+\frac{5}{36}=3\frac{5}{36}$.

2	8, 18, 24
2	4, 9, 12
2	2, 9, 6
3	1, 9, 3
	1, 3, 1

LCM = $2\times2\times2\times3\times3 = 72$

1.10 Properties of Addition of Rational Numbers

You studied the properties of the operation of addition over integers in class VI. These properties hold good for addition in rational numbers also.

Let $\frac{a}{b}$ and $\frac{c}{d}$, be any two unique rational numbers. Then,

■ **Property 1. Closure :** $\frac{a}{b}+\frac{c}{d}$ *is a unique rational number.*

For example :

(i) $\frac{3}{4}+\frac{5}{7}=\frac{41}{28}$, which is a rational number.

(ii) $\frac{-7}{12}+\frac{5}{6}=\frac{(-7)+5\times2}{12}=\frac{-7+10}{12}=\frac{3}{12}$, which is a rational number.

■ **Property 2. Commutative :** $\frac{a}{b}+\frac{c}{d}=\frac{c}{d}+\frac{a}{b}$

i.e., two rational numbers can be added in any order.

For example :

(i) $\dfrac{1}{2}+\dfrac{3}{5}=\dfrac{5+6}{10}=\dfrac{11}{10}$ (ii) $\dfrac{7}{8}+\left(\dfrac{-5}{12}\right)=\dfrac{7\times 3+(-5)\times 2}{24}=\dfrac{21-10}{24}=\dfrac{11}{24}$

$\dfrac{3}{5}+\dfrac{1}{2}=\dfrac{6+5}{10}=\dfrac{11}{10}$ $\dfrac{-5}{12}+\dfrac{7}{8}=\dfrac{-5\times 2+7\times 3}{24}=\dfrac{-10+21}{24}=\dfrac{11}{24}$

$\therefore\quad \dfrac{1}{2}+\dfrac{3}{5}=\dfrac{3}{5}+\dfrac{1}{2}.$ $\therefore\quad \dfrac{7}{8}+\left(\dfrac{-5}{12}\right)=\dfrac{-5}{12}+\dfrac{7}{8}.$

- **Property 3. Associative :** For any three rational numbers $\dfrac{a}{b},\dfrac{c}{d},\dfrac{e}{f}$, we have $\left(\dfrac{a}{b}+\dfrac{c}{d}\right)+\dfrac{e}{f}=\dfrac{a}{b}+\left(\dfrac{c}{d}+\dfrac{e}{f}\right).$

i.e., while adding three or more rational numbers, they can be grouped in any order.

For example : Suppose we have to find the sum of $\dfrac{1}{2}, -\dfrac{1}{3}$ and $\dfrac{-3}{5}$. Then,

$$\left(\dfrac{1}{2}+\dfrac{-1}{3}\right)+\dfrac{-3}{5}=\dfrac{3-2}{6}+\left(\dfrac{-3}{5}\right)=\dfrac{1}{6}+\dfrac{-3}{5}=\dfrac{1\times 5+(-3)\times 6}{30}=\dfrac{5-18}{30}=\dfrac{-13}{30}$$

$$\dfrac{1}{2}+\left(\dfrac{-1}{3}+\dfrac{-3}{5}\right)=\dfrac{1}{2}+\dfrac{-1\times 5+(-3)\times 3}{15}=\dfrac{1}{2}+\dfrac{-5-9}{15}=\dfrac{1}{2}+\dfrac{-14}{15}$$

$$=\dfrac{1\times 15+(-14)\times 2}{30}=\dfrac{15-28}{30}=\dfrac{-13}{30}$$

$$\therefore\quad \left(\dfrac{1}{2}+\dfrac{-1}{3}\right)+\dfrac{-3}{5}=\dfrac{1}{2}+\left(\dfrac{-1}{3}+\dfrac{-3}{5}\right).$$

Remark. The associative property enables us to add three or more rational numbers by re-arranging and grouping them in a convenient form so that the sum may be found more easily. The following examples will illustrate this point.

Ex. 1. *Simplify :* $\dfrac{2}{5}+\dfrac{8}{3}+\dfrac{-11}{15}+\dfrac{4}{5}+\dfrac{-2}{3}.$

Sol. (a) You may group pairs of numbers with a common denominator

$$\dfrac{2}{5}+\dfrac{8}{3}+\dfrac{-11}{15}+\dfrac{4}{5}+\dfrac{-2}{3}=\left(\dfrac{2}{5}+\dfrac{4}{5}\right)+\left(\dfrac{8}{3}+\dfrac{-2}{3}\right)+\dfrac{-11}{15}$$

$$=\dfrac{2+4}{5}+\dfrac{8-2}{3}+\dfrac{-11}{15}=\dfrac{6}{5}+\dfrac{6}{3}+\dfrac{-11}{15}$$

$$=\dfrac{6\times 3+6\times 5+1\times(-11)}{15}=\dfrac{18+30-11}{15}=\dfrac{37}{15}.$$

Ex. 2. *Evaluate:* $\dfrac{7}{20}+\dfrac{17}{-45}+\dfrac{-11}{-30}+\dfrac{-8}{15}.$

Sol. $\dfrac{7}{20}+\dfrac{17}{-45}+\dfrac{-11}{-30}+\dfrac{-8}{15}=\dfrac{7}{20}+\dfrac{-17}{45}+\dfrac{11}{30}+\dfrac{-8}{15}$

     | Writing in standard form |

$$=\left(\dfrac{7}{20}+\dfrac{11}{30}\right)+\left(\dfrac{-8}{15}+\dfrac{-17}{45}\right)$$

| Grouping pairs of numbers having denominators with common divisors |

$$=\dfrac{7\times 3+11\times 2}{60}+\dfrac{-8\times 3+(-17)}{45}$$

$$= \frac{21+22}{60} + \frac{-24-17}{45} = \frac{43}{60} + \frac{-41}{45}$$

$$= \frac{43\times3+(-41)\times4}{180} = \frac{129-164}{180} = \frac{-35}{180} = \frac{-7}{36}.$$

■ **Property 4. Property of zero :** *The sum of any rational number and 0, is the rational number itself,*

i.e., if $\frac{a}{b}$ is any rational number, then

$$\frac{a}{b} + 0 = 0 + \frac{a}{b} = \frac{a}{b}.$$

Remark. 0 is called the **additive identity** or the **identity element** for the addition of rational numbers.

For example :

(i) $\frac{7}{8} + 0 = \frac{7}{8} + \frac{0}{8} = \frac{7+0}{8} = \frac{7}{8}$ (ii) $\frac{-8}{19} + 0 = \frac{-8}{19} + \frac{0}{19} = \frac{-8+0}{19} = \frac{-8}{19}$

(iii) $0 + \frac{17}{-18} = \frac{0}{18} + \frac{-17}{18} = \frac{0-17}{18} = \frac{-17}{18}.$

Ex. 3. *Simplify :* $\frac{4}{7} + 0 + \frac{-8}{9} + \frac{-13}{7} + \frac{17}{21}.$

Sol. $\frac{4}{7} + 0 + \frac{-8}{9} + \frac{-13}{7} + \frac{17}{21} = \left(\frac{4}{7} + 0\right) + \frac{-8}{9} + \left(\frac{-13}{7} + \frac{17}{21}\right) = \frac{4}{7} + \frac{-8}{9} + \frac{-13}{7} + \frac{17}{21}$

$$= \left(\frac{4}{7} + \frac{-13}{7}\right) + \frac{-8}{9} + \frac{17}{21} = \frac{-9}{7} + \frac{-8}{9} + \frac{17}{21}$$

$$= \frac{-9\times9+(-8)\times7+17\times3}{63}$$

$$= \frac{-81-56+51}{63}$$

$$= \frac{-137+51}{63} = \frac{-86}{63}.$$

7	7, 9, 21
3	1, 9, 3
	1, 3, 1

∴ LCM of 7, 9, 21
   $= 7 \times 3 \times 3 = 63$

■ **Property 5. (Negative of a rational number):** *If $\frac{a}{b}$ is a rational number, then $-\frac{a}{b}$ is a rational number such that*

$$\frac{a}{b} + \left(-\frac{a}{b}\right) = \left(-\frac{a}{b}\right) + \frac{a}{b} = 0.$$

$-\frac{a}{b}$ is called **negative of** $\frac{a}{b}$. It is also called the **additive inverse** of $\frac{a}{b}$.

Remarks 1. It follows from the above that if $-\frac{a}{b}$ is the negative of a, then $\frac{a}{b}$ is the negative of

$$-\frac{a}{b}, i.e., \frac{a}{b} = -\left(-\frac{a}{b}\right).$$

2. We have $0 + 0 = 0 = 0 + 0$, so 0 is the additive inverse of itself, that is, **–0 = 0.**

It may be noted that 0 is the only rational number which is its own additive inverse.

Ex. 4. *Write the additive inverse of :*

(a) $\frac{3}{7}$ (b) $\frac{-14}{19}$ (c) $\frac{9}{-16}$ (d) $\frac{-21}{-40}.$

Sol. (a) Additive inverse of $\frac{3}{7} = \frac{-3}{7}$ (b) Additive inverse of $\frac{-14}{19} = -\left(\frac{-14}{19}\right) = \frac{14}{19}$.

(c) We may write $\frac{9}{-16} = \frac{9 \times (-1)}{-16 \times (-1)} = \frac{-9}{16}$ $\therefore$ Additive inverse of $\frac{9}{-16}$ is $-\left(\frac{-9}{16}\right) = \frac{9}{16}$.

(d) We may write $\frac{-21}{-40} = \frac{(-21) \times (-1)}{(-40) \times (-1)} = \frac{21}{40}$ $\therefore$ Additive inverse of $\frac{-21}{-40} = \frac{-21}{40}$.

1.11 Subtraction

If $\frac{a}{b}$ and $\frac{c}{d}$ are two rational numbers, then

$$\frac{a}{b} - \frac{c}{d} = \frac{a}{b} + \left(\textbf{additive inverse of } \frac{c}{d}\right)$$

$$= \frac{a}{b} + \left(-\frac{c}{d}\right)$$

For example : $\frac{3}{7} - \frac{5}{7} = \frac{3}{7} + \left(\text{additive inverse of } \frac{5}{7}\right) = \frac{3}{7} + \left(\frac{-5}{7}\right) = \frac{3 + (-5)}{7} = -\frac{2}{7}$.

$$\frac{-7}{12} - \frac{1}{8} = \frac{-7}{12} + \left(\text{additive inverse of } \frac{1}{8}\right) = \frac{-7}{12} + \left(-\frac{1}{8}\right)$$

> LCM of 12 and 8 is 24

$$= \frac{-7 \times 2 + (-1) \times 3}{24} = \frac{-14 - 3}{7} = \frac{-17}{24}.$$

$$\frac{1}{3} - \left(-\frac{1}{4}\right) = \frac{1}{3} + \left(\text{additive inverse of } -\frac{1}{4}\right) = \frac{1}{3} + \left(\frac{1}{4}\right) = \frac{1 \times 4 + 1 \times 3}{12} = \frac{4 + 3}{12} = \frac{7}{12}.$$

$$3\frac{1}{2} - 1\frac{1}{3} = (3 - 1) + \frac{1}{2} - \frac{1}{3} = 2 + \frac{3 \times 1 - 1 \times 2}{6} = 2 + \frac{3 - 2}{6} = 2 + \frac{1}{6} = 2\frac{1}{6}.$$

1.12 Properties of Subtraction

1. **Closure property.** *If $\frac{a}{b}$ and $\frac{c}{d}$ are any two rational numbers, then $\frac{a}{b} - \frac{c}{d}$ is also a rational number.*

   For example : $\frac{4}{5} - \frac{3}{10} = \frac{4 \times 2 - 3 \times 1}{10} = \frac{8 - 3}{10} = \frac{5}{10} = \frac{1}{2}$, is a rational number.

2. **Existence of right identity.** In case of addition, we have $\frac{a}{b} + 0 = 0 + \frac{a}{b} = \frac{a}{b}$, but in case of subtraction, for any rational number $\frac{a}{b}$, $\frac{a}{b} - 0 = \frac{a}{b}$ but $0 - \frac{a}{b} = -\frac{a}{b}$ (not equal to $\frac{a}{b}$). Therefore, 'only the right identity exists for subtraction'.

Ex. 5. *Subtract :* (a) $\frac{2}{3}$ *from* $\frac{7}{8}$ (b) $\frac{-5}{9}$ *from* $\frac{-3}{7}$.

Sol. (a) $\frac{7}{8} - \frac{2}{3} = \frac{7}{8} + \left(-\frac{2}{3}\right) = \frac{7 \times 3 + (-2) \times 8}{24} = \frac{21 - 16}{24} = \frac{5}{24}$.

(b) $\frac{-3}{7} - \left(\frac{-5}{9}\right) = -\frac{3}{7} + \left(\text{additive inverse of } \frac{-5}{9}\right)$

> Additive inverse of $\frac{-5}{9}$ is $\frac{5}{9}$

$$= -\frac{3}{7} + \frac{5}{9}$$

$$= \frac{(-3) \times 9 + 5 \times 7}{63} = \frac{-27 + 35}{63} = \frac{8}{63}.$$

Shortcut : $-\left(-\dfrac{a}{b}\right) = \dfrac{a}{b}$

Ex. 6. *The sum of two rational numbers is –3. If one of them is $\dfrac{-11}{5}$, find the other.*

Sol. Let the other rational number be x. Then

$$x + \left(\frac{-11}{5}\right) = -3 \quad \Rightarrow \quad x = -3 - \left(\frac{-11}{5}\right).$$

$$\Rightarrow \qquad x = -3 + \frac{11}{5} = \frac{-3}{1} + \frac{11}{5} = \frac{-3 \times 5 + 11}{5} = \frac{-15 + 11}{5} = \frac{-4}{5}.$$

Hence, the other number is $\dfrac{-4}{5}$.

Ex. 7. *What number should be added to $\dfrac{-4}{7}$ to get $\dfrac{5}{9}$?*

Sol. Let the required number be x. Then

$$\frac{-4}{7} + x = \frac{5}{9} \quad \Rightarrow \quad x = \frac{5}{9} - \left(-\frac{4}{7}\right) = \frac{5}{9} + \frac{4}{7}$$

$$\Rightarrow \qquad x = \frac{5 \times 7 + 4 \times 9}{63} = \frac{35 + 36}{63} = \frac{71}{63}.$$

Hence, the required number is $\dfrac{71}{63}$.

Ex. 8. *What should be subtracted from $\dfrac{-7}{11}$ to get –2?*

Sol. Let the required number be x. Then

$$\frac{-7}{11} - x = -2 \quad \Rightarrow \quad \frac{-7}{11} = x - 2$$

$$\Rightarrow \qquad x = \frac{-7}{11} + 2 = \frac{-7 + 2 \times 11}{11} = \frac{-7 + 22}{11} = \frac{15}{11}.$$

EXERCISE 1 (b)

1. Add the following rational numbers :

(a) $\dfrac{3}{7}$ and $\dfrac{2}{7}$ (b) $-\dfrac{11}{13}$ and $\dfrac{9}{13}$ (c) $\dfrac{-1}{6}$ and $\dfrac{3}{10}$ (d) $\dfrac{-5}{12}$ and $\dfrac{-7}{18}$

(e) $\dfrac{6}{15}$ and $\dfrac{-7}{25}$ (f) $\dfrac{13}{14}$ and $\dfrac{9}{-7}$ (g) $3\dfrac{3}{4}$ and $4\dfrac{1}{3}$ (h) $2\dfrac{5}{7}$ and $\dfrac{-3}{-14}$

2. Simplify :

(a) $\dfrac{5}{6} + \dfrac{7}{18} + \dfrac{-11}{12}$ (b) $\dfrac{7}{15} + \dfrac{-9}{25} + \dfrac{-3}{10}$ (c) $\dfrac{-2}{3} + 1\dfrac{5}{6} + \dfrac{-3}{2}$ (d) $4\dfrac{1}{5} + \left(-5\dfrac{3}{10}\right) + 1\dfrac{1}{2}$

3. Verify the following :

(a) $\dfrac{3}{4} + \dfrac{-2}{5} = \dfrac{-2}{5} + \dfrac{3}{4}$ (b) $\dfrac{-3}{4} + \dfrac{-7}{8} = \dfrac{-7}{8} + \dfrac{-3}{4}$ (c) $-8 + \dfrac{-11}{-12} = \dfrac{-11}{-12} + (-8)$

(d) $\dfrac{9}{-14} + \dfrac{17}{-21} = \dfrac{17}{-21} + \dfrac{9}{-14}.$

4. Verify that :

(a) $\left(\dfrac{-5}{8}+\dfrac{9}{8}\right)+\dfrac{13}{8}=\dfrac{-5}{8}+\left(\dfrac{9}{8}+\dfrac{13}{8}\right)$

(b) $\left(\dfrac{7}{2}+\dfrac{-4}{3}\right)+\dfrac{3}{5}=\dfrac{7}{2}+\left(\dfrac{-4}{3}+\dfrac{3}{5}\right)$

(c) $-20+\left(\dfrac{3}{-5}+\dfrac{-7}{-10}\right)=\left(-20+\dfrac{3}{-5}\right)+\dfrac{-7}{-10}.$

5. Fill in the blanks :

(a) $\left(\dfrac{-4}{15}\right)+\left(\dfrac{-21}{10}\right)=\left(\dfrac{-21}{10}\right)+(\ldots\ldots).$

(b) $-10+\dfrac{-17}{12}=\dfrac{-17}{12}+(\ldots\ldots)$

(c) $\left(\dfrac{-7}{8}+\dfrac{5}{-12}\right)+\dfrac{9}{16}=(\ldots\ldots)+\left(\dfrac{5}{-12}+\dfrac{9}{16}\right)$

(d) $-25+\left(\dfrac{11}{2}+\dfrac{7}{-4}\right)=\left(-25+\dfrac{11}{2}\right)+(\ldots\ldots)$

(e) $\dfrac{18}{-7}+\left(\dfrac{-5}{12}+\dfrac{-6}{5}\right)=\left(\dfrac{18}{-7}+\ldots\ldots\right)+\dfrac{-6}{5}$

(f) $\dfrac{2}{-3}+\ldots\ldots=\ldots\ldots+\dfrac{2}{-3}=\dfrac{-2}{3}.$

(g) $\dfrac{-4}{-5}+\ldots\ldots=\ldots\ldots+\dfrac{-4}{-5}=\dfrac{4}{5}.$

6. Find the additive inverse of each of the following :

(a) $\dfrac{2}{3}$ (b) $\dfrac{17}{9}$ (c) -23 (d) $\dfrac{-17}{9}$ (e) $\dfrac{8}{-29}$ (f) 0

(g) $\dfrac{-15}{-11}$ (h) $\dfrac{-21}{-30}$ (i) $\dfrac{21}{-40}$

7. Arrange and simplify :

(a) $\dfrac{1}{2}+\dfrac{-3}{5}+\dfrac{3}{2}$

(b) $\dfrac{28}{17}+\dfrac{35}{17}+\dfrac{-16}{17}+\dfrac{-23}{17}$

(c) $\dfrac{2}{3}+\dfrac{-3}{5}+\dfrac{1}{6}+\dfrac{-8}{15}$

(d) $\dfrac{3}{5}+\dfrac{5}{3}+\dfrac{-11}{5}+\dfrac{-2}{3}$

(e) $\dfrac{4}{3}+\dfrac{3}{5}+\dfrac{-2}{3}+\dfrac{-11}{5}$

(f) $\dfrac{4}{9}+\dfrac{5}{3}+\dfrac{-4}{5}+\dfrac{7}{9}+\dfrac{-2}{3}+\dfrac{9}{5}$

(g) $\dfrac{-8}{5}+0+\dfrac{-11}{6}+\dfrac{17}{12}+\dfrac{9}{10}$

8. Verify that $-(-x)=x$, **when** $x=$ (a) $\dfrac{7}{6}$ (b) $\dfrac{-8}{9}.$

9. Verify that $-(x+y)=(-x)+(-y)$, **when**   (a) $x=\dfrac{3}{4},\ y=\dfrac{6}{7}$ (b) $x=\dfrac{-3}{4},\ y=\dfrac{-6}{7}.$

10. Subtract :

(a) $\dfrac{1}{5}$ from $\dfrac{3}{5}$

(b) $\dfrac{4}{9}$ from $\dfrac{-1}{6}$

(c) $\dfrac{-4}{15}$ from $\dfrac{3}{10}$

(d) $\dfrac{3}{-4}$ from $\dfrac{4}{5}$

(e) $-\dfrac{1}{16}$ from $-\dfrac{3}{8}$

(f) $\dfrac{-4}{5}$ from $\dfrac{9}{8}$

11. The sum of two rational numbers is $\dfrac{5}{18}$. If one of the numbers is $\dfrac{1}{8}$, find the other.

12. What number should be added to $\dfrac{-5}{16}$ to get $\dfrac{7}{24}$?

13. What number should be subtracted from $\dfrac{7}{-8}$ to get $\dfrac{-13}{12}$?

14. What should be subtracted from $\left(\dfrac{3}{4}+\dfrac{1}{3}+\dfrac{2}{5}\right)$ to get $\dfrac{1}{2}$?

15. Simplify :

(a) $\dfrac{-5}{7}+\dfrac{1}{12}+\dfrac{3}{4}+\dfrac{-1}{3}+\dfrac{10}{7}+\dfrac{-1}{6}$

(b) $\dfrac{-2}{9}+\dfrac{1}{3}+\dfrac{11}{9}+\dfrac{-5}{6}+\dfrac{-2}{3}+\dfrac{13}{6}$

1.13 Multiplication

If $\dfrac{a}{b}$ and $\dfrac{c}{d}$ are two rational numbers, then

$$\left(\frac{a}{b}\times\frac{c}{d}\right)=\left(\frac{a\times c}{b\times d}\right)$$

For example :

$$\frac{3}{25}\times\frac{10}{9}=\frac{\cancel{3}^1\times\cancel{10}^2}{\cancel{25}_5\times\cancel{9}_3}=\frac{1\times 2}{5\times 3}=\frac{2}{15}.$$

$$\frac{-1}{4}\times\frac{1}{3}=\frac{-1\times 1}{4\times 3}=\frac{-1}{12}.$$

$$\frac{-3}{4}\times\frac{-8}{15}=\frac{-\cancel{3}^1\times-\cancel{8}^2}{\cancel{4}_1\times\cancel{15}_5}=\frac{-1\times-2}{1\times 5}=\frac{2}{5}.$$

$$-2\frac{1}{3}\times 3\frac{3}{4}=\frac{-7}{3}\times\frac{15}{4}=\frac{-7\times\cancel{15}^5}{\cancel{3}_1\times 4}=\frac{-7\times 5}{1\times 4}=\frac{-35}{4}=-8\frac{3}{4}.$$

1.14 Properties of Multiplication of Rational Numbers

■ **Property 1.** (*Closure*). **The product of two rational numbers is always a rational number**

i.e., if $\dfrac{a}{b}$ and $\dfrac{c}{d}$ are any two rational numbers, then $\left(\dfrac{a}{b}\times\dfrac{c}{d}\right)$ is also a rational numbers.

For example :

(i) $\dfrac{1}{3}\times\dfrac{5}{9}=\dfrac{1\times 5}{3\times 9}=\dfrac{5}{27}$, which is a rational number.

(ii) $\dfrac{-3}{8}\times\dfrac{7}{5}=\dfrac{-3\times 7}{8\times 5}=\dfrac{-21}{40}$, which is a rational number.

(iii) $\dfrac{-11}{9}\times\dfrac{-4}{7}=\dfrac{-11\times-4}{9\times 7}=\dfrac{44}{63}$, which is a rational number.

■ **Property 2.** (*Commutativity*). *Two rational numbers can be multiplied in any order.*

Thus, if $\dfrac{a}{b}$ *and* $\dfrac{c}{d}$ *are any rational numbers, then*

$$\left(\frac{a}{b}\times\frac{c}{d}\right)=\left(\frac{c}{d}\times\frac{a}{b}\right)$$

For example :

(i) $\dfrac{2}{3}\times\dfrac{4}{5}=\dfrac{2\times 4}{3\times 5}=\dfrac{8}{15};\quad \dfrac{4}{5}\times\dfrac{2}{3}=\dfrac{4\times 2}{5\times 3}=\dfrac{8}{15}\quad \therefore\quad \dfrac{2}{3}\times\dfrac{4}{5}=\dfrac{4}{5}\times\dfrac{2}{3}.$

(ii) $\dfrac{-5}{8}\times\dfrac{-9}{7}=\dfrac{-5\times-9}{8\times 7}=\dfrac{45}{46};\quad \dfrac{-9}{7}\times\dfrac{-5}{8}=\dfrac{-9\times-5}{7\times 8}=\dfrac{45}{56}\quad \therefore\quad \dfrac{-5}{8}\times\dfrac{-9}{7}=\dfrac{-9}{7}\times\dfrac{-5}{8}.$

■ **Property 3. (*Associativity*).** *While multiplying three or more rational numbers, they can be grouped in any order. Thus, if $\frac{a}{b}$, $\frac{c}{d}$ and $\frac{e}{f}$ are three rational numbers, then*

$$\left(\frac{a}{b} \times \frac{c}{d}\right) \times \frac{e}{f} = \frac{a}{b} \times \left(\frac{c}{d} \times \frac{e}{f}\right)$$

For example : Let us consider the product of $\frac{-4}{5}, \frac{3}{7}$ and $\frac{-8}{11}$.

We have $\left(\frac{-4}{5} \times \frac{3}{7}\right) \times \left(\frac{-8}{11}\right) = \frac{-4 \times 3}{5 \times 7} \times \frac{-8}{11} = \frac{-12}{35} \times \frac{-8}{11} = \frac{-12 \times -8}{35 \times 11} = \frac{96}{385}$.

$-\frac{4}{5} \times \left(\frac{3}{7} \times \frac{-8}{11}\right) = \frac{-4}{5} \times \frac{3 \times -8}{7 \times 11} = \frac{-4}{5} \times \frac{-24}{77} = \frac{-4 \times -24}{5 \times 77} = \frac{96}{385}$.

$\therefore \quad \left(\frac{-4}{5} \times \frac{3}{7}\right) \times \frac{-8}{11} = \frac{-4}{5} \times \left(\frac{3}{7} \times \frac{-8}{11}\right)$

■ **Property 4. (*Property of 1*).** *If $\frac{a}{b}$ is a rational number, then $\frac{a}{b} \times 1 = 1 \times \frac{a}{b} = \frac{a}{b}$.*

For example :

(i) $\frac{59}{134} \times 1 = \frac{59}{134} \times \frac{1}{1} = \frac{59 \times 1}{134 \times 1} = \frac{59}{134}$. (ii) $1 \times \frac{-598}{3247} = \frac{1}{1} \times \frac{-598}{3247} = \frac{1 \times (-598)}{1 \times 3247} = \frac{-598}{3247}$.

Remark. 1 is called the **multiplicative identity** for rational numbers.

■ **Property 5. (*Multiplication by 0*).** *Every rational number multiplied with 0 gives 0. Thus if $\frac{a}{b}$ is any rational number, then $\frac{a}{b} \times 0 = 0 = 0 \times \frac{a}{b}$.*

For example :

(i) $\frac{8}{9} \times 0 = \frac{8}{9} \times \frac{0}{1} = \frac{8 \times 0}{9 \times 1} = \frac{0}{9} = 0$; and $0 \times \frac{8}{9} = \frac{0}{1} \times \frac{8}{9} = \frac{0 \times 8}{1 \times 9} = \frac{0}{9} = 0$ $\therefore \frac{8}{9} \times 0 = 0 = 0 \times \frac{8}{9}$.

(ii) $\frac{-7}{16} \times 0 = \frac{-7}{16} \times \frac{0}{1} = \frac{-7 \times 0}{16 \times 1} = \frac{0}{16} = 0$ and $0 \times \frac{-7}{16} = \frac{0}{1} \times \frac{-7}{16} = \frac{0 \times -7}{1 \times 16} = \frac{0}{16} = 0$ $\therefore \frac{-7}{16} \times 0 = 0 = 0 \times \frac{-7}{16}$.

■ **Property 6. (*Distributivity of multiplication over addition*).** *The multiplication of rational numbers is distributive over addition.*

Thus, if $\frac{a}{b}$, $\frac{c}{d}$ and $\frac{e}{f}$ are rational numbers then $\frac{a}{b} \times \left(\frac{c}{d} + \frac{e}{f}\right) = \frac{a}{b} \times \frac{c}{d} + \frac{a}{b} \times \frac{e}{f}$.

For example : Consider any three rational numbers, $\frac{4}{5}$, $-\frac{3}{4}$ and $\frac{5}{6}$.

We have $\frac{4}{5} \times \left(\frac{-3}{4} + \frac{5}{6}\right) = \frac{4}{5} \times \left(\frac{-3 \times 3 + 5 \times 2}{12}\right) = \frac{4}{5} \times \left(\frac{-9 + 10}{12}\right)$

$= \frac{4}{5} \times \frac{1}{12} = \frac{{}^1\!\!\!\!\!\diagup\!\!A \times 1}{5 \times 12_3} = \frac{1 \times 1}{5 \times 3} = \frac{1}{15}$

and $\frac{4}{5} \times \frac{-3}{4} + \frac{4}{5} \times \frac{5}{6} = \frac{{}^1\!A \times -3}{5 \times A_1} + \frac{{}^2\!A \times 5^1}{{}_1\!5 \times 6_3} = \frac{1 \times -3}{5 \times 1} + \frac{2 \times 1}{1 \times 3}$

$$= \frac{-3}{5} + \frac{2}{3} = \frac{-3 \times 3 + 2 \times 5}{15} = \frac{-9 + 10}{15} = \frac{1}{15}$$

$$\therefore \qquad \frac{4}{5} \times \left(\frac{-3}{4} + \frac{5}{6} \right) = \frac{4}{5} \times \frac{-3}{4} + \frac{4}{5} \times \frac{5}{6}.$$

■ **Property 7.** (*Existence of multiplicative inverse*). *Every non-zero rational number* $\frac{a}{b}$ *has its multiplicative inverse* $\frac{b}{a}$.

Thus, $\qquad \left(\frac{a}{b} \times \frac{b}{a} \right) = \left(\frac{b}{a} \times \frac{a}{b} \right) = 1,$

$\frac{a}{b}$ is called the reciprocal of $\frac{a}{b}$. It is denoted by $\left(\frac{a}{b} \right)^{-1}$. Thus, $\left(\frac{a}{b} \right)^{-1} = \frac{b}{a}$.

The reciprocal of 0 does not exist, Reciprocal of 1 is 1 and the reciprocal of (–1) is –1.

For example : The reciprocal of 15 is $\frac{1}{15}$, of –3 is $-\frac{1}{3}$, of $\frac{5}{6}$ is $\frac{6}{5}$ and of $\frac{-15}{16}$ is $\frac{-16}{15}$.

$$\left(\frac{1}{8} \right)^{-1} = 8, \quad \left(-\frac{8}{7} \right)^{-1} = -\frac{7}{8}, \quad (-5)^{-1} = -\frac{1}{5}.$$

1.15 Division

If $\frac{a}{b}$ and $\frac{c}{d}$ are two rational numbers such that $\frac{c}{d} \neq 0$, then $\frac{a}{b} \div \frac{c}{d} = \frac{a}{b} \times$ reciprocal of $\frac{c}{d} = \frac{a}{b} \times \frac{d}{c}$.

For example : $\qquad \frac{1}{8} \div \frac{9}{2} = \frac{1}{8_4} \times \frac{2^1}{9} = \frac{1 \times 1}{4 \times 9} = \frac{1}{36}$.

$$-2\frac{1}{3} \div 3\frac{3}{4} = \frac{-7}{3} \div \frac{15}{4} = \frac{-7}{3} \times \frac{4}{15} = \frac{-7 \times 4}{3 \times 15} = \frac{-28}{45}.$$

$$-2\frac{2}{7} \div (-8) = \frac{-16}{7} \div (-8) = \frac{-16^2}{7} \times \frac{-1}{8_1} = \frac{-2 \times -1}{7 \times 1} = \frac{2}{7}.$$

1.16 Properties of Division

■ **Property 1.** *If* $\frac{a}{b}$ *and* $\frac{c}{d}$ *are two rational numbers such that* $\frac{c}{d} \neq 0$, *then* $\frac{a}{b} \div \frac{c}{d}$ *is always a rational number.* That is, the set of all non-zero rational numbers is **closed** under division.

For example : $\frac{27}{16} \div \frac{9}{8} = \frac{27}{16} \times \frac{8}{9} = \frac{^3 27 \times 8^1}{^2 16 \times 9_1} = \frac{3 \times 1}{2 \times 1} = \frac{3}{2}$ is a rational number.

■ **Property 2.** *For any rational number* $\frac{a}{b}$, *we have*

$$\frac{a}{b} \div 1 = \frac{a}{b} \quad and \quad \frac{a}{b} \div (-1) = -\frac{a}{b}.$$

For example : $\frac{8}{21} \div 1 = \frac{8}{21}$, $\frac{8}{21} \div (-1) = \frac{8}{21} \div \frac{-1}{1} = \frac{8}{21} \times \frac{1}{-1} = \frac{8 \times 1}{21 \times -1} = \frac{8}{-21} = \frac{-8}{21}$.

■ **Property 3.** *For every non-zero rational number* $\frac{a}{b}$, *we have*

(i) $\frac{a}{b} \div \frac{a}{b} = 1$ \quad (ii) $\frac{a}{b} \div \left(-\frac{a}{b} \right) = -1$ \quad (iii) $-\frac{a}{b} \div \frac{a}{b} = -1.$

EXERCISE 1 (c)

1. Multiply :

(a) $\dfrac{6}{7}$ by $\dfrac{2}{3}$ (b) $\dfrac{-9}{11}$ by $\dfrac{22}{63}$ (c) $\dfrac{-12}{13}$ by $\dfrac{-5}{18}$

(d) $\dfrac{-90}{11}$ by $\dfrac{-55}{72}$ (e) $5\dfrac{1}{7}$ by $-2\dfrac{1}{3}$ (f) $\dfrac{18}{35}$ by $-3\dfrac{1}{8}$

2. Simplify :

(a) $\left(\dfrac{-6}{7}\times\dfrac{-28}{18}\right)+\left(\dfrac{-11}{13}\times\dfrac{65}{22}\right)$ (b) $\left(\dfrac{-4}{5}\times\dfrac{15}{8}\right)+\left(\dfrac{-1}{3}\times\dfrac{-9}{7}\right)-\left(\dfrac{2}{9}\times\dfrac{27}{14}\right)$

Verify the statements given in Q. 3 to 5 :

3. (a) $\dfrac{4}{5}\times\dfrac{7}{9}=\dfrac{7}{9}\times\dfrac{4}{5}$ (b) $\dfrac{8}{7}\times\dfrac{9}{-10}=\dfrac{9}{-10}\times\dfrac{8}{7}$

4. (a) $\left(\dfrac{3}{4}\times\dfrac{1}{2}\right)\times\dfrac{5}{7}=\dfrac{3}{4}\times\left(\dfrac{1}{2}\times\dfrac{5}{7}\right)$ (b) $\left(-\dfrac{7}{6}\times\dfrac{-2}{5}\right)\times\dfrac{3}{8}=\dfrac{-7}{6}\times\left(\dfrac{-2}{5}\times\dfrac{3}{8}\right)$

5. (a) $\dfrac{2}{3}\times\left(\dfrac{4}{5}+\dfrac{7}{8}\right)=\left(\dfrac{2}{3}\times\dfrac{4}{5}\right)+\left(\dfrac{2}{3}\times\dfrac{7}{8}\right)$ (b) $\dfrac{-6}{15}\times\left(\dfrac{7}{8}+\dfrac{-5}{12}\right)=\left(\dfrac{-6}{15}\times\dfrac{7}{8}\right)+\left(\dfrac{-6}{15}\times\dfrac{-5}{12}\right)$

6. Fill in the blanks :

(a) $\dfrac{-18}{37}\times\dfrac{11}{40}=\dfrac{11}{40}\times\ldots\ldots\ldots\ldots$ (b) $-19\times\dfrac{-5}{12}=\dfrac{-5}{12}\times\ldots\ldots\ldots\ldots$

(c) $\left(\dfrac{6}{11}\times\dfrac{-20}{21}\right)\times\left(\dfrac{-7}{8}\right)=\ldots\ldots\ldots\ldots\times\left(\dfrac{-20}{21}\times\dfrac{-7}{8}\right)$ (d) $\dfrac{-21}{40}\times\left(\dfrac{3}{7}\times\dfrac{17}{-24}\right)=\left(\dfrac{-21}{40}\times\dfrac{17}{-24}\right)\times\ldots\ldots\ldots\ldots$

(e) $\dfrac{1}{8}\times\left(\dfrac{-2}{5}+\dfrac{6}{17}\right)=\dfrac{1}{8}\times\dfrac{-2}{5}+\ldots\ldots\ldots\ldots$

7. Use the distributivity of multiplication of rational numbers over addition to simplify :

(a) $\dfrac{7}{4}\times\left(\dfrac{5}{8}+\dfrac{1}{2}\right)$ (b) $\dfrac{-3}{8}\times\left(\dfrac{4}{7}+\dfrac{-11}{7}\right)$ (c) $\dfrac{-2}{5}\times\left(\dfrac{3}{8}-25\right)$

8. Find the multiplicative inverse, _i.e._, the reciprocal of

(a) 6 (b) -23 (c) $\dfrac{11}{20}$ (d) $\dfrac{-19}{16}$ (e) $\dfrac{11}{-5}$

(f) $\dfrac{-7}{-8}$ (g) $-1\times\dfrac{-3}{10}$ (h) $\dfrac{4}{5}\times\dfrac{15}{8}$ (i) $\dfrac{-4}{5}\times\dfrac{-2}{7}$ (j) $0\times\dfrac{2}{9}$

9. By taking $x=-\dfrac{1}{3}$, $y=-\dfrac{3}{5}$, $z=-\dfrac{4}{9}$, verify the following :

(a) $x\times y=y\times x$ (b) $x\times(y\times z)=(x\times y)\times z$ (c) $x\times(y+z)=x\times y+x\times z$

(d) $(x+y)^{-1}\neq x^{-1}+y^{-1}$ (e) $(x-y)^{-1}=x^{-1}-y^{-1}$ is false

(f) $(x\times y)^{-1}=x^{-1}\times y^{-1}$ is true   (g) $\left|x^{-1}\right|=\left|x\right|^{-1},\left|y^{-1}\right|=\left|y\right|^{-1},\left|z^{-1}\right|=\left|z\right|^{-1}$.

10. Name the property of multiplication illustrated by the following statements :

(a) $3\times\dfrac{1}{3}=1$ (b) $\dfrac{1}{3}\times0=0$ (c) $\dfrac{5}{23}\times\dfrac{-7}{39}=\dfrac{-7}{39}\times\dfrac{5}{23}$ (d) $\dfrac{5}{6}\times1=\dfrac{5}{6}$

(e) $\frac{5}{7} \times \left(-2 + \frac{1}{3} \right) = \left(\frac{5}{7} \times -2 \right) + \left(\frac{5}{7} \times \frac{1}{3} \right)$ (f) $1 \times 1 = 1$ (g) $0 \times \frac{-7}{8} = \frac{-7}{8} \times 0$

(h) $\frac{-1}{2} \times \left(\frac{1}{3} \times \frac{-1}{4} \right) = \left(\frac{-1}{2} \times \frac{1}{3} \right) \times \frac{-1}{4}$ (i) $\left(\frac{-8}{9} \times \frac{1}{-5} \right) + \left(\frac{-8}{9} \times \frac{-7}{11} \right) = \frac{-8}{9} \times \left(\frac{1}{-5} + \frac{-7}{11} \right)$

(j) $\frac{-9}{20} \times \frac{20}{-9} = 1$.

11. What two properties of multiplication are involved, if we wish to show that $5 \times \frac{1}{5} a = a$?

12. **What four properties of multiplication are involved in the following :**

$32 \times \frac{1}{4} = (8 \times 4) \times \frac{1}{4} = 8 \times \left(4 \times \frac{1}{4} \right) = 8 \times 1 = 8$

13. Find a, if a is a rational number and $a \times a = a$.

14. Name two rational numbers that are their own reciprocals.

15. **Simplify the following and express the result in standard form :**

(a) $\frac{-4}{7} \times \left(\frac{-18}{11} \right) \times \left(\frac{44}{9} \right) \times (-14)$ (b) $(-36) \times \left(\frac{-35}{76} \right) \times \left(\frac{19}{15} \right) \times \left(\frac{3}{-2} \right)^{-1}$

16. **Fill in the blanks :**

(a) The product of a rational number and its reciprocal is ....

(b) The number 0 is .... the reciprocal of any number.

(c) Zero has .... reciprocal.

(d) Reciprocal of $\frac{1}{a}$, $a \neq 0$ is ....   (e) $(8 \times 19)^{-1} = 8^{-1} \times$ ....   (f) $\left(\left(\frac{3}{7} \right)^{-1} \right)^{-1} =$ ....

EXERCISE 1 (d)

1. **Divide :**

(a) $\frac{5}{9}$ by 15   (b) $\frac{7}{18}$ by $\frac{-14}{51}$ (c) $\frac{10}{33}$ by $\frac{2}{-11}$

(d) $\frac{-3}{16}$ by $\frac{-15}{18}$ (e) -18 by $\frac{(-36)}{37}$ (f) $\frac{-24}{50}$ by $\frac{-4}{75}$

2. **Verify, whether the following are true or false :**

(a) $\frac{24}{35} \div \frac{20}{21} = \frac{20}{21} \div \frac{24}{35}$ (b) $\frac{10}{21} \div \frac{8}{9} = \frac{8}{9} \div \frac{10}{21}$

(c) $\left(\frac{2}{5} \div \frac{26}{15} \right) \div \frac{39}{12} = \frac{2}{5} \div \left(\frac{26}{15} \div \frac{39}{12} \right)$ (d) $\frac{26}{15} \div \left(\frac{1}{5} + \frac{7}{3} \right) = \frac{26}{15} \div \frac{1}{5} + \frac{26}{15} \div \frac{7}{3}$

(e) $\frac{-22}{7} \div \left(\frac{9}{14} - \frac{5}{21} \right) = \left(\frac{-22}{7} \div \frac{9}{14} \right) - \left(\frac{-22}{7} \div \frac{5}{21} \right)$

(f) $\left(\frac{9}{5} + \frac{4}{25} \right) \div \left(\frac{-5}{7} \right) = \frac{9}{5} \div \left(\frac{-5}{7} \right) + \frac{4}{25} \div \left(\frac{-5}{7} \right)$ (g) $\left(\frac{9}{20} - \frac{17}{40} \right) \div \frac{10}{3} = \left(\frac{9}{20} \div \frac{10}{3} \right) - \left(\frac{17}{40} \div \frac{10}{3} \right)$

3. Fill in the blanks :

(a) $\dfrac{-3}{8} \div \dfrac{-3}{8} = $ ....

(b) .... $\div (-1) = \dfrac{8}{15}$

(c) $\dfrac{12}{13} \div $ .... $= (-1)$

(d) $\dfrac{6}{7} \div $ .... $= \dfrac{6}{7}$

(e) .... $\div (1) = \dfrac{-9}{17}$

(f) $\left(\dfrac{-13}{25}\right) \div $ .... $= 1$

4. Evaluate :

(a) $\left(\dfrac{5}{9} \div \dfrac{15}{36}\right) \div \left(-\dfrac{5}{6}\right)$

(b) $\left(\dfrac{-3}{29} \div \dfrac{9}{87}\right) \div \dfrac{-1}{7}$

1.17 To Find Rational Numbers between two given Rational Numbers

An important result : If $\dfrac{a}{b}$ and $\dfrac{c}{d}$ are two rational numbers, such that $\dfrac{a}{b} < \dfrac{c}{d}$, than $\dfrac{1}{2}\left(\dfrac{a}{b} + \dfrac{c}{d}\right)$ is a rational number lying between $\dfrac{a}{b}$ and $\dfrac{c}{d}$.

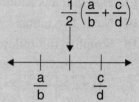

Ex. 1. Find a rational number between $\dfrac{1}{3}$ and $\dfrac{1}{4}$.

Sol. Required rational number $= \dfrac{1}{2}\left(\dfrac{1}{3} + \dfrac{1}{4}\right) = \dfrac{1}{2}\left(\dfrac{4+3}{12}\right) = \dfrac{1}{2} \times \dfrac{7}{12} = \dfrac{7}{24}$.

To find many rational numbers between two given distinct rational numbers.

Ex. 2. Find four rational numbers between $\dfrac{1}{6}$ and $\dfrac{1}{3}$.

Sol. Let q_1, q_2, q_3 and q_4 be the four required rational numbers. Then,

$$q_1 = \dfrac{1}{2}\left(\dfrac{1}{6} + \dfrac{1}{3}\right) = \dfrac{1}{2}\left(\dfrac{1+2}{6}\right) = \dfrac{1}{4};$$

$$q_2 = \dfrac{1}{2}\left(\dfrac{1}{4} + \dfrac{1}{3}\right) = \dfrac{1}{2}\left(\dfrac{3+4}{12}\right) = \dfrac{7}{24};$$

$$q_3 = \dfrac{1}{2}\left(\dfrac{7}{24} + \dfrac{1}{3}\right) = \dfrac{1}{2}\left(\dfrac{7+8}{24}\right) = \dfrac{5}{16};$$

$$q_4 = \dfrac{1}{2}\left(\dfrac{5}{16} + \dfrac{1}{3}\right) = \dfrac{1}{2}\left(\dfrac{15+16}{48}\right) = \dfrac{31}{96}.$$

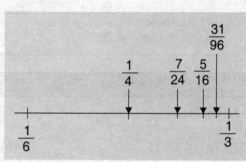

Hence, four rational numbers between $\dfrac{1}{6}$ and $\dfrac{1}{3}$ are $\dfrac{1}{4}, \dfrac{7}{24}, \dfrac{5}{16}$ **and** $\dfrac{31}{96}$.

Method 1.

Let the given rational numbers be a and b $(a < b)$. Then,

$$q_1 = \dfrac{1}{2}(a+b),\ q_2 = \dfrac{1}{2}(q_1+b),\ q_3 = \dfrac{1}{2}(q_2+b),\ q_4 = \dfrac{1}{2}(q_3+b),\ \text{and so on.}$$

In this manner, we can find as many rational numbers as we please between two given distinct rational numbers.

Method 2. *Alternatively,* we can find the required rational numbers by finding the equivalent rational numbers, having a sufficiently large common denominator depending on how many rational numbers, we have to find.

Ex. 3. *Find 7 rational numbers, between $\frac{1}{3}$ and $\frac{1}{2}$.*

Sol. If write $\frac{1}{3} = \frac{30}{90}$ and $\frac{1}{2} = \frac{45}{90}$, then 31, 32, ... 44 are 14 integers between 30 and 45.

Therefore, $\frac{30}{90} < \frac{31}{90} < \frac{32}{90} < \text{.........} < \frac{44}{90} < \frac{45}{90}$. or $\frac{1}{3} < \frac{31}{90} < \frac{32}{90} < \text{.........} < \frac{44}{90} < \frac{1}{2}$.

i.e., $\frac{31}{90}, \frac{32}{90}, \text{..........} \frac{44}{90}$ are 14 rational numbers between $\frac{1}{2}$ and $\frac{1}{3}$.

If we write $\frac{1}{3} = \frac{60}{180}$ and $\frac{1}{2} = \frac{90}{180}$, we can find up to 29 rational numbers between $\frac{1}{3}$ and $\frac{1}{2}$.

Ex. 4. *Find (i) 7 rational numbers (ii) 70 rational numbers, (iii) 100 rational numbers between $\frac{1}{3}$ and $\frac{3}{5}$.*

Sol. (*i*) Taking the equivalent rationals, $\frac{10}{30}$ for $\frac{1}{3}$ and $\frac{18}{30}$ for $\frac{3}{5}$, we find that seven integers between 10 and 18 are 11, 12, 13, ... 16, 17.

Therefore, $\frac{10}{30} < \frac{11}{30} < \frac{12}{30} < \text{.........} < \frac{16}{30} < \frac{17}{30} < \frac{18}{30}$.

i.e., $\frac{1}{3} < \frac{11}{30} < \frac{12}{30} < \text{.........} < \frac{17}{30} < \frac{3}{5}$.

Hence, the seven required rational numbers between $\frac{1}{3}$ and $\frac{3}{5}$ are $\frac{11}{30}, \frac{12}{30}, \text{..........}, \frac{17}{30}$.

(*ii*) Take the equivalent rational numbers $\frac{100}{300}$ for $\frac{1}{3}$ and $\frac{180}{300}$ for $\frac{3}{5}$, we find that the integers lying between 100 and 180 are 101, 102, 103, ..., 179.

Therefore, the seventy rational numbers between $\frac{1}{3}$ and $\frac{3}{5}$, may be taken as $\frac{101}{300}, \frac{102}{300}, \frac{103}{300}, \text{..........} \frac{170}{300}$.

(*iii*) Taking the equivalent rational numbers $\frac{1000}{3000}$ for $\frac{1}{3}$ and $\frac{1800}{3000}$ for $\frac{3}{5}$, we may have the 100 integers between 1000 and 1800 as 1001, 1002, ... 1100.

Hence, the 100 rational numbers between $\frac{1}{3}$ and $\frac{3}{5}$ are $\frac{1001}{3000}, \frac{1002}{3000}, \frac{1003}{3000}, \text{.......} \frac{1099}{3000}, \frac{1100}{3000}$.

> **Note :** By taking a larger and larger common denominator, we can find more and more rational numbers between $\frac{1}{3}$ and $\frac{3}{5}$. Suppose we take $\frac{1}{3} = \frac{10,000}{30,000}$ and $\frac{3}{5} = \frac{18,000}{30,000}$ then we can find more than 1000 rational numbers between $\frac{1}{3}$ and $\frac{3}{5}$.

Ex. 5. *Insert :* (*i*) *14 Rational numbers between $\frac{-4}{13}$ and $\frac{11}{13}$;*

          (*ii*) *70 rational numbers between $\frac{-4}{13}$ and $\frac{11}{13}$;*

          (*iii*) *100 rational numbers between $\frac{-4}{13}$ and $\frac{11}{13}$;*

Sol. (*i*) –3, –2, ..., 10 are the 14 integers lying between –4 and 11. Clearly,

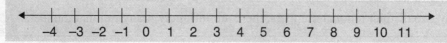

$-4 < -3 < -2 < -1 < 0 < 1 < 2 < 3 < 4 < 5 < 6 < 7 < 8 < 9 < 10 < 11.$

$\therefore \quad \dfrac{-4}{13} < \dfrac{-3}{13} < \dfrac{-2}{13} < \dfrac{-1}{13} < \dfrac{0}{13} < \dfrac{1}{13} < \dfrac{2}{13} < \dfrac{3}{13} < \dfrac{4}{13} < \dfrac{5}{13} < \dfrac{6}{13} < \dfrac{7}{13} < \dfrac{8}{13} < \dfrac{9}{13} < \dfrac{10}{13} < \dfrac{11}{13}$

$\therefore$ 14 rational numbers between $\dfrac{-4}{13}$ and $\dfrac{11}{13}$ are

$\dfrac{-3}{13}, \dfrac{-2}{13}, \dfrac{-1}{13}, \dfrac{0}{13}, \dfrac{1}{13}, \dfrac{2}{13}, \dfrac{3}{13}, \dfrac{4}{13}, \dfrac{5}{13}, \dfrac{6}{13}, \dfrac{7}{13}, \dfrac{8}{13}, \dfrac{9}{13}, \dfrac{10}{13}.$

(ii) Taking the equivalent fractions with common denominator of $\dfrac{-4}{13}$ and $\dfrac{11}{13}$ as

$\dfrac{-4}{13} = \dfrac{-4 \times 5}{13 \times 5} = \dfrac{-20}{65}, \quad \dfrac{11}{13} = \dfrac{11 \times 5}{13 \times 5} = \dfrac{55}{65}$

We have $\dfrac{-20}{65} < \dfrac{-19}{65} < \dfrac{-18}{65} < \ldots\ldots < \dfrac{-1}{65} < 0, \dfrac{1}{65} < \dfrac{2}{65} < \dfrac{3}{65} < \ldots\ldots, < \dfrac{55}{65}.$

Seventy rational numbers between $\dfrac{-4}{13}$ and $\dfrac{11}{13}$ are :

$\dfrac{-19}{65}, \dfrac{-18}{65}, \dfrac{-17}{65}, \ldots\ldots, \dfrac{-2}{65}, \dfrac{-1}{65}, \dfrac{0}{65}, \dfrac{1}{65}, \dfrac{2}{65} \ldots\ldots \dfrac{50}{65}.$

(iii) Taking the equivalent fractions with common denominator of $\dfrac{-4}{13}$ and $\dfrac{11}{13}$ as

$\dfrac{-4}{13} = \dfrac{-4 \times 10}{13 \times 10} = \dfrac{-40}{130}$ and $\dfrac{11}{13} = \dfrac{11 \times 10}{13 \times 10} = \dfrac{110}{130}$, we have

$\dfrac{-40}{130} < \dfrac{-39}{130} < \dfrac{-38}{130} < \ldots\ldots < \dfrac{-1}{130} < 0 < \dfrac{1}{130} < \dfrac{2}{130} < \dfrac{3}{130} < \ldots\ldots < \dfrac{110}{130}.$

$\therefore$ One hundred rational numbers between $\dfrac{-4}{13}$ and $\dfrac{11}{13}$ are

$\dfrac{-39}{130}, \dfrac{-38}{130}, \dfrac{-37}{130}, \ldots\ldots \dfrac{-1}{130}, 0, \dfrac{1}{130}, \dfrac{2}{130}, \ldots\ldots \dfrac{60}{130}.$

EXERCISE 1 (e)

1. Find a rational number between a and b, if :

(a) $a = \dfrac{1}{5}, b = \dfrac{1}{4}$ (b) $a = \dfrac{1}{8}, b = \dfrac{7}{12}$ (c) $a = \dfrac{-5}{6}, b = -\dfrac{2}{5}$ (d) $a = -\dfrac{4}{9}, b = \dfrac{11}{6}$

2. Find two rational numbers between -2 and 2.   **3.** Find three rational numbers between -2 and $-\dfrac{7}{2}$.

4. Find four rational numbers between -1 and $-\dfrac{1}{2}$.   **5.** Find six rational numbers between -1 and 0.

6. Insert 10 rational numbers between $\dfrac{-3}{11}$ and $\dfrac{8}{11}$.   **7.** Insert 100 rational numbers between $\dfrac{-3}{13}$ and $\dfrac{9}{13}$.

8. Find (i) Six (ii) Sixty (iii) Six hundred rational between $\dfrac{-5}{8}$ and $\dfrac{3}{8}$.

9. State true or false :

(a) Between any two distinct integers, there is always an integer.

(b) Between any two distinct rational numbers, there is always a rational number.

(c) Between any two distinct rational numbers, there are infinitely many rational numbers.

1.18 Word Problems

Ex. 1. *The product of two number is $\frac{5}{9}$. If one of the numbers is $\frac{-35}{24}$, find the other?*

Sol. Product $= \frac{5}{9}$, One number $= -\frac{35}{24}$

∴ The other number $= \frac{5}{9} \div \left(\frac{-35}{24}\right) = \frac{\overset{1}{\cancel{5}}}{\cancel{9}_3} \times \frac{\overset{8}{\cancel{24}}}{-\cancel{35}_7} = \frac{1 \times 8}{3 \times -7} = \frac{8}{-21} = \frac{-8}{21}$.

Ex. 2. *Radhika had a certain amount of money in her piggy bank. She spent Rs $10\frac{1}{4}$ in the school canteen, gave Rs $15\frac{1}{2}$ to her friend and bought a gift worth Rs $25\frac{3}{4}$ for her brother. Radhika then had a balance of Rs $200\frac{1}{8}$. How much did she have to begin with.*

Sol. To begin with Radhika had

$$= \text{Rs } 10\frac{1}{4} + \text{Rs } 15\frac{1}{2} + \text{Rs } 25\frac{3}{4} + \text{Rs } 200\frac{1}{8}$$

$$= \text{Rs } \left[(10 + 15 + 25 + 200) + \left(\frac{1}{4} + \frac{1}{2} + \frac{3}{4} + \frac{1}{8}\right)\right]$$

$$= \text{Rs } \left[250 + \frac{2 + 4 + 6 + 1}{8}\right] = \text{Rs } \left[250 + \frac{13}{8}\right]$$

$$= \text{Rs } \left[250 + 1\frac{5}{8}\right] = \textbf{Rs } \mathbf{251\frac{5}{8}}.$$

Ex. 3. *A recipe for French toast calls for $\frac{3}{4}$ litres of milk. If you want to make only $\frac{2}{3}$ of the recipe, how much milk should you use?*

Sol. Amount of milk required $= \left(\frac{2}{3} \times \frac{3}{4}\right)l = \frac{1}{2}l.$

Ex. 4. *The area of a rectangle is $45\frac{5}{16}$ cm^2. If one edge is $6\frac{1}{4}$ cm, find the other.*

Sol. Area of the rectangle $= 45\frac{5}{16}$ cm$^2 = \frac{725}{16}$ cm^2

One edge $= 6\frac{1}{4}$ cm $= \frac{25}{4}$ cm.

∴ The other edge $= \left(\frac{725}{16} \div \frac{25}{4}\right)$cm $= \left(\frac{725}{16} \times \frac{4}{25}\right)$cm $= \frac{29}{4}$ cm $= 7\frac{1}{4}$**cm**.

EXERCISE 1 (f)

1. The product of two rational numbers is –12. If one of the number is –8, find the other.

2. By what rational number should $\frac{-7}{85}$ be multiplied to obtain $\frac{1}{17}$?

3. Divide the sum of $\frac{3}{8}$ and $\frac{-5}{12}$ by the reciprocal of $\frac{-15}{8} \times \frac{16}{27}$.

4. By what rational number should $\dfrac{-15}{56}$ be divided to get $\dfrac{-5}{7}$?

5. The perimeter of an isosceles triangle is $10\dfrac{3}{4}$ cm. If one of its equal sides is $2\dfrac{5}{6}$ cm, find the third side.

6. The area of a rectangular table top is $5\dfrac{3}{8}$ m². If one of the sides measures $2\dfrac{1}{4}$ m, find the length of the other side.

7. The cost of $12\dfrac{3}{5}$ kg of mangoes is Rs $330\dfrac{3}{4}$. What is the cost of 1 kg of mango.

8. A train covers $80\dfrac{4}{5}$ km in 1 hour. How much distance will it cover is $4\dfrac{3}{4}$ hours?

9. What is the perimeter of a quadrilateral whose four sides measure $3\dfrac{1}{6}$ cm, $2\dfrac{3}{4}$ cm, $4\dfrac{5}{12}$ cm and $2\dfrac{1}{2}$ cm.

10. If $\dfrac{1}{3}$ of a number exceeds its $\dfrac{2}{7}$ by 1, find the number.

11. Rohit travelled $1\dfrac{1}{8}$ km from home to school, $\dfrac{5}{6}$ km from school to skating rink, $\dfrac{2}{3}$ km from skating rink to work and $\dfrac{5}{16}$ km from work to his home. How many km did Rohit travel.

12. Concert tickets usually cost Rs $120\dfrac{4}{5}$ per person. For students they are priced at $\dfrac{1}{4}$ of the normal cost. How much will 6 tickets cost for students?

13. In the last three months Mr. Sharma lost $5\dfrac{1}{2}$ kg, gained $2\dfrac{1}{4}$ kg and then lost $3\dfrac{3}{4}$ kg. If he now weighs 95 kg, how much did Mr. Sharma weigh to begin with.

14. If $12\dfrac{1}{2}$ m of rope is to be divided into $1\dfrac{1}{4}$ m pieces, how many pieces will be there?

15. If a triangle has a base of $10\dfrac{3}{4}$ cm and a height of $15\dfrac{3}{4}$ cm, what is its area?

LOOKING BACK
Summary of Key Facts

1. Property of closure : If x and y are any two rational numbers, then

   (a) $\dfrac{a}{b} + \dfrac{c}{d}$ is a rational number ; *e.g.* $\dfrac{1}{2} + \dfrac{3}{4} = \dfrac{5}{4}$ is a rational number

   (b) $\dfrac{a}{b} - \dfrac{c}{d}$ is a rational number ; *e.g.* $\dfrac{1}{2} - \dfrac{3}{4} = \dfrac{-1}{4}$ is a rational number.

   (c) $\dfrac{a}{b} \times \dfrac{c}{d}$ is a rational number. *e.g.* $\dfrac{1}{2} \times \dfrac{3}{4} = \dfrac{3}{8}$ is a rational number.

   (d) $\dfrac{a}{b} \div \dfrac{c}{d} \left(\dfrac{c}{d} \neq 0 \right)$ is a rational number. $\dfrac{1}{2} \div \dfrac{3}{4} = \dfrac{2}{3}$ is a rational number.

2. Commutative Law : For any rational numbers $\dfrac{a}{b}, \dfrac{c}{d}$

   (a) $\dfrac{a}{b} + \dfrac{c}{d} = \dfrac{c}{d} + \dfrac{a}{b}$ (comm. law of addition) *e.g.* $\dfrac{5}{7} + \dfrac{-8}{9} = \dfrac{-8}{9} + \dfrac{5}{7}$

(b) $\frac{a}{b} \times \frac{c}{d} = \frac{c}{d} \times \frac{a}{b}$ (comm. law of multiplication) e.g. $\frac{5}{7} \times \frac{-8}{9} = \frac{-8}{9} \times \frac{5}{7}$

This law does not hold for the operations of subtraction and division, i.e., $\frac{a}{b} - \frac{c}{d} \neq \frac{c}{d} - \frac{a}{b}$ and $\frac{a}{b} \div \frac{c}{d} \neq \frac{c}{d} \div \frac{a}{b}$.

3. **Associative Law :** For any rational numbers x, y, z ;

(a) $\frac{a}{b} + \frac{c}{d} + \frac{e}{f} = \frac{a}{b} + \frac{c}{d} + \frac{e}{f}$ (associative law of addition). e.g. $\left(\frac{1}{2} + \frac{-3}{4}\right) + \frac{4}{5} = \frac{1}{2} + \left(\frac{-3}{4} + \frac{4}{5}\right)$

(b) $\frac{a}{b} \times \frac{c}{d} \times \frac{e}{f} = \frac{a}{b} \times \frac{c}{d} \times \frac{e}{f}$ (associative law of multiplication) e.g. $\left(\frac{1}{2} \times \frac{-3}{4}\right) \times \frac{4}{5} = \frac{1}{2} \times \left(\frac{-3}{4} \times \frac{4}{5}\right)$

4. **Distributive law :**

(a) $\frac{a}{b} \times \left(\frac{c}{d} + \frac{e}{f}\right) = \frac{a}{b} \times \frac{c}{d} + \frac{a}{b} \times \frac{e}{f}$ (distributive law of multiplication over addition).

e.g. $\frac{-3}{4} \times \left(\frac{8}{7} + \frac{5}{-2}\right) = \frac{-3}{4} \times \frac{8}{7} + \left(\frac{-3}{4} \times \frac{5}{-2}\right)$

(b) $\frac{a}{b} \times \left(\frac{c}{d} - \frac{e}{f}\right) = \frac{a}{b} \times \frac{c}{d} - \frac{a}{b} \times \frac{e}{f}$ (distributive law of multiplication over subtraction).

e.g. $\frac{-3}{4} \times \left(\frac{8}{7} - \frac{5}{-2}\right) = \left(\frac{-3}{4} \times \frac{8}{7}\right) - \left(\frac{-3}{4} \times \frac{5}{-2}\right)$

5. **Identity element.** For a rational number $\frac{a}{b}$, $(b \neq 0)$,

(a) $\frac{a}{b} + 0 = 0 + \frac{a}{b} = \frac{a}{b}$. Zero is called the additive identity.

(b) $\frac{a}{b} - 0 = \frac{a}{b}$.

(c) $\frac{a}{b} \times 1 = 1 \times \frac{a}{b} = \frac{a}{b}$ × 1 is called the multiplicative identity.

(d) $\frac{a}{b} \div 1 = \frac{a}{b}$.

6. **Multiplication by Zero.** For any rational number $\frac{a}{b}$, $\frac{a}{b} \times 0 = 0 \times \frac{a}{b} = 0$.

We cannot divide by zero, i.e., $\frac{a}{b} \div 0$ is not defined.

7. **Additive and Multiplicative Inverse.** For any rational number $\frac{a}{b}$,

(a) $\frac{a}{b} + \left(-\frac{a}{b}\right) = \left(-\frac{a}{b}\right) + \frac{a}{b} = 0$. $-\frac{a}{b}$ is called the additive inverse of $\frac{a}{b}$.

(b) $\frac{a}{b} \times \left(\frac{a}{b}\right)^{-1} = 1 = \left(\frac{a}{b}\right)^{-1} \times \frac{a}{b} = 1$. $\left(\frac{a}{b}\right)^{-1}$ or $\frac{1}{a/b}$ is called the multiplicative inverse or reciprocal of $\frac{a}{b}$.

e.g., $\frac{7}{5}$ is the multiplicative inverse or reciprocal of $\frac{5}{7}$.

(c) $\left(\left(\frac{a}{b}\right)^{-1}\right)^{-1} = \frac{a}{b}$, i.e., the reciprocal of the reciprocal of any rational number is the rational number itself.

e.g. reciprocal of $\frac{-9}{8}$ is $\frac{-8}{9}$ and reciprocal of $\frac{-8}{9}$ is $\frac{-9}{8}$, i.e., $\left(\left(\frac{-9}{8}\right)^{-1}\right)^{-1} = \frac{-9}{8}$.

8. If $\frac{a}{b}$ and $\frac{c}{d}$ are any two rational numbers, then $\frac{1}{2}\left(\frac{a}{b}+\frac{c}{d}\right)$ is a rational number, lying between $\frac{a}{b}$ and $\frac{c}{d}$

  e.g., A rational number lying between $-\frac{3}{2}$ and $\frac{5}{8}$ is $\frac{1}{2}\left(-\frac{3}{2}+\frac{5}{8}\right)=\frac{1}{2}\left(\frac{-3\times4+5}{8}\right)=\frac{1}{2}\left(\frac{-7}{8}\right)=\frac{-7}{16}$.

9. Between two rational numbers $\frac{a}{b}$ and $\frac{c}{d}$, infinitely many rational numbers can be found.

MENTAL MATHS – 1

1. Add $\frac{2}{-7}$ and $\frac{11}{7}$

2. **Subtract** (i) $\frac{13}{17}$ from $\frac{18}{17}$ (ii) $\frac{-4}{9}$ from $\frac{7}{18}$.

3. **State the additive inverse of** (i) $\frac{2}{3}$ (ii) $\frac{8}{-15}$ (iii) 0 (iv) –1.

4. The sum of the two numbers is $\frac{5}{8}$. If one of the numbers is $\frac{3}{4}$, find the other.

5. **Simplify :** $\frac{-8}{14}\times\frac{7}{2}$

6. **Multiply :** $\frac{-9}{17}$ by $\frac{-85}{18}$

7. $\frac{-3}{17}\times0=\frac{-3}{17}$. True or False?

8. $\frac{6}{35}\div0=0$, True or False?

9. How much is $\frac{-6}{37}\times(-1)$?

10. **State the reciprocal of** (i) $\frac{7}{18}$ (ii) $\frac{9}{-19}$ (iii) –20

11. Evaluate $\left|\frac{-4}{5}+\frac{9}{20}\right|$

12. $\left(\frac{p}{q}\right)\times\left(\frac{p}{q}\right)^{-1}=1$. True or False?

13. **What is the reciprocal of** $\frac{1}{a}$ if (i) $a = 0$ (ii) $a \neq 0$?

14. State the multiplicative inverse of $\left|\frac{-4}{5}\right|$.

Divide :

15. 1 by $\frac{1}{4}$ 16. 0 by $\frac{-28}{19}$ 17. $\frac{5}{7}$ by $\frac{5}{-7}$

18. State the reciprocal of $\left|-\frac{7}{9}\right|$.

Find a rational number between :

19. –3 and 7   20. $\frac{2}{9}$ and $\frac{5}{9}$

21. **Fill in the blanks :**

  (i) $\left(\frac{5}{7}\right)+\left(\frac{-11}{12}\right)=\left(\frac{-11}{12}\right)+$ ....

  (ii) $\frac{1}{2}\times\left(\frac{1}{3}+\frac{1}{4}\right)=\frac{1}{2}\times\frac{1}{3}+\frac{1}{2}\times$ ....

22. $x \div (y + z) = x \div y + x \div z$. True or False?

MULTIPLE CHOICE QUESTIONS – 1

1. What number should be added to $\frac{-3}{4}$ to get $\frac{+7}{6}$?

  (a) $\frac{11}{24}$ (b) $\frac{10}{25}$ (c) $\frac{23}{12}$ (d) $\frac{9}{24}$

2. The property of rational number illustrated by the mathematical expression $\left(\frac{2}{7}+\frac{-3}{8}\right)\times\frac{5}{11}=\left(\frac{2}{7}\times\frac{5}{11}\right)+\left(\frac{-3}{8}\times\frac{5}{11}\right)$ is

  (a) Associativity of Addition   (b) Distributivity of Multiplication over Addition
  (c) Associativity of Multiplication   (d) Commutativity.

3. $\frac{3}{8}\div\left(\frac{-51}{24}\div\frac{17}{12}\right)$ is equal to :

(a) $\dfrac{3}{4}$ (b) $-\dfrac{1}{4}$ (c) $\dfrac{1}{4}$ (d) $\dfrac{5}{48}$

4. The rational number equivalent to $\dfrac{-24}{45}$ is :

(a) $\dfrac{12}{20}$ (b) $\dfrac{8}{15}$ (c) $\dfrac{-6}{9}$ (d) $\dfrac{4}{11}$

5. Which of the following rational number is in standard form?

(a) $\dfrac{-14}{30}$ (b) $\dfrac{6}{-7}$ (c) $\dfrac{-39}{125}$ (d) $\dfrac{-21}{78}$

6. $\dfrac{-6}{11}$ lies :

(a) to left of 0 on the number line

(b) to the right of 0 on the number line

(c) sometimes to the left and sometimes to the right of 0 in the number line

(d) none of these

7. $\dfrac{-6}{7} \times (\ldots\ldots) = \dfrac{4}{5}$

(a) $\dfrac{3}{10}$ (b) $-\dfrac{21}{45}$ (c) $\dfrac{-14}{15}$ (d) $\dfrac{14}{15}$

8. The smallest rational number in $\dfrac{4}{-9}, \dfrac{-5}{12}, \dfrac{7}{18}, \dfrac{-2}{3}$ is

(a) $\dfrac{4}{-9}$ (b) $\dfrac{-9}{12}$ (c) $\dfrac{7}{-18}$ (d) $\dfrac{-2}{3}$

9. The reciprocal of a negative rational number a is

(a) $-a$ (b) $\dfrac{1}{a}$ (c) $-\dfrac{1}{a}$ (d) none of these

10. The area of a rectangle is $6\dfrac{1}{3}$ cm^2. If its length is $6\dfrac{1}{4}$ cm, its breadth is

(a) $1\dfrac{1}{5}$ cm (b) $1\dfrac{1}{75}$ cm (c) $3\dfrac{1}{15}$ cm (d) $4\dfrac{1}{5}$ cm

ANSWERS

EXERCISE 1 (a)

1. (a) $\dfrac{4}{10}, \dfrac{6}{15}, \dfrac{8}{20}, \dfrac{10}{25}$ (b) $\dfrac{-10}{18}, \dfrac{-15}{27}, \dfrac{-20}{36}, \dfrac{-25}{45}$ (c) $\dfrac{16}{-22}, \dfrac{24}{-33}, \dfrac{32}{-44}, \dfrac{40}{-55}$ (d) $\dfrac{-24}{26}, \dfrac{-36}{39}, \dfrac{-48}{52}, \dfrac{-60}{65}$

2. $\dfrac{-63}{24}$ **3.** $\dfrac{4}{-12}$ **4.** (a) < (b) < (c) < (d) < (e) > (f) > **5.** (a) $-\dfrac{25}{28}, -\dfrac{1}{2}, -\dfrac{3}{7}, -\dfrac{5}{14}$

(b) $\dfrac{-11}{15}, \dfrac{-3}{10}, -\dfrac{1}{5}, \dfrac{13}{20}$ **6.** (a) $\dfrac{5}{8}$ (b) $\dfrac{7}{10}$ (c) 0 (d) $\dfrac{11}{12}$ (e) $\dfrac{16}{19}$

(f) $\dfrac{25}{64}$ (g) 8 (h) $\dfrac{11}{56}$ (i) $\dfrac{13}{30}$ (j) 125 **7.** (a) < (b) >

8. (a) $\dfrac{-11}{13}, \dfrac{11}{13}$ (b) $-7, 7$ (c) $\dfrac{-23}{27}, \dfrac{23}{27}$ **11.** (a) T (b) F (c) F (d) T

(e) F (f) T (g) T

EXERCISE 1 (b)

1. (a) $\dfrac{5}{7}$ (b) $-\dfrac{2}{13}$ (c) $\dfrac{2}{15}$ (d) $\dfrac{-29}{36}$ (e) $\dfrac{3}{25}$ (f) $\dfrac{-5}{14}$ (g) $8\dfrac{1}{12}$

(h) $2\dfrac{13}{14}$ 2. (a) $\dfrac{11}{36}$ (b) $\dfrac{-29}{150}$ (c) $-\dfrac{1}{3}$ (d) $\dfrac{2}{5}$ 5. (a) $\dfrac{-4}{15}$ (b) -10

(c) $\dfrac{-7}{8}$ (d) $\dfrac{7}{-4}$ (e) $\dfrac{-5}{12}$ (f) 0 (g) 0 6. (a) $\dfrac{-2}{3}$ (b) $\dfrac{-17}{9}$

(c) 23 (d) $\dfrac{17}{9}$ (e) $\dfrac{8}{29}$ (f) 0 (g) $\dfrac{-15}{11}$ (h) $\dfrac{-21}{30}$ (i) $\dfrac{21}{40}$

7. (a) $1\dfrac{2}{5}$ (b) $1\dfrac{7}{17}$ (c) $\dfrac{-3}{10}$ (d) $\dfrac{-3}{5}$ (e) $\dfrac{-14}{15}$ (f) $3\dfrac{2}{9}$ (g) $-1\dfrac{7}{60}$

10. (a) $\dfrac{2}{5}$ (b) $\dfrac{-11}{18}$ (c) $\dfrac{17}{30}$ (d) $\dfrac{31}{20}$ (e) $\dfrac{-5}{16}$ (f) $\dfrac{77}{40}$ 11. $\dfrac{11}{72}$

12. $\dfrac{29}{48}$ 13. $\dfrac{5}{24}$ 14. $\dfrac{59}{60}$ 15. (a) $1\dfrac{1}{21}$ (b) 2.

EXERCISE 1 (c)

1. (a) $\dfrac{4}{7}$ (b) $\dfrac{-2}{7}$ (c) $\dfrac{10}{39}$ (d) $\dfrac{25}{4}$ (e) -12 (f) $\dfrac{-45}{28}$ 2. (a) $\dfrac{-7}{6}$

(b) $\dfrac{-3}{2}$ 6. (a) $\dfrac{-18}{37}$ (b) -19 (c) $\dfrac{6}{11}$ (d) $\dfrac{3}{7}$ (e) $\dfrac{1}{8}\times\dfrac{6}{17}$ 7. (a) $\dfrac{63}{32}$

(b) $\dfrac{3}{8}$ (c) $\dfrac{197}{20}$ 8. (a) $\dfrac{1}{6}$ (b) $-\dfrac{1}{23}$ (c) $\dfrac{20}{11}$ (d) $\dfrac{16}{-19}$ (e) $\dfrac{-5}{11}$

(f) $\dfrac{8}{7}$ (g) $\dfrac{10}{3}$ (h) $\dfrac{2}{3}$ (i) $\dfrac{35}{8}$ (j) does not exist.

10. (a) Closure (b) Multiplication by 0 (c) Commutativity (d) Property of 1
(e) Distributivity of multiplication over addition. (f) Property of 1 (g) Multiplication by 0
(h) Associativity (i) Distributivity of multiplication over addition (j) Reciprocal

11. Closure and multiplication by 1. 12. Closure, Associativity in '×', multiplicative inverse and property of 1.

13. 1 14. $1, -1$ 15. (a) -64 (b) -14

16. (a) 1 (b) not (c) no (d) a (e) 19^{-1} (f) $\dfrac{3}{7}$

EXERCISE 1 (d)

1. (a) $\dfrac{1}{27}$ (b) $\dfrac{-17}{12}$ (c) $\dfrac{-5}{3}$ (d) $\dfrac{9}{40}$ (e) $\dfrac{37}{2}$ (f) 9

3. (a) 1 (b) $\dfrac{-8}{15}$ (c) $\dfrac{-12}{13}$ (d) 1 (e) $\dfrac{-9}{17}$ (f) $\dfrac{-13}{25}$

4. (a) $\dfrac{-8}{5}$ (b) 7

EXERCISE 1 (e)

1. (a) $\dfrac{9}{40}$ (b) $\dfrac{17}{48}$ (c) $\dfrac{-37}{60}$ (d) $\dfrac{25}{36}$ 2. $0, 1$ 3. $\dfrac{-11}{4}, \dfrac{-25}{8}, \dfrac{-53}{16}$

4. $\dfrac{-7}{8}, \dfrac{-3}{4}, \dfrac{-5}{8}, \dfrac{-9}{16}$ 5. $-\dfrac{1}{2}, -\dfrac{1}{4}, -\dfrac{1}{8}, -\dfrac{1}{16}, -\dfrac{1}{32}, -\dfrac{1}{64}$ 6. (a) $\dfrac{-2}{11}, \dfrac{-1}{11}, \dfrac{0}{11}, \dfrac{1}{11}, \dfrac{2}{11}, \dfrac{3}{11}, \dfrac{4}{11}, \dfrac{5}{11}, \dfrac{6}{11}, \dfrac{7}{11}$

7. $\dfrac{-29}{130}, \dfrac{-28}{130}, ..., \dfrac{-1}{130}, 0, \dfrac{1}{130}, \dfrac{2}{130}, ..., \dfrac{70}{130}$ 8. (a) $\dfrac{-4}{8}, \dfrac{-3}{8}, \dfrac{-2}{8}, \dfrac{-1}{8}, 0, \dfrac{1}{8}$ (b) $\dfrac{-49}{80}, \dfrac{-48}{80}, ..., 0, ..., \dfrac{10}{80}$.

(c) $\dfrac{-499}{800}, \dfrac{-498}{800}, ..., 0, \dfrac{1}{800}, ..., \dfrac{99}{800}, \dfrac{100}{800}$ 9. (a) False (b) True (c) True.

EXERCISE 1 (f)

1. $\dfrac{3}{2}$ 2. $\dfrac{-5}{7}$ 3. $\dfrac{5}{108}$ 4. $\dfrac{3}{8}$ 5. $5\dfrac{1}{12}$ cm 6. $\dfrac{43}{18}$ m 7. Rs $26\dfrac{1}{4}$

8. $383\dfrac{4}{5}$ km 9. $12\dfrac{5}{6}$ cm 10. 21 11. $2\dfrac{15}{16}$ km 12. Rs $181\dfrac{1}{5}$ 13. 102 kg 14. 10

15. $84\dfrac{21}{32}$ cm^2

MENTAL MATHS – 1

1. $\dfrac{9}{7}$ 2. (i) $\dfrac{5}{17}$ (ii) $\dfrac{15}{18}$ 3. (i) $\dfrac{-2}{3}$ (ii) $\dfrac{8}{15}$ (iii) 0 (iv) 1

4. $-\dfrac{1}{8}$ 5. -2 6. $\dfrac{5}{2}$ 7. False 8. False 9. $\dfrac{6}{37}$

10. (i) $\dfrac{18}{7}$ (ii) $\dfrac{-19}{6}$ (iii) $\dfrac{1}{-20}$ 11. $\dfrac{7}{20}$ 12. True 13. (i) does not exist (ii) a

14. $\dfrac{5}{4}$ 15. 4 16. 0 17. -1 18. $\dfrac{9}{7}$ 19. 6 20. $\dfrac{3}{9}$

21. (i) $\dfrac{5}{7}$ (ii) $\dfrac{1}{4}$ 22. False.

MULTIPLE CHOICE QUESTIONS – 1

1. (c) 2. (b) 3. (b) 4. (b) 5. (c) 6. (a)
7. (c) 8. (d) 9. (b) 10. (b)

HISTORICAL NOTE

1. The Lilavati explains the process of division as follows. After reversing the numerator and denominator of the divisor, the remaining process of division of fractions is that of multiplication.

2. The Babylonians also used reciprocals in order to divide two numbers. They wrote $a \div b = a : \left(\dfrac{1}{b}\right)$ and developed tables of reciprocals.

2. Exponents

2.1 Introduction

You have learnt in class VII that if we multiply an integer by itself again and again, then it can be written in a short form in *exponential or power notation.*

For example : $4 \times 4 \times 4 = 4^3$ $\qquad (-3) \times (-3) \times (-3) \times (-3) \times (-3) = (-3)^5$

In the same manner, we can write

$$\frac{1}{2} \times \frac{1}{2} \times \frac{1}{2} \times \frac{1}{2} \times \frac{1}{2} \times \frac{1}{2} \times \frac{1}{2} = \left(\frac{1}{2}\right)^7$$

$$\frac{-5}{7} \times \frac{-5}{7} \times \frac{-5}{7} \times \frac{-5}{7} = \left(\frac{-5}{7}\right)^4$$

$$\left(-\frac{5}{7}\right)^4 \text{ means } \frac{-5}{7} \times \frac{-5}{7} \times \frac{-5}{7} \times \frac{-5}{7}$$

EXPONENT — BASE

$\left(-\dfrac{5}{7}\right)$ raised to the power four

A numeral such as $\left(\dfrac{1}{2}\right)^7$ is called an **exponential expression.**

In $\left(\dfrac{1}{2}\right)^7, \dfrac{1}{2}$ is called the base and 7 the exponent. We read $\left(\dfrac{1}{2}\right)^7$ as $\dfrac{1}{2}$ raised to the power 7.

In general,

For any rational number 'a' and a positive integer n, we define
a^n *as* $a \times a \times a \times a \times \text{................. } \times a$ *(n times)*
a^n *is called the nth power of 'a' and is also read as 'a raised to the power of n'.*

The rational number '*a*' is called the **base** and *n* is called the **exponent** or **power** or **index.**

Now look at the following illustrations :

$$(-1)^2 = -1 \times -1 = 1, \quad (-1)^3 = -1 \times -1 \times -1 = -1$$

$$(-2)^6 = -2 \times -2 \times -2 \times -2 \times -2 \times -2 = 64$$

$$(-2)^7 = -2 \times -2 \times -2 \times -2 \times -2 \times -2 \times -2 = -128$$

$$\left(-\frac{1}{3}\right)^4 = -\frac{1}{3} \times -\frac{1}{3} \times -\frac{1}{3} \times -\frac{1}{3} = \frac{1}{81}, \qquad \left(-\frac{1}{3}\right)^5 = -\frac{1}{3} \times -\frac{1}{3} \times -\frac{1}{3} \times -\frac{1}{3} \times -\frac{1}{3} = -\frac{1}{243}.$$

Also, we have

$$\left(\frac{5}{6}\right)^3 = \frac{5}{6} \times \frac{5}{6} \times \frac{5}{6} = \frac{5 \times 5 \times 5}{6 \times 6 \times 6} = \frac{5^3}{6^3} = \frac{125}{216}.$$

$$\left(\frac{-3}{2}\right)^5 = \frac{-3}{2} \times \frac{-3}{2} \times \frac{-3}{2} \times \frac{-3}{2} \times \frac{-3}{2} = \frac{-3 \times -3 \times -3 \times -3 \times -3}{2 \times 2 \times 2 \times 2 \times 2} = \frac{(-3)^5}{2^5} = \frac{-243}{32}.$$

Do you observe that

I. (1) A negative rational number raised to an even power is positive, *e.g.* $\left(\dfrac{-2}{3}\right)^2 = \dfrac{4}{9}$.

(2) A negative rational number raised to an odd power is negative, *e.g.* $\left(\dfrac{-2}{3}\right)^3 = \dfrac{-8}{27}$.

(3) When the power of –1 is any even natural number, the product is always 1.

(4) When the power of –1 is any odd natural number, the product is always –1.

$$(-1)^{\text{odd natural number}} = -1, \quad (-1)^{\text{even natural number}} = 1$$

Thus, $\qquad\qquad (-1)^{47} = -1, \; (-1)^{193} = -1, \; (-1)^{50} = 1, \; (-1)^{376} = 1$

II. If $\dfrac{p}{q}$ is any rational number and n is any integer, then $\left(\dfrac{p}{q}\right)^n = \dfrac{p^n}{q^n}$; *e.g.*, $\left(\dfrac{5}{7}\right)^2 = \dfrac{5^2}{7^2}; = \dfrac{25}{49}$.

Ex. 1. *Express each of the following powers of rational numbers as a rational number :*

(i) $\left(\dfrac{2}{5}\right)^4$ (ii) $\left(\dfrac{-3}{7}\right)^3$ (iii) $\left(-\dfrac{3}{4}\right)^4$

Sol. (i) $\left(\dfrac{2}{5}\right)^4 = \dfrac{2}{5} \times \dfrac{2}{5} \times \dfrac{2}{5} \times \dfrac{2}{5} = \dfrac{2 \times 2 \times 2 \times 2}{5 \times 5 \times 5 \times 5} = \dfrac{\mathbf{16}}{\mathbf{625}}$.

(ii) $\left(\dfrac{-3}{7}\right)^3 = \dfrac{-3}{7} \times \dfrac{-3}{7} \times \dfrac{-3}{7} = \dfrac{-3 \times -3 \times -3}{7 \times 7 \times 7} = \dfrac{\mathbf{-27}}{\mathbf{343}}$.

(iii) $\left(\dfrac{-3}{4}\right)^4 = \dfrac{-3}{4} \times \dfrac{-3}{4} \times \dfrac{-3}{4} \times \dfrac{-3}{4} = \dfrac{-3 \times -3 \times -3 \times -3}{4 \times 4 \times 4 \times 4} = \dfrac{\mathbf{81}}{\mathbf{256}}$.

Ex. 2. *Express in power notation :*

(i) $\dfrac{16}{81}$ (ii) $\dfrac{-27}{343}$ (iii) $-\dfrac{1}{243}$

Sol. (i) $\dfrac{16}{81} = \dfrac{2 \times 2 \times 2 \times 2}{3 \times 3 \times 3 \times 3} = \dfrac{2^4}{3^4} = \left(\dfrac{2}{3}\right)^4$.

Result used :
$\dfrac{p^n}{q^n} = \left(\dfrac{p}{q}\right)^n$

(ii) $\dfrac{-27}{343} = \dfrac{-3 \times -3 \times -3}{7 \times 7 \times 7} = \dfrac{(-3)^3}{7^3} = \left(\dfrac{-3}{7}\right)^3$.

(iii) $-\dfrac{1}{243} = \dfrac{-1}{243} = \dfrac{-1}{3 \times 3 \times 3 \times 3 \times 3} = \dfrac{(-1)^5}{3^5} = \left(\dfrac{-1}{3}\right)^5$.

3	243
3	81
3	27
3	9
	3

Ex. 3. *Find value of*

(i) $2x^2 + y^3$ *for* $x = \dfrac{-1}{3}$ *and* $y = \dfrac{-2}{3}$. (ii) $a^6 - (b + 1)^3$ *when* $a = \dfrac{1}{2}$, $b = \dfrac{-3}{4}$.

Sol. (i) $\qquad 2x^2 + y^3 = \left(2 \times \left(\dfrac{-1}{3}\right)^2\right) + \left(\dfrac{-2}{3}\right)^3 = \left(2 \times \dfrac{(-1)^2}{3 \times 3}\right) + \dfrac{(-2)^3}{3^3}$

$$= 2 \times \dfrac{1}{9} + \dfrac{-8}{27} = \dfrac{2}{9} + \dfrac{-8}{27} = \dfrac{2 \times 3 + -8 \times 1}{27} = \dfrac{6 + (-8)}{27} = \dfrac{-2}{27}.$$

(ii) $\quad a^6 - (b+1)^3 = \left(\dfrac{1}{2}\right)^6 - \left(\dfrac{-3}{4}+1\right)^3 = \dfrac{1}{2\times2\times2\times2\times2\times2} - \left(\dfrac{-3}{4}+\dfrac{1}{1}\right)^3$

$\qquad = \dfrac{1}{64} - \left(\dfrac{-3\times1+1\times4}{4}\right)^3 = \dfrac{1}{64} - \left(\dfrac{-3+4}{4}\right)^3 = \dfrac{1}{64} - \left(\dfrac{1}{4}\right)^3$

$\qquad = \dfrac{1}{64} - \dfrac{1\times1\times1}{4\times4\times4} = \dfrac{1}{64} - \dfrac{1}{64} = \dfrac{1-1}{64} = \dfrac{0}{64} = \mathbf{0}.$

Ex. 4. *Find the value of*

(a) $\left(\dfrac{-3}{5}\right)^4 \times \left(\dfrac{1}{3}\right)^3$
(b) $(-2)^5 \div \left(-\dfrac{1}{3}\right)^4.$

Sol. (a) $\left(\dfrac{-3}{5}\right)^4 \times \left(\dfrac{1}{3}\right)^3 = \dfrac{-3}{5}\times\dfrac{-3}{5}\times\dfrac{-3}{5}\times\dfrac{-3}{5}\times\dfrac{1}{3}\times\dfrac{1}{3}\times\dfrac{1}{3} = \dfrac{-1}{5}\times\dfrac{-1}{5}\times\dfrac{-1}{5}\times\dfrac{-3}{5} = \dfrac{3}{\mathbf{625}}.$

(b) $(-2)^5 \div \left(-\dfrac{1}{3}\right)^4 = \dfrac{(-2)^5}{\left(-\dfrac{1}{3}\right)^4} = \dfrac{(-2)\times(-2)\times(-2)\times(-2)\times(-2)}{\left(-\dfrac{1}{3}\right)\times\left(-\dfrac{1}{3}\right)\times\left(-\dfrac{1}{3}\right)\times\left(-\dfrac{1}{3}\right)}$

$\qquad = \dfrac{-32}{\dfrac{1}{81}} = -32\times81 = \mathbf{-2592}.$

Ex. 5. *Simplify :*

(a) $\left[\left(\dfrac{1}{2}\right)^2 - \left(\dfrac{1}{4}\right)^3\right] \times 2^3$
(b) $(3^2 - 2^2) \div \left(\dfrac{1}{5}\right)^2.$

Sol. (a) $\left[\left(\dfrac{1}{2}\times\dfrac{1}{2}\right) - \left(\dfrac{1}{4}\times\dfrac{1}{4}\times\dfrac{1}{4}\right)\right] \times (2\times2\times2) = \left[\dfrac{1}{4} - \dfrac{1}{64}\right]\times8 = \left(\dfrac{16-1}{64}\right)\times8 = \dfrac{15}{64}\times8 = \dfrac{\mathbf{15}}{\mathbf{8}}.$

(b) $(3^2 - 2^2) \div \left(\dfrac{1}{5}\right)^2 = (9-4)\div\left(\dfrac{1}{5\times5}\right) = 5\div\dfrac{1}{25} = 5\times25 = \mathbf{125}.$

Ex. 6. *Find the reciprocal of* (i) $(-2)^4$ (ii) $\left(-\dfrac{3}{8}\right)^3$ (iii) $\left(\dfrac{-7}{11}\right)^{105}$ *and express them in exponential form.*

Sol. (i) Reciprocal of $(-2)^4 = \dfrac{1}{(-2)^4} = \dfrac{1^4}{(-2)^4} = \left(\dfrac{1}{-2}\right)^4 = \left(-\dfrac{1}{2}\right)^4.$

$\qquad\qquad\qquad\qquad\qquad\qquad\qquad\qquad\qquad\qquad\qquad\qquad \boxed{\because \dfrac{1}{-2} = \dfrac{-1}{2}}$

(ii) $\left(-\dfrac{3}{8}\right)^3 = \dfrac{(-3)^3}{8^3}$ $\therefore$ Reciprocal of $\left(-\dfrac{3}{8}\right)^3 = \dfrac{8^3}{(-3)^3} = \left(\dfrac{8}{-3}\right)^3 = \left(\dfrac{-8}{3}\right)^3.$

$\qquad\qquad\qquad\qquad\qquad\qquad\qquad\qquad\qquad\qquad\qquad\qquad \boxed{\because \dfrac{8}{-3} = \dfrac{-8}{3}}$

(iii) $\left(\dfrac{-7}{11}\right)^{105} = \dfrac{(-7)^{105}}{11^{105}}$ $\therefore$ Reciprocal of $\left(\dfrac{-7}{11}\right)^{105} = \dfrac{11^{105}}{(-7)^{105}} = \left(\dfrac{11}{-7}\right)^{105} = \left(\dfrac{-11}{7}\right)^{105}.$

EXERCISE 2 (a)

1. Express each of the following in exponential form :

(i) $\dfrac{2}{3} \times \dfrac{2}{3} \times \dfrac{2}{3} \times \dfrac{2}{3}$ (ii) $\dfrac{3}{8} \times \dfrac{3}{8} \times \dfrac{3}{8} \times \dfrac{3}{8} \times \dfrac{3}{8}$ (iii) $\dfrac{-5}{7} \times \dfrac{-5}{7} \times \dfrac{-5}{7} \times \dfrac{-5}{7} \times \dfrac{-5}{7} \times \dfrac{-5}{7}$

(iv) $\dfrac{-11}{8} \times \dfrac{-11}{8} \times \dfrac{-11}{8} \times \dfrac{-11}{8} \times \dfrac{-11}{8} \times \dfrac{-11}{8} \times \dfrac{-11}{8} \times \dfrac{-11}{8} \times \dfrac{-11}{8}$

2. Express each of the following as a rational number of the form $\dfrac{p}{q}$:

(i) $\left(\dfrac{5}{9}\right)^2$ (ii) $\left(\dfrac{4}{7}\right)^3$ (iii) $\left(\dfrac{-2}{3}\right)^7$ (iv) $\left(\dfrac{-5}{2}\right)^3$ (v) $\left(\dfrac{-1}{2}\right)^8$

3. Express each of the following rational numbers in power notation :

(i) $\dfrac{9}{64}$ (ii) $\dfrac{49}{25}$ (iii) $\dfrac{-8}{27}$ (iv) $-\dfrac{1}{216}$ (v) $\dfrac{-32}{243}$ (vi) $\dfrac{81}{625}$

4. Find the value of :

(i) $\left(\dfrac{1}{3}\right)^3 \times \left(\dfrac{3}{2}\right)^2$ (ii) $\left(\dfrac{-2}{3}\right)^4 \times \left(\dfrac{-3}{4}\right)^3$ (iii) $\left(-\dfrac{1}{5}\right)^3 \times \left(-\dfrac{1}{5}\right)^2$ (iv) $\left(\dfrac{4}{-5}\right)^2 \times (-5)^3$

(v) $\left(-\dfrac{1}{3}\right)^5 \div \left(\dfrac{2}{3}\right)^3$ (vi) $\left(-\dfrac{1}{5}\right)^3 \times (-1)^{85} \times \left(\dfrac{2}{5}\right)^2$ (vii) $\left(\dfrac{1}{2}\right)^4 \div \left(\dfrac{1}{3}\right)^4 + \left(-\dfrac{1}{2}\right)^3$

(viii) $\left(\left(\dfrac{-3}{5}\right)^3 + \dfrac{7}{25}\right) \div \left(\dfrac{5}{2}\right)^3$ (ix) $(12^2 - 5^3) \times \dfrac{(-1)^{40}}{19}$

5. Find the reciprocal of :

(i) $\dfrac{16}{125}$ (ii) $\dfrac{-27}{64}$ (iii) $(-2)^4$ (iv) $\left(\dfrac{-3}{7}\right)^2$

(v) $\left(-\dfrac{11}{4}\right)^3$ (vi) $\left(\dfrac{-7}{4}\right)^{208}$ (vii) $\left(-\dfrac{1}{10}\right)^{47}$ (viii) $\left(-\dfrac{3}{17}\right)^{89}$

6. Find the absolute value of :

(i) $\left(\dfrac{3}{4}\right)^3$ (ii) $-\left(\dfrac{7}{8}\right)^2$ (iii) $\left(-\dfrac{2}{3}\right)^4$ (iv) $\left(\dfrac{-3}{2}\right)^5$

7. Evaluate $b^2 - 9(b-1)^2$ if $b = 1.1$.   (Hint : Put $b = 1.1 = \dfrac{11}{10}$)

2.2 Laws of Exponents

Law I : If $\dfrac{a}{b}$ be any non-zero rational number and m, n be positive integers, then

$$\left(\dfrac{a}{b}\right)^m \times \left(\dfrac{a}{b}\right)^n = \left(\dfrac{a}{b}\right)^{m+n}$$

For example : $\left(\dfrac{-2}{7}\right)^3 \times \left(\dfrac{-2}{7}\right)^6 = \left(\dfrac{-2}{7}\right)^{6+3} = \left(\dfrac{-2}{7}\right)^9$.

$\left(\dfrac{9}{11}\right)^4 \times \left(\dfrac{9}{11}\right)^5 \times \left(\dfrac{9}{11}\right)^{11} = \left(\dfrac{9}{11}\right)^{4+5+11} = \left(\dfrac{9}{11}\right)^{20}$.

Law II : *If $\frac{a}{b}$ be any non-zero rational number and m, n are positive integers, then*

$$\left[\left(\frac{a}{b}\right)^m\right]^n = \left(\frac{a}{b}\right)^{mn}$$

For example :

$$\left[\left(\frac{3}{5}\right)^3\right]^3 = \left(\frac{3}{5}\right)^{3\times3} = \left(\frac{3}{5}\right)^9.$$

$$\left[\left(\frac{-5}{13}\right)^4\right]^5 = \left(\frac{-5}{13}\right)^{4\times5} = \left(\frac{-5}{13}\right)^{20} = \left(\frac{5}{13}\right)^{20}.$$

$$\because \quad (-1)^{\text{even integer}} = 1$$

Law III : *For all non-zero rational number $\frac{a}{b}$ and $\frac{c}{d}$, if m is a positive integer, then*

$$\left(\frac{a}{b}\right)^m \times \left(\frac{c}{d}\right)^m = \left(\frac{a}{b} \times \frac{c}{d}\right)^m$$

For example :

$$7^3 \times \left(\frac{3}{14}\right)^3 = \left(7 \times \frac{3}{14}\right)^3 = \left(\frac{3}{2}\right)^3 = \frac{27}{8}.$$

$$\left(\frac{7}{11}\right)^6 \times \left(\frac{-11}{7}\right)^6 = \left(\frac{7}{11} \times \frac{-11}{7}\right)^6 = (-1)^6 = 1.$$

$$\because \quad (-1)^{\text{even integer}} = 1$$

Law IV : *For all non-zero rational numbers $\frac{a}{b}$ and all positive integers m and n,*

$$\left(\frac{a}{b}\right)^m \div \left(\frac{a}{b}\right)^n = \left(\frac{a}{b}\right)^{m-n}$$

For example :

$$\left(\frac{-3}{8}\right)^7 \div \left(\frac{-3}{8}\right)^2 = \left(\frac{-3}{8}\right)^{7-2} = \left(\frac{-3}{8}\right)^5.$$

2.3 Zero and Negative Integral Exponents

For any non-zero rational number a, we have

	We have	But we already know that	This suggests that we should define
(i)	$\dfrac{a^5}{a^5} = a^{5-5} = a^0$	$\dfrac{a^5}{a^5} = 1$	$a^0 = 1$
(ii)	$\dfrac{a^3}{a^9} = a^{3-9} = a^{-6}$	$\dfrac{a^3}{a^9} = \dfrac{1}{a^{9-3}} = \dfrac{1}{a^6}$	a^{-6} as $\dfrac{1}{a^6}$

Therefore, to make $\dfrac{a^m}{a^n} = a^{m-n}$, true for all cases, we define *zero exponent* and *negative integer exponent* as :

Let $\frac{a}{b}$ be any non-zero rational number, and let n be any positive integer.

┌──── zero exponent

$\left(\dfrac{a}{b}\right)^0$ means 1

┌──── negative integer exponent

$\left(\dfrac{a}{b}\right)^{-n}$ means $\dfrac{1}{\left(\dfrac{a}{b}\right)^n}$, *i.e.,* $\left(\dfrac{b}{a}\right)^n$

Law V : *For any non-zero rational number $\frac{a}{b}$, and a positive integer n,*

$$\left(\frac{a}{b}\right)^{-n} = \left(\frac{b}{a}\right)^{n}$$

$$\left(\frac{a}{b}\right)^{-n} = \frac{1}{\left(\frac{a}{b}\right)^{n}} = \frac{1}{\frac{a^n}{b^n}} = \frac{b^n}{a^n} = \left(\frac{b}{a}\right)^{n}$$

$$\boxed{\because \quad a^{-n} = \frac{1}{a^n}, \left(\frac{p}{q}\right)^{n} = \frac{p^n}{q^n}}$$

For example : $\quad (-5)^{-1} = \left(\frac{-5}{1}\right)^{-1} = \left(\frac{1}{-5}\right)^{1} = \frac{1}{-5} = -\frac{1}{5}, \quad \left(\frac{2}{3}\right)^{-3} = \left(\frac{3}{2}\right)^{3} = \frac{3^3}{2^3} = \frac{27}{8}.$

2.4 Laws of Exponents for all Integral Powers

We defined a^0 and a^{-n} so that $\frac{a^m}{a^n} = a^{m-n}$ holds true for all integers m and n. Also, with these definitions, the other properties (laws) of exponents hold for all integral powers (positive, negative and zero). We restate all the laws of exponents as :

Let $\frac{a}{b}$ and $\frac{c}{d}$ be any non-zero rational numbers, and let m and n be any integers, then

1. $\left(\frac{a}{b}\right)^{m} \cdot \left(\frac{a}{b}\right)^{n} = \left(\frac{a}{b}\right)^{m+n}$

2. $\left(\frac{a}{b} \times \frac{c}{d}\right)^{m} = \left(\frac{a}{b}\right)^{m} \times \left(\frac{c}{d}\right)^{m}$

3. $\left[\left(\frac{a}{b}\right)^{m}\right]^{n} = \left(\frac{a}{b}\right)^{mn}$

4. $\frac{(a/b)^{m}}{(a/b)^{n}} = \left(\frac{a}{b}\right)^{m-n}$

5. $\left(\frac{a/b}{c/d}\right)^{n} = \left[\frac{(a/b)^{n}}{(c/d)^{n}}\right]$

6. $\left(\frac{a}{b}\right)^{-n} = \left(\frac{b}{a}\right)^{n}$

Ex. 1. *Simplify and express with positive exponents :*

    (i) $\left(\frac{5}{7}\right)^{3} \times \left(\frac{5}{7}\right)^{-5}$ **(ii)** $\left(\frac{-7}{9}\right)^{-8} \times \left(\frac{-7}{9}\right)^{-11} \times \left(\frac{-7}{9}\right)$

Sol. *(i)* $\left(\frac{5}{7}\right)^{3} \times \left(\frac{5}{7}\right)^{-5} = \left(\frac{5}{7}\right)^{3+(-5)}$

$$= \left(\frac{5}{7}\right)^{-2} = \left(\frac{7}{5}\right)^{2}.$$

$$\boxed{\because \left(\frac{a}{b}\right)^{m} \times \left(\frac{a}{b}\right)^{n} = \left(\frac{a}{b}\right)^{m+n}}$$

$$\boxed{\because \left(\frac{a}{b}\right)^{-n} = \left(\frac{b}{a}\right)^{n}}$$

    (ii) $\left(-\frac{7}{9}\right)^{-8} \times \left(-\frac{7}{9}\right)^{-11} \times \left(-\frac{7}{9}\right) = \left(-\frac{7}{9}\right)^{(-8)+(-11)+1} = \left(-\frac{7}{9}\right)^{-18} = \left(-\frac{9}{7}\right)^{18}.$

Ex. 2. *Simplify and express with positive exponents :*

    (i) $\left(\frac{3}{11}\right)^{4} \div \left(\frac{3}{11}\right)^{-3}$ **(ii)** $\left(-\frac{5}{9}\right)^{-6} \div \left(-\frac{5}{9}\right)^{5}$ **(iii)** $\left(\frac{-4}{7}\right)^{-4} \div \left(\frac{-4}{7}\right)^{-10}$

Sol. (i) $\left(\dfrac{3}{11}\right)^4 \div \left(\dfrac{3}{11}\right)^{-3} = \left(\dfrac{3}{11}\right)^{4-(-3)} = \left(\dfrac{3}{11}\right)^{4+3} = \left(\dfrac{3}{11}\right)^7.$

> $\because \left(\dfrac{p}{q}\right)^m \div \left(\dfrac{p}{q}\right)^n = \left(\dfrac{p}{q}\right)^{m-n}$

(ii) $\left(-\dfrac{5}{9}\right)^{-6} \div \left(\dfrac{-5}{9}\right)^5 = \left(\dfrac{-5}{9}\right)^{-6-5} = \left(\dfrac{-5}{9}\right)^{-11} = \left(\dfrac{9}{-5}\right)^{11} = \left(\dfrac{-9}{5}\right)^{11}.$

> $\because \left(\dfrac{a}{b}\right)^{-n} = \left(\dfrac{b}{a}\right)^n$

(iii) $\left(\dfrac{-4}{7}\right)^{-4} \div \left(\dfrac{-4}{7}\right)^{-10} = \left(\dfrac{-4}{7}\right)^{-4-(-10)} = \left(\dfrac{-4}{7}\right)^{-4+10} = \left(\dfrac{-4}{7}\right)^6.$

Ex. 3. *Simplify :*

(i) $\left[\left(\dfrac{2}{5}\right)^{-3}\right]^4$ (ii) $\left[\left(\dfrac{-6}{11}\right)^{-5}\right]^{-3}$ (iii) $\left(-\dfrac{2}{3}\right)^{-4} \times \left(\dfrac{1}{8}\right)^{-4}$ (iv) $\left(\dfrac{5}{7}\right)^{-1} \times \left(\dfrac{7}{3}\right)^{-1}$

Sol. (i) $\left[\left(\dfrac{2}{5}\right)^{-3}\right]^4 = \left(\dfrac{2}{5}\right)^{-3\times4} = \left(\dfrac{2}{5}\right)^{-12} = \left(\dfrac{5}{2}\right)^{12}.$

> $\because \left[\left(\dfrac{a}{b}\right)^m\right]^{} = \left(\dfrac{a}{b}\right)^{mn}$
>
> $\because \left(\dfrac{a}{b}\right)^{-m} = \left(\dfrac{b}{a}\right)^m$

(ii) $\left[\left(\dfrac{-6}{11}\right)^{-5}\right]^{-3} = \left(\dfrac{-6}{11}\right)^{-5\times-3} = \left(\dfrac{-6}{11}\right)^{15}.$

(iii) $\left(\dfrac{2}{3}\right)^{-4} \times \left(\dfrac{1}{8}\right)^{-4} = \left(-\dfrac{2}{3} \times \dfrac{1}{8}\right)^{-4} = \left(-\dfrac{1}{12}\right)^{-4} = \left(\dfrac{12}{-1}\right)^4 = (-12)^4 = (-1)^4 (12)^4 = \mathbf{12^4}.$

> $\because (-1)^4 = 1$

(iv) $\left(\dfrac{5}{7}\right)^{-1} \times \left(\dfrac{7}{3}\right)^{-1} = \left(\dfrac{5}{7} \times \dfrac{7}{3}\right)^{-1} = \left(\dfrac{5}{3}\right)^{-1} = \dfrac{3}{5}.$

Ex. 4. *Simplify :*

(i) $[4^{-1} \div 3^{-1}]^{-2}$ (ii) $(5^{-1} \times 3^{-1})^{-1} \div 6^{-1}$ (iii) $(6^{-1} - 8^{-1})^{-1} + (2^{-1} - 3^{-1})^{-1}$

Sol. (i) $[4^{-1} \div 3^{-1}]^{-2} = \left(\dfrac{1}{4} \div \dfrac{1}{3}\right)^{-2} = \left(\dfrac{1}{4} \times \dfrac{3}{1}\right)^{-2} = \left(\dfrac{3}{4}\right)^{-2} = \left(\dfrac{4}{3}\right)^2 = \dfrac{16}{9}.$

> $\because a^{-1} = \dfrac{1}{a}$

(ii) $(5^{-1} \times 3^{-1})^{-1} \div 6^{-1} = \left(\dfrac{1}{5} \times \dfrac{1}{3}\right)^{-1} \div \dfrac{1}{6} = \left(\dfrac{1}{15}\right)^{-1} \div \dfrac{1}{6} = \dfrac{15}{1} \div \dfrac{1}{6} = \dfrac{15}{1} \times \dfrac{6}{1} = \mathbf{90}.$

> $\because a^{-1} = \dfrac{1}{a}$

(iii) $(6^{-1} - 8^{-1})^{-1} + (2^{-1} - 3^{-1})^{-1} = \left(\dfrac{1}{6} - \dfrac{1}{8}\right)^{-1} + \left(\dfrac{1}{2} - \dfrac{1}{3}\right)^{-1}$

> $\because a^{-1} = \dfrac{1}{a}$

$\qquad\qquad = \left(\dfrac{4-3}{24}\right)^{-1} + \left(\dfrac{3-2}{6}\right)^{-1} = \left(\dfrac{1}{24}\right)^{-1} + \left(\dfrac{1}{6}\right)^{-1} = 24 + 6 = \mathbf{30.}$

Ex. 5. *Find x so that* $\left(\dfrac{5}{7}\right)^{-3} \times \left(\dfrac{5}{7}\right)^{-11} = \left(\dfrac{5}{7}\right)^{7x}.$

Sol. $\left(\dfrac{5}{7}\right)^{-3} \times \left(\dfrac{5}{7}\right)^{-11} = \left(\dfrac{5}{7}\right)^{7x} \Rightarrow \left(\dfrac{5}{7}\right)^{-3+(-11)} \Rightarrow \left(\dfrac{5}{7}\right)^{-14} = \left(\dfrac{5}{7}\right)^{7x}$

In an equation, when bases on both sides are equal, their powers must also be equal.

$\therefore \quad -14 = 7x \quad \Rightarrow \quad x = -\dfrac{14}{7} \Rightarrow x = -2.$

Ex. 6. *Find the value of m if* $\left(\frac{2}{9}\right)^3 \times \left(\frac{2}{9}\right)^{-6} = \left(\frac{2}{9}\right)^{2m-1}$ *.*

Sol. $\left(\frac{2}{9}\right)^3 \times \left(\frac{2}{9}\right)^{-6} = \left(\frac{2}{9}\right)^{2m-1} \Rightarrow \left(\frac{2}{9}\right)^{3+(-6)} = \left(\frac{2}{9}\right)^{2m-1} \Rightarrow \left(\frac{2}{9}\right)^{-3} = \left(\frac{2}{9}\right)^{2m-1}$

In an equation, when bases on both sides are equal, their powers must also be equal.

$\therefore \quad 2m - 1 = -3 \quad$ or $\quad 2m = -3 + 1 \quad \Rightarrow \quad 2m = -2 \quad \Rightarrow \quad m = \frac{-2}{2} = \mathbf{-1}$.

Ex. 7. *Find the reciprocal of the rational number* $\left(\frac{1}{2}\right)^{-2} \div \left(\frac{2}{3}\right)^{-3}$ *.*

Sol. $\left(\frac{1}{2}\right)^{-2} \div \left(\frac{2}{3}\right)^{-3} = \left(\frac{2}{1}\right)^2 \div \left(\frac{3}{2}\right)^3 = \frac{2^2}{1^2} \div \frac{3^3}{2^3} = 4 \div \frac{27}{8} = 4 \times \frac{8}{27} = \frac{32}{27}$

Reciprocal of $\frac{32}{27}$ is $\frac{27}{32}$ $\quad \therefore \quad$ Reciprocal of the given expression is $\frac{27}{32}$.

Ex. 8. *If* $\frac{p}{q} = \left(\frac{3}{2}\right)^{-2} \div \left(\frac{6}{7}\right)^0$ *, find the value of* $\left(\frac{p}{q}\right)^{-3}$ *.*

Sol. $\frac{p}{q} = \left(\frac{3}{2}\right)^{-2} \div \left(\frac{6}{7}\right)^0 = \left(\frac{2}{3}\right)^2 \div 1 = \frac{4}{9}$

> Using $\left(\frac{a}{b}\right)^{-n} = \left(\frac{b}{a}\right)^n$ and $\left(\frac{a}{b}\right)^0 = 1$

$\therefore \quad \left(\frac{p}{q}\right)^{-3} = \left(\frac{4}{9}\right)^{-3} = \left[\left(\frac{2}{3}\right)^2\right]^{-3} = \left(\frac{2}{3}\right)^{2 \times -3} = \left(\frac{2}{3}\right)^{2 \times -3} = \left(\frac{2}{3}\right)^{-6} = \left(\frac{3}{2}\right)^6$.

Ex. 9. *By what number should* $\left(\frac{p}{q}\right)^{-3}$ *be multiplied so that the product is* $\left(\frac{4}{27}\right)^{-1}$ *?*

Sol. Let the required number be x. Then,

$$x \times \left(\frac{2}{3}\right)^{-2} = \left(\frac{4}{27}\right)^{-1} \quad \Rightarrow \quad x \times \left(\frac{3}{2}\right)^2 = \frac{27}{4} \Rightarrow x \times \frac{9}{4} = \frac{27}{4}$$

$$\Rightarrow \quad x = \frac{27}{4} \div \frac{9}{4} \Rightarrow x = \frac{27}{4} \times \frac{4}{9} \Rightarrow x = \mathbf{3}.$$

Hence, the required number is **3**.

Ex. 10. *By what number should* $\left(\frac{5}{4}\right)^{-3}$ *be divided so that the quotient may be* $\left(\frac{15}{16}\right)^{-2}$ *?*

Sol. Let the required number be x. Then,

$$\left(\frac{5}{4}\right)^{-3} \div x = \left(\frac{15}{16}\right)^{-2} \Rightarrow \left(\frac{4}{5}\right)^3 \times \frac{1}{x} = \left(\frac{16}{15}\right)^2$$

$$\Rightarrow \quad \left(\frac{4}{5}\right)^3 = \left(\frac{16}{15}\right)^2 \times x \Rightarrow x = \left(\frac{4}{5}\right)^3 \div \left(\frac{16}{15}\right)^2$$

$$\Rightarrow \quad x = \frac{64}{125} \div \frac{256}{225} \Rightarrow x = \frac{64}{125} \times \frac{225}{256} = \frac{9}{20}$$

The required number is $\frac{9}{20}$.

EXERCISE 2 (b)

1. Express as a rational number :

(i) 5^{-1} (ii) $\left(\dfrac{1}{2}\right)^{-6}$ (iii) $\left(\dfrac{3}{4}\right)^{-4}$ (iv) $\left(-\dfrac{4}{5}\right)^{-2}$ (v) $(-x)^{-1}$

2. Simplify and express with positive exponents :

(i) $\left(\dfrac{4}{9}\right)^{-3} \times \left(\dfrac{4}{9}\right)^{11} \times \left(\dfrac{4}{9}\right)^{-10}$

(ii) $\left(-\dfrac{7}{11}\right)^{-6} \div \left(\dfrac{-7}{11}\right)^{-2}$

(iii) $\left(\dfrac{-8}{3}\right)^{-7} \div \left(\dfrac{-8}{3}\right)^{4}$

(iv) $\left[\left(\dfrac{9}{11}\right)^{-3} \times \left(\dfrac{9}{11}\right)^{-7}\right] \div \left(\dfrac{9}{11}\right)^{-3}$

(v) $\left[\left(\dfrac{3}{5}\right)^{-2}\right]^{-4}$

(vi) $\left[\left\{\left(-\dfrac{2}{3}\right)^{-3}\right\}^{-4}\right]^{-2}$

3. Evaluate :

(i) $\left(\dfrac{-3}{4}\right)^{-2} \times \left(\dfrac{-6}{5}\right)^{-2}$

(ii) $\left(\dfrac{11}{7}\right)^{-4} \times \left(\dfrac{7}{44}\right)^{-4}$

(iii) $(-16)^{-3} \times \left(\dfrac{1}{20}\right)^{-3}$

4. Evaluate :

(i) $(3^{-1} \div 4^{-1})^2$

(ii) $(4^{-1} + 8^{-1}) \div \left(\dfrac{2}{3}\right)^{-1}$

(iii) $\left(\dfrac{2}{3}\right)^{-2} \times \left(\dfrac{3}{4}\right)^{-3} \times \left(\dfrac{-7}{8}\right)^{0}$

(iv) $\left(-\dfrac{1}{4}\right)^{-3} \div \left(\dfrac{3}{8}\right)^{-2}$

5. Find x such that :

(i) $\left(\dfrac{7}{4}\right)^{-3} \times \left(\dfrac{7}{4}\right)^{-5} = \left(\dfrac{7}{4}\right)^{x-2}$

(ii) $\left(\dfrac{125}{8}\right) \times \left(\dfrac{125}{8}\right)^{x} = \left(\dfrac{5}{2}\right)^{18}$

(iii) $\left(\dfrac{35}{11}\right)^{4} \times \left(\dfrac{11}{7}\right)^{4} = 5^{x}$

(iv) $\left(\left(\dfrac{-3}{7}\right)^{4} \times \left(\dfrac{-3}{7}\right)^{8}\right)^{-5} = \left(\left(\dfrac{-3}{7}\right) \times \left(\dfrac{-3}{7}\right)^{5}\right)^{x}$

6. If $x = \left[\left(\dfrac{2}{3}\right)^{2}\right]^{3} \times \left(\dfrac{1}{3}\right)^{-2} \times 3^{-1} \times \dfrac{1}{6}$, find the reciprocal of x.

7. Find the reciprocal of the following rational numbers :

(i) $\left(\dfrac{-3}{7}\right)^{-3} \div \left(\dfrac{-3}{7}\right)^{-4}$

(ii) $\left(\left(\dfrac{8}{11}\right)^{2}\right)^{-5} \times \left(\dfrac{11}{8}\right)^{-12}$

8. If $3^{2x+1} \div 9 = 27$, find x.

9. By what number should $\left(\dfrac{-3}{2}\right)^{-3}$ be multiplied, so that the product is $\left(\dfrac{9}{8}\right)^{-2}$?

10. By what number should $\left(\dfrac{5}{4}\right)^{-2}$ be divided, so that the quotient $\left(\dfrac{1}{2}\right)^{-3}$?

11. Simplify $\left[\left\{\left(\dfrac{-2}{5}\right)^{-7}\times\left(\dfrac{-2}{5}\right)^{9}\right\}\div\left(\dfrac{-2}{5}\right)^{2}\right]$ and express the result as a power of 5.

Simplify :

12. $\left[\left(-\dfrac{1}{3}\right)^{8}\div\left(-\dfrac{1}{3}\right)^{5}\right]-\left[\left(\dfrac{-1}{3}\right)^{5}\div\left(\dfrac{-1}{3}\right)^{3}\right]$

13. $(2^{-1}\div5^{-1})^{2}\times\left(\dfrac{-5}{8}\right)^{-2}$

14. $\left[\left(\dfrac{1}{3}\right)^{-3}-\left(\dfrac{1}{2}\right)^{-3}\right]\div\left(\dfrac{1}{4}\right)^{-3}$

15. If $x=\left(\dfrac{5}{8}\right)^{-2}\times\left(\dfrac{12}{15}\right)^{-2}$, find the value of x^{-3}.

LOOKING BACK
Summary of Key Facts

1. A rational number when multiplied by itself repeatedly can be written in short form in

exponential notation, _e.g,_ $\dfrac{4}{5}\times\dfrac{4}{5}\times\dfrac{4}{5}\times$ .... 100 times $=\left(\dfrac{4}{5}\right)^{100}$.

2. **Laws of exponents :**

Let $\dfrac{a}{b}$ and $\dfrac{c}{d}$ be any non-zero rational numbers and let _m_ and _n_ be any integers, then

(_i_) $\left(\dfrac{a}{b}\right)^{m}\times\left(\dfrac{a}{b}\right)^{n}=\left(\dfrac{a}{b}\right)^{m+n}$ 　　(_ii_) $\left(\dfrac{a}{b}\times\dfrac{c}{d}\right)^{m}=\left(\dfrac{a}{b}\right)^{m}\times\left(\dfrac{c}{d}\right)^{m}$ 　　(_iii_) $\left(\dfrac{a}{b}\right)^{m}\div\left(\dfrac{a}{b}\right)^{n}=\left(\dfrac{a}{b}\right)^{m-n}$

(_iv_) $\left(\left(\dfrac{a}{b}\right)^{m}\right)^{n}=\left(\dfrac{a}{b}\right)^{mn}$ 　　(_v_) $\left(\dfrac{a}{b}\right)^{0}=1$ 　　(_vi_) $\left(\dfrac{a}{b}\right)^{-n}=\left(\dfrac{b}{a}\right)^{n}$

MENTAL MATHS – 2

1. **Express in power notation :**

(_i_) $\left(\dfrac{3}{5}\right)^{-1}\times\left(\dfrac{3}{5}\right)^{-1}\times\left(\dfrac{3}{5}\right)^{-1}\times\left(\dfrac{3}{5}\right)^{-1}$

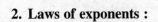

(_ii_) $\left(\dfrac{-2}{7}\right)^{-3}\times\left(\dfrac{-2}{7}\right)^{-3}\times\left(\dfrac{-2}{7}\right)^{-3}$

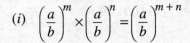

2. Express $\left(\dfrac{-3}{4}\right)^{-2}$ as a rational number.

3. **Express as an exponent of a rational number :**

(_i_) $\dfrac{16}{81}$ 　　(_ii_) $\dfrac{-1}{216}$ 　　(_iii_) $\dfrac{1}{1000000}$

4. **Find the value of :**

(_i_) $(-5)^{-1}$ 　　(_ii_) $\left(\dfrac{1}{3}\right)^{-1}+\left(\dfrac{1}{5}\right)^{-1}-\left(\dfrac{1}{6}\right)^{-1}$

5. Simplify : $\left(\dfrac{2}{3}\right)^{-2}\times\left(-\dfrac{7}{8}\right)^{0}$

6. If $\dfrac{a}{b}=\left(\dfrac{2}{3}\right)^{-3}\times\left(\dfrac{5}{6}\right)^{0}$, find the value of $\left(\dfrac{a}{b}\right)^{-3}$

7. Find the value of _x_ if $\left(\dfrac{5}{6}\right)^{7}\times\left(\dfrac{5}{6}\right)^{-9}=\left(\dfrac{5}{6}\right)^{2x}$

8. By what number should $(-3)^{7}$ be divided so that the quotient is (_i_) $(-3)^{2}$ (_ii_) $(-3)^{2}$.

9. Find the reciprocal of $\left(\dfrac{2}{5}\right)^{-3}$

10. Express $\left(\left(\dfrac{-3}{7}\right)^{-3}\right)^{2}$ with a positive exponent.

MULTIPLE CHOICE QUESTIONS – 2

1. $\left(\dfrac{3}{2}\right)^{-3}$ is equal to :

(i) $\dfrac{4}{9}$ (ii) $\dfrac{8}{27}$ (iii) $-\dfrac{27}{8}$ (iv) $\dfrac{27}{8}$

2. $\left(-\dfrac{2}{7}\right)^{-4} \div \left(-\dfrac{2}{7}\right)^{-8}$ is equal to :

(i) $\left(-\dfrac{2}{7}\right)^{-12}$ (ii) $\left(-\dfrac{2}{7}\right)^{4}$ (iii) $\left(-\dfrac{2}{7}\right)^{-4}$ (iv) $\left(-\dfrac{2}{7}\right)^{12}$

3. $\left\{\left(-\dfrac{1}{3}\right)^{(-2)}\right\}^{(-2)}$ is equal to :

(i) 81   (ii) –9   (iii) $\dfrac{1}{81}$ (iv) $-\dfrac{1}{27}$

4. $(16)^{0.16} \times (16)^{0.04} \times (2)^{0.2}$ is equal to

(i) 1   (ii) 2   (iii) 4   (iv) 16

5. The value of $(8^{-1} - 9^{-1})^{-1} \div (4^{-1} - 9^{-1})^{-1}$ is :

(i) 5   (ii) 10   (iii) 25   (iv) 14

6. If $\left(\dfrac{4}{11}\right)^{x-1} = \left(\dfrac{11}{4}\right)^{x-5}$, then x is equal to :

(i) 3   (ii) 0   (iii) –1   (iv) 2

7. If $\left(\dfrac{x}{y}\right)^{-3} = \left(\dfrac{2}{7}\right)^{-3} \left(\dfrac{21}{16}\right)^{-3}$, then $\left(\dfrac{x}{y}\right)^{-2}$ is equal to

(i) $\dfrac{3}{8}$ (ii) $-\dfrac{8}{3}$ (iii) $\dfrac{9}{84}$ (iv) $\dfrac{64}{9}$

8. If $\left(\dfrac{2}{3}\right)^{-6} \times \left(\dfrac{16}{81}\right)^{3} = \left(\dfrac{2}{3}\right)^{2x-2}$, the value of x is :

(i) 2   (ii) –2   (iii) 4   (iv) 3

9. If m and n are whole numbers such that $m^n = 121$, then the value of $(m-1)^{n+1}$ is :

(i) 1   (ii) 10   (iii) 121   (iv) 1000

10. If $\left(\dfrac{3}{8}\right)^{-5} \times \left(\dfrac{16}{21}\right)^{-5} = \left(\dfrac{2}{7}\right)^{x}$, then the value of x^2 is :

(i) $\dfrac{1}{5}$ (ii) 25   (iii) $\dfrac{4}{49}$ (iv) $-\dfrac{1}{25}$

ANSWERS

EXERCISE 2 (a)

1. (i) $\left(\dfrac{2}{3}\right)^4$ (ii) $\left(\dfrac{3}{8}\right)^5$ (iii) $\left(\dfrac{-5}{7}\right)^6$ (iv) $\left(\dfrac{-11}{8}\right)^9$

2. (i) $\dfrac{25}{81}$ (ii) $\dfrac{64}{343}$ (iii) $\dfrac{-128}{2187}$ (iv) $\dfrac{-125}{8}$ (v) $\dfrac{1}{256}$

3. (i) $\left(\dfrac{3}{8}\right)^2$ (ii) $\left(\dfrac{7}{5}\right)^2$ (iii) $\left(-\dfrac{2}{3}\right)^3$ (iv) $\left(-\dfrac{1}{6}\right)^3$ (v) $\left(\dfrac{-2}{3}\right)^5$ (vi) $\left(\dfrac{3}{5}\right)^4$

4. (i) $\dfrac{1}{12}$ (ii) $-\dfrac{1}{12}$ (iii) $-\dfrac{1}{3125}$ (iv) -80 (v) $-\dfrac{1}{72}$ (vi) $\dfrac{4}{3125}$ (vii) $\dfrac{79}{16}$

  (viii) $\dfrac{64}{15625}$ (ix) 1

5. (i) $\dfrac{125}{16}$ (ii) $\dfrac{64}{-27}$ (iii) $\left(\dfrac{1}{-2}\right)^4$ (iv) $\left(\dfrac{7}{-3}\right)^2$ (v) $\left(\dfrac{4}{-11}\right)^3$ (vi) $\left(\dfrac{4}{-7}\right)^{208}$ (vii) $\left(\dfrac{10}{-1}\right)^{47}$

  (viii) $\left(\dfrac{17}{-3}\right)^{89}$

6. (i) $\dfrac{27}{64}$ (ii) $\dfrac{49}{64}$ (iii) $\dfrac{16}{81}$ (iv) $\dfrac{243}{32}$ 7. 1.12

EXERCISE 2 (b)

1. (i) $\dfrac{1}{5}$ (ii) 32 (iii) $\dfrac{256}{81}$ (iv) $\dfrac{25}{16}$ (v) $-\dfrac{1}{x}$

2. (i) $\left(\dfrac{9}{4}\right)^2$ (ii) $\left(\dfrac{11}{-7}\right)^4$ (iii) $\left(\dfrac{-3}{8}\right)^{11}$ (iv) $\left(\dfrac{11}{9}\right)^7$ (v) $\left(\dfrac{3}{5}\right)^8$ (vi) $\left(\dfrac{-3}{2}\right)^{24}$

3. (i) $\dfrac{100}{81}$ (ii) 256 (iii) $\dfrac{-125}{64}$ 4. (i) $\dfrac{16}{9}$ (ii) $\dfrac{1}{4}$ (iii) $\dfrac{16}{3}$ (iv) -9

5. (i) $x = -6$ (ii) $x = 5$ (iii) $x = 4$ (iv) $x = -10$ 6. $\dfrac{729}{32}$

7. (i) $-\dfrac{7}{3}$ (ii) $\left(\dfrac{11}{8}\right)^2$ 8. $x = 2$ 9. $\dfrac{-8}{3}$ 10. $\dfrac{2}{25}$ 11. 5^0 12. $\dfrac{-4}{27}$

13. 16 14. $\dfrac{19}{64}$ 15. $\dfrac{1}{64}$

MENTAL MATHS – 2

1. (i) $\left(\dfrac{3}{5}\right)^{-4}$ (ii) $\left(\dfrac{-2}{7}\right)^{-9}$ 2. $\dfrac{16}{9}$ 3. (i) $\left(\dfrac{2}{3}\right)^4$ (ii) $\left(-\dfrac{1}{6}\right)^3$ (iii) $\left(\dfrac{1}{10}\right)^6$

4. (i) $-\dfrac{1}{5}$ (ii) 2 5. $\dfrac{9}{4}$ 6. $\left(\dfrac{2}{3}\right)^9$ 7. $x = -1$

8. (i) $(-3)^5$ (ii) $(-3)^9$ 9. $\left(\dfrac{2}{5}\right)^3$ 10. $\left(-\dfrac{7}{3}\right)^6$

MULTIPLE CHOICE QUESTIONS – 2

1. (ii)   2. (ii)   3. (iii)   4. (iii)   5. (ii)   6. (i)   7. (iv)

8. (iii)   9. (iv)   10. (ii)

3. Squares and Square Roots

3.1 Squares

If a number is multiplied by itself, the product so obtained is called the square of that number.

For example :

$3 \times 3 = 3^2 = 9$ We say that 9 is the square of 3.

$16 \times 16 = 16^2 = 256$ We say that 256 is the square of 16.

$0.7 \times 0.7 = (0.7)^2 = 0.49$ We say that 0.49 is the square of 0.7.

$\dfrac{4}{5} \times \dfrac{4}{5} = \left(\dfrac{4}{5}\right)^2 = \dfrac{16}{25}$ We say that $\dfrac{16}{25}$ is the square of $\dfrac{4}{5}$.

The **square of number** *is a number raised to the power 2.*

3.2. Perfect Square

The numbers 1, 4, 9, 16, 25, 36 are the squares of natural numbers 1, 2, 3, 4, 5, 6 respectively and are called perfect squares or square numbers.

> *A natural number is called a* **perfect square** *or a square number if it is the square of some natural number.*

Test : *A given number is a perfect square if its prime factors can be expressed in* **pairs of equal factors.**

Ex. 1. *Is 900 a perfect square? If so, find the number whose square is 900.*

Sol. Resolving into prime factors, we find that

$$900 = \underline{2 \times 2} \times \underline{3 \times 3} \times \underline{5 \times 5}$$

2	900
2	450
3	225
3	75
5	25
5	5
	1

Since, 900 can be grouped into pairs of equal factors therefore, 900 is a perfect square.

Also, $900 = (2 \times 3 \times 5) \times (2 \times 3 \times 5) = (30 \times 30) = (30)^2$

So, **900** is the square of 30.

Ex. 2. *Show that 3675 is not a perfect square.*

Sol. $3675 = 3 \times 5 \times 5 \times 7 \times 7$

Grouping the factors into pairs of equal factors, we find that 3 is left.

So, 3675 is not a perfect square.

Remark. If we multiply or divide 3675 by the factor 3 which cannot be paired, the product or the quotient is a perfect square.

3	3675
5	1225
5	245
7	49
7	7
	1

Thus, $3675 \times 3 = 11025 = (3 \times 3) \times (5 \times 5) \times (7 \times 7) = (3 \times 5 \times 7) \times (3 \times 5 \times 7)$

$$= 105 \times 105 = 105^2$$

Also, $3675 \div 3 = 1225 = (5 \times 5) \times (7 \times 7)$ is a perfect square.

EXERCISE 3 (a)

1. Using the prime factorization method show that the following numbers are perfect squares? In each case, find the number whose square is the given number.

   (*i*) 100   (*ii*) 784   (*iii*) 3600   (*iv*) 8100

2. Using the prime factorization method, find which of the following numbers are not perfect squares.

   (*i*) 400   (*ii*) 768   (*iii*) 6300   (*iv*) 1296   (*v*) 8000   (*vi*) 9025

3. Find the smallest number by which each of the given numbers must be multiplied so that the product is a perfect square.

   (*i*) 512   (*ii*) 700   (*iii*) 1323   (*iv*) 35280

4. Find the smallest number by which each of the given numbers should be divided so that the result is a perfect square.

   (*i*) 180   (*ii*) 1575   (*iii*) 6912   (*iv*) 19200

3.3 Table of Squares

The following table contains squares of numbers 1 to 100. Memorise at least the squares of number 1 to 30 and a few other selected numbers. Such memorisation of figures is always useful and creates confidence.

Number	Square	Number	Square	Number	Square	Number	Square
1	1	26	676	51	2601	76	5776
2	4	27	729	52	2704	77	5929
3	9	28	784	53	2809	78	6084
4	16	29	814	54	2916	79	6241
5	25	30	900	55	3025	80	6400
6	36	31	961	56	3136	81	6561
7	49	32	1024	57	3249	82	6724
8	64	33	1089	58	3364	83	6889
9	81	34	1156	59	3481	84	7056
10	100	35	1225	60	3600	85	7225
11	121	36	1296	61	3721	86	7396
12	144	37	1369	62	3844	87	7569
13	169	38	1444	63	3969	88	7744
14	196	39	1521	64	4096	89	7921
15	225	40	1600	65	4225	90	8100
16	256	41	1681	66	4356	91	8281
17	289	42	1764	67	4489	92	8464
18	324	43	1849	68	4624	93	8649
19	361	44	1936	69	4761	94	8836
20	400	45	2025	70	4900	95	9025
21	441	46	2116	71	5041	96	9216
22	484	47	2209	72	5184	97	9409
23	529	48	2304	73	5329	98	9604
24	576	49	2401	74	5476	99	9801
25	625	50	2500	75	6525	100	10,000

3.4 Properties of Square Numbers

- **Property 1**

  A number having 2, 3, 7 or 8 at the unit's place is never a perfect square; i.e., a square number never ends in 2, 3, 7 or 8.

  If you have a look at the table of squares, you will observe that all squares of numbers have 0, 1, 4, 5, 6, or 9 at units place. None of the square numbers ends in 2, 3, 7 or 8.

  > **Test :** Look at the unit's place of a number. If it ends in 2, 3, 7 and 8, then it is not a perfect square.

For example : The numbers 732, 2093, 82097 and 236918 are not perfect squares.

  Remark. A number having a digit other than, 2, 3, 7, and 8 at the unit's place is not necessarily a perfect square. It may or may not be a perfect square. For example, 91, 2305, 2504, 26490 are not perfect squares.

- **Property 2**

  The number of zeros at the end of a perfect square is always even.

For example :

The numbers $100 (= 10^2)$; $90,000 (= 300)^2$; $3,60,00,000 (= 6,000)^2$ are all perfect squares, while none of the numbers 80,5000, 81,00000 is a perfect square.

> **Note :** Numbers ending in an even number of zeros are not necessarily perfect squares. Thus, 2900, 63,0000, 97,000000 are not perfect squares.

- **Property 3**

  Squares of even numbers are always even numbers and squares of odd numbers are always odd numbers.

  You may verify this fact from the table of squares. Thus,

  $(33)^2 = 1089,$ $(84)^2 = 7056,$ $(315)^2 = 99225,$ $(836)^2 = 698896,$
  odd   even   odd   even

- **Property 4 A**

  The square of a natural other than one is either a multiple of 3 or exceeds a multiple of 3 by 1. In other words, a perfect square leaves a remainder 0 or 1 when divided by 3.

- **Property 4 B**

  The square of a natural number other than one is either a multiple of 4 or exceeds a multiple of 4 by 1.

  Thus, $5^2 = 25 = 3 \times 8 + 1 =$ multiple of 3 + 1.   Also $25 = 4 \times 6 + 1 =$ multiple of 4 + 1
  $21^2 = 441 = 3 \times 147 =$ multiple of 3.   Also $441 = 4 \times 110 + 1 =$ multiple of 4 + 1

> **Test :** (1) *If a number when divided by 3 leaves remainder 2, then it is not a perfect square.*
> (2) *If a number when divided by 4 leaves remainder 2 or 3, then it is not a perfect square.*

  Remark. If a number leaves remainder 0 or 1 when divided by 3 or 4, it is not necessarily a perfect square. But if it leaves a remainder other than 0 and 1, it is not a perfect square.

- **Property 5**

  If n is a perfect square, then 2n can never be a perfect square.

- **Property 6**

  A perfect square number is never negative.

- **Property 7.** *For every natural number n, we have*

  The sum of first n odd natural numbers = n^2.

  Thus, $1^2 = 1$ = sum of first 1 odd natural number = 1^2

  $2^2 = 4 = 1 + 3$ = sum of first two odd natural numbers = $4 = 2^2$

  $3^2 = 9 = 1 + 3 + 5$ = sum of first three odd natural numbers = $1 + 3 + 5 = 9 = 3^2$, and so on.

- **Property 8**

  For every natural number n, $(n + 1)^2 - n^2 = (n + 1) + n$

  i.e., the difference of squares of two consecutive natural number is equal to their sum.

  Proof

  For any natural number *n*, we have

  $$(n + 1)^2 - n^2 = (n + 1 + n)(n + 1 - n)$$
  $$= n + 1 + n$$

Using $(a + b)(a - b) = a^2 - b^2$

  Thus, $14^2 - 13^2 = 14 + 13 = 27, 28^2 - 27^2 = 28 + 27 = 55$

3.5 Pythagorean Triplets

A triplet (*m, n, p*) of three natural numbers *m, n* and *p* is called a Pythagorean triplet, if $m^2 + n^2 = p^2$.

For example :

(3, 4, 5), (5, 12, 13), (8, 15, 17) *etc.* are Pythagorean triplets, because

$3^2 + 4^2 = 9 + 16 = 25 = 5^2$, $5^2 + 12^2 = 25 + 144 = 169 = 13^2$, $8^2 + 15^2 = 64 + 225 = 289 = 17^2$.

- **Property 9**

  For any natural number m greater than 1, $(2m, m^2 - 1, m^2 + 1)$ is a Pythagorean triplet.

For example :

Taking *m* = 4, we find that $2 \times 4, 4^2 - 1, 4^2 + 1$, *i.e.*, 8, 15, 17 is a Pythagorean triplet.

Ex. 1. *The following numbers are not perfect squares. Give reason.*

  (i) *1057*   **(ii)** *23453*   **(iii)** *7928*   **(iv)** *222222*   **(v)** *64000*

  (vi) *505050*

Sol. (*i*) to (*iv*). We know that the natural numbers ending in the digits 2, 3, 7 or 8 are not perfect squares therefore, 1057, 23453, 7928 and 222222 are not perfect squares.

  (*v*), (*vi*) We know that the numbers ending in an odd number of consecutive zeros are not perfect squares. Therefore, 64000 and 505050 are not perfect squares.

Ex. 2. *What will be the unit's digit of the squares of the following numbers :*

  (i) *81*   **(ii)** *272*   **(iii)** *799*   **(iv)** *3853*   **(v)** *1234*

  (vi) *26387*   **(vii)** *52698*   **(viii)** *99880*   **(ix)** *12796*   **(x)** *45535*

Sol. From the property of squares, we know that the unit's digit of the square of a natural number is the unit's digit of the square of the digit at unit's place of the given natural number. Applying this property, we have

	Since	**Unit's digit of**		**Since**	**Unit's digit of**		**Since**	**Unit's digit of**
(*i*)	$(1)^2 = 1$,	$(81)^2 = 1$	(*ii*)	$(2)^2 = 4$,	$(272)^2$ is 4	(*iii*)	$(9)^2 = 81$,	$(799)^2$ is 1
(*iv*)	$(3)^2 = 9$,	$(3853)^2 = 9$	(*v*)	$(4)^2 = 16$,	$(1234)^2$ is 6	(*vi*)	$(7)^2 = 49$,	$(26387)^2$ is 9
(*vii*)	$(8)^2 = 64$,	$(52698)^2$ is 4	(*viii*)	$(0)^2 = 0$,	$(99880)^2$ is 0	(*ix*)	$(6)^2 = 36$,	$(12796)^2$ is 6
(*x*)	$(5)^2 = 25$,	$(45535)^2$ is 5						

Ex. 3. *Which of the following triplets are Pythagorean?*

(i) *(6,8,10)*   (ii) *(16, 63, 65)*   (iii) *(24, 144, 145)*

Sol. For three numbers to be Pythagorean triplet, they should be expressible as $(2m, m^2 - 1, m^2 + 1)$.

(i) Let $m = 3$, then $2m = 6$, $m^2 - 1 = 3^2 - 1 = 8$, $m^2 + 1 = 3^2 + 1 = 10$

So (6, 8, 10) is a Pythagorean triplet.

(ii) Let $m = 8$, then $2m = 16$, $m^2 - 1 = 8^2 - 1 = 63$, $m^2 + 1 = 8^2 + 1 = 65$. So (16, 63, 65) is a Pythagorean triplet.

(iii) Let $m = 12$, then $2m = 24$, $m^2 - 1 = 12^2 - 1 = 143$, $m^2 + 1 = 12^2 + 1 = 145$

So (24, 144, 145) is not a Pythagorean triplet.

EXERCISE 3 (b)

1. The following numbers are not perfect squares. Give reasons.

  (i) 2367   (ii) 35943   (iii) 4368   (iv) 333222

2. The following numbers are not perfect squares. Give reasons.

  (i) 57000   (ii) 30710   (iii) 57322

3. What will be the unit's digit of the squares of the following numbers?

  (i) 539   (ii) 731   (iii) 8593   (iv) 23904   (v) 39487

  (vi) 73568   (vii) 39065   (viii) 793126   (ix) 5980

4. Determine whether squares of the following numbers are even or odd.

  (i) 537   (ii) 31298   (iii) 900265   (iv) 700312

  (Hint : Apply property 3 of square numbers)

5. Fill in the blanks :

  (i) $19^2 - 18^2 = $ ....   (ii) $30^2 - 29^2 = $ ....   (iii) $87^2 - 86^2 = $ ....

  (Hint : Apply property 8)

6. Express each of the following perfect squares as the sum of odd numbers.

  (i) 16   (ii) 25   (iii) 49   (iv) 81

7. Without adding, find the sum :

  (i) $1 + 3 + 5 + 7 + 9$ (ii) $1 + 3 + 5 + 7 + 9 + 11$ (iii) $1 + 3 + 5 + 7 + 9 + 11 + 13 + 15 + 17$

  (Hint : Apply property 7)

8. Which of the following triplets are Pythagorean?

  (i) (10, 24, 26)   (ii) (14, 48, 50)   (iii) (18, 79, 82)   (iv) (22, 120, 122)   (v) (20, 98, 101)

9. Write true (T) or false (F) for the following statements.

  (i) The number of digits in a square number is even.

  (ii) The square of a prime number is prime.

  (iii) The sum of two square numbers is a square number.

  (iv) The difference of two square numbers is a square number.

  (v) The product of two square numbers is a square number.

  (vi) No square number is negative.

  (vii) There is no square number between 50 and 60.

  (viii) There are fourteen square numbers up to 200.

SQUARE ROOTS

3.6 Meaning of Square Root

The square root of a number n is that number which when multiplied by itself gives n as the product.

For example :

$5 \times 5 = 25$, so 5 is the square root of 25. We write $\sqrt{25} = 5$

The symbol $\sqrt{}$ is used to indicate square root.

$11 \times 11 = 121$, so $\sqrt{121} = 11$. $\qquad$ $17 \times 17 = 289$ so $\sqrt{289} = 17$.

$0.7 \times 0.7 = 0.49$ so $\sqrt{0.49} = 0.7$. $\qquad$ $0.25 \times 0.25 = 0.0625$ so $\sqrt{0.0625} = 0.25$.

$\dfrac{3}{8} \times \dfrac{3}{8} = \dfrac{9}{64}$ so $\sqrt{\dfrac{9}{64}} = \dfrac{3}{8}$. $\qquad$ $\dfrac{10}{19} \times \dfrac{10}{19} = \dfrac{100}{361}$ so $\sqrt{\dfrac{100}{361}} = \dfrac{10}{19}$.

3.7 Finding Square Root of a Perfect Square

Method. By Prime Factorization.

One way to find the square root of perfect squares is by resolving the given number into prime factors.

Ex. 1. *Find the square root of 576.*

Sol. By prime factorization, we get

$$576 = (2 \times 2) \times (2 \times 2) \times (2 \times 2) \times (3 \times 3)$$

$\therefore \qquad \sqrt{576} = 2 \times 2 \times 2 \times 3 = \textbf{24}.$

Make pairs of factors.

Pickup one factor from each pair.

2	576
2	288
2	144
2	72
2	36
2	18
3	9
3	3
	1

Ex. 2. *Find the square root of $\sqrt{7744}$.*

Sol. **Step 1.** *Split the given number into prime factors*

$$7744 = 2 \times 2 \times 2 \times 2 \times 2 \times 2 \times 11 \times 11$$

Step 2. *Form pairs of like factors*

$$= (2 \times 2) \times (2 \times 2) \times (2 \times 2) \times (11 \times 11)$$

Step 3. From each pair, pick out one prime factor.

Ist pair	2nd pair	3rd pair	4th pair
(2×2) $\times$	(2×2) $\times$	(2×2) $\times$	(11×11)
Pick out one 2	Pick out one 2	Pick out one 2	Pick out one 11

Step 4. *Multiply the factors so picked.*

The product is the square root of the given number.

$$\sqrt{7744} = 2 \times 2 \times 2 \times 11 = \textbf{88}.$$

2	7744
2	3872
2	1936
2	968
2	484
2	242
11	121
	11

Note : You may write $7744 = 2^6 . 11^2$ then

$$\sqrt{7744} = \sqrt{2^6 \times 11^2} = 2^3 \times 11 = 8 \times 11 = \textbf{88}$$

It may be noted that the *even* powers of a number are squares.

Ex. 8. *Simplify* $= \sqrt{900} + \sqrt{0.09} + \sqrt{0.000009}$.

Sol. If p and q are natural numbers, then $\sqrt{pq} = \sqrt{p} \times \sqrt{q}$

$$\sqrt{900} = \sqrt{9 \times 100} = \sqrt{9} \times \sqrt{100} = 3 \times 10 = 30$$

$$\sqrt{0.09} = \sqrt{0.3 \times 0.3} = 0.3$$

$$\sqrt{0.000009} = \sqrt{0.003 \times 0.003} = 0.003$$

$$\therefore \quad \sqrt{900} + \sqrt{0.09} + \sqrt{0.000009} = 30 + 0.3 + 0.003 = \mathbf{30.303}.$$

> **Think !**
> 0.09 contains 2 decimal places so one of its equal factors will contain one decimal place.
> 0.000009 contains 6 decimal places so one of its equal factors will contain 3 decimal places.

EXERCISE 3 (c)

Find by prime factorization the square root of the following numbers.

1. 144	**2.** 2500	**3.** 256	**4.** 3600	**5.** 1936	**6.** 2916
7. 2704	**8.** 7056	**9.** 9025	**10.** 9216	**11.** 7744	**12.** 9801

Find the square root of the following fractions.

13. $\dfrac{25}{49}$ **14.** $\dfrac{196}{484}$ **15.** $\dfrac{1225}{2025}$ **16.** $1\dfrac{396}{9604}$ **17.** 0.01 **18.** 0.0009

19. 0.000004 **20.** 0.00000049

Simplify :

21. $\sqrt{(5^2 - 4^2)}$ **22.** $\sqrt{(5^2 + 12^2)}$ **23.** $(-8)^2 - \sqrt{64}$ **24.** $\left(\dfrac{1}{2}\right)^2 + \sqrt{0.25}$

25. $\left(-\sqrt{\dfrac{4}{9}}\right)\left(-\sqrt{\dfrac{81}{100}}\right)$ **26.** $\sqrt{400} + \sqrt{0.04} + \sqrt{0.000004}$

1.8 Finding Square Root of a Perfect Square By the Long Division Method

Sometimes it is not easy or convenient to write the factors of a number. In such cases, we use the method of long division to find the square root.

Ex. 1. *Find the square root of 7396.*

Sol. **Step 1.** Begin on the right. Mark off the digits in pairs from right to left ($\leftarrow$).

Step 2. Take the first pair of digits, and find the nearest perfect square. The largest perfect square less then 73 is 64, the square of 8. Write 8 on top as quotient and also in the division. Subtract $8 \times 8 = 64$ from 73. The remainder is 9.

Step 3. Bring down the next pair 96. Double 8, the number in the quotient and place the double i.e. 16 as the next divisor as shown. Divide 16 into 96 to obtain 6. Write 6 in the quotient to the right of 8, and to the right of 6 in the divisor. Multiply 166 by 6 and place the product under 996. Subtract. The remainder is zero. Therefore 86 is the exact square root.

```
          8  6
     8 | 73 96
         64 ↓
    166 | 9 96
          9 96
             0
```

$$\therefore \quad \sqrt{7396} = \mathbf{86.}$$

Ex. 1. *Find the square root of 17424.*

Sol.

```
        1  3  2
1    | 1 74 24
     |   1 ↓ ↓
23   |   74
     |   69 ↓ ↓
262  |      524
     |      524
     |        0
```

Mark off the digits in pairs from right to left
←

Step 1. $1^2 = 1$

Step 2. Twice $1 = 2$

Step 3. 2 goes into 7 three times. Put 3 on top and in the divisor as shown, $23 \times 3 = 69$

Step 4. Double 13. You get 26. First digit of 26 which is 2, goes into the first digit of 524 which is 5, 2 times. Place 2 on top and in the divisor as shown, $2 \times 262 = 524$.

Step 5. Subtract : The remainder is 0.

Therefore, $\sqrt{17424} = \mathbf{132}$.

Ex. 4. *Find the square root of* $56\dfrac{569}{1225}$.

Sol. *(i)* $56\dfrac{569}{1225} = \dfrac{69169}{1225}$

$\therefore \sqrt{56\dfrac{569}{1225}} = \sqrt{\dfrac{69169}{1225}} = \dfrac{\sqrt{69169}}{\sqrt{1225}}$

Using $\sqrt{\dfrac{a}{b}} = \dfrac{\sqrt{a}}{\sqrt{b}}$

We find the square roots of 69169 and 1225 separately.

```
          2  6  3
2    |  6 91 69
     |  4 ↓
46   |  2 91
     |  2 76 ↓
523  |    15 69
     |    15 69
     |        0
```

```
        3  5
3    | 12 25
     |  9 ↓
65   |  3 25
     |  3 25
     |     0
```

Thus $\sqrt{69169} = 263$

$\sqrt{1225} = 35$

$\therefore \dfrac{\sqrt{69169}}{\sqrt{1225}} = \dfrac{263}{35}$

Hence, $\sqrt{56\dfrac{569}{1225}} = \dfrac{263}{35} = 7\dfrac{18}{35}$.

3.9 Finding the Number of Digits in the Square Root of a Perfect Square

The number of digits in the square root of a perfect square depends on the number of digits in the perfect square. Thus

	Number of digits in the perfect square	*Number of digits in the square root*
$\sqrt{1225} = 35$	4	$2 = \dfrac{4}{2}$
$\sqrt{961} = 31$	3	$2 = \dfrac{3+1}{2}$
$\sqrt{67600} = 260$	5	$3 = \dfrac{5+1}{2}$
$\sqrt{288369} = 537$	6	$3 = \dfrac{6}{2}$

In general, if a perfect square contains *n* digits then, its square root will contain $\frac{n}{2}$ digits, when *n* is even and $\frac{n+1}{2}$ digits, when *n* is odd.

3.10 Finding Square Root of Perfect Square Decimal Numbers by Division Method

A slight variation in method is necessary when it is required to find the square root of a decimal.

While finding the square root of a natural number, say, 46656, you make pairs by counting from **right to left** and if in the last, one digit is left, you leave it by itself. For example, while finding the square root of 276676 and 46656, we form pairs as under:

$\overleftarrow{27}\ \overleftarrow{66}\ \overleftarrow{76}$ $\qquad\qquad\qquad$ $4\ \overleftarrow{66}\ \overleftarrow{56}$

In case of a decimal number, we count from left to the right for the decimal portion and from right to the left for the integral portion.

If the last period of the decimal number contains only one figure we may add zero to it. This is because two digits are necessary to make up a period, while the addition of a zero at the right of a decimal figure does not change its value. For example, while finding the square roots of 0.00 00 2601, 492.84, 998.56, 252.70729 the periods will be formed as under :

$0.\overrightarrow{00}\ \overrightarrow{00}\ \overrightarrow{26}\ \overrightarrow{01},\ 4\ \overleftarrow{92}\cdot\overrightarrow{84},\ \overleftarrow{998}\cdot\overrightarrow{56},\ 2\ \overleftarrow{52}\cdot\overrightarrow{70}\ \overrightarrow{72}\ \overrightarrow{90}$

$\qquad\qquad\qquad\qquad\qquad\qquad\qquad\qquad$ └── **one zero is added**

The square root of a decimal will contain as many decimal places as there are periods, or half as many decimal places as the given number.

The operations in obtaining the square root of a decimal number are the same as for whole numbers.

Follow the steps in the following example :

Ex.1. *Find the square root of 3881.29*

Sol. **Step 1.** Beginning at the decimal point, mark off points to the left and right.

Step 2. 6 is the largest whole-number square root that is contained in 38 which constitutes the first period. Write 6 on top as quotient and also in the divisor. Subtract 6 × 6 = 36 from 38. The remainder is 2.

Step 3. Bring down the next pair 81. Double 6 (the number in the quotient) and place the double *i.e.,* 12 as the next divisor as shown. Divide 12 into 28 to obtain 2. Write 2 as the next number in the quotient and also place 2 next to 12 in the divisor as shown. Multiply 122 by 2 and place the product under 281. Subtract. The remainder is 37.

	6 2 . 3
6	38 81 . 29
	36 ↓
122	2 81
	2 44 ↓
1243	37 29
	37 29
	0

Step 4. Place the decimal point in the quotient after 2 because the next pair is a decimal part.

Step 5. Bring down 29 to make 3729 the next dividend. Double 62 (the number in the quotient) and place the double *i.e.* 124 as the next divisor as shown. Divide 124 into 372 to obtain 3. Write 3 as the next number in the quotient and also place 3 next to 124 in the divisor. Multiply 1243 by 3 and place the product under 3729. Subtract. The remainder is zero.

$\therefore\ \sqrt{3881.29}\ = \mathbf{62.3}$

Ex. 2. *Find the square root of 6432.04.*

Sol.

Put 0 at both places as shown

```
                    8   0 . 2
             8 │ 64 32 . 04
               │ 64
          1602 │    32 04
               │    32 04
               │        0
```

In the above example, since 16 does not divide 3, put a zero both in the root (quotient) and the divisor and bring down the next pair 04 also.

> **Note :** When a divisor is larger than the corresponding dividend, write zero in the trial divisor and bring down the root period.

Ex. 3. *Find the value of $\sqrt{3136}$ and use it to find the value of $\sqrt{31.36} + \sqrt{0.3136}$.*

Sol.

```
                   5   6
            5 │ 31 36
              │ 25
         106  │    6 36
              │    6 36
              │       0
```

$$\sqrt{3136} = 56$$

$$\therefore \quad \sqrt{31.36} = 5.6 \text{ and } \sqrt{0.3136} = 0.56$$

$$\therefore \quad \sqrt{31.36} + \sqrt{0.316} = 5.6 + 0.56 = \mathbf{6.16}.$$

We can also work out as under

$$\sqrt{31.36} + \sqrt{0.3136} = \sqrt{\frac{3136}{100}} + \sqrt{\frac{3136}{10000}} = \frac{\sqrt{3136}}{10} + \frac{\sqrt{3136}}{100}$$

$$= \frac{56}{10} + \frac{56}{100} = 5.6 + 0.56 = \mathbf{6.16}.$$

Ex. 4. *Find the square roots of 3364 and 1936 and hence find the value of $\dfrac{\sqrt{0.3364} + \sqrt{0.1936}}{\sqrt{0.3364} - \sqrt{0.1936}}$.*

$$\therefore \quad \sqrt{3364} = 58 \text{ and } \sqrt{1936} = 44$$

Now, $\dfrac{\sqrt{0.3364} + \sqrt{0.1936}}{\sqrt{0.3364} - \sqrt{0.1936}}$

$$= \frac{\sqrt{\dfrac{3364}{10000}} + \sqrt{\dfrac{1936}{10000}}}{\sqrt{\dfrac{3364}{10000}} - \sqrt{\dfrac{1936}{10000}}} = \frac{\dfrac{58}{100} + \dfrac{44}{100}}{\dfrac{58}{100} - \dfrac{44}{100}} = \frac{\dfrac{58+44}{100}}{\dfrac{58-44}{100}}$$

$$= \frac{58+44}{58-44} = \frac{102}{14} = \frac{51}{7} = 7\frac{2}{7}.$$

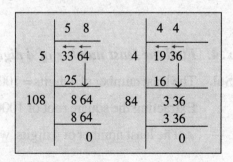

```
               5   8              4   4
        5 │ 33 64          4 │ 19 36
          │ 25               │ 16
      108 │   8 64        84 │  3 36
          │   8 64           │  3 36
          │      0           │     0
```

EXERCISE 3 (d)

Find the square root of each of the following numbers by long division.

1. 2304	**2.** 1225	**3.** 2209	**4.** 3481	**5.** 4225
6. 6724	**7.** 7921	**8.** 8649	**9.** 9801	**10.** 15129

Find the square of each of the following decimal numbers by long division.

11. 655.36   **12.** 1324.96   **13.** 1831.84   **14.** 3564.09   **15.** 4556.25

16. 6099.61   **17.** 7903.21   **18.** 9273.69

Evaluate :

19. $\sqrt{\dfrac{2809}{4096}}$ **20.** $\sqrt{\dfrac{1849}{5776}}$ **21.** $\sqrt{1\dfrac{869}{1156}}$ **22.** $\sqrt{2\dfrac{1337}{3844}}$

23. Find the value of $\sqrt{9216}$ and from this value calculate $\sqrt{92.16} + 9.216$.

24. Find the square roots of 2116 and 1764 and hence find the value of $\dfrac{\sqrt{0.2116} + \sqrt{0.1764}}{\sqrt{0.2116} - \sqrt{0.1764}}$.

25. Simplify : $\dfrac{\sqrt{59.29} - \sqrt{5.29}}{\sqrt{59.29} + \sqrt{5.29}}$

3.11 Simple Problems on Square Roots

Ex. 1. *Find the least number which must be subtracted from 2361 to make it a perfect square.*

Sol. From the working shown, we find that if 57 be subtracted from the given number the square root of the remainder will be 48.

Hence the required number is **57**.

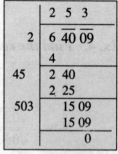

Ex. 2. *Find the least number which must be added to 4931 to make it a perfect square.*

Sol. We observe that the given number is greater than $(70)^2$ but less than $(71)^2$.

The number to be added $= (71)^2 - 4931 = 5041 - 4931 = \textbf{110}.$

Ex. 3. *A General wishing to draw up his 64 019 men in the form of a solid square, found that he had 10 men over. Find the number of men in the front row.*

Sol. Number of men arranged in a solid square $= 64\,019 - 10 = 64\,009$

$\therefore$ Number of men in the front row $= \sqrt{64009} = \textbf{253}.$

Ex. 4. *Find the least number of 4 digits, which is a perfect square.*

Sol. The least number of 4 digits $= 1000$

Extracting the square root of 1000, we find that $(31)^2 < 1000 < (32)^2$

$\therefore$ The least number of 4 digits, which is a perfect square $= (32)^2 = \textbf{1024}.$

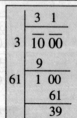

Ex. 5. *Find the greatest number of 4 digits, which is a perfect square.*

Sol. The greatest number of 4 digits $= 9999$

Extracting the square root of 9999, we find that $(99)^2$ is less than 9999

by 198.

Hence, the required number $= 9999 - 198 = \textbf{9801}.$

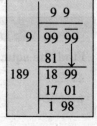

Ex. 6. *Find the least number which is a perfect square and which is also divisible by 16, 18 and 45.*

Sol. L.C.M. of 16, 18, and 45

$$= 2 \times 9 \times 8 \times 5$$
$$= 2^2 \times 3^2 \times 2^2 \times 5 = 720$$

∴ In order to get the required number, we should multiply 720 by 5.

Hence, the required numbers is 720×5 or **3600.**

2	16, 18, 45
9	8, 9, 45
	8, 1, 5

EXERCISE 3 (e)

1. 3600 soldiers are asked to stand in different rows. Every row has as many soldiers as there are rows. Find the number of rows.
2. Find the perimeter of a square whose area is 6889 m^2.
3. In a school show 576 students line up to form a square. Find the number of students in each row.
4. A society collected Rs 8836, each member contributing as many rupees as there were members. Find the number of members of the society.
5. In a basket there are 1250 flowers. A man goes for worship and puts as many flowers as there are temples in the city. Thus he needs 8 baskets of flowers. Find the number of temples in the city.
6. What should be subtracted from 6249 to get a perfect square number? What is this perfect square number? Also, find its square root.
7. What least number must be added to 594 to make the sum a perfect square?
8. What would be added to 7912 to make the sum a perfect square?
9. Find the least number which must be subtracted from 4494 to make it a perfect square.
10. Find the least number of four digits which is a perfect square.
11. A General arranges his soldiers in rows to form a perfect square. He finds that in doing so, 60 soldiers are left out. If the total number of soldiers be 8160, find the number of soldiers in each row.
12. A gardener arranges his plants in rows to form a perfect square. He finds that in doing so, 4 plants are left out. If the total number of plants be 3604, find the number of plants in each row.

3.12 Square Root of Numbers which are not Perfect Squares

Now we will see how to find the square root of numbers which are not perfect squares. As the numbers are not perfect squares, we will not get an exact square root, so we shall determine approximate square roots. To find approximate square roots we add zeros after the decimal point or after the last figure if the original number is already in decimal form.

To get the square root of a number upto two decimal places, we calculate the square root upto three places of decimal *i.e.*, after the decimal point we should have six digits (3 periods). Then we round the answer up or down to 2 places of decimal, seeing the digit at the third decimal place as equal to, greater or lesser than 5.

Ex. 1. *Find the square root of (i) 7 (ii) 0.7 to two decimal places.*

Sol. (i)

```
          2 . 6 4 5
   2 | 7 . 00 00 00
     |   4
  46 |   3 00
     |   2 76
 524 |      24 00
     |      20 96
5285 |       3 04 00
     |       2 64 25
     |         39 75
```

(ii)

```
          0 . 8 3 6
    8 | 0 . 70 00 00
      |     64
  163 |      6 00
      |      4 89
 1666 |      1 11 00
      |        99 96
      |        11 04
```

$$\therefore \qquad \sqrt{7} \; = \; 2.645 \text{ to 3 dp} \qquad\qquad \therefore \qquad \sqrt{0.7} \; = \; 0.836 \text{ to 3 dp}$$
$$= \; \textbf{2.65} \text{ to 2 dp} \qquad\qquad\qquad\qquad\qquad = \; \textbf{0.84} \text{ to 2 dp}$$

Ex. 2. *Find the square of 25.63 correct to two places of decimal.*

Ex. 3. *Find the square root of 1869 to 2 decimal places.*

Sol.

```
            5 . 0 6 2
      ┌─────────────────────
    5 │ 25 . 63  00  00
      │ 25    ↓    ↓
      ├─────────────────────
 1006 │      63 00
      │      60 36   ↓
      ├─────────────────────
10122 │        2 64 00
      │        2 02 44
      │          ─────────
      │          61 56
```

```
            4 3 . 2 3 1
      ┌──────────────────────────
    4 │ 18 69 . 00  00  00
      │ 16  ↓
      ├──────────────────────────
   83 │  2 69
      │  2 49     ↓
      ├──────────────────────────
  862 │      20 00
      │      17 24   ↓
      ├──────────────────────────
 8643 │       2 76 00
      │       2 59 29   ↓
      ├──────────────────────────
86461 │          16 71 00
      │           8 64 61
      │          ─────────
      │           8 06 39
```

$$\therefore \qquad \sqrt{25.63} \; = \; 5.062 \text{ to 3 dp} \qquad\qquad \therefore \qquad \sqrt{1869} \; = \; 43.231 \text{ to 3 dp}$$
$$= \; \textbf{5.06} \text{ to 2 dp} \qquad\qquad\qquad\qquad\qquad = \; \textbf{43.23} \text{ to 2 dp}$$

1.13 Square Root of Fractions (when the numerator and denominator are not perfect squares)

Method. *First divide the number by the denominator and convert the given fraction into a decimal number.*

Ex. 5. *Find the square root of $3\frac{3}{7}$ correct to 2 places of decimals.*

Sol.

$$\begin{array}{r} 7\,\overline{)\;3.000\;000} \\ \hline 0.428\;571... \end{array} \qquad\qquad \therefore \quad \frac{3}{7} = 0.428571$$

$$3\frac{3}{7} = 3.428571$$

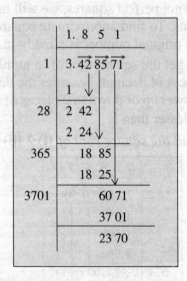

$$\therefore \quad \sqrt{3\frac{3}{7}} = 1.851 \,(\text{to 3 dp}) = \textbf{1.85} \,(\text{to 2 dp})$$

Ex. 6. *Find the square root of* $10\frac{2}{3}$ *correct to two places of decimals.*

Sol. $3\,\overline{)\,2.00000000}$ $\therefore \frac{2}{3} = 0.666666$
       $\overline{0.666666...}$

$\therefore 10\frac{2}{3} = 10.666666$

$\therefore \sqrt{10\frac{2}{3}} = 3.265$ to 3 dp

              $= 3.27$ to 2 dp

	3. 2 6 5
3	10. 66 66 66
	9
62	1 66
	1 24
646	42 66
	38 76
6525	3 90 66
	3 26 25
65309	64 41

EXERCISE 3 (f)

Find the square root of each of the following numbers correct to two places of decimal :

1. 3   **2.** 5   **3.** 17   **4.** 23   **5.** 66   **6.** 73

7. 478   **8.** 789   **9.** 2000   **10.** 6153

Find the square root of each of the following decimal numbers correct to 2 places of decimal :

11. 1.1   **12.** 3.8   **13.** 7.83   **14.** 13.26   **15.** 74.9   **16.** 175.01

17. 423.74   **18.** 683.95   **19.** 5893.27   **20.** 7136.8

Find the square root of each of the following fractional numbers correct to 2 places of decimal :

21. $\frac{4}{7}$ **22.** $\frac{13}{11}$ **23.** $1\frac{7}{8}$ **24.** $1\frac{5}{9}$ **25.** $83\frac{7}{11}$ **26.** $431\frac{2}{5}$

27. $697\frac{1}{2}$ **28.** $1007\frac{3}{4}$.

LOOKING BACK
Summary of Key Facts

1. If a number is multiplied by itself, the product so obtained is called the **square** of that number. It is a number raised to the power 2.

Thus, $7 \times 7 = 7^2 = 49$, 49 is the square of 7. The number 7 is called the **square root** of 49.

2. The square of a natural number is called a **perfect square**.

3. Properties of Squares.

  (*i*)   A perfect square is never negative.

  (*ii*) A square number never ends in 2, 3, 7 or 8.

  (*iii*) The number of zeros at the end of a perfect square is always even.

  (*iv*) The square of an even number is even.

  (*v*)   The square of an odd number is odd.

  (*vi*) For any natural number *n*,

  n^2 = sum of the first n odd natural numbers. (*e.g.* $4^2 = 1 + 3 + 5 + 7$)

4. Properties of square root.

    (i)   If a number ends in an odd number of zeros, then it does not have a square root.

    (ii)   The square root of an even square number is even and square root of an odd square number is odd.

    (iii)   If p and q are perfect squares ($q \neq 0$), then

        (a) $\sqrt{p \times q} = \sqrt{p} \times \sqrt{q}$ (b) $\sqrt{\dfrac{p}{q}} = \dfrac{\sqrt{p}}{\sqrt{q}}$.

5. Finding the square root.

    (i)   The square root of a perfect square number can be obtained by finding the prime factorization of the square number, pairing equal factors and picking out one prime factor out of each pair.

         Thus, $900 = \underline{2 \times 2} \times \underline{3 \times 3} \times \underline{5 \times 5}$ and so $\sqrt{900} = 2 \times 3 \times 5 = 30$.

    (ii)   The square root of a number may also be found by division method.

    (iii)   The pairing of numbers in the division method starts from the decimal point. For the integral part, it goes from right to left and for the decimal part, it goes from left to right as shown below :

$$\overleftarrow{1}\ \overleftarrow{66}\ \overleftarrow{41} \quad \overrightarrow{59}\ \overleftarrow{37}\ \overleftarrow{28} \quad \overleftarrow{397}.\overrightarrow{00}\ \overrightarrow{37}\ \overrightarrow{48}\ \overrightarrow{00}$$

    (iv)   If a positive number is not a perfect square then an approximate value of its square root may be obtained by the division method.

    (v)   If p and q are not perfect squares, then to find $\sqrt{\dfrac{p}{q}}$, we may express $\dfrac{p}{q}$ as a decimal number and then use the division method. e.g., $\sqrt{\dfrac{7}{8}} = \sqrt{0.875}$, $\sqrt{2\dfrac{1}{12}} = \sqrt{\dfrac{25}{12}} = \sqrt{2.0833}$

6. We may also find $\sqrt{\dfrac{p}{q}}$ by making the denominator free from the radical sign.

    e.g. $\sqrt{\dfrac{2}{7}} = \dfrac{\sqrt{2}}{\sqrt{7}} = \dfrac{\sqrt{2}}{\sqrt{7}} \times \dfrac{\sqrt{7}}{\sqrt{7}} = \dfrac{\sqrt{2 \times 7}}{7} = \dfrac{\sqrt{14}}{7}$.

7. If n is not a perfect square, then $\sqrt{n}$ is not a rational number, e.g., $\sqrt{2}, \sqrt{3}, \sqrt{7}$ are not rational numbers.

MENTAL MATHS – 3

1. square of 4 = ...

2. square of 6 ...

3. square of 8 = ...

4. square of $\dfrac{5}{9}$ = ...

5. square of 0.3 is ...

6. square of 0.12 is ...

7. $15^2 - 14^2 = ...$

8. $99^2 - 98^2 = ...$

9. square of 0.07 = ...

10. Without adding, find the sum of $1 + 3 + 5 + 7 + 9 + 11 + 13 + 15 + 17$

11. $\sqrt{0.0081} = ...$

12. Find the square root of 10000000000.

13. Why is each of the following numbers not a perfect square?

    (i) 372   (ii) 59307   (iii) 71298   (iv) 39000

14. Find the least number which should be subtracted from 18 to make it a perfect square.

MULTIPLE CHOICE QUESTIONS – 3

1. $\sqrt{1296} = (?)^2$

    (*i*)   6   (*ii*)   1296   (*iii*)   625   (*iv*)   36

2. The value of $\sqrt{212 + \sqrt{154 + \sqrt{225}}}$ is

    (*i*)   13   (*ii*)   15   (*iii*)   25   (*iv*)   12

3. $\dfrac{2707}{\sqrt{?}} = 27.07$

    (*i*)   10   (*ii*)   100   (*iii*)   1000   (*iv*)   10000

4. If $\sqrt{1 + \dfrac{x}{144}} = \dfrac{13}{12}$, then x is equal to :

    (*i*)   1   (*ii*)   12   (*iii*)   13   (*iv*)   15   (*v*)   25

5. $\sqrt{\dfrac{0.289}{0.00121}}$ is equal to :

    (*i*) $\dfrac{170}{11}$ (*ii*) $\dfrac{17}{110}$ (*iii*) $\dfrac{17}{11}$ (*iv*) $\dfrac{0.17}{11}$

6. $\sqrt{\dfrac{0.081 \times 0.484}{0.0064 \times 6.25}}$ is equal to

    (*i*)   9   (*ii*)   0.9   (*iii*)   99   (*iv*)   0.99

7. The least number by which 1445 must be divided to get a perfect square, is :

    (*i*)   15   (*ii*)   7   (*iii*)   5   (*iv*)   9

8. If $\dfrac{x}{\sqrt{2.25}} = 550$, then the value of x is :

    (*i*)   825   (*ii*)   82.5   (*iii*)   3666.66   (*iv*)   2

9. If $\sqrt{4096} = 64$, then the value of $\sqrt{40.96} + \sqrt{0.4096} + \sqrt{0.004096}$ is

    (*i*)   64.64   (*ii*)   6.664   (*iii*)   7.104   (*iv*)   64.64

10. The least number which must be added to 157 to make it a perfect square is :

    (*i*)   17   (*ii*)   12   (*iii*)   8   (*iv*)   10

ANSWERS

EXERCISE 3 (a)

1. (*i*)   10   (*ii*)   28   (*iii*)   60   (*iv*) 90   **2.** (*ii*), (*iii*) and (*v*)
3. (*i*)   2   (*ii*)   7   (*iii*)   3   (*iv*) 5
4. (*i*)   5   (*ii*)   7   (*iii*)   3   (*iv*) 3

EXERCISE 3 (b)

1. (*i*)   It ends in 7   (*ii*)   It ends in 3   (*iii*)   It ends is 8   (*iv*)   It ends in 2
2. (*i*)   and   (*ii*) have odd number of consecutive zeros at the end   (*iii*) It ends in 2
3. (*i*)   1   (*ii*)   1   (*iii*)   9   (*iv*)   6   (*v*)   9   (*vi*)   4   (*vii*)   5
    (*viii*)   6   (*ix*)   0   **4.** (*i*)   odd   (*ii*)   even   (*iii*)   odd   (*iv*)   even
5. (*i*) $19 + 18 = 37$ (*ii*) $30 + 29 = 59$ (*iii*) $87 + 86 = 173$

6. (i) $1+3+5+7$ (ii) $1+3+5+7+9$ (iii) $1+3+5+7+9+11+13$
   (iv) $1+3+5+7+9+11+13+15+17$ 7.   (i) 25 (ii)   36 (iii)   81
8. (i), (ii), (iv)   9. (i) F   (ii) F   (iii) F   (iv) F   (v) T   (vi) T
  (vii) T   (viii) T

EXERCISE 3 (c)

1. 12   2. 50   3. 16   4. 60   5. 44   6. 54   7. 52

8. 84   9. 95   10. 96   11. 88   12. 99   13. $\frac{5}{7}$ 14. $\frac{14}{22}$

15. $\frac{35}{45}$ 16. $1\frac{2}{98}$ 17. 0.1   18. 0.03   19. 0.002   20. 0.0007   21. 3

22. 13   23. 56   24. 0.75   25. $\frac{3}{5}$ 26. 20.202

EXERCISE 3 (d)

1. 48   2. 35   3. 47   4. 59   5. 65   6. 82   7. 89
8. 93   9. 99   10. 123   11. 25.6   12. 36.4   13. 42.8   14. 59.7

15. 67.5   16. 78.1   17. 88.9   18. 96.3   19. $\frac{53}{64}$ 20. $\frac{43}{76}$ 21. $1\frac{11}{34}$

22. $1\frac{33}{62}$ 23. 96; 18.816   24. 46 ; 42 ; 22   25. 0.54

EXERCISE 3 (e)

1. 60   2. 332 m   3. 24   4. 94   5. 100   6. 8 ; 79   7. 31
8. 9   9. 5   10. 1024   11. 90   12. 60

EXERCISE 3 (f)

1. 1.73   2. 2.24   3. 4.12   4. 4.80   5. 8.12   6. 8.54   7. 21.86
8. 28.09   9. 44.72   10. 78.44   11. 1.05   12. 1.95   13. 2.80   14. 3.64
15. 8.65   16. 13.23   17. 20.58   18. 26.15   19. 76.77   20. 84.48   21. 0.76
22. 1.09   23. 1.37   24. 1.25   25. 9.15   26. 20.77   27. 26.41   28. 31.75

MENTAL MATHS – 3

1. 16   2. 36   3. 64   4. $\frac{25}{81}$ 5. 0.09   6. 0.0144   7. 29
8. 197   9. 0.0049   10. 81   11. 0.09   12. 100000   13. (i) It ends in 2
  (ii) It ends in 7 (iii) It ends is 8 (iv) it has odd number of consecutive zeros at the end   14. 2

MULTIPLE CHOICE QUESTIONS – 3

1. (iv)   2. (ii)   3. (iv)   4. (v)   5. (i)   6. (iv)   7. (iii)
8. (i)   9. (iii)   10. (ii)

4. Cubes and Cube Roots

4.1 Cubes

The cube of a number is the number raised to the power 3. Thus,

cube of $2 = 2^3 = 2 \times 2 \times 2 = 8$,   cube of $5 = 5^3 = 5 \times 5 \times 5 = 125$.

4.2 Perfect Cube

We know that $2^3 = 8$, $3^3 = 27$, $6^3 = 216$, $7^3 = 343$, $10^3 = 1000$.

The numbers 8, 27, 216, 343, 1000, ... are called perfect cubes. A natural number is said to be a perfect cube, if it is the cube of some natural number. That is,

A natural number n is a perfect cube if there exists a natural number m such that $m \times m \times m = n$.

> **Test.** *A given natural number is a perfect cube if in its prime factorisation; every prime occurs three times or a multiple of three times, i.e., if it is expressible as the product of **triplets** of the same prime factors.*

The cubes of first 20 natural numbers are given below. You may learn them by heart.

Number	Cube	Number	Cube	Number	Cube	Number	Cube
1	1	6	216	11	1331	16	4096
2	8	7	343	12	1728	17	4913
3	27	8	512	13	2197	18	5832
4	64	9	729	14	2744	19	6859
5	125	10	1000	15	3375	20	8000

Ex. 1. *Examine if (i) 200 (ii) 864 are perfect cubes.*

Sol. **Method.**

1. *Find the prime factorisation of the given number.*
2. *Group together triplets of the same prime factors.*
3. *If no number is left out, the number is a perfect cube.*
4. *If some factor is left out as a single factor or a double factor, then the number is not a perfect cube.*

2	200
2	100
2	50
5	25
5	5
	1

2	864
2	432
2	216
2	108
2	54
3	27
3	9
3	3
	1

(i) $200 = 2 \times 2 \times 2 \times 5 \times 5$

If we form triplets of equal factors, the number 2 forms a group of three while the factor 5 does not do so, therefore, 200 is not a perfect cube.

(ii) $864 = 2 \times 2 \times 2 \times 2 \times 2 \times 3 \times 3 \times 3$

Here, the second group of 2's does not form a triplet, hence 864 is not a perfect cube.

Ex. 2. *Show that 729 is a perfect cube.*

Sol. Resolving 729 into prime factors, we have

$729 = 3 \times 3 \times 3 \times 3 \times 3 \times 3$

Here, we find that the prime factor 3 of the given number can be grouped into threes and no factor is left out. Hence, 729 is a perfect cube

Also, 729 is the cube of 3×3, *i.e.*, **$729 = (9)^3$.**

3	729
3	243
3	81
3	27
3	9
3	3
	1

Ex. 3. *What is the smallest number by which 1323 may be multiplied so that the product is a perfect cube ?*

Sol. Resolving 1323 into prime factors, we have

$1323 = 3 \times 3 \times 3 \times 7 \times 7$

Since one more 7 is required to make a triplet of 7, the smallest number by which 1323 should be multiplied to make it a perfect cube is **7**.

3	1323
3	441
3	147
7	49
7	7
	1

Ex. 4. *What is the smallest number by which 1375 should be divided so that the quotient may be a perfect cube?*

Sol. Resolving 1375 into prime factors, we have

$1375 = 5 \times 5 \times 5 \times 11$

The factor 5 makes a triplet, and 11 is left out. So, clearly 1375 should be divided by **11** to make it a perfect cube.

5	1375
5	275
5	55
11	11
	1

4.3 Properties of Cubes of Numbers

From the table of cubes given above, it is easy to observe that

1. Cubes of all odd natural numbers are odd. Thus $3^3 = 27, 5^3 = 125, 7^3 = 343, 9^3 = 729$ etc.
2. Cubes of all even natural numbers are even. Thus $2^3 = 8, 4^3 = 64, 6^3 = 216, 8^3 = 512$ etc.
3. **Cubes of Negative Integers**

   The cube of a negative integer is always negative

   e.g.,
   $(-1) = (-1) \times (-1) \times (-1) = (1) \times (-1) = 1.$
   $(-2)^5 = -2 \times -2 \times -2 \times -2 \times -2 = (-2 \times -2) \times (-2 \times -2) \times -2$
   $= 4 \times 4 \times -2 = -32.$

4. **Cube of a rational number**

   For any rational number $\frac{a}{b}$, we have $\left(\frac{a}{b}\right)^3 = \frac{a^3}{b^3}$.

   Thus $\left(\frac{2}{3}\right)^3 = \frac{2^3}{3^3} = \frac{8}{27}$, $\left(\frac{-4}{5}\right)^3 = \frac{(-4)^3}{5^3} = \frac{-64}{125}$.

EXERCISE 4 (a)

Find the cubes of the following numbers :

1. (*a*) 8   (*b*) 13   (*c*) 27   (*d*) 400   (*e*) 103

2. (*a*) $\frac{3}{5}$ (*b*) $\frac{-4}{9}$ (*c*) $2\frac{5}{7}$ (*d*) $1\frac{6}{17}$ (*e*) $-\frac{11}{8}$

3. (*a*) 0.3   (*b*) 0.5   (*c*) – 2.4   (*d*) 0.08   (*e*) 0.001

4. **Which of the following numbers are perfect cubes?**

   64, 125, 243, 729, 1331, 864, 4096, 74088

   (**Hint** : Resolve into prime factors and see if you can group these factors into triplets of equal numbers)

5. What is the smallest number by which 675 should be multiplied so that the product is a perfect cube?

6. What is the smallest number by which 2916 should be divided so that the quotient is a perfect cube?

7. Write cubes of all natural numbers between 1 and 10 and verify the following statements.

   (*a*) Cubes of all odd natural numbers are odd.

   (*b*) Cubes of all even natural numbers are even.

8. Write cubes of five natural numbers which are multiples of 3 and verify the following:

   'The cube of a natural number which is a multiple of 3 is a multiple of 27'.

9. Write cubes of 4 natural numbers which are multiples of 5 and verify the following:

   'The cube of a natural number which is a multiple of 5 is a multiple of 125'.

4.4 Cube Root

The cube root of a number *a* is that number which when multiplied by itself three times gives *a*,

i.e.,   If $a \times a \times a = a^3$ then $\sqrt[3]{a^3} = a$

> **Note :**
>
> 1. Cube root is denoted by the symbol $\sqrt[3]{}$
>
> 2. Cube root of a negative number is negative, *i.e.,* $\sqrt[3]{-a^3} = -a$
>
> 3. Cube root of product of two integers: $\sqrt[3]{a.b} = \sqrt[3]{a}.\sqrt[3]{b}$
>
> 4. Cube root of a rational number: $\sqrt[3]{\dfrac{a}{b}} = \dfrac{\sqrt[3]{a}}{\sqrt[3]{b}}$ $(b \neq 0)$.

4.5 Finding the Cube Root

Method 1. Prime Factorisation Method

Step 1. *Resolve the given number into prime factors.*

Step 2. *Form groups of threes of like factors.*

Step 3. *Take out one factor from each group and multiply.*

Ex. 1. *Find the cube root of*

   (**i**) *64*   (**ii**) $4\dfrac{12}{125}$ (**iii**) *–0.729*

Sol. (*i*) Resolving into prime factors

$$64 = \underbrace{2 \times 2 \times 2} \times \underbrace{2 \times 2 \times 2}$$

$$\sqrt[3]{64} = 2 \times 2$$

$$= \mathbf{4.}$$

Picking out one factor from each group of three like factors.

2	64
2	32
2	16
2	8
2	4
2	2
	1

(ii) $4\frac{12}{125} = \frac{512}{125} = \frac{(2\times2\times2)\times(2\times2\times2)\times(2\times2\times2)}{5\times5\times5}$

2	512
2	256
2	128
2	64
2	32
2	16
2	8
2	4
2	2
	1

3	729
3	243
3	81
3	27
3	9
3	3
	1

$\therefore \quad \sqrt[3]{4\frac{12}{125}} = \sqrt[3]{\frac{512}{125}} = \frac{\sqrt[3]{512}}{\sqrt[3]{125}} = \frac{2\times2\times2}{5} = \frac{8}{5}$.

(iii) $-0.729 = -\frac{729}{1000} = \frac{(3\times3\times3)\times(3\times3\times3)}{10\times10\times10}$

$\sqrt[3]{\frac{-729}{1000}} = -\frac{\sqrt[3]{729}}{\sqrt[3]{1000}} = \frac{3\times3}{10} = -\frac{9}{10} = \mathbf{-0.9}$.

Ex. 2. *Find the value of* $\sqrt[3]{968} \times \sqrt[3]{1375}$.

Sol. $\sqrt[3]{968} \times \sqrt[3]{1375} = \sqrt[3]{968\times1375}$

Resolving 968 and 6125 into prime factors, we have

2	968
2	484
2	242
11	121
11	11
	1

5	1375
5	275
5	55
11	11
	1

$\therefore \quad 968 \times 1375 = 2\times2\times2\times11\times11\times5\times5\times5\times11$

$= \underline{2\times2\times2} \times \underline{11\times11\times11} \times \underline{5\times5\times5}$

$\therefore \quad \sqrt[3]{968\times1375} = 2\times11\times5 = \mathbf{110}$.

EXERCISE 4 (b)

1. **Find the cube roots of the following numbers by prime factorisation method :**

(i) 8   (ii) 27   (iii) 125   (iv) 216   (v) 343

(vi) 1331   (vii) 2744   (viii) 5832   (ix) 8000   (x) 3375

2. **Find the cube roots of the following :**

(i) –729   (ii) –1728   (iii) –9261   (iv) –2197

3. **Find the cube roots of the following :**

(i) $\frac{125}{343}$ (ii) $\frac{-729}{2197}$ (iii) $\frac{-3375}{4913}$ (iv) $\frac{125}{2744}$ (v) $5\frac{23}{64}$

4. **Evaluate :**

(i) $\sqrt[3]{0.216}$ (ii) $\sqrt[3]{4.096}$ (iii) $\sqrt[3]{0.003375}$

5. Show that $\sqrt[3]{27} \times \sqrt[3]{125} = \sqrt[3]{27\times125}$.

6. Find the value of (i) $\sqrt[3]{392} \times \sqrt[3]{448}$, (ii) $\sqrt[3]{3375\times729}$

7. Find the smallest number by which 1323 must be multiplied so that the product is a perfect cube. Also find the cube root of the product.

8. Find the smallest number by which –17496 must be divided so that the quotient is a perfect cube. Also find the cube root of the quotient.

LOOKING BACK
Summary of Key Facts

1. The cube of a number is the number raised to the power 3, *e.g.*, cube of $7 = 7^3 = 7 \times 7 \times 7 = 343$.

2. A number n is a perfect cube if it can be expressed as $n = m^3$ for some natural number m, *e.g.*, 8 is a perfect cube as 8 can be expressed as $8 = 2^3$.

3. (*i*) The cube of an even number is even, *e.g.*, $4^3 = 64$.

   (*ii*) The cube of an odd number is odd, *e.g.*, $5^3 = 125$.

4. The cube root of a number n is the number whose cube is n. It is denoted by $\sqrt[3]{n}$, *e.g.*, $6^3 = 6 \times 6 \times 6 = 216$, therefore, cube root of $216 = \sqrt[3]{216} = 6$.

5. The cube root of a number can be found by resolving the number into prime factors, making groups of 3 equal factors picking out one of the equal factors from each group and multiplying the factors so picked.

   e.g., $1728 = \underline{2 \times 2 \times 2} \times \underline{2 \times 2 \times 2} \times \underline{3 \times 3 \times 3}$ so $\sqrt[3]{1728} = 2 \times 2 \times 3 = 12$

6. The cube root of a negative perfect cube is negative *e.g.*, $\sqrt[3]{-8} = -2$.

7. For any integer a and b, we have

   (*i*) $\sqrt[3]{ab} = \sqrt[3]{a} \times \sqrt[3]{b}$ (*ii*) $\sqrt[3]{\dfrac{a}{b}} = \dfrac{\sqrt[3]{a}}{\sqrt[3]{b}}$

   e.g., (*i*) $\sqrt[3]{4} \times \sqrt[3]{54} = \sqrt[3]{4 \times 54} = \sqrt[3]{2 \times 2 \times 2 \times 3 \times 3 \times 3} = 2 \times 3 = 6$, (*ii*) $\sqrt[3]{\dfrac{8}{27}} = \dfrac{\sqrt[3]{8}}{\sqrt[3]{27}} = \dfrac{2}{3}$.

MENTAL MATHS – 4

1. Is 8000 a perfect cube? Yes/No

2. Write the cubes of first five natural numbers.

3. What is the smallest number by which 4 should be multiplied to make it a perfect cube.

4. What is the smallest number by which 81 should be divided to make it a perfect square?

5. Find the cube root of $\dfrac{27}{64}$.

6. Find the cube root of 0.008.

7. Find the cube root of – 27000.

8. Identify the perfect cubes in the following 27, 64, 125, 98, 100, – 8000, – 9000.

9. Simplify $(10)^2 - 4^3$.

10. $\sqrt[3]{0.001} \times 10$.

MULTIPLE CHOICE QUESTIONS – 4

1. The cube root of 0.000512 is :

   (*i*) 0.5 (*ii*) 0.08 (*iii*) 0.008 (*iv*) 8

2. $\sqrt[3]{\sqrt{.000064}} = ?$

   (*i*) 0.02 (*ii*) 0.2 (*iii*) 2 (*iv*) .04

3. The largest four digit number which is a perfect cube is :

   (*i*) 9999 (*ii*) 9261 (*iii*) 8000 (*iv*) 9899

4. $\sqrt[3]{-125 \times 64}$ is equal to

(i) 10   (ii) –20   (iii) 20   (iv) 40

5. By what least number should 675 be multiplied so as to obtain a number which is a perfect cube?

(i) 5   (ii) 6   (iii) 7   (iv) 8

6. By what least number should 4000 be divided so as to obtain a number which is a perfect cube?

(i) 8   (ii) 4   (iii) 12   (iv) 6

7. $\sqrt[3]{-6\frac{29}{125}}$ is

(i) $-2\frac{1}{5}$ (ii) $-1\frac{4}{5}$ (iii) $1\frac{4}{5}$ (iv) $2\frac{2}{5}$.

8. The cube root of $(-6^3 \times -7^3)$ is

(i) 216   (ii) –42   (iii) 42   (iv) 21

9. The cube root of an odd number is always an

(i) an even number   (ii) a prime number   (iii) an odd number

(iv) sometimes even and sometimes odd number.

10. If $\frac{\sqrt[3]{0.512}}{x} = \sqrt[3]{1000}$, then the value of x is

(i) 0.8   (ii) 0.08   (iii) 0.008   (iv) 80

ANSWERS

EXERCISE 4 (a)

1. (a) 512   (b) 2197   (c) 19683   (d) 64000000   (e) 1092727.

2. (a) $\frac{27}{125}$ (b) $\frac{-64}{729}$ (c) $\frac{6859}{343}$ (d) $\frac{12167}{4913}$ (e) $\frac{-1331}{512}$.

3. (a) 0.027   (b) 0.125   (c) –13.824   (d) 0.000512   (e) 0.000000001.

4. 64, 125, 729, 1331, 4096, 74088   5. 5   6. 4

EXERCISE 4 (b)

1. (i) 2   (ii) 3   (iii) 5   (iv) 6   (v) 7   (vi) 11   (vii) 14

(viii) 18   (ix) 20   (x) 15   2. (i) –9   (ii) –12   (iii) –21   (iv) –13

3. (i) $\frac{5}{7}$ (ii) $\frac{-9}{13}$ (iii) $\frac{-15}{17}$ (iv) $\frac{5}{14}$ (v) $1\frac{3}{4}$

4. (i) 0.6   (ii) 1.6   (iii) 0.15   6. (i) 56   (ii) 135   7. 7; 21   8. 3; –18

MENTAL MATHS – 4

1. Yes   2. 1, 8, 27, 64, 125   3. 2   4. 3   5. $\frac{3}{4}$ 6. 0.2

7. – 30   8. 27, 64, 125, –8000   9. 36   10. 1

MULTIPLE CHOICE QUESTIONS – 4

1. (ii)   2. (ii)   3. (ii)   4. (ii)   5. (i)   6. (ii)   7. (ii)

8. (iii)   9. (iii)   10. (ii)

HISTORICAL NOTE
Aryabhata - 1

1. **Aryabhata - 1** was the first Indian to have given a scientific basis to **Astronomy**. He was also a great mathematician. He was born on March 21, 476 - a little over 1,515 years ago at Kusumapura, near Pataliputra (Modern Patna). He recorded all his thoughts, theories and calculations in his book 'Aryabhatiya' which he wrote when he was only 23 years of age. He made important contributions to **Astronomy** and all branches of mathematics- Algebra, Geometry and Arithmetic.

2. He was the first to propound the theory that the earth was spherical and that it revolved round the sun.

3. He could calculate 1500 years ago that the length of one day and one night was 23 hours, 56 minutes and 4.1 seconds. Modern scientists have calculated this same period to be 23 hours, 56 minutes and 4.091 seconds.

4. He gave an accurate value of π(Pi).

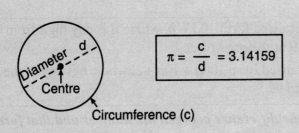

$$\pi = \frac{c}{d} = 3.14159$$

Aryabhata wrote

100 + 4 multiply by 8 add to 62,000. This is approximately the measure of the circumference of a circle whose diameter is 20,000, which mathematically can be written as :

$$\frac{62832}{20000} = 3.1416.$$

Note that Aryabhata-I added this ratio was approximate. It is even today that with the help of computers an exact value has not been found.

5. India's first artificial satellite was named after him. Its launching coincided with his 1500th birth anniversary.

5. Playing with Numbers

5.1 Writing a Number is Generalised Form

- **Look at the Following**

$$47 = 10 \times 4 + 7, \quad 54 = 10 \times 5 + 4, \quad 80 = 10 \times 8 + 0,$$
$$125 = 100 \times 1 + 10 \times 2 + 5, \quad 356 = 100 \times 3 + 10 \times 5 + 6, \quad 700 = 100 \times 7 + 10 \times 0 + 0$$

In the above, the given numbers have been expressed in expanded form, using the place values of the digits at various position in the numbers. If you study the rule or the patterns it would be easy for you to observe the following :

> 'A 2 digit number can be expressed in the generalised form $10a + b$, where a is any digit from 1 to 9 in the tens place and b is any of the digits 0 to 9 at the ones place.'
>
> 'A 3 digit number can be expressed in the generalised form $100a + 10b + c$, where a is any of the digits 1 to 9 and b and c are any of the digits from 0 to 9.'

Ex. 1. *The sum of the digits of a number is 13, and the difference between the number and that formed by reversing the digits is 27. Find the numbers.*

Sol. Let the original number be $10a + b$. When the digits are reversed, that is the digit a occupies the units place and the digit b occupies the tens place, then the new number formed is $10b + a$.

$10a + b \Rightarrow 10b + a$
The digits are reversed — New number formed

It is given in the problem that the sum of the digits is 10, *i.e.*,

$$a + b = 13 \Rightarrow b = 13 - a. \tag{i}$$

The difference between the old number and the new number is 27, *i.e.*,

$$(10a + b) - (10b + a) = 27 \Rightarrow 9a - 9b = 27 \Rightarrow a - b = 3 \tag{ii}$$

Substituting in (2) $b = 13 - a$, we have

$$a - (13 - a) = 3 \Rightarrow 2a - 13 = 3$$

$$\Rightarrow \qquad 2a = 13 + 3 = 16 \Rightarrow a = \frac{16}{2} = \mathbf{8}$$

$\therefore$ From (1), $b = 13 - 8 = 5$

Hence, the original number $= 10a + b = 10 \times 8 + 5 = 80 + 5 = \mathbf{85}$.

The number formed on reversing the digits = 58.

Ex. 2. *The middle digit of a number between 100 and 1000 is zero, and the sum of the other digits is 11. If the digits be reversed, the number so formed exceeds the original number by 495, find it.*

Sol. A three digit number in the generalised form is $100a + 10b + c$. Since the middle digit is 0, let the number be $100x + y$. If the digits are reversed the number so formed will be $100y + x$.

It is given that (the difference of the numbers is 495.)

$$\therefore \quad 100x + y - (100y + x) = 495 \Rightarrow 100x + y - 100y - x = 495$$

$$\Rightarrow \qquad 99x - 99y = 495 \Rightarrow x - y = 5 \tag{1}$$

64

Also, It is given that the sum of the digits is 11,

$$\therefore \qquad\qquad x + y = 11 \qquad\qquad\qquad\qquad ...(2)$$

Solving (1) and (2), we get $x = 8$, $y = 3$. Hence the number is **308**.

EXERCISE 5 (a)

1. The sum of the digits of a two-digit number is 9. The number is 6 times the units digit. Find the number.

2. The sum of the digits of a two-digit number is 7. If the digits are reversed, the new number increased by 3 equals 4 times the original number. Find the original number.

3. The sum of a number of two digits and of the number formed by reversing the digits is 110, and the difference of the digits is 6. Find the number.

4. A certain number between 10 and 100 is 8 times the sum of its digits, and if 45 be subtracted from it the digits will be reversed. Find the number.

5. A number consists of three digits, the right hand being zero. If the left hand and the middle digits be interchanged the number is diminished by 180. If the left-hand digit be halved and the middle and right-hand digits be interchanged the number is diminished by 454. Find the number. (**Hint :** Let the original number be $100a + 10b + 0$, *i.e.*, $100a + 10b$, then, by the first condition

$(100a + 10b) - (100b + 10a) = 180 \implies a - b = 2$

By the second condition, new number $= 100 \times \dfrac{a}{2} + 0 + b = 50a + b$

and so $(100a + 10b) - (50a + b) = 454 \implies 50a + 9b = 454$)

5.2 Test of Divisibility for Numbers Expressed in the Generalised Form

1. **Test of divisibility by 2.** A number is divisible by 2 if its units digit is even, *i.e.*, if its units digit is any of the digits 0, 2, 4, 6 or 8.

   For a number in the generalised form :

   (*i*) **A two-digit number $10a + b$ is divisible by 2 if '*b*' is any of the digits 0, 2, 4, 6 or 8.**

   (*ii*) **A three-digit number $100a + 10b + c$ is divisible by 2 if '*c*' is any of the digits 0, 2, 4, 6 or 8.**

For example : The numbers 12, 42, 68, 96, 120, 246, 854 are all divisible by 2.

2. **Test of divisibility by 3.** A number is divisible by 3, if the sum of its digits is divisible by 3.

   For a number in the generalised form :

   (*i*) **A two-digit number $10a + b$ is divisible by 3 if $(a + b)$ is divisible by 3.**

   (*ii*) **A three-digit number $100a + 10b + c$ is divisible if $(a + b + c)$ is divisible by 3.**

For example : 21, 54, 93, 123, 351, 762 are all divisible by 3 but none of the numbers 22, 56, 76, 359, 835 is divisible by 3.

3. **Test of divisibility by 5.** A number is divisible by 5, if its units digit is either 0 or 5.

   For a number in the generalised form :

   (*i*) **A two-digit number $10a + b$ is divisible by 5 if '*b*' is either 0 or 5.**

   (*ii*) **A three-digit number $100a + 10b + c$ is divisible by 5, if '*c*' is divisible by 5.**

For example : The numbers 15, 35, 80, 110, 325 are all divisible by 5.

4. **Test of divisibility by 9.** A number is divisible by 9 if the sum of its digits is divisible by 9.

   For a number in the generalised form :

   (*i*) A two-digit number $10a + b$ is divisible by 9 if '$a + b$' is divisible by 9.

(ii) A three-digits number $100a + 10b + c$ is divisible by 9 if '$a + b + c$' is divisible by 9.

For example : The numbers $18, 27, 63, 225, 801$ are all divisible by 9.

5. **Test of divisibility by 10.** A number is divisible by 10, if its units digit is 0.

For a number in the generalised form :

(i) A two-digit number $10a + b$ is divisible by 10, if 'b' is equal to 0.

(ii) A three-digit number $100a + 10b + c$ is divisible by 10, if 'c' is equal to 0.

For example : The numbers $20, 70, 320, 580, 900$ are divisible by 10.

EXERCISE 5 (b)

1. **Which of the following numbers are divisible by 2?**
   $57, 34, 60, 93, 126, 365, 890, 992$

2. **Which of the following numbers are divisible by 3?**
   $42, 73, 84, 105, 314, 726, 814, 915$

3. **Which of the following numbers are divisible by 5?**
   $30, 49, 75, 210, 305, 640, 704, 985$

4. **Which of the following numbers are divisible by 9?**
   $36, 90, 157, 243, 514, 810, 719, 936$

5. **Which of the following numbers are divisible by 10?**
   $75, 80, 140, 400, 670, 895, 985, 990.$

5.3 Number Puzzles and Games

Ex. 1. *If we delete the numeral occurring in both the numerator and the denominator of the fraction $\frac{26}{65}$, we don't change its value because $\frac{26}{65} = \frac{2}{5}$. What other fractions consisting of two digits figures in the numerator and denominator can be similarly reduced?*

Sol. The fraction has the general form $\frac{10x + y}{10y + z} = \frac{x}{z}$

$\Rightarrow \qquad 10xz + yz = 10yx + zx$ (cross multiplying) $\Rightarrow 9xz = y(10x - z)$.

y must be 3 or a product of 3 because otherwise $(10x - z)$ must be divisible by 9, which is impossible except for the case $x = z$. The fractions we are looking for are $\frac{26}{65}$, $\frac{16}{64}$, $\frac{19}{95}$, and $\frac{49}{98}$.

Ex. 2. *Ask your friend to think of a four digit number, and then to subtract from it each of the number's digits. For example, if your friend chooses 5901 and then takes away 5, 9, 0, 1, the resultant number will be 5886. Now ask your friend to give you the digit of the new number leaving out any one of the four digits. Suppose he tells you the number 886, you can astonish your friend by telling the missing digit? Explain how you can do it.*

Sol. The trick depends on the following two facts :

(i) Any number minus its digits is divisible by 9.

(ii) A number is divisible by 9, if the sum of its digits is divisible by 9.

$$
\begin{aligned}
&(1000a + 100b + 10c + d \\
&= \frac{-(a + b + c + d)}{999a + 99b + 9c} \\
&= 9(111a + 11b + c)
\end{aligned}
$$

Here $8 + 8 + 6 = 22$. We need to add 5 to 22 so that the sum of the digits becomes 9. Then the number would be divisible 9. Here the missing digit is 5.

Ex. 3. *Can you have all the whole numbers from 1 through 20 using up to three squares to name each number, e.g., 5 = 2² + 1² and 19 = 4² + 2² – 1.*

Sol. $1 = 1^2$, $2 = 1^2 + 1^2$, $3 = 2^2 - 1^2$, $4 = 3^2 - 2^2 - 1^2$, $6 = 2^2 + 1^2 + 1^2$, $7 = 3^2 - 1^2 - 1^2$, $8 = 2^2 + 2^2$, $9 = 5^2 - 4^2$, $10 = 3^2 + 1^2$, $11 = 3^2 + 1^2 + 1^2$, $12 = 4^2 - 2^2$, $13 = 3^2 + 2^2$, $14 = 3^2 + 2^2 + 1^2$, $15 = 4^2 - 1^2$, $16 = 4^2$, $17 = 4^2 + 1^2$, $18 = 4^2 + 1^2 + 1^2$, $20 = 4^2 + 2^2$.

Magic square. In a Magic square, the sum along any column, row, or diagonal is the same.

Ex. 4. *Complete the magic square given here so that the sum of the number in each row or in each column or along each diagonal is 15.*

8	1	
		5

Sol. (1) The number in the upper right hand corner = $(15 - (8 + 1) = 15 - 9 = $ **6**

(2) The bottom number in the second column = $15 - (1 + 5) = 15 - 6 = $ **9**

(3) The number in the lower right hand corner = $15 - (8 + 5) = 15 - 13 = $ **2**

(4) The number in the lower left hand corner = $15 - (2 + 9) = 15 - 11 = $ **4**

(5) The number in the right hand corner in the middle row = $15 - (3 + 5)$
    $= 15 - 8 = $ **7**.

The completed magic square often filling in the missing numerals is as shown.

8	1	6
3	5	7
4	9	2

Cross number puzzles. Cross number puzzles are similar to crossword puzzles. They differ in that digits are used to form numerals instead of using letters to form words.

Ex. 5. *Complete the cross number puzzle with the help of the given clues :*

Horizontal	*Vertical*
a. $0.7 \times 8 \times 0.09$	*a.* 64% of 9200
c. $94.9 - 2.1$	*b.* 0.6×75
e. 80% of 6600	*c.* $1079.2 - 90.2$
g. 0.5×168	*d.* 0.4×50
i. 0% of 125	*f.* $512 + 1722$
j. $10^4 - 1037$	*k.* 896×7
m. $550 - 26$	*l.* $(0.36 \times 10^4) + 192$
n. 100% of 79	*o.* $10^2 \times 9$
q. $360 + 30$	*p.* $(3 \times 10^1) + (3 \times 10^0)$
r. $8.34 - 5.22$	*q.* 70% of 50.
s $8 \times 5 \times 13$	

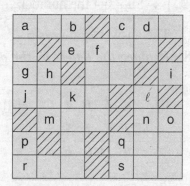

Sol.

5	0	4		9	2	8
8		5	2	8	0	
8	4		2	9		0
8	9	6	3		3	
	5	2	4		7	9
3		7		3	9	0
3	1	2		5	2	0

Ex. 6. *Use each of the digits 1 – 9 in only one of the circles so that the sum along each side of the triangle is 21. There are several correct solutions.*

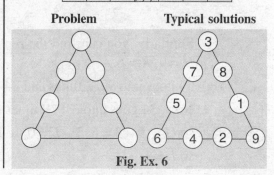

Problem   Typical solutions

Fig. Ex. 6

Patterns

Ex. 7. *Observe the following patterns :*
$$1 \times 9 - 1 = 8$$
$$21 \times 9 - 1 = 188$$
$$321 \times 9 - 1 = 2888$$
$$4321 \times 9 - 1 = 38888$$
Find the value of $87654321 \times 9 - 1$.

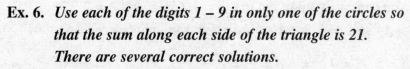

Sol. There are as many eights in the answer as the first digit (from the right) in the given number which is to be multiplied by 9. Also the left most digit in the answer is one less than the first digit in the number.

$$\therefore \qquad 87654321 \times 9 - 1 = 7 \quad 88888888$$

one less   8 eights

Number Tricks

Have you ever had a "number trick" played on you and wondered how it was done? Many of these tricks or puzzles can be explained mathematically.

Ex. 7. *Suppose you ask a friend to choose a number. Then, if your directions are followed correctly, you will be able to state the answer which your friend has obtained without knowing the original number.*

Sol.

Directions	Mathematical Explanation
• Select any number	n
• Add 8	$n + 8$
• Multiple by 3.	$3(n + 8) = 3n + 24$
• Subtract 6	$3n + 24 - 6 = 3n + 18$
• Divide by 3.	$\dfrac{3n+18}{3} = n + 6$
• Subtract the number you started with	$n + 6 - n = 6$

The answer is always 6.

Ex. 8. *Replace the letters by the numerals to make correctly worked example.*

```
                                                         A B C
(i)    A 6 B 4 C   (ii) 1 A 3 B 5   (iii)      1 A 7   (iv) 34)9 9 9 6
     + 1 7 2 5 5        – 5 C 7 D          ×    3 1 2        D 8 0 0
       9 D 0 E 8          6 6 6 6               B 5 C        3 1 E 6
                                             D 2 E 0         F 0 G 0
                                           3 F G 0 0         I 3 H
                                           3 H K 2 4         L J K
                                                              0
```

Sol. *(i)* $C = 8 - 5 = 3$, $E = 4 + 5 = 9$, $B = 10 - 2 = 8$, $D = 1 + 6 + 7 = 14$, so $D = 4$, $A = 9 - (1 + 1)$ $= 9 - 2 = 7$.

(ii) $D = 15 - 6 = 9$, Then obviously, you can easily make out that $B = 4$, $C = 6$, and $A = 2$.

(iii) To find C, we observe that $2 \times 7 = 14$ so $C = 4$, $2 \times A + 1$ (carried from units place) = 5.

$$\Rightarrow \qquad 2A + 1 = 5 \quad \Rightarrow \quad 2A = 5 - 1 = 4 \quad \Rightarrow \quad A = \frac{4}{2} = 2,$$

Similarly, you can find the replacements for other letters as $B = 2$, $D = 1$, $E = 7$, $F = 8$, $G = 1$, $H = 9$, $K = 6$.

(iv) 34 goes into 99, 2 times and $34 \times 2 = 68$, so $A = 2$ and $D = 6$, $9 - 0 = E \Rightarrow E = 9$.

Now, 34 goes into 319. 9 times ($34 \times 9 = 319$), so $B = 9$, $H = 6 - 0 = 6$, $E (= 9) - G = 3$, so $G = 9 - 3 = 6$, $3 - F = 0$, so $F = 3$. $H (= 6) - K = 0$, so $K = 6$, $3 - J = 0$, so $J = 3$, $1 - L = 0$, so $L = 1$.

The completed solutions after replacing letters by numerals are :

```
                                                              2 9 4
(i)    7 6 8 4 3     (ii) 1 2 3 4 5   (iii)   1 2 7    (iv) 34) 9 9 9 6
     + 1 7 2 5 5          - 5 6 7 9        ×   3 1 2          6 8 0 0
       9 4 0 9 8            6 6 6 6            2 5 4          3 1 9 6
                                            1 2 7 0          3 0 6 0
                                        3 8 1 0 0              1 3 6
                                        3 9 6 2 4              1 3 6
                                                                   0
```

Ex. 9. *An ancient faded document containing an arithmetical problem, written in the old parchment was found. The dots indicate the unrecognizable figures, which you have to find.*

Sol. The position of the two dots in the third line indicates that the divisor x is a two-digit figure, one that divides into the first three digits of the dividend without a remainder. In that case, the fact that both the fourth and fifth digit of the dividend are carried down together would prove that in the quotient the 8 must be preceded by a 0. It is also clear that the two dots in the third line represent a two-digit figure into which another two-digit figure namely x, divides 8 times. On the other hand the divisor x divides less than 10 times into a three digit figure, represented by three dots in the fifth row. Only one two-digit number, namely 12, fulfils both these conditions, and therefore, the divisor x must be 12·x must be bigger than the first two digits of the figure represented by the three dots in the third line because otherwise the third digit of the figure would have been carried to the line below. Therefore, the first digit of the figure can only be 1, and that allows us to conclude that the figure is 108, which is divisible by 12 without remainder. Now it is easy to reconstruct the whole division.

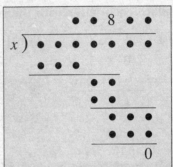

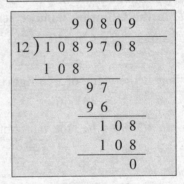

Ex. 10. *Given the adjoining addition sum, cross out nine of the digits so that the total of the numbers is 1111. The solution is not unique. See how many ways you can do it.*

```
  1 1 1
  3 3 3
  5 5 5
  7 7 7
+ 9 9 9
```

Sol. Three sample solutions are

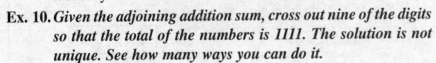

Test Your I.Q.

Ex. 11. *What should come in place of the question mark (?) in the number series 15, 32, 31, 60, 177, 704, 3515?*

(A) *21090*   (B) *21054*   (C) *21085*   (D) *21000*   (E) *None of these*

Sol.

32   31   60   177   704   3515   **? (21084)**

$\times 1 - 1$ $\times 2 - 2$ $\times 3 - 3$ $\times 4 - 4$ $\times 5 - 5$ $\times 6 - 6$

Answer is (E).

Ex. 12. *In a row of boys, A sits to the left of B and is at the fifteenth position from left while position of B is fourth from right. There are three boys between A and B. If C sits immediately next to the left of A, what is the position of C from the right?*

    (A) *9th*   **(B)** *10th*   **(C)** *11th*   **(D)** *12th.*

Sol. According to the question,

Left → C A | | | B ← Right
            15th   4th

So the position of C from the right is 9th.

EXERCISE 5 (c)

1. Replace each letter with the correct numeral :

(a)
```
  4 A 7 2
  B 8 5 C
  9 2 D 6
  -------
  E 7 7 5
```

(b)
```
  A 2 4 6
- 5 2 B 7
  -------
  1 C D E
```

(c)
```
      1 2 A
    ×   B 1 5
    ---------
      C 2 5
    D E F 0
  2 G 0 0 0
  ---------
  H 6 8 K J
```

(d)
```
           B 3
      37 ) A 5 1
           7 4 0
           -----
           1 C D
           E F G
           -----
               0
```

2. What should come in place of the question mark (?) in the following number series ?

(a) 563 582 620 677 753 848

(b) 17 17 51 255 1785 16065?

3. What is the value of x in figure III.

(a) 4   (b) 16   (c) 25   (d) 36

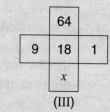

Fig. Q. 3

4. If $ab\,\overline{)\,252\,}\,(ba$, the values of a and b are : (A) 1, 2 (B) 2, 3 (C) 1, 3 (D) None of these

```
      2 4
      ---
      1 2
      1 2
      ---
        0
```

5. The missing number is :

    (A) 17   (B) 30   (C) 71   (D) 16

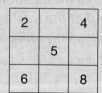

Fig. Q. 7

6. In a digital display which digit can display all 10 digits from 0 to 9.

    (A) nine   (B) six   (C) zero   (D) eight

7. Complete the magic square so that the sum of the numbers in each row, each column and along the diagonals may be 15.

8. Write the nine, non-repetitive digits in the circles of this triangle in such a way as to have a total of 20 on each side.

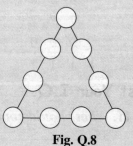

Fig. Q.8

9. The magic hexagon has a total of 19 hexagons within it. All sets of 3, 4 and 5 hexagons in a row add to 38. Fill in the missing figures. No number should be repeated.

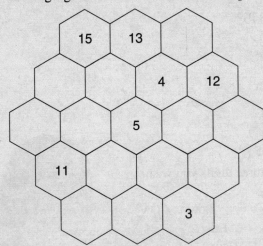

Fig. Q. 9

Fig. Q. 10. How rumours spread

10. **Rumours :** Rumours spread very fast. Sometimes an incident witnessed by just a few persons becomes the talk of the town within less than two hours. Suppose a man comes at about 8 a.m. to a town with a population of about 50,000 and conveys an interesting news to just three persons. This takes up, say, 15 minutes. Within 2 hours it becomes a talk of the town. Show, how it is possible.

11. **Number Patterns**

$$0 \times 9 + 1 = 1$$
$$1 \times 9 + 2 = 11$$
$$12 \times 9 + 3 = 111$$
$$123 \times 9 + 4 = 1111$$
$$1234 \times 9 + 5 = 11111$$
$$12345 \times 9 + 6 = 111111$$
$$123456 \times 9 + 7 = 1111111$$
$$1234567 \times 9 + 8 = 11111111$$
$$12345678 \times 9 + 9 = 111111111$$
$$123456789 \times 9 + 10 = 1111111111$$

Investigate a similar number pattern where the first two lines are :

$$1 \times 8 + 1 = 9$$
$$12 \times 8 + 2 = 98$$

12. ● Choose any four digits, for example, 6, 8, 9, and 2.
    ● Repeat the first digit at the end.
    ● Find the difference between the pairs of digits next to each other. Always repeat the first digit at the end.
    ● Continue the pattern until all the numbers are the same.

Try the above Pattern with these numbers.

1. 4, 5, 5, 2   2. 9, 4, 3, 8

3. 4, 8, 7, 6   4. 8, 6, 3, 2

5. Try the same pattern using any four digits you wish.

Fig. Q. 12

13. You may want to try this with you calculator.

- Enter any three digits in your calculator.   753
- Repeat the three digits to get a six-digits number.   753753
- Divide by 13.   57981
- Divide by 11.   5271
- Divide by 7.   753
- You will find that your result is your original number.

Try Pattern II with these numbers.

1. 347   **2.** 952   **3.** 885

4. 409   **5.** Try the same pattern using any three digits you wish.

14. Blaise Pascal (1623–1662) was a famous French mathematician and philosopher. One of his most important discoveries is known as Pascal's Triangle. See if you can discover the secret of this pattern of numbers.

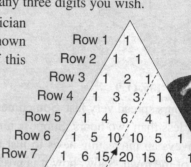

Solve.

1. Write Row 8 of Pascal's Triangle.
2. Write Row 9 of Pascal's Triangle.
3. Write Row 10 of Pascal's Triangle.
4. What is the sum of the numbers in Row 1 of Pascal's Triangle?
5. What is the sum of the numbers in Row 3 of Pascal's Triangle?
6. Find the sum of the numbers in Row 8 of Pascal's Triangle without adding.

Fig. Q. 14

15. Sudoko : Fill in the grid so that every horizontal row, every vertical column and every 3 × 3 box contains the digits 1–9, without repeating the numbers in the same row, column or box. You can't change the digits already given in the grid.

16. One way of expressing 10 as a combination of five as is $9 + \dfrac{99}{99} = 10$. Find the further ways of doing so.

17. A clock takes three seconds to strike 3O' clock. How long does it take to strike 6O'clock?

18. What is the smallest integer that can be written with two digits?

19. Write 1 by using all the ten digits.

20. Write 10 with five 9's. Do it in at least two ways.

21. Write 100 by using all the ten digits.

22. Show four different ways of writing 100 with five identical digits.

23. What is the biggest number that can be written with four 1's?

24. Calculate the length of the strip of all the millimetre squares in one square metre; if placed one alongside the other.

25. Calculate the height of a pole made up of all the millimetre cubes in one cubic metre, if placed one atop another.

Fig. Q. 15

Fig. Q. 17

ANSWERS

EXERCISE 5 (a)

1. 36 **2.** 16 **3.** 28 **4.** 72 **5.** 860

EXERCISE 5 (b)

1. 34, 60, 126, 890, 992   **2.** 42, 84, 105, 726, 915   **3.** 30, 75, 210, 305, 640, 985

4. 36, 90, 243, 810, 936   **5.** 80, 140, 400, 670, 990

EXERCISE 5 (c)

1. (*a*) A = 6, B = 3, C = 7, D = 4, E = 1   (*b*) A = 7, B = 8, C = 9, D = 9, E = 9

(*c*) A = 5, B = 2, C = 6, D = 1, E = 2, F = 5, G = 5, H = 2, K = 7, J = 5

(*d*) A = 8, B = 2, C = 1, D = 1, E = 1, F = 1, G = 1.

2. (*a*) **Ans. 962**

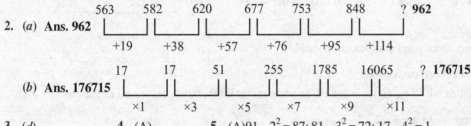

(*b*) **Ans. 176715**

3. (*d*)   **4.** (A)   **5.** (A) $91 - 2^2 = 87$; $81 - 3^2 = 72$; $17 - 4^2 = 1$

2	9	4
7	5	3
6	1	8

6. (D) **8** ; $\frac{1}{2}$ is zero, one side is 1, then **2, 3, 4, 5, 6, 7, 9**   **7.**

8. (*a*) Write the nine more repetitive digits in the circles of this triangle in such a way as to have a total of 20 in each side.

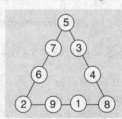

9. (Magic Hexagon) The missing numbers, going across from top to bottom are : 10, 14, 8, 9, 6, 2, 16, 1, 7, 19, 18, 17.

10. At 8.15 a.m. the news is known to just four persons: the newcomer and three local residents. Each of the three hastens to tell it to three others. That takes another 15 minutes. In other words, half an hour later the news is the common knowledge of 4 + (3 × 3) = 13 persons. In their turn, each of the nine persons who have learnt the news last pass it on to three friends. By 8.45 a.m. the news is known to 13 + (3 × 9) = 40 residents. If the rumour continues to spread in the same manner, *i.e.,* if everyone who hears it passes it on to three others within the next 15 minutes, the result will be as follows :

By 9 a.m. the news will be known to 40 + (3 × 27) = 121 persons

By 9.15 a.m. the news will be known to 121 + (3 × 81) = 364 persons

By 9.30 a.m. the news will be known to 364 + (3 × 243) = 1,093 persons

In other words, within one and a half hours the news will be known to almost 1,100 persons. That does not seem too much for a town with a population of 50,000. In fact, some may think it will take quite a long time before the whole town knows it. Let us see how fast it will continue to spread :

By 9.45 a.m. the news will be known to 1,093 + (3 × 729) = 3,280 persons

By 10 a.m. the news will be known to 3,280 + (3 × 2,187) = 9,841 persons

In the next 15 minutes it will be the property of more than half of the town's population : 9,841 + (3 × 6,561) = 29,524 persons. And this means that the news that only one man knew at 8 a.m. will be known to the entire town before it is 10.30 a.m.

14. (1) 1, 7, 21, 35, 35, 21, 7, 1   (2) 1, 8, 28, 56, 70, 56, 26, 6, 1   (3) 1, 9, 36, 64, 126, 126, 64, 36, 9, 1

15.

8	5	6	9	3	4	7	1	2
1	7	3	5	2	8	9	4	6
9	2	4	1	7	6	3	8	5
4	8	9	7	1	5	2	6	3
6	1	7	2	8	3	5	9	4
2	3	5	4	6	9	8	7	1
7	4	1	3	9	2	6	5	8
3	9	8	6	5	1	4	2	7
5	6	2	8	4	7	1	3	9

16. $9+9-9+\dfrac{9}{9}$, $\left(9+\dfrac{9}{9}\right)\times\dfrac{9}{9}$, $9+\dfrac{9+9}{9+9}$, $9+\dfrac{9\times9}{9\times9}$, $9+\dfrac{\frac{9}{9}}{\frac{9}{9}}$, $\dfrac{99}{9}-\dfrac{9}{9}$, $\dfrac{9}{0.9}+9-\sqrt{(9\times9)}$, $\dfrac{9}{0.9}\times\dfrac{\sqrt{(9\times9)}}{9}$.

$9^{\frac{9}{9}}+\dfrac{9}{9}$, $\sqrt{9}+\sqrt{9}+\sqrt{9}+\dfrac{9}{9}$. Many more combinations are possible.

17. 7.5 seconds. It takes 1.5 seconds between each strike.

18. The smallest digit that can be written with two digits is not 10, as some might think, but 1, expressed as follows :

$\dfrac{1}{1},\dfrac{2}{2},\dfrac{3}{3},\dfrac{4}{4}$, etc. upto $\dfrac{9}{9}$ other expressions are $1^0, 2^0, 3^0, 4^0$, etc., up to 9^0.

19. We will have to present it as the sum of two fractions : $\dfrac{148}{296}+\dfrac{35}{70}=1$. The other ways are 123456789^0, 234567^{9-8-1}, etc.

20. The two ways are: $9\dfrac{99}{99}=10$, and $\dfrac{99}{9}-\dfrac{9}{9}=10$. Several other possible solutions are $\left(9\dfrac{9}{9}\right)^{\frac{9}{9}}=10$, $9+99^{9-9}=10$, etc.

21. Here are four solutions : $70+24\dfrac{9}{18}+5\dfrac{3}{6}=100$, $80\dfrac{27}{54}+19\dfrac{3}{6}=100$, $87+9\dfrac{4}{5}+3\dfrac{12}{60}=100$, $50\dfrac{1}{2}+49\dfrac{38}{76}=100$.

22. It is easy to write 100 by using five identical digits: 1s, 3s or the simplest way: 5s. Here we see the four ways :

$111-11=100$, $\quad 33\times3+\dfrac{3}{3}=100$, $\quad 5\times5\times5-5\times5=100$, $\quad (5+5+5+5)\times5=100$.

23. Perhaps you may at once say that it is 1,111. But it is possible to write a number many many times greater, namely 11^{11}. If you are able to calculate it, you will find that it exceeds, the number 2,80,000,000,000. Therefore, it is 250 million times greater than 1,111.

24. 1 sq m = 1000 thousand sq mm = (1000 × 1000) sq m. One thousand millimetre squares placed. One alongside the other will stretch out 1 metre; 1000 thousand squares will therefore be 1,000 metres long, *i.e.*, 1 kilometre long.

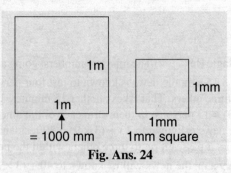

Fig. Ans. 24

25. You will be stunned at the answer. The pole would be 1000 km high. Let us calculate it. A cubic metre is equal to 1,000 cubic millimetres × 1000 × 1000. One thousand millimetre cubes placed one atop another will make a pole 1 kilometre in height. And since we have 1,000 times more cubes, we shall have a pole that is 1,000 kilometres long.

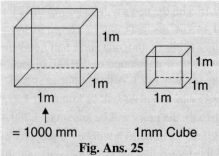

Fig. Ans. 25

6. Algebraic Expressions and Special Products

6.1 Review

Let us recall the important and basic definitions of algebra which you have studied in Class 6.

1. **Constants and Variables :** *A symbol in algebra having a fixed value is called a constant, whereas a symbol which can be given or assigned a varied number of values is called a variable.*

   $4, 0.35, \dfrac{5}{7}, -\dfrac{6}{9}$ are all fixed values and hence are constants.

   Variables are generally represented by letters of the English alphabet, *i.e.*, *x, y, z,* etc. They can be assigned any value.

2. **Algebraic Expression :** *A combination of constants and variables connected by the basic mathematical operators, i.e., +, −, ÷, × is called an algebraic expression.*

   For example : $4xy, 2x^2 - y, 4x - 2y + 3z, \dfrac{p}{q}, a^2 + b^2$ etc. are all algebraic expressions.

3. **Term :** *The various parts of an algebraic expression connected by + or − sign are called terms of the expression.*

   For example : $2x + 4y^2 - 3z$ has three terms, namely, $+ 2x, + 4y^2, - 3z$; $2xy - 4y^2$ has two terms namely $+ 2xy$ and $- 4y^2$.

4. **Like terms and Unlike terms :** *The terms having the same literal factors are called like terms and those having different literal factors are called unlike terms.*

   For example : $- 6x^2y$ and $4yx^2$ are like terms whereas

   $2xy, - 3x^2y, 4xy^2$ are unlike terms.

5. **Coefficients :** The numerical part is called the **numerical coefficient** and literal part or the variable part is called the **literal coefficient**.

   For example : In $24xy$, 24 is the numerical coefficient and xy is the literal coefficient.

6.2 Types of Algebraic Expressions

(*i*) **Monomials :** Expressions with a single term are called monomials.

For example : $- 3xy, 4y^2, 2z$ are all monomials.

(*ii*) **Binomials :** Expressions with two terms are called binomials.

For example : $4x + 3y, 2x^2y - 4y, a + \dfrac{1}{a}$ etc. are binomials.

(*iii*) **Trinomials :** Expressions with three terms are called trinomials.

For example : $2x + 4y - 3z, 4x^2y + 6xy - 7xy^2$ are trinomials.

(*iv*) **Multinomials :** Expressions with two or more terms are called multinomials.

6.3 Polynomials

1. **Polynomial in one variable :** An algebraic expression of the form $a + bx + cx^2 + dx^3$, where a, b, c and d are constants and x is a variable is called a polynomial. **The powers of the variable involved are non-negative integers.**

   The degree of the polynomial is the greatest power of the variable present in the polynomial.

For example : $6 + 8a$ is a polynomial of degree 1 and $4x^3 - 2x + 3$ is a polynomial of degree 3.

2. **Polynomial in two or more variables :** It is an algebraic expression involving two or more variables with non-negative integral powers :

   In such a polynomial, the degree of any term is the sum of the powers of the variables in that term. The greatest sum is the degree of the polynomial.

For example :   (i) $4x + 4y^2 + 4xy$ is a polynomial in x and y and its degree is 2.

               (ii) $11x^2y^2 + 4xy - 2xy^2$ is a polynomial in x and y of degree 4.

> **Note :** Terms where the powers of the variable are negative, i.e., x^{-1} or $\dfrac{1}{x}, \dfrac{1}{y^2}, \dfrac{x}{y}, \dfrac{x^2}{y}$ do not make a polynomial.

For example :

1. $10 + 3x + 2x^2 - \dfrac{1}{5}x^3 + \sqrt{2}x^4$ is a polynomial in one variable x.

2. $5x^3 + 3x^2y - \sqrt{5}xy^2 + 21y^3$ is a polynomial in two variables x and y.

3. $7 + 3x^{-2} + x^3$ is not a polynomial since it contains a term with negative exponent.

4. $4x^3 - 2x^{\frac{3}{2}} + 7x^2 + 8$ is not a polynomial as it contains a term with power $\dfrac{3}{2}$ which is not a positive integer.

5. A polynomial is said to be simplified, or in **simplest form**, when no two of its terms are similar. For example, $7x^2 - 3x + 2$ is in simplest form, but $5y^2 + 9y - 2y + 3$ is not in simplest form. Its simplified form will be $5y^2 + 7y + 3$. It is obtained on combining $9y$ and $-2y$.

6. The terms of a polynomial are said to be in **ascending or descending order** if they increase or decrease in degrees respectively.

Thus

(i)   The terms of the polynomial $7x^3 - 2x^2 + 5x - 11$ are in descending order.

(ii)   The terms of the polynomial $3 - 5x + 2x^2 - 8x^3$ are in ascending order.

OPERATIONS ON POLYNOMIALS

6.4 Addition and Subtraction of Polynomials (Revision)

You have already done addition and subtraction of algebraic expressions in your previous class. We give here a few solved examples and a few unsolved questions to help you in revising and strengthening the above concepts.

Method 1. For addition or subtraction of two or more polynomials :

1. *We collect the like terms together.*

2. *Find the sum or difference of the numerical coefficients of these terms.*

3. *The resulting expression should be in the simplest form and can be written in the ascending or descending order of the terms.*

Ex. 1. *Add :* $-5x^2y^2$, $-\dfrac{11}{5}x^2y^2$, $7x^2y^2$, $\dfrac{2}{3}x^2y^2$.

Sol. $\left(-5x^2y^2\right)+\left(-\dfrac{11}{5}x^2y^2\right)+7x^2y^2+\dfrac{2}{3}x^2y^2$

$$=\left(-5-\dfrac{11}{5}+7+\dfrac{2}{3}\right)x^2y^2=\left(\dfrac{-75-33+105+10}{15}\right)x^2y^2=\dfrac{7}{15}x^2y^2.$$

$$\begin{array}{r} -9x^2y \\ -7x^2y \\ + \\ \hline -2x^2y \end{array}$$

Ex. 2. *Subtract :* $-7x^2y$ *from* $-9x^2y$.

Sol. Required difference $= -9x^2y - (-7x^2y) = -9x^2y + 7x^2y = (-9+7)x^2y = \mathbf{-2x^2y}.$

Ex. 3. *Add together :* $7a - 3b + 5c$, $2a - 3b - 4c$ *and* $c - 4a + b$.

Sol. **First method.**

Sum $= (7a - 3b + 5c) + (2a - 3b - 4c) + (c - 4a + b)$

$= (7a + 2a - 4a) + (-3b - 3b + b) + (5c - 4c + c)$

$= \mathbf{5a - 5b + 2c}.$

Note : After practice, you may collect the similar terms mentally and write the sum directly.

Second method. By arranging like terms in columns and adding them up, we have

$$\begin{array}{l} 7a - 3b + 5c \\ 2a - 3b - 4c \\ -4a + b + c \\ \hline \end{array}$$

Sum $= \mathbf{5a - 5b + 2c}$

Ex. 4. *Add :* $-7x^2 - 3xy + 10y^2$, $8xy + 2x^2 - 11y^2$ *and* $8y^2 - 3x^2 + 6xy$.

Sol. Arranging the terms in descending powers of x and putting like terms under each other and adding column wise we have

$$\begin{array}{l} -7x^2 - 3xy + 10y^2 \\ 2x^2 + 8xy - 11y^2 \\ -3x^2 + 6xy + 8y^2 \\ \hline \end{array}$$

Sum $= \mathbf{-8x^2 + 11xy + 7y^2}$

Think !

$-7 + 2 - 3 = -10 + 2 = -8$
$-3 + 8 + 6 = -3 + 14 = +11$
$10 - 11 + 8 = (10 + 8) - 11$
$= 18 - 11 = 7$

Ex. 5. *Subtract :* $13xy - 6x^2 + 4a^2 - 1$ *from* $25x^2 + 16xy - 3b^2 - 2$.

Sol. Arranging the terms properly (writing like terms one below the other), changing the signs in the subtrahend and adding the columns, we have

$$\begin{array}{l} 25x^2 + 16xy - 3b^2 - 2 \\ -6x^2 + 13xy \quad\quad -1 + 4a^2 \\ +\quad\quad -\quad\quad\quad\quad +\quad - \\ \hline 31x^2 + 3xy - 3b^2 - 1 - 4a^2 \end{array}$$

We may also set our work as under :

$(25x^2 + 16xy - 3b^2 - 2) - (13xy - 6x^2 + 4a^2 - 1)$

$= 25x^2 + 16xy - 3b^2 - 2 - 13xy + 6x^2 - 4a^2 + 1$

$= \mathbf{31x^2 + 3xy - 3b^2 - 1 - 4a^2}.$

Think !

In the first column, the sign of $-6x^2$ is changed. Then $25 + 6 = 31$. In the second column, the sign of $13xy$ is changed. Then $16 - 13 = 3$, $-3b^2$ remains unchanged. In the fifth column -1 becomes $+1$. Then $-2 + 1 = -1$. In the last column the sign of $4a^2$ is changed.

Changing signs of the subtrahend combining like terms mentally we have $25x^2 + 6x^2 = 31x^2$, $+16xy - 13xy = 3xy$, $-2 + 1 = -1$.

Ex. 6. *Simplify : 5a + 7a + 2b + 8b – a + 1.*

Sol. Combining mentally like terms together we have

$$5a + 7a - a = 11a \text{ and } 2b + 8b = 10b$$

$\therefore$ Given expression $= 5a + 7a - a + 2b + 8b + 1 = \mathbf{11a + 10b + 1.}$

EXERCISE 6 (a)

1. Add :

   (i) $5xy, -2xy, -11xy, 8xy$ (ii) $3a^2b, -5a^2b, 10a^2b, -7a^2b$ (iii) $a + b, 3a + 2b$

   (iv) $3a - 2b + c, 5a + 8b - 7c$ (v) $4x^2 - 5xy + 3y^2, 8x^2 + 7xy - 6y^2, -2x^2 - 9xy + 13y^2$

2. Subtract :

   (i) $3x - 5$ from $8x - 17$ (ii) $-8xy$ from $7xy$

  (iii) $2x^2 - 5x + 10$ from $5x^2 - 11x + 19$ (iv) $3y^2 - 8y + 7$ from $9y^2 + 5y + 6$

   (v) $-7p + 2q - 3r + 5$ from $2p - 3q - 7r - 11.$ (vi) $2x^3 + 5x^2 - 6x + 2$ from $3x^3 - x^2 + 4x - 2$

  (vii) $5m^3 - 3m^2 + 7m - 8$ from $8m^3 - 9m^2 + 5m - 2.$

3. Two adjacent sides of a rectangle are $3x^2 - 5y^2$ and $7x^2 - xy$. Find its perimeter.

4. The perimeter of a triangle is $7p^2 - 8p + 9$ and two of its sides are $2p^2 - p + 1$ and $11p^2 - 3p + 5$. Find the third side of the triangle.

6.5 Multiplication

Recollect the following rules for the multiplication of positive and negative numbers.

Rule	Illustration	
$(+x) \times (+y) = (+xy)$	$(+5) \times (+3) = +15$	Product is positive
$(-x) \times (-y) = (+xy)$	$(-5) \times (-3) = +15$	
$(+x) \times (-y) = (-xy)$	$(+5) \times (-3) = -15$	Product is negative
$(-x) \times (+y) = (-xy)$	$(-5) \times (+3) = -15$	

6.6 Multiplication of Monomials

   Rule 1. (*i*) *Multiply numerical coefficients,* (*ii*) *Multiply literal coefficients,* (*iii*) *Multiply results.*

For example :

  (1) $3x \times 5y = (3 \times 5) \times (x \times y) = 15 \times xy = 15xy.$

  (2) $2a \times 3b \times 5c = (2 \times 3 \times 5) \times (a \times b \times c) = 30abc.$

   Rule 2. *To multiply the powers of the same base, keep the base and add the exponents.*

Thus, $a \cdot a^2 = a^{1+2} = a^3, x^3 \cdot x^5 \cdot x = x^{3+5+1} = x^9.$

     $a^3b^4 \cdot a^2b^7 = a^5b^{11}, 3^2 \cdot 3^3 \cdot x \cdot x^4 \cdot x^5 \cdot y^2 \cdot y = 3^5 x^{10} y^3.$

Remember, when multiplying powers, that a is the same as a^1, b is the same as b^1.

To find the power of a base, keep the base and multiply the exponents.

Thus, $(x^3)^4 = x^{3\times4} = x^{12}$, since $(x^3)^4 = (x^3)(x^3)(x^3)(x^3)$

         $(2^5)^3 = 2^{5\times3} = 2^{15}$, since $(2^5)^3 = (2^5)(2^5)(2^5).$

For example :

Write	*Think*	*Write*	*Think*
x^4 $\times\, x^7$ $\overline{x^{11}}$	Add exponents (coefficients understood to be 1 in each term).	$5a$ $\times\, 4a^6$ $\overline{20a^7}$	Multiply coefficients. Add exponents (exponent in the first term understood to be 1).
$3xy$ $\times\, 7xy^2$ $\overline{21x^2y^3}$	Multiply coefficients. Add exponents for product of powers	$(4xy)\,(8yz)$ $= 32\,xy^2z$	x and z unchanged—no like factors to combine with them. Write variables in alphabetical order.

Ex. 1. Find the product : (i) $4a^2b \times -6a^3b^2c$, (ii) $-\dfrac{6}{8}x^4yz \times 24x^2y^2z^3$.

Sol. (i) $\quad 4a^2b \times -6a^3b^2c = (4 \times -6) \times (a^2b \times a^3b^2c)$
$$\qquad\qquad\qquad\quad = -24a^5b^3c.$$

> **Think !**
> $a^2 \times a^3 = a^{2+3} = a^5, b \times b^2 = b^{1+2} = b^3$

(ii) $\quad \dfrac{-6}{8}x^4yz \times 24x^2y^2z^3 = \left(\dfrac{-6}{8} \times 24\right) \times \left(x^4yz \times x^2y^2z^3\right)$
$$\qquad\qquad\qquad\qquad\quad = -18x^6y^3z^4.$$

> **Think !**
> $x^4 \times x^2 = x^{4+2} = x^6, y \times y^2 = y^{1+2} = y^3,$
> $z \times z^3 = z^{1+3} = z^4$

Ex. 2. Multiply $\dfrac{-5}{8}x^2y^3$ **by** $\dfrac{-16}{15}x^3y$ **and verify your result for** $x = -1, y = 2$.

Sol. $\dfrac{-5}{8}x^2y^3 \times \dfrac{16}{15}x^3y = \left(\dfrac{\cancel{5}^1}{\cancel{8}_1}\right) \times \dfrac{\cancel{16}^2}{\cancel{15}_3} \times (x^2 \times x^3 \times y^3 \times y)$

> Add the exponents of x, $(2 + 3 = 5)$
> Add the exponents of y, $(3 + 1 = 4)$

$$\qquad\qquad\quad = \dfrac{-1 \times 2}{1 \times 3}x^5y^4 = \dfrac{-2}{3}x^5y^4.$$

EXERCISE 6 (b)

1. Multiply:

 (i) b by a (ii) $-x$ by y (iii) $-x$ by $-3y$ (iv) $-y^2$ by -1

 (v) $-a^2b^2$ by -3 (vi) $-2xy$ by $-6z$ (vii) $4mn$ by $(-1)^7 p^2q$ (viii) $-\dfrac{2}{7}a^2c$ by $\left(\dfrac{16}{21}\right)bd^2$.

2. (i) a^4 by a^3 (ii) $4y^2$ by $3y^5$ (iii) $-3w^4$ by $-10w^5$ (iv) $-7m^4$ by $13\,m^6$

 (v) $-3x^2y$ by $-5xy^2$ (vi) $-3mn$ by $4mn$ (vii) $-3axy$ by $15a^2y$ (viii) $\dfrac{-3}{8}x^4yz$ by $-16a^2y^4b^3$

 (ix) $\left(\dfrac{-17}{8}x^3y^2\right) \times \left(\dfrac{-16}{51}x^2y\right)$ (x) $\left(-\dfrac{1}{20}x^4y^3\right) \times (-5x^7y^2)$ (xi) $\left(-\dfrac{4}{13}x\right)\left(\dfrac{65}{16}x^2y\right)(-4)$

Find the products :

3. $(xy^2)\,(-2x)\,(+3xy)\,(-4x^2y)$ **4.** $(-2xy)\,(-3x^3y^2)\left(-\dfrac{1}{6}x^2y^7\right)$

5. $(-2p)\,(-3q)\,(-r)\,(-4\,pqr)$ **6.** $\left(\dfrac{5}{2}x^2y^3\right) \times (-y^2z) \times (-2x^3yz^7) \times \left(\dfrac{-1}{5}xyz\right)$

7. Find the value

 (i) $(2.4a^7b^3) \times 1.5a^3b$ when $a = 1$ and $b = 0.6$ (ii) $(-10m^2n^6) \times (-20\,mn^{15})$ for $m = 1.2$ and $n = -1$.

6.7 Multiplication of a Polynomial by a Monomial

Extended distributive law : $a(b + c + d + ...) = ab + ac + ad + ...$

Using this law, we can multiply a polynomial by a monomial as under :

(1) *Write the polynomial inside parentheses and the monomial outside the parentheses.*

(2) *Now multiply each term of the polynomial by this monomial.*

(3) *The result is the sum of the products obtained in (2).*

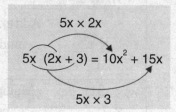

For example :

(1) $5(a + b) = 5a + 5b$

(2) $-x(y - 7z) = -x(y) + (-x)(-7z) = -xy + 7xz.$

(3) $-5x(x^2 + 3x - 7) = -5x(x^2) + (-5x)(3x) + (-5x)(-7) = -5x^3 - 15x^2 + 35x.$

(4) $100x(0.01x^3 - 0.02x) = 100x \times 0.01x^3 - 100x \times 0.02x = 100x \times \dfrac{1}{100}x^3 - 100x \times \dfrac{2}{100}x = x^4 - x^2.$

(5) $-(m - 7) = (-1)(m - 7) = (-1)m + (-1)(-7) = -m + 7.$

In the last example, it is understood that the multiplier is -1.

In the above, you have multiplied a polynomial by a monomial **horizontally**. You may multiply **vertically** as under :

Ex. 1.
$$\begin{array}{r} y^2 + 7y - 8 \\ \times\ 2y \\ \hline 2y^3 + 14y^2 - 16y \\ \hline \end{array}$$

Ex. 2.
$$\begin{array}{r} x^3 - 5x^2 - 7 \\ \times\ - x^2 \\ \hline -x^5 + 5x^4 + 7x^2 \\ \hline \end{array}$$

Ex. 3.
$$\begin{array}{r} 7a + 3b - 4c + 6 \\ \times\ -3abc \\ \hline -21a^2bc - 9ab^2c + 12abc^2 - 18abc \\ \hline \end{array}$$

Ex. 4. *Simplify :* (i) $a^2(b^2 - c^2) + b^2(c^2 - a^2) + c^2(a^2 - b^2)$

(ii) $x^2(x - 3y^2) - xy(y^2 - 2xy) - x(y^3 - 5x^2)$

(iii) $a^2b(a - b^2) + ab^2(4ab - 2a^2) - a^3b(1 - 2b).$

Sol. (i) $a^2(b^2 - c^2) + b^2(c^2 - a^2) + c^2(a^2 - b^2)$

$= a^2b^2 - a^2c^2 + b^2c^2 - b^2a^2 + c^2a^2 - c^2b^2$

$= (a^2b^2 - b^2a^2) + (-a^2c^2 + c^2a^2) + (b^2c^2 - c^2b^2)$

$= (a^2b^2 - a^2b^2) + (-c^2a^2 + c^2a^2) + (b^2c^2 - b^2c^2)$

$= 0 + 0 + 0 = \mathbf{0}.$

> Collecting like terms
> By commutative law
> $b^2a^2 = a^2b^2,\ a^2c^2 = c^2a^2,\ c^2b^2 = b^2c^2$

(ii) $x^2(x - 3y^2) - xy(y^2 - 2xy) - x(y^3 - 5x^2)$

$= x^3 - 3x^2y^2 - xy^3 + 2x^2y^2 - xy^3 + 5x^3$

$= (x^3 + 5x^3) + (-3x^2y^2 + 2x^2y^2) + (-xy^3 - xy^3)$

$= \mathbf{6x^3 - x^2y^2 - 2xy^3}.$

> Collecting like terms

(iii) $a^2b(a - b^2) + ab^2(4ab - 2a^2) - a^3b(1 - 2b)$

$= a^3b - a^2b^3 + 4a^2b^3 - 2a^3b^2 - a^3b + 2a^3b^2$

$= (a^3b - a^3b) + (-a^2b^3 + 4a^2b^3) + (-2a^3b^2 + 2a^3b^2)$

$= 0 + 3a^2b^3 + 0 = \mathbf{3a^2b^3}.$

> Collecting like terms

EXERCISE 6 (c)

Find the products :

1. $5(x + 3)$
2. $7(2x - 3)$
3. $-4(5y + 7)$
4. $-6(-m - 3)$
5. $-2(2x^2 + 3xy - 4y^2)$
6. $x(x + 1)$
7. $2y(-y^2 + 3y - 4)$
8. $-y^2(3y^2 - 5)$
9. $ab(3a - 5b)$
10. $5mn(3m - 2n)$
11. $-x^2y(2xy + 3x - y - 7)$
12. $2x^2(x^2 + 5x - 6)$
13. $-y(y^3 - 5y)$
14. $x^2y(3x^2y^2 - 5xy + 7)$
15. $-2c^2(4c^3 - 10c^2 - 8c + 9)$
16. $-x^2y^2(x^4 + x^2y^2 - y^4)$
17. $10x^2y(0.2xy - 0.7y)$
18. $100x(0.01x - 0.19yz)$

19. Evaluate the product :

    (i) $27y^2\left(1 - \dfrac{1}{3}y\right)$ for $y = -2$ (ii) $mn(m^2 + n^2)$ for $m = 2$ and $n = 0.1$

Simplify :

20. $x(y - z) + y(z - x) + z(x - y)$
21. $42a^2 - 8a(a - 1) - 7a(1 + 5a) + a(a - 1)$
22. $x^2(3 - 5y^2) + x(xy^2 - 3x) - 2y(y - 2x^2y)$.

6.8 Multiplication of Binomials

Suppose we have to multiply two binomials $(a + b)$ and $(c + d)$. We can do so by using the distributive law of multiplication over addition twice as shown below.

$$(a + b) \times (c + d) = a \times (c + d) + b \times (c + d) \qquad \text{Applying distributive law.}$$
$$= (a \times c + a \times d) + (b \times c + b \times d) \qquad \text{Applying distributive law again.}$$
$$= ac + ad + bc + bd$$

Thus, to multiply any two binomials, we multiply each term of one binomial by each term of the other and add the products.

Remark. This method is known as the horizontal method.

Ex. 1. *Multiply $3a + 2b$ and $5a + 7b$.*

Sol. $(3a + 2b)(5a + 7b) = 3a(5a + 7b) + 2b(5a + 7b)$
$$= 15a^2 + 21ab + 10ab + 14b^2$$
$$= \mathbf{15a^2 + 31ab + 14b^2}.$$

Second Method : (*Column Method*). Recall that you can multiply two whole numbers by writing them one below the other. Likewise you can multiply two binomials by writing them one below the other as shown below :

$$\begin{array}{r} 3a + 2b \\ \times\ \ 5a + 7b \\ \hline 15a^2 + 10ab \\ +\ 21ab + 14b^2 \\ \hline \mathbf{15a^2 + 31ab + 14b^2} \end{array}$$

$$\begin{array}{r} 387 \\ \times\ 26 \end{array}$$

First, multiply $3a + 2b$ by $5a$
Next, multiply $3a + 2b$ by $7b$
Finally, add like terms

The product is : $\mathbf{15a^2 + 31ab + 14b^2}$

Ex. 2 *Multiply $(2x^2 + 3y^2)$ by $(5x^2 - y^2)$.*

Sol. *Horizontal method :*

$$(2x^2 + 3y^2)(5x^2 - y^2) = 2x^2(5x^2 - y^2) + 3y^2(5x^2 - y^2)$$
$$= 10x^4 - 2x^2y^2 + 15x^2y^2 - 3y^4 = \mathbf{10x^4 + 13x^2y^2 - 3y^4}.$$

Column Method :

$$2x^2 + 3y^2$$
$$\times \quad 5x^2 - y^2$$
$$\overline{\qquad\qquad\qquad}$$
$$10x^4 + 15x^2y^2$$
$$- 2x^2y^2 - 3y^4$$
$$\overline{\qquad\qquad\qquad}$$

The product is : $\mathbf{10x^4 + 13x^2y^2 - 3y^4}$

> 1. Multiply by $5x^2$
> 2. Multiply by $(-y^2)$
> 3. Add

Ex. 3. *Multiply* $(3x^2y - 5xy^2)$ *by* $\left(\dfrac{1}{5}x^2 + \dfrac{1}{3}y^2\right)$.

Sol. *Horizontal method :*

$$\left(\frac{1}{5}x^2 + \frac{1}{3}y^2\right)(3x^2y - 5xy^2) = \frac{1}{5}x^2(3x^2y - 5xy^2) + \frac{1}{3}y^2(3x^2y - 5xy^2)$$

$$= \frac{3}{5}x^4y - x^3y^2 + x^2y^3 - \frac{5}{3}xy^4.$$

Column method :

$$3x^2y - 5xy^2$$
$$\frac{1}{5}x^2 + \frac{1}{3}y^2$$
$$\overline{\qquad\qquad\qquad}$$
$$\frac{3}{5}x^4y - x^3y^2$$
$$+ \quad x^2y^3 - \frac{5}{3}xy^4$$
$$\overline{\qquad\qquad\qquad\qquad}$$

Product is : $\dfrac{3}{5}x^4y - x^3y^2 + x^2y^3 - \dfrac{5}{3}xy^4$

> 1. Multiply by $\dfrac{1}{5}x^2$
> 2. Multiply by $\dfrac{1}{3}y^2$
> 3. Add

Remarks. As you can yourself observe, in this case the horizontal method is more convenient.

Ex. 4 *Simplify :* $(5x - 3y)(-x + 7y) - (2x + 5y)(3x - 4y)$.

Sol. We have

$(5x - 3y)(-x + 7y) - (2x + 5y)(3x - 4y)$

$\qquad = 5x(-x + 7y) - 3y(-x + 7y) - [2x(3x - 4y) + 5y(3x - 4y)]$

$\qquad = (-5x^2 + 35xy + 3xy - 21y^2) - (6x^2 - 8xy + 15xy - 20y^2)$

$\qquad = (-5x^2 + 38xy - 21y^2) - (6x^2 + 7xy - 20y^2)$

$\qquad = -5x^2 + 38xy - 21y^2 - 6x^2 - 7xy + 20y^2$

$\qquad = (-5x^2 - 6x^2) + (38xy - 7xy) - 21y^2 + 20y^2 = \mathbf{-11x^2 + 31xy - y^2}.$

Remark. As part of a problem, whenever you have to find the product of two binomials, you can shorten and quicken your work by **multiplying the two binomials mentally.**

Thus, if you have to find the product $(2x + y)(3x - y)$, you can do so by first multiplying the terms of the second binomial by first term and then by second term of the first binomial.

First multiply by $2x$

$(2x + y)(3x - 2y)$

Then multiply by y.

$\qquad = 6x^2 - 4xy + 3xy - 2y^2$

$\qquad = \mathbf{6x^2 - xy - 2y^2}.$

> $-4xy$ and $3xy$ can also be combined mentally to obtain $-xy$

$$(3a^2 - 4b^2c)\,(5a^2 - 7b^2c) = 15a^4 - 21a^2b^2c - 20a^2b^2c + 28b^4c^2$$

$$= 15a^4 - 41a^2b^2c + 28b^4c^2.$$

EXERCISE 6 (d)

Multiply :

1. $(x + 2)\,(x + 5)$ **2.** $(x - 4)\,(x + 9)$ **3.** $(x - 7)\,(x - 9)$ **4.** $(x^2 + 5)\,(x^2 - 6)$

5. $(3x + 8)\,(3x - 8)$ **6.** $(5x - 3y)\,(3x + 4y)$ **7.** $(a^2 - b^2)\,(a^2 + b^2)$ **8.** $(5x^2 + 2y^2)\,(3x^2 - 7y^2)$

9. $\left(3x + \dfrac{5y}{7}\right)\left(2x - \dfrac{3y}{7}\right)$ **10.** $\left(\dfrac{1}{7}x - \dfrac{1}{8}y\right)(7x^2 - 8y^2)$ **11.** $(m^3 - n^3)\,(m^2 + n^2)$ **12.** $(a^2 + b^4)\,(a^2 - b^2)$

13. Multiply $(4x^2 + 3y)$ by $(3x^2 - 4y)$ and verify the result for $x = 1$, $y = 2$

14. Find the product of $\left(x + \dfrac{2}{7}x^2\right)$ and $(7x - x^2)$ and verify the result for $x = -2$.

Simplify :

15. $\dfrac{2}{7}(14x^2 - 21y^2)\,(-5x^2 - 3y^2)$ **16.** $(2x - 3)\,(5x + 2) + (3x - 7)\,(4x - 1)$

17. $\dfrac{1}{2}(2x^2 - 8xy)\,(7x^2 + 8xy) - \dfrac{1}{3}(3x^2 + 6xy)\,(-6x^2 + 5xy)$

Multiply the following mentally :

18. $(x + 4)\,(x + 5)$ **19.** $(x + 7)\,(x - 7)$ **20.** $(2x - 5)\,(x + 3)$

21. $(8m + 5)\,(3m - 4)$ **22.** $(6t - 3)\,(2t - 7)$

6.9 Multiplication of a Binomial and a Trinomial

Recall that a trinomial is an algebraic expression containing three terms. The distributive law of multiplication can be extended to the product of algebraic expressions containing any number of terms. Thus, we have

$$(a + b)\,(x + y + z) = a(x + y + z) + b(x + y + z)$$

$$= ax + ay + az + bx + by + bz$$

Rule. Multiply each term of the binomial with every term of the trinomial and add all the products so obtained.

Ex. 1. *Find the product* $(3x - 2)\,(2x^2 + 3x - 5)$.

Sol. *Horizontal Method :*

$$\text{Product} = (3x - 2)\,(2x^2 + 3x - 5)$$

$$= 3x(2x^2 + 3x - 5) - 2\,(2x^2 + 3x - 5)$$

$$= 6x^3 + 9x^2 - 15x - 4x^2 - 6x + 10$$

$$= 6x^3 + (9x^2 - 4x^2) - 15x - 6x + 10$$

$$= 6x^3 + 5x^2 - 21x + 10.$$

> Multiplying the terms of the first bracket by $3x$ and those of the second bracket by -2

> Collecting lime terms.

Column Method :

$$2x^2 + 3x - 5$$
$$\underline{\qquad 3x - 2}$$
$$6x^3 + 9x^2 - 15x \qquad \longleftarrow$$
$$\underline{\qquad -4x^2 - 6x + 10} \qquad \longleftarrow$$

The product is : $\qquad 6x^3 + 5x^2 - 21x + 10 \qquad \longleftarrow$

Step 1. Multiply by $3x$
Step 2. Multiply by -2
Step 3. Add the products

Ex. 2. *Find the product* $(x + y) (x^2 - xy + y^2)$.

Sol. *Horizontal Method :*

Product $= (x + y) (x^2 - xy + y^2)$

$\qquad = x(x^2 - xy + y^2) + y(x^2 - xy + y^2)$

$\qquad = x^3 - x^2y + xy^2 + x^2y - xy^2 + y^3 \qquad \longleftarrow$

$\qquad = x^3 + (-x^2y + x^2y) + (xy^2 - xy^2) + y^3 \qquad \longleftarrow$

$\qquad = x^3 + y^3. \qquad \longleftarrow$

Multiplying terms of first bracket by x and those of second bracket by y
Grouping like terms.
All other terms cancel out.

Column Method :

$$x^2 - xy + y^2$$
$$\underline{\qquad x + y}$$
$$x^3 - x^2y + xy^2 \qquad \longleftarrow$$
$$\underline{\qquad + x^2y - xy^2 + y^3} \qquad \longleftarrow$$
$$x^3 + 0 + 0 + y^3 \qquad \longleftarrow$$

Step 1. Multiply by x
Step 2. Multiply by y
Step 3. Add

$\therefore$ Product $= x^3 + y^3.$

Remark. The same method applies to multiplication of algebraic expressions containing more than three terms.

Ex. 3. *Multiply* $3x^2 - x^3 + x + 1$ *by* $1 + x$.

Sol. *Horizontal Method :*

Product $= (1 + x) (3x^2 - x^3 + x + 1)$

$\qquad = 1 (3x^2 - x^3 + x + 1) + x(3x^2 - x^3 + x + 1)$

$\qquad = 3x^2 - x^3 + x + 1 + 3x^3 - x^4 + x^2 + x \qquad \longleftarrow$

$\qquad = -x^4 - x^3 + 3x^3 + 3x^2 + x^2 + x + x + 1 \qquad \longleftarrow$

$\qquad = -x^4 + 2x^3 + 4x^2 + 2x + 1.$

Arranging in descending powers of x.
Combining like terms.

Column Method :

It is always best to arrange the given polynomials in descending order of exponents.

$$-x^3 + 3x^2 + x + 1$$
$$\underline{\qquad x + 1}$$
$$-x^4 + 3x^3 + x^2 + x$$
$$\underline{\qquad - x^3 + 3x^2 + x + 1}$$

Product $= \qquad -x^4 + 2x^3 + 4x^2 + 2x + 1$

Step 1. Multiply by x
Step 2. Multiply by 1
Step 3. Add

Ex. 4. *Multiply : $(5x^2 - 7x + 2)$ by $(2x^2 - 3x - 5)$.*

Sol. *Horizontal Method :*

Product $= (5x^2 - 7x + 2)(2x^2 - 3x - 5)$

$= 5x^2(2x^2 - 3x - 5) - 7x(2x^2 - 3x - 5) + 2(2x^2 - 3x - 5)$

$= 10x^4 - 15x^3 - 25x^2 - 14x^3 + 21x^2 + 35x + 4x^2 - 6x - 10$ ⟵ | Carry out the multiplication of each bracket.

$= 10x^4 + (-15x^3 - 14x^3) + (-25x^2 + 21x^2 + 4x^2) + (35x - 6x) - 10$ ⟵ | Combine like terms

$= 10x^4 - 29x^3 + 0 + 29x - 10 = \mathbf{10x^4 - 29x^3 + 29x - 10}.$

Column Method :

$$
\begin{array}{r}
5x^2 - 7x + 2 \\
2x^2 - 3x - 5 \\
\hline
10x^4 - 14x^3 + 4x^2 \\
-15x^3 + 21x^2 - 6x \\
-25x^2 + 35x - 10 \\
\hline
\end{array}
$$

⟵ 1. Multiply by $2x^2$
⟵ 2. Multiply by $(-3x)$
⟵ 3. Multiply by (-5)

Product $= 10x^4 - 29x^3 + 0 + 29x - 10$ ⟵ 4. Add

$= \mathbf{10x^4 - 29x^3 + 29x - 10}.$

Ex. 5. *Simplify : $(5x - 7)(2x + 3)(7x - 8)$.*

Sol. $(5x - 7)(2x + 3)(7x - 8)$

$= [(5x - 7)(2x + 3)](7x - 8)$ | First multiply the terms of the first two brackets.

$= [5x(2x + 3) - 7(2x + 3)](7x - 8)$

$= (10x^2 + 15x - 14x - 21)(7x - 8)$

$= (10x^2 + x - 21)(7x - 8)$ ⟵ | Now multiply the product of the first two brackets and those of the third bracket.

$= 7x(10x^2 + x - 21) - 8(10x^2 + x - 21)$

$= 70x^3 + 7x^2 - 147x - 80x^2 - 8x + 168$

$= 70x^3 + 7x^2 - 80x^2 - 147x - 8x + 168$ | Combine like terms

$= \mathbf{70x^3 - 73x^2 - 155x + 168}.$

If you find the column method more convenient, you may work out as under :

$$
\begin{array}{r}
2x + 3 \\
5x - 7 \\
\hline
10x^2 + 15x \\
-14x - 21 \\
\hline
10x^2 + x - 21 \\
\end{array}
\qquad
\begin{array}{r}
10x^2 + x - 21 \\
7x - 8 \\
\hline
70x^3 + 7x^2 - 147x \\
-80x^2 - 8x + 168 \\
\hline
70x^3 - 73x^2 - 155x + 168 \\
\end{array}
$$

EXERCISE 6 (e)

Find the products :

1. $(x + 2)(x^2 + x + 1)$
2. $(2x + 3)(3x^2 - x - 2)$
3. $(4x - 5)(2x^2 - 7x - 3)$
4. $(3x - 7)(5x^2 - 2x + 3)$
5. $(x - y)(x^2 + xy + y^2)$
6. $(x^2 - 2)(9x^2 - 2x + 5)$
7. $(x - 3)(x^3 + 3x^2 - 7x + 1)$
8. $(x^2 - 5)(x^3 - 2x^2 + 4x + 3)$
9. $(x + y - 3)(4x - 7y + 2)$
10. $(x^2 - 7x + 2)(x^2 + 5x - 4)$
11. $(2x + 3)(3x - 2)(x - 5)$
12. $(4x - 5)(x - 1)(2x + 7)$
13. $(2 - x)(5 - 3x)(1 - 7x)$
14. $(2 - x^2)(1 - 3x^2)(5 - 2x^2)$

Simplify :

15. $(3x - 4)(2x^2 - 5x + 1) - (2x - 1)(3x^2 + 7x - 5)$

16. $(x + 1)(x^3 - 3x^2 + 4x - 5) - (3x - 2)(x^3 - x^2 + 5x - 7)$

DIVISION

6.10 Dividing Powers

When dividing powers having the same base, arrange them into a fraction and apply the formula $x^m \div x^n = x^{m-n}$, where x is a variable and m and n are positive integers.

Thus, $x^5 \div x^2 = x^{5-2} = x^3$, $x^7 \div x^7 = x^{7-7} = x^0 = 1$, $x^3 \div x^8 = x^{3-8} = x^{-5} = \dfrac{1}{x^5}$.

> **Note :** You should be able to write such results as $\dfrac{x^7}{x^2} = x^5$, $\dfrac{x^4}{x^{11}} = \dfrac{1}{x^7}$, $\dfrac{x^6}{x^6} = 1$, etc., directly.

6.11 Dividing Monomial by a Monomial

Ex. 1. *Divide :*   **(i)** $35x^2y^3$ *by* $-5x^3y^2$ **(ii)** $-18a^3bc^3$ *by* $-6abc^5$

Sol.   *(i)*   1. *Arrange in fractional form.*   3. *Divide literal coefficients*

           2. *Divide numerical coefficients.*   4. *Multiply the results.*

1. $\dfrac{35x^2y^3}{-5x^3y^2}$ $\left(\dfrac{Dividend}{Divisor}\right)$ 3. $\dfrac{x^2y^3}{x^3y^2} = \dfrac{y}{x}$

2. $\dfrac{35}{-5} = -7$ 4. $-7 \times \dfrac{y}{x} = \dfrac{-7y}{x}$

> **Think !**
> $\dfrac{x^2}{x^3} = x^{2-3} = x^{-1} = \dfrac{1}{x}$,
> $\dfrac{y^3}{y^2} = y^{3-2} = y^1 = y$

In actual working you may combine steps 2 and 3 and arrange your work as under :

$$35x^2y^3 \div (-5x^3y^2) = \frac{35x^2y^3}{-5x^3y^2} = \frac{-7y}{x}.$$

(ii) $\dfrac{-18a^3bc^3}{-6abc^5} = \dfrac{3a^2}{c^2}$

> **Think !**
> $\dfrac{-18}{-6} = 3$, $\dfrac{a^3}{a} = a^2$, $\dfrac{b}{b} = 1$, $\dfrac{c^3}{c^6} = \dfrac{1}{c^2}$

EXERCISE 6 (f)

Divide :

1. (i) $x^5 \div x^3$)   (ii) $y^7 \div y^3$ (iii) $a^9 \div a^4$ (iv) $x^3 \div x$
2. (i) $a \div a$ (ii) $r^7 \div r^7$ (iii) $m^2 \div m^2$
3. (i) $x^3 \div x^7$ (ii) $y \div y^4$ (iii) $15y^3 \div 3y^{10}$
4. (i) $-56abc \div 7$ (ii) $-8x \div (-2)$ (iii) $-14ab \div 7a$
5. $a^3b^4 \div a^2b$ 6. $a^3b^7 \div a^4b^6$ 7. $-54x^4y^5 \div 6x^2y^3$ 8. $84a^2b^5 \div 12a^2b^2$
9. $75x^2y^5z \div 15xy^2z$ 10. $-108m^6n^2x \div 12m^3x$ 11. $-33abc^2 \div (-33abc^2)$ 12. $-7x^7y^3 \div (-7y^3)$
13. $\dfrac{-36a^2b^3c^4}{18a^4b^2c^7}$ 14. $\dfrac{-8m^3np}{-np}$

6.12 Dividing a Polynomial by a Monomial

Method. *Divide each term of the polynomial by the monomial and combine the result.*

Ex. 1. *Simplify : $(12x + 36) \div 4$.*

Sol. Quotient $= \dfrac{12x+36}{4} = \dfrac{12x}{4} + \dfrac{36}{4} = $ **$3x + 9$.**

Ex. 2. *Simplify : $(3x^2 - x) \div (-x)$.*

Sol. Quotient $= \dfrac{3x^2 - x}{-x} = \dfrac{3x^2}{-x} + \dfrac{-x}{-x} = $ **$-3x + 1$.**

Ex. 3. *Simplify : $(-12a^3b + 18a^2b^2 - 24ab^3) \div -6ab$.*

Sol. Quotient $= \dfrac{-12a^3b+18a^2b^2-24ab^3}{-6ab} = \dfrac{-12a^3b}{-6ab} + \dfrac{18a^2b^2}{-6ab} + \dfrac{-24ab^3}{-6ab}$

$$= 2a^2 - 3ab + (4b^2) = \mathbf{2a^2 - 3ab + 4b^2}.$$

EXERCISE 6 (g)

Divide:

1. $8x + 4$ by 2   2. $3x + 6y$ by 3   3. $7a - 14$ by -7 4. $6y - 3$ by 3
5. $5m + 15$ by -5 6. $9m + 9$ by 9   7. $12y^2 + 36$ by -4 8. $21t - 7$ by 7
9. $-40x - 30$ by -10 10. $18x^2 - 24$ by -6 11. $-36a + 48$ by -12 12. $3b - 3$ by -3
13. $x^3 - x^2$ by x 14. $5c^2 - c$ by $-c$ 15. $10a^3 + 12ab$ by $2a$ 16. $2t - 6t^2$ by $-t$
17. $x^4y - 2x^3y^2 + x^5y^5$ by x^2y 18. $x^8 + x^2$ by x^2 19. $9x^2y^2 + 3x^2y - 6xy^2$ by $3xy$
20. $4x^2y - 7xy^2 - y^2$ by $-x^2y^2$ 21. $6a^2b^2 - 3abc + 9abd$ by $-\dfrac{1}{3}ab$ 22. $-10x^3y^2 + 15x^2y^3 - 5x^2y^2$ by $\dfrac{-5}{2}x^2y^2$

6.13 Dividing Polynomials by Polynomials

Ex. 1. *Divide $2x^2 - 11x + 12$ by $x - 4$.*

 Method

 Step 1. *Set up in the form of long division in which the polynomials are arranged in descending order, leaving space for missing terms.*

 2. *Divide the first term of the dividend $(2x^2)$ by the first term of the divisor (x) and write the quotient above the line.*

3. *Multiply the first term of the quotient ($2x$) by each term of the divisor ($x - 4$) and write the product below the dividend.*

4. *Subtract like terms and bring down one or more terms as needed.*

5. *Now use the remainder $-3x + 12$ as the new dividend and repeat steps 2 to 4.*

6. *Stop when the remainder becomes zero or when there is no term in the remainder into which the first term of the divisor will divide evenly.*

Sol.   (*By Steps*)

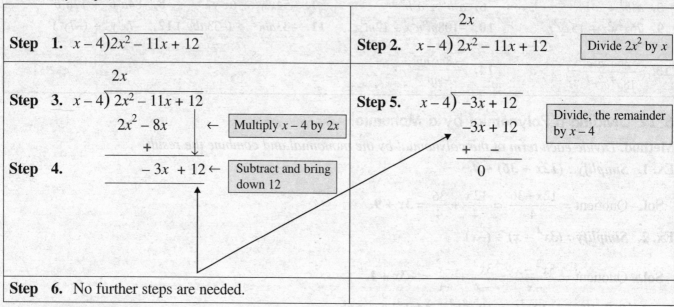

Step 6. No further steps are needed.

Full Solution

$$
\begin{array}{r}
2x - 3 \\
x - 4 \overline{)\ 2x^2 - 11x + 12} \\
2x^2 - 8x \\
\underline{-\quad +\quad\quad} \\
-3x + 12 \\
-3x + 12 \\
\underline{+\quad -\quad\quad} \\
0
\end{array}
$$

Remark. You know that if a number say 7 divides another number 28 exactly, then 7 is a factor of 28, Similarly, in the above example, $2x^2 - 11x + 12$ is divided by $x - 4$ and the remainder is zero, so ($x - 4$) **is a factor** of $2x^2 - 11x + 12$.

Ex. 2. *Divide $6x^3 - x + 19x^2 - 29$ by $2x + 3$.*

  Sol.   First arrange the dividend in descending powers of x.

$$
\begin{array}{r}
3x^2 + 5x\ \ - 8 \\
2x + 3 \overline{)\ 6x^3 + 19x^2 - x - 29} \\
6x^3 + 9x^2 \\
\underline{-\quad -\quad\quad\quad} \\
10x^2 - x \\
10x^2 + 15x \\
\underline{-\quad\quad -\quad\quad} \\
-16x - 29 \\
-16x - 24 \\
\underline{+\quad\quad +\quad} \\
-5
\end{array}
$$

The quotient is $3x^2 + 5x - 8$ with a remainder of -5. The quotient may also be written as

$$3x^2 + 5x - 8 + \frac{-5}{2x+3} \quad \text{or} \quad 3x^2 + 5x - 8 - \frac{5}{2x+3}.$$

6.14 Division Algorithm

We know that if a number is divided by another number then

Dividend = Divisor × Quotient + Remainder

Then, if 48 is divided by 5, then

$$48 = 5 \times 9 + 3$$

Remainder
Quotient
Dividend
Divisor

$$5 \overline{)\,48\,}(9$$
$$\underline{-45}$$
$$3$$

Similarly, if a polynomial is divided by another polynomial, then

Dividend = Divisor × Quotient + Remainder

This is generally called the 'division algorithm'.

Thus in Example 2 above let us check whether this algorithm holds or not, *i.e.*, whether the following is true or not.

$$6x^3 + 19x^2 - x - 29 = (2x + 3) \ (3x^2 + 5x - 8) + (-5)$$

Divisor   Quotient   Remainder

Divisor × Quotient + Remainder $= 2x(3x^2 + 5x - 8) + 3(3x^2 + 5x - 8) - 5$

$$= 6x^3 + 10x^2 - 16x + 9x^2 + 15x - 24 - 5$$

$$= 6x^3 + (10x^2 + 9x^2) - 16x + 15x - 29$$

$$= 6x^3 + 19x^2 - x - 29 = \text{Dividend}.$$

So the division algorithm holds.

Ex. 3. *Using division show that $x^2 + 2 - 3x$ is a factor of $2 - 3x^2 + x - x^3 + x^4$.*

Sol. Arrange the expressions according to descending powers of x.

$$x^2 - 3x + 2 \overline{)\, x^4 - \ x^3 - \ 3x^2 + x + 2 \,}(x^2 + 2x + 1$$
$$\underline{x^4 - 3x^3 + 2x^2}$$
$$\underline{-\ \ + \ \ \ -}$$
$$2x^3 - 5x^2 + x$$
$$2x^3 - 6x^2 + 4x$$
$$\underline{-\ \ + \ \ \ -}$$
$$x^2 - 3x + 2$$
$$x^2 - 3x + 2$$
$$\underline{-\ \ + \ \ \ -}$$
$$0$$

Since the remainder is zero, therefore, $x^2 - 3x + 2$ is a factor of $x^4 - x^3 - 3x^2 + x + 2$.

Remark. The quotient $x^2 + 2x + 1$ is also a factor of the given expression.

Ex. 4. *Find whether $4z^2 - 5$ is a factor of $4z^4 + 7z^2 + 15$ or not.*

Sol. We divide $4z^4 + 7z^2 + 15$ by $4z^2 - 5$.

$$4z^2 - 5 \overline{)\, 4z^4 + 7z^2 + 15 \,}(z^2 + 3$$
$$\underline{4z^4 - 5z^2}$$
$$\underline{-\ \ +}$$
$$12z^2 + 15$$
$$12z^2 - 15$$
$$\underline{-\ \ +}$$
$$30$$

$\therefore$ Remainder = 30. Since the remainder is not 0, so $4z^2 - 5$ is not a factor of $4z^4 + 7z^2 + 15$.

Ex. 5. *Divide $x^4 - 3x^3 - 13x^2 + 12x + 4$ by $x^2 - x + 2$, and verify that*

Dividend = Divisor × Quotient + Remainder.

Sol. Arrange the divisor and the dividend according to descending powers of x.

$$
\begin{array}{r}
x^2 - x + 2 \overline{)\, x^4 - 3x^3 - 13x^2 + 12x + 4} \,(x^2 - 2x - 17 \\
x^4 - x^3 + 2x^2 \\
-\quad+\quad- \\
\hline
-2x^3 - 15x^2 + 12x \\
-2x^3 + 2x^2 - 4x \\
+\quad-\quad+ \\
\hline
-17x^2 + 16x + 4 \\
-17x^2 + 17x - 34 \\
+\quad-\quad+ \\
\hline
-x + 38
\end{array}
$$

Verification :

Divisor × Quotient + Remainder,

$= (x^2 - x + 2)(x^2 - 2x - 17) + (-x + 38)$

$= x^2(x^2 - 2x - 17) - x(x^2 - 2x - 17)$
$\qquad\qquad + 2(x^2 - 2x - 17) - x + 38$

$= x^4 - 2x^3 - 17x^2 - x^3 + 2x^2 + 17x$
$\qquad\qquad + 2x^2 - 4x - 34 - x + 38$

$= x^4 - 2x^3 - x^3 - 17x^2 + 2x^2 + 2x^2$
$\qquad\qquad + 17x - 4x - x - 34 + 38$
$\qquad\qquad$ (Collecting like terms)

$= x^4 - 3x^3 - 13x^2 + 12x + 4 =$ Dividend.

Hence verified.

The quotient $= x^2 - 2x - 17$ and the remainder $= -x + 38$.

■ If one or more terms are missing in the dividend, be sure to leave a blank space for each such term.

Ex. 6. *Divide $x^3 - 8$ by $x - 2$, $x \neq 2$.*

Sol.

$$
\begin{array}{r}
x - 2 \overline{)\, x^3 \qquad\qquad\quad -8} \,(x^2 + 2x + 4 \\
x^3 - 2x^2 \\
-\quad+ \\
\hline
2x^2 \\
2x^2 - 4x \\
-\quad+ \\
\hline
+4x - 8 \\
4x - 8 \\
-\quad+ \\
\hline
0
\end{array}
$$

Note: Since the remainder is 0, so $x - 2$ is a factor of $x^3 - 8$.

∴ Quotient $= x^2 + 2x + 4$.

Ex. 7. *What must be subtracted from $x^4 + 6x^3 + 13x^2 + 13x + 8$ so that the resulting polynomial is exactly divisible by $(x^2 + 3x + 2)$.*

Sol.

$$
\begin{array}{r}
x^2 + 3x + 2 \overline{)\, x^4 + 6x^3 + 13x^2 + 13x + 8} \,(x^2 + 3x + 2 \\
x^4 + 3x^3 + 2x^2 \\
-\quad-\quad- \\
\hline
3x^3 + 11x^2 + 13x + 8 \\
3x^3 + 9x^2 + 6x \\
-\quad-\quad- \\
\hline
2x^2 + 7x + 8 \\
2x^2 + 6x + 4 \\
-\quad-\quad- \\
\hline
x + 4
\end{array}
$$

Quotient $= x^2 + 3x + 2$

Remainder $= x + 4$

So, if, we subtract the remainder $x + 4$ from $x^4 + 6x^3 + 13x^2 + 13x + 8$, it will be exactly divisible by $x^2 + 3x + 2$.

EXERCISE 6 (h)

Divide:

1. $a^2 + 6a + 1$ by $a + 1$
2. $x^2 - 3x + 2$ by $x - 1$
3. $x^2 + 4x - 21$ by $x + 7$
4. $14 - 17x + 5x^2$ by $2 - x$
5. $14x^2 + 13x - 15$ by $7x - 4$
6. $x^3 + 3 - 4x + 2x^2$ by $x - 2$
7. $x^4 + 4x - 2x^2 + x^3 - 10$ by $x - 2$
8. $8x^2 + 21x + x^3 + 18$ by $6 + 5x + x^2$
9. $5x + 24x^2 + 4x^3 - 75$ by $7x - 15 + 2x^2$
10. $2y^4 + 7y^2 + 8y^3 + 4y + 3$ by $(y + 3)$.

11. $6x^5 + 4x^4 - 27x^3 - 7x^2 + 27x + \dfrac{3}{2}$ by $(2x^2 - 3)$.

Using division find whether or not the first polynomial is a factor of the second:

12. $x - 7$; $x^2 - 3x - 28$
13. $2x - 3$; $6x^3 + x^2 - 19x + 6$
14. $x - 6$; $x^2 - 12x + 40$
15. $2y - 5$; $4y^4 - 10y^3 - 10y^2 + 30y - 15$
16. $2y^2 - 6$; $6y^5 - 28y^3 + 3y^2 + 30y - 9$

Divide and in each case check your answer using the relation 'Dividend = Divisor × Quotient + Remainder'.

17. $6p^3 + 5p^2 + 4$ by $(2p + 1)$
18. $x^3 + 4x - 3$ by $(x + 5)$
19. $9x^3 + 3x^2 - 5x + 7$ by $(3x - 1)$
20. $3x^5 - 2x^4 + x^2 - 2$ by $(x^2 + x + 1)$
21. What should be subtracted from $8x^4 + 14x^3 - 2x^2 + 7x - 8$ so that the resulting polynomial is exactly divisible by $4x^2 + 3x - 2$.
22. What should be added to $6x^5 + 4x^4 - 27x^3 - 7x^2 - 27x - 6$ so that the resulting polynomial is exactly divisible by $(2x^2 - 3)$.

SPECIAL PRODUCTS
(Some Special Identities)

6.15 Meaning of an Identity

Consider the mathematical sentence $(x + 3)^2 = x^2 + 6x + 9$. On putting various values of x, you find that L.H.S. = R.H.S. for all values of x. Such a mathematical sentence containing an unknown variable x which is satisfied for all values of x is called an identity.

x	L.H.S.	R.H.S.
1	16	16
2	25	25
3	36	36
4	49	49

6.16 Square of a Binomial

Two simple binomials are $a + b$ and $a - b$. The first two identities relate to finding the square of these binomials, _i.e._, $(a + b)^2$ and $(a - b)^2$.

$(a+b)^2 = (a+b)(a+b)$

$= a(a+b) + b(a+b)$

$= a^2 + ab + ab + b^2$

$= a^2 + 2ab + b^2$ [since $ba = ab$]

Thus, we have the following identity.

Aid to Memory :

$(a + b)^2 = a^2 + 2ab + b^2$

1. _Square the first term of the binomial._
2. _Double the product of the two terms._
3. _Square the second term of the binomial._

Identity 1: $(a+b)^2 = a^2 + 2ab + b^2$

Also, $(a-b)^2 = (a-b)(a-b) = a(a-b) - b(a-b)$

$= a^2 - ab - ba + b^2$

$= a^2 - 2ab + b^2$ \qquad\qquad [Since $ba = ab$]

Thus, we have the second identity as under:

Identity 2 : $(a-b)^2 = a^2 - 2ab + b^2$.

Note that the signs of the square terms, *i.e.*, a^2 and b^2 are always plus. The sign of the term containing twice the product ab is the same as the sign between the two terms of the binomial.

Remark. Because each of the expressions $a^2 + 2ab + b^2$ and $a^2 - 2ab + b^2$ is a trinomial that can be obtained by squaring a binomial, a polynomial that can be written in one of these forms is called a **trinomial square.** For example, since

$$m^2 + 6m + 9 = m^2 + 2(3)m + 3^2 = (m+3)^2,$$

the trinomial $m^2 + 6m + 9$ is a trinomial square. It is also called a **perfect square trinomial.**

Ex. 1. *Find the following products:*

    (i) $(x + 3)(x + 3)$ **(ii)** $(2x + 3y)(2x + 3y)$ **(iii)** $(3x^2 + 5y^2)(3x^2 + 5y^2)$

Sol.   (*i*) $(x+3)(x+3) = (x+3)^2$

$$= (x)^2 + 2 \times x \times 3 + (3)^2$$

> $(1\text{st term})^2 + 2\,(1\text{st term})\,(2\text{nd term}) + (2\text{nd term})^2$

$$= x^2 + 6x + 9.$$

  (*ii*) $(2x+3y)(2x+3y) = (2x+3y)^2$

$$= (2x)^2 + 2 \times 2x \times 3y + (3y)^2 = 4x^2 + 12xy + 9y^2.$$

  (*iii*) $(3x^2 + 5y^2)(3x^2 + 5y^2) = (3x^2 + 5y^2)^2$

$$= (3x^2)^2 + 2 \times (3x^2) \times (5y^2) + (5y^2)^2 = 9x^4 + 30x^2y^2 + 25y^4.$$

Ex. 2. *Find the following products :*

    (i) $(a - 7)(a - 7)$ **(ii)** $(3x - 5)(3x - 5)$ **(iii)** $(5x^3 - 2y^2)(5x^3 - 2y^2)$

Sol.   (*i*) $(a-7)(a-7) = (a-7)^2$

$$= (a)^2 - 2 \times a \times 7 + (7)^2$$

> $(1\text{st term})^2 - 2 \times 1\text{st term} \times 2\text{nd term} + (2\text{nd term})^2$

$$= a^2 - 14a + 49.$$

  (*ii*) $(3x-5)(3x-5) = (3x-5)^2$

$$= (3x)^2 - 2 \times 3x \times 5 + (5)^2 = 9x^2 - 30x + 25.$$

  (*iii*) $(5x^3 - 2y^2)(5x^3 - 2y^2) = (5x^3 - 2y^2)^2$

$$= (5x^3)^2 - 2 \times (5x^3) \times (2y^2) + (2y^2)^2$$

$$= 25x^6 - 20x^3y^2 + 4y^4.$$

> $\because (x^3)^2 = x^{3 \times 2} = x^6$

Ex. 3. *Write down the squares of :*

    (i) $3m + \dfrac{1}{2}$ **(ii)** $2x + \dfrac{1}{x}$ **(iii)** $5m - \dfrac{1}{5m}$ **(iv)** $16a - \dfrac{1}{4}$

Sol. (i) $\left(3m+\dfrac{1}{2}\right)^2$

$$= (3m)^2 + 2^1 \times 3m \times \dfrac{1}{2_1} + \left(\dfrac{1}{2}\right)^2$$

$$= 9m^2 + 3m + \dfrac{1}{4}.$$

(ii) $\left(2x+\dfrac{1}{x}\right)^2$

$$= (2x)^2 + 2 \times 2x \times \dfrac{1}{x} + \left(\dfrac{1}{x}\right)^2$$

$$= 4x^2 + 4 + \dfrac{1}{x^2}.$$

(iii) $\left(5m-\dfrac{1}{5m}\right)^2$

$$= (5m)^2 - 2 \times 5m \times \dfrac{1}{5m} + \left(\dfrac{1}{5m}\right)^2$$

$$= 25m^2 - 2 + \dfrac{1}{25m^2}.$$

(iv) $\left(16a-\dfrac{1}{4}\right)^2$

$$= (16a)^2 - 2 \times 16^4 a \times \dfrac{1}{4_1} + \left(\dfrac{1}{4}\right)^2$$

$$= 256a^2 - 8a + \dfrac{1}{16}.$$

Ex. 4. _Simplify :_

(i) $\left(4z+\dfrac{5}{2}\right)^2$ (ii) $\left(3z^7+\dfrac{1}{z^7}\right)^2$ (iii) $\left(\dfrac{1}{2}x^2-\dfrac{7}{3}y^3\right)^2$ (iv) $\left(9y^2-\dfrac{1}{2}z^2\right)^2$

Sol. (i) $\left(4z+\dfrac{5}{2}\right)^2$

$$= (4z)^2 + 2^1 \times 4z \times \dfrac{5}{2_1} + \left(\dfrac{5}{2}\right)^2$$

$$= 16z^2 + 20z + \dfrac{25}{4}.$$

(ii) $\left(3z^7+\dfrac{1}{z^7}\right)^2$

$$= (3z^7)^2 + 2 \times 3z^7 \times \dfrac{1}{z^7} + \left(\dfrac{1}{z^7}\right)^2$$

$$= 9z^{14} + 6 + \dfrac{1}{z^{14}}.$$

$$\boxed{\because (z^7)^2 = z^{7\times2} = z^{14}}$$

(iii) $\left(\dfrac{1}{2}x^2-\dfrac{7}{3}y^3\right)^2$

$$= \left(\dfrac{1}{2}x^2\right)^2 - 2 \times \dfrac{1}{2}x^2 \times \dfrac{7}{3}y^3 + \left(\dfrac{7}{3}y^3\right)^2$$

$$= \dfrac{1}{4}x^4 - \dfrac{7}{3}x^2y^3 + \dfrac{49}{9}y^6.$$

(iv) $\left(9y^2-\dfrac{1}{2}z^2\right)^2$

$$= (9y^2)^2 - 2 \times 9y^2 \times \dfrac{1}{2}z^2 + \left(\dfrac{1}{2}z^2\right)^2$$

$$= 81y^4 - 9y^2z^2 + \dfrac{1}{4}z^4.$$

EXERCISE 6 (i)

Find the following products:

1. (i) $(x+2)(x+2)$ (ii) $(3x+5)(3x+5)$ (iii) $\left(\dfrac{3}{4}x^2+5\right)\left(\dfrac{3}{4}x^2+5\right)$

2. (i) $(y-9)(y-9)$ (ii) $\left(7t-\dfrac{1}{2}u\right)\left(7t-\dfrac{1}{2}u\right)$ (iii) $(5x^2-4y^2)(5x^2-4y^2)$

Write down the squares of:

3. (i) $p+5$ (ii) $2t+9$ (iii) $5c+2d$ (iv) $9m+\dfrac{1}{4}$ (v) $3x+\dfrac{1}{3x}$

   (vi) $(2y^2+5z^2)$ (vii) $\left(7x^3+\dfrac{1}{7}y^3\right)$ (viii) $\left(\dfrac{1}{2}a^4+\dfrac{1}{3}b^7\right)$

4. (i) $t-3$ (ii) $9t-11$ (iii) $7p-8q$ (iv) $8m-\dfrac{1}{2}$

(v) $12x - \dfrac{1}{5x}$ (vi) $3m^3 - 7n^4$ (vii) $x^3 - \dfrac{1}{x^3}$ (viii) $\dfrac{1}{5}p^5 - \dfrac{1}{2}q^6$

5. Simplify:

(i) $(a+8)^2$ (ii) $(x+1)^2$ (iii) $(d-6)^2$ (iv) $(7-y)^2$ (v) $(a^2+b^2)^2$

(vi) $(m^2-n^2)^2$ (vii) $(mn-xy)^2$ (viii) $(2ax+9y)^2$ (ix) $(a^3b-xy^3)^2$ (x) $(0\cdot3x+4)^2$

(xi) $\left(\dfrac{1}{4}x^3+2\right)^2$ (xii) $\left(\dfrac{3}{5}a-10b\right)^2$ (xiii) $\left(\dfrac{1}{3}b^2-3c^2\right)^2$ (xiv) $\left(2x^2+\dfrac{1}{3x^2}\right)^2$ (xv) $\left(5m^3-\dfrac{1}{5m^3}\right)^2$.

6.17 Applications

$$\left(x+\frac{1}{x}\right)^2 = (x)^2 + 2\times x\times\frac{1}{x}+\left(\frac{1}{x}\right)^2$$
$$= x^2+2+\frac{1}{x^2}$$
$$\boxed{x^2+\frac{1}{x^2} = \left(x+\frac{1}{x}\right)^2 - 2}$$

$$\left(x-\frac{1}{x}\right)^2 = (x)^2 - 2\times x\times\frac{1}{x}+\left(\frac{1}{x}\right)^2$$
$$= x^2-2+\frac{1}{x^2}$$
$$\boxed{x^2+\frac{1}{x^2} = \left(x-\frac{1}{x}\right)^2 + 2}$$

Ex. 5. If $x+\dfrac{1}{x}=3$, find the value of

     (i) $x^2+\dfrac{1}{x^2}$ **(ii)** $x^4+\dfrac{1}{x^4}$.

Sol. Given: $x+\dfrac{1}{x}=3$

(i) $\left(x+\dfrac{1}{x}\right)^2=3^2$ | Squaring both sides

$\Rightarrow x^2+2\times x\times\dfrac{1}{x}+\dfrac{1}{x^2}=9$

$\Rightarrow x^2+2+\dfrac{1}{x^2}=9$

$\Rightarrow x^2+\dfrac{1}{x^2}=9-2=\mathbf{7}.$

(ii) Now, squaring again both sides, we get

$\left(x^2+\dfrac{1}{x^2}\right)^2=7^2$

$\Rightarrow x^4+2\times x^2\times\dfrac{1}{x^2}+\dfrac{1}{x^4}=49$

$\Rightarrow x^4+2+\dfrac{1}{x^4}=49$

$\Rightarrow x^4+\dfrac{1}{x^4}=49-2=\mathbf{47}.$

Ex. 6. *Evaluate the following, using identities:*

     (i) $(103)^2$ **(ii)** 98^2 **(iii)** $(10.3)^2$ **(iv)** $(99.5)^2$

Sol. (i) $(103)^2=(100+3)^2=(100)^2+2\times100\times3+(3)^2$ | Using $(a+b)^2=a^2+2ab+b^2$

$\qquad =10000+600+9=\mathbf{10,609}.$

(ii) $98^2=(100-2)^2=(100)^2-2\times100\times2+(2)^2$ | Using $(a-b)^2=a^2-2ab+b^2$

$\qquad =10000-400+4=\mathbf{9,604}.$

$\qquad$ (iii) $(10.4)^2 = (10 + 0.4)^2$ $\qquad\qquad$ (iv) $(99.5)^2 = (100 - 0.5)^2$

$\qquad\qquad = (10)^2 + 2 \times 10 \times 0.4 + (0.4)^2$ $\qquad\qquad (100)^2 - 2 \times 100 \times 0.5 + (0.5)^2$

$\qquad\qquad = 100 + 8 + 0.16$ $\qquad\qquad\qquad = 10000 - 100 + 0.25$

$\qquad\qquad = \mathbf{108.16}.$ $\qquad\qquad\qquad = 9900 + 0.25 = \mathbf{9900.25}.$

Ex. 8. *If* $x^2 + \dfrac{1}{x^2} = 38$, *find the value of*

$\qquad$ **(i)** $x - \dfrac{1}{x}$ $\qquad\qquad$ **(ii)** $x^4 + \dfrac{1}{x^4}.$

Sol. We have :

$\qquad$ (i) $\left(x - \dfrac{1}{x}\right)^2 = x^2 + \dfrac{1}{x^2} - 2 = 38 - 2 = 36 = 6^2$ $\quad$ (ii) $x^2 + \dfrac{1}{x^2} = 38 \implies \left(x^2 + \dfrac{1}{x^2}\right)^2 = 38^2$ $\boxed{\text{Squaring both sides}}$

$\qquad\qquad \therefore \ x - \dfrac{1}{x} = \mathbf{6}.$ $\qquad\qquad\qquad \implies x^4 + \dfrac{1}{x^4} + 2 = 1444 \implies x^4 + \dfrac{1}{x^4} = 1444 - 2 = \mathbf{1442}.$

EXERCISE 6 (j)

Using the identity for square of a binomial, evaluate the following:

1. $(102)^2$ $\quad$ **2.** $(53)^2$ $\quad$ **3.** $(501)^2$ $\quad$ **4.** $(807)^2$ $\quad$ **5.** $(709)^2$ $\quad$ **6.** $(59)^2$

7. $(48)^2$ $\quad$ **8.** $(199)^2$ $\quad$ **9.** $(698)^2$ $\quad$ **10.** $(999)^2$ $\quad$ **11.** $(77)^2$ $\quad$ **12.** $(497)^2$

Find the value of the expression:

13. $25x^2 + 70x + 49$ if $x = -1$ $\qquad\qquad$ **14.** $49x^2 - 84xy + 36y^2$ if $x = 2, y = 3$

15. If $\left(x + \dfrac{1}{x}\right) = 12,$ find the value of $\left(x^2 + \dfrac{1}{x^2}\right).$

16. If $\left(x + \dfrac{1}{x}\right) = 5,$ find the values of $\left(x^2 + \dfrac{1}{x^2}\right)$ and $\left(x^4 + \dfrac{1}{x^4}\right).$

17. If $x - \dfrac{1}{x} = 7,$ find the value of $\left(x^2 + \dfrac{1}{x^2}\right).$ $\qquad$ **18.** If $x - \dfrac{1}{x} = 8,$ find the values of $\left(x^2 + \dfrac{1}{x^2}\right)$ and $\left(x^4 + \dfrac{1}{x^4}\right).$

19. If $x^2 + \dfrac{1}{x^2} = 27,$ find the value of (i) $x - \dfrac{1}{x}$ $\quad$ (ii) $x^4 + \dfrac{1}{x^4}.$

20. If $x + y = 9$ and $xy = 16,$ find the value of $(x^2 + y^2)$ $\quad$ **21.** If $x - y = 6$ and $xy = 10,$ find the value of $(x^2 + y^2).$

6.18 To Find the Product of the Sum and the Difference of the Same Two Terms

$\qquad$ The multiplication at the right shows the steps used to find the product of the binomials $a + b$ and $a - b$. Notice that two terms of the product, ab and $-ab$, are opposites, and so their sum is zero.

$\qquad$ 1. *Square the first term.*

$\qquad$ 2. *Square the second term.*

$\qquad$ 3. *Subtract the second square from the first by placing a minus sign between the two squares.*

$(a + b)(a - b)$

$= a(a - b) + b(a - b)$

$= a^2 - ab + ba - b^2$

$= a^2 \ - \ b^2$

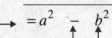

Thus we have

$$(a+b)(a-b) = a^2 - b^2$$

Note that there are only two terms in the product.

> **Remark.** You can mentally find the product of two numbers if you recognize that one factor is the sum of two particular numbers and the other factor is the difference of these numbers.

Ex. 1. *Find the products:*

    (i) $(x+6)(x-6)$ (ii) $(4-x)(4+x)$ (iii) $(2b+3c)(2b-3c)$

    (iv) $\left(\dfrac{1}{2}ab - x^2\right)\left(\dfrac{1}{2}ab + x^2\right)$ (v) $(5x^2 - 7y^2)(5x^2 + 7y^2)$ (vi) $\left(x^3 + \dfrac{1}{x^3}\right)\left(x^3 - \dfrac{1}{x^3}\right)$

Sol.   (i) $(x+6)(x-6) = x^2 - 6^2 = \mathbf{x^2 - 36}$.

    (ii) $(4-x)(4+x) = (4)^2 - x^2 = \mathbf{16 - x^2}$.

    (iii) $(2b+3c)(2b-3c) = (2b)^2 - (3c)^2 = \mathbf{4b^2 - 9c^2}$.

    (iv) $\left(\dfrac{1}{2}ab - x^2\right)\left(\dfrac{1}{2}ab + x^2\right) = \left(\dfrac{1}{2}ab\right)^2 - (x^2)^2 = \mathbf{\dfrac{1}{4}a^2b^2 - x^4}$.

    (v) $(5x^2 - 7y^2)(5x^2 + 7y^2) = (5x^2)^2 - (7y^2)^2 = \mathbf{25x^4 - 49y^4}$.

    (vi) $\left(x^3 + \dfrac{1}{x^3}\right)\left(x^3 - \dfrac{1}{x^3}\right) = \left(x^3\right)^2 - \left(\dfrac{1}{x^3}\right)^2 = \mathbf{x^6 - \dfrac{1}{x^6}}$.

Ex. 2. *Find the continued product $(x + 3)(x - 3)(x^2 + 9)$.*

Sol. $(x+3)(x-3)(x^2+9)$.

    $= \left[(x+3)(x-3)\right](x^2+9)$ Associative Law

    $= (x^2 - 9)(x^2 + 9) = \left(x^2\right)^2 - (9)^2 = \mathbf{x^4 - 81}$.

Ex. 3. *Using the identity for difference of two squares, find the product of 51×49.*

Sol. $51 \times 49 = (50+1)(50-1) = (50)^2 - 1^2 = 2500 - 1 = \mathbf{2499}$.

Ex. 4. *Simplify: $279 \times 279 - 21 \times 21$.*

Sol. $279 \times 279 - 21 \times 21 = (279)^2 - (21)^2$

                         $= (279+21)(279-21) = 300 \times 258 = \mathbf{77400}$.

EXERCISE 6 (k)

Find the following products:

1. (i) $(x+2)(x-2)$ (ii) $(d-8)(d+8)$ (iii) $(7-p)(7+p)$ (iv) $(4a-3b)(4a+3b)$

    (v) $(5+9m)(5-9m)$ (vi) $(ab+9)(ab-9)$ (vii) $(x^2-y^2)(x^2+y^2)$ (viii) $\left(\dfrac{2}{5}ab - c\right)\left(\dfrac{2}{5}ab + c\right)$

    (ix) $\left(\dfrac{2}{b} - \dfrac{5}{c}\right)\left(\dfrac{2}{b} + \dfrac{5}{c}\right)$

2. (i) $(a+1)(a-1)(a^2+1)$

(ii) $(a+x)(a-x)(a^2+x^2)$

(iii) $\left(x-\dfrac{1}{x}\right)\left(x+\dfrac{1}{x}\right)\left(x^2+\dfrac{1}{x^2}\right)$

(iv) $\left(x^3-\dfrac{1}{x^3}\right)\left(x^3+\dfrac{1}{x^3}\right)\left(x^6+\dfrac{1}{x^6}\right)$.

3. Using the identity for difference of two squares, find the values of:

(i) 18×22 (ii) 71×69 (iii) 101×99 (iv) 53×29

(v) $(84)^2-(76)^2$ (vi) $(203)^2-(197)^2$ (vii) $(121)^2-(119)^2$ (viii) $(169)^2-(131)^2$

4. Find the value of x, if :

(i) $13x=(58)^2-(45)^2$ (ii) $24x=(99)^2-(87)^2$

5. Simplify:

(i) $179\times179-21\times21$ (ii) $1\cdot62\times1\cdot62-0\cdot38\times0\cdot38$ (iii) $\dfrac{297\times297-203\times203}{94}$ (**Hint :** $94 = 297-203$)

(iv) $\dfrac{23\cdot71\times23\cdot71-16\cdot29\times16\cdot29}{0\cdot742}$.

LOOKING BACK
Summary of Key Facts

1. Algebraic expressions in which the variables involved have only non-negative integral exponents are called **polynomials**.

e.g. $5x^2 - 3x + 2$ is a polynomial while $3x^{-2} + 5x^{-1} + 7 + 4x$ and $x^{\frac{1}{2}} + 9x^2 - 3$ are not polynomials.

2. A polynomial that involves only one variable is called a **polynomial in one variable.**

3. (i) Polynomials having only one term are called **monomials**.

(ii) Polynomials having only two terms are called **binomials.**

(iii) Polynomials having only three terms are called **trinomials**.

4. (i) The highest exponent of the variable in a polynomial in one variable is called the degree of the polynomial.

e.g. degree of the polynomial $5x^4 - 3x^3 + 7x^2 + 9$ is 4.

(ii) A constant is a polynomial of degree zero.

(iii) In a polynomial in more than one variable, the highest sum of the powers of the variables is called the degree of the polynomial.

e.g. degree of the polynomial $5 - 3x^7 + 8x^3y^7 - 2xy^6$ is $3 + 7$, i.e., 10.

5. The standard form of a polynomial in one variable is that in which the terms of the polynomial are written in the decreasing or **descending order** of the exponents of the variable.

6. A polynomial is said to be **linear, quadratic, cubic** or **biquadratic** if its degree is 1, 2, 3, or 4 respectively.

7. (i) The **product of two monomials** is the product of their coefficients and literals in the two monomials, the exponent of each literal being the sum of its exponents in the given monomials.

e.g., $5a^3b^4c^7 \times -8a^5b^{25}c^{30} = (5\times-8)\times a^{3+5}.b^{4+25}c^{7+30} = -40a^8b^{29}c^{37}$.

(ii) The **product of a monomial and a binomial** is obtained on multiplying each term of the binomial by the monomial and adding up the two products.

e.g., $-5x^2y(3x^2+5y^2) = (-5x^2y)(3x^2)+(-5x^2y)(5y^2) = -15x^4y - 25x^2y^3$.

(*iii*) The **product of two binomials is a binomial** obtained on multiplying each term of one binomial by each term of the other binomial and adding up the products.

e.g., $(5x + 7y)(3x - 2y) = 5x(3x - 2y) + 7y(3x - 2y) = 15x^2 - 10xy + 21xy - 14y^2 = 15x^2 + 11xy - 14y^2$.

(*iv*) The product of a binomial and a polynomial (trinomial, expression containing 4 or more terms) is obtained on multiplying each term of the binomial with each term of the polynomial and adding up.

e.g. $(2m - 3n)(2m^2 - 5mn + 7n^2) = (2m)(2m^2 - 5mn + 7n^2) - 3n(2m^2 - 5mn + 7n^2)$

$$= 4m^3 - 10m^2n + 14mn^2 - 6m^2n + 15mn^2 - 21n^3 = 4m^3 - 16m^2n + 29mn^2 - 21n^3.$$

8.   (*i*) If a polynomial is divided by another polynomial then we have, **dividend = (divisor × quotient + remainder)**.

    (*ii*) If on dividing a polynomial (called dividend) a zero remainder is obtained then the dividing polynomial (called divisor) is a **factor** of the dividend. In such cases, dividend = divisor × quotient

    (*iii*) Before performing long division, the divisor and the dividend must be written in standard form.

    (*iv*) While performing long division, like terms are written one below the other, leaving gaps whenever necessary.

    (*v*) The degree of the remainder is always less than that of the divisor.

9. **Special Products :**

   (i) $(x + a)(x + b) = x^2 + (a + b)x + ab$ (ii) $(a + b) = a^2 + 2ab + b^2$ (iii) $(a - b)^2 = a^2 - 2ab + b^2$

   (iv) $a^2 + b^2 = (a + b)^2 - 2ab$ (v) $x^2 + \dfrac{1}{x^2} = \left(x + \dfrac{1}{x}\right)^2 - 2$ (vi) $(a + b)^2 = (a - b)^2 + 4ab$

  (vii) $(a - b)^2 = (a + b)^2 - 4ab$ (viii) $(a + b)^2 + (a - b)^2 = 2(a^2 + b^2)$

   (ix) Expression of the form $a^2 + 2ab + b^2 = (a + b)^2$ and $a^2 - 2ab + b^2 = (a - b)^2$ are called perfect squares. They are of the form (1st term)^2 ± 2(sq. root of 1st term) (square root 2nd term) + (2nd term)^2.

   (x) $(a + b)(a - b) = a^2 - b^2$.

MENTAL MATHS – 5

Simplify :

1. $7a + 5a$ **2.** $-6m - 15m$ **3.** $4x - 10y + 7x + 3y$ **4.** $-3abc - 5cab - 7bca$

5. $5t - 2(t - 4)$

Find the product:

6. $3a^3$ and $5a^2$ **7.** $11ab$ and $-8bc$ **8.** $\left(\dfrac{7}{9} p^2 qr\right) \times (18pq^2)\left(-\dfrac{3}{14} r^3\right)$

9. $(a^{1000})(b^{9999})(abc)(0)$ **10.** $(x^3)(x^{20})(x^{17})(x^{60})(x^0)$ **11.** $7a(2a + 3)$ **12.** $5x(2x^2 - 7xy^2)$

13. $(-3xy)(x^2 - y^2)$ **14.** $(x + 5)(x + 6)$ **15.** $(3m + 2n)(2m - 3n)$

16. Divide $-21x^3y^2$ by $-3xy$ **17.** State the quotient of $7p^3 - 6p^2 + 12p$, if it is divided by $3p$.

18. What is the quotient if $21y^3p^4q^2$ is divided by $7y^2p^3q$.

19. Expand : (*i*) $(x + 3)^2$ (*ii*) $(2x - 3y)^2$

20. Multiply using a suitable identity :

   (*i*) $(x + 8)(x + 8)$ (*ii*) $(3a + 5b)(3a + 5b)$ (*iii*) $(2x + 7)(2x - 7)$ (*iv*) $\left(\dfrac{5}{9}x + \dfrac{1}{2}y\right)\left(\dfrac{5}{9}x - \dfrac{1}{2}y\right)$

Evaluate suitable identify :

21. 19^2 **22.** $135^2 - 125^2$ **23.** $100^2 - 99^2$ **24.** $5.68 \times 5.68 - 4.32 \times 4.32$

MULTIPLE CHOICE QUESTIONS – 5

1. $\dfrac{-5}{3}x^2 - \dfrac{3}{4}x^2 - \dfrac{4}{3}x^2 - \dfrac{1}{4}x^2 + x^2$ is equal to :

    (i) $-5x^2$ (ii) $4x^2$ (iii) $-6x^2$ (iv) $-3x^2$

2. When $x = 1$, $y = 2$, $z = 3$, the value of the sum of $5x^2$, $-2x^3 z$ and $3y^4$ is :

    (i) 40   (ii) 10   (iii) -37 (iv) 47

3. A boy attempts $x + y$ sums, of which only $y - 2z$ are correct. The number of wrong sums is :

    (i) $-x + 2z$ (ii) $-2y - 2z$ (iii) $x + 2z$ (iv) $2y + 2z$

4. The value of $(-1.4\ a^2 b) \times (-0.5\ abc^2)$ is

    (i) $7a^3 b^2 c^2$ (ii) $-0.07\ a^3 b^2 c^3$ (iii) $0.7\ a^3 b^2 c^2$ (iv) $70\ a^2 b^3 c^2$

5. $(a - b)\ (a - b) - (a + b)\ (a - b)$ is equal to :

    (i) $2a^2 - 2b^2$ (ii) $2b^2 - 2ab$ (iii) $a^2 + 2ab$ (iv) $2b^2 + 2ab - 2a^2$

6. If $-100\ a^4 t^2 y$ is divided by $\dfrac{1}{4} a t^2 y$, the quotient is :

    (i) $-25a^5 t^4 y^2$ (ii) $25a^3$ (iii) $-400\ a^3$ (iv) $400\ a^5 t^4 y^2$

7. $2a(a - b) - b(3b - 2a)$ is equal to :

    (i) $3a^2 - 2b^2$ (ii) $2a^2 - 3b^2$ (iii) $-2a^2 + 3b^2$ (iv) $-3a^2 - 2b^2$

8. The degree of the polynomial $2\dfrac{1}{2}x^5 - y + 6y^3 + 4x^2 y^3$ is :

    (i) 3   (ii) 2   (iii) 5   (iv) 1

9. $(18a^4 x^2 - 24ax^5) \div (-6ax^2)$ is equal to :

    (i) $54a^3 x^2 - 4a^2 x^7$ (ii) $3a^3 - 4x^3$ (iii) $-3a^3 + 4x^3$ (iv) $4a^3 - 3x^3$

10. The quotient when $10 + x^2 - 7x$ is divided by $x - 2$ is :

    (i) $5 - x$ (ii) $x - 5$ (iii) $x + 5$ (iv) $-x - 5$

ANSWERS

EXERCISE 6 (a)

1. (i) 0 (ii) $a^2 b$ (iii) $4a + 3b$ (iv) $8a + 6b - 6c$ (v) $10x^2 - 7xy + 10y^2$

2. (i) $5x - 12$ (ii) $15xy$ (iii) $3x^2 - 6x + 9$ (iv) $6y^2 + 13y - 1$

    (v) $p - 5q - 4r - 16$ (vi) $x^3 - 6x^2 + 10x - 4$ (vii) $3m^3 - 6m^2 - 2m + 6$

3. $20x^2 - 2xy - 10y^2$ **4.** $-6p^2 - 4p + 3$

EXERCISE 6 (b)

1. (i) ab (ii) $-xy$ (iii) $3xy$ (iv) y^2 (v) $3a^2 b^2$ (vi) $12xyz$

    (vii) $-4\ mnp^2 q$ (viii) $\dfrac{-32}{147} a^2 bcd^2$

2. (i) a^7 (ii) $12y^7$ (iii) $30\ w^9$ (iv) $-91m^{10}$ (v) $15x^3 y^3$ (vi) $-12m^2 n^2$

    (vii) $-45a^2 xy^2$ (viii) $6a^2 b^3 x^4 y^5 z$ (ix) $\dfrac{2}{3}x^5 y^3$ (x) $\dfrac{1}{4}x^{11} y^5$ (xi) $5x^3 y$ **3.** $24x^5 y^4$ **4.** $-x^6 y^{10}$

5. $24p^2 q^2 r^2$ **6.** $-x^6 y^7 z^9$ **7.** (i) 0.46656 (ii) -345.60

EXERCISE 6 (c)

1. $5x + 15$ **2.** $14x - 21$ **3.** $-20y - 28$ **4.** $6m + 18$ **5.** $-4x^2 - 6xy + 8y^2$ **6.** $x^2 + x$

7. $-2y^3 + 6y^2 - 8y$ **8.** $-3y^4 + 5y^2$ **9.** $3a^2 b - 5ab^2$ **10.** $15m^2 n - 10mn^2$ **11.** $-2x^3 y^2 - 3x^3 y + x^2 y^2 + 7x^2 y$

12. $2x^4 + 10x^3 - 12x^2$ 13. $-y^4 + 5y^2$ 14. $3x^4y^3 - 5x^3y^2 + 7x^2y$ 15. $-8c^5 + 20c^4 + 16c^3 - 18c^2$

16. $-x^6y^2 - x^4y^4 + x^2y^6$ 17. $2x^3y^2 - 7x^2y^2$ 18. $x^2 - 19xyz$

19. (i) 180   (ii) 0.802   (iii) 59.8   20. 0   21. 0   22. $-2y^2$

EXERCISE 6 (d)

1. $x^2 + 7x + 10$ 2. $x^2 + 5x - 36$ 3. $x^2 - 16x + 63$ 4. $x^4 - x^2 - 30$ 5. $9x^2 - 64$

6. $15x^2 + 11xy - 12y^2$ 7. $a^4 - b^4$ 8. $15x^4 - 29x^2y^2 - 14y^4$ 9. $6x^2 + \frac{1}{7}xy - \frac{15}{49}y^2$

10. $x^3 - \frac{7}{8}x^2y - \frac{8}{7}y^2x + y^3$ 11. $m^5 + m^3n^2 - m^2n^3 - n^5$ 12. $a^4 - a^2b^2 + a^2b^4 - b^6$

13. $12x^4 - 7x^2y - 12y^2$ 14. $7x^2 + x^3 - \frac{2}{7}x^4$ 15. $-20x^4 + 18x^2y^2 + 18y^4$

16. $22x^2 - 42x + 1$ 17. $13x^4 - 13x^3y - 42x^2y^2$ 18. $x^2 + 9x + 20$ 19. $x^2 - 49$

20. $2x^2 + x - 15$ 21. $24m^2 - 17m - 20$ 22. $12t^2 - 48t + 21$

EXERCISE 6 (e)

1. $x^3 + 3x^2 + 3x + 2$ 2. $6x^3 + 7x^2 - 7x - 6$ 3. $8x^3 - 38x^2 + 23x + 15$

4. $15x^3 - 41x^2 + 23x - 21$ 5. $x^3 - y^3$ 6. $9x^4 - 2x^3 - 13x^2 + 4x - 10$

7. $x^4 - 16x^2 + 22x - 3$ 8. $x^5 - 2x^4 - x^3 + 13x^2 - 20x - 15$ 9. $4x^2 - 3xy - 10x + 23y - 7y^2 - 6$

10. $x^4 - 2x^3 - 37x^2 + 38x - 8$ 11. $6x^3 - 25x^2 - 31x + 30$ 12. $8x^3 + 10x^2 - 53x + 35$

13. $10 - 81x + 80x^2 - 21x^3$ 14. $10 - 39x^2 + 29x^4 - 6x^6$ 15. $-34x^2 + 40x - 9$ 16. $-2x^4 + 3x^3 - 16x^2 + 30x - 19$

EXERCISE 6 (f)

1. (i) x^2 (ii) y^4 (iii) a^5 (iv) x^2 2. (i) 1   (ii) 1   (iii) 1

3. (i) $\frac{1}{x^4}$ (ii) $\frac{1}{y^3}$ (iii) $\frac{5}{y^7}$ 4. (i) $-8abc$ (ii) $4x$ (iii) $-2b$

5. ab^3 6. $\frac{b}{a}$ 7. $-9x^2y^2$ 8. $7b^3$ 9. $5xy^3$ 10. $-9m^2n^2$

11. 1   12. x^7 13. $\frac{-2b}{a^2c^3}$ 14. $8m^3$

EXERCISE 6 (g)

1. $4x + 2$ 2. $x + 2y$ 3. $-a + 2$ 4. $2y - 1$ 5. $-m - 3$ 6. $m + 1$ 7. $-3y^2 - 9$

8. $3t - 1$ 9. $4x + 3$ 10. $-3x^2 + 4$ 11. $3a - 4$ 12. $-b + 1$ 13. $x^2 - x$ 14. $-5c + 1$

15. $5a^2 + 6b$ 16. $-2 + 6t$ 17. $x^2 - 2xy + x^3y^4$ 18. $x^6 + 1$ 19. $3xy + x - 2y$

20. $\frac{-4}{y} + \frac{7}{x} + \frac{1}{x^2}$ 21. $-18ab + 9c - 27d$ 22. $4x - 6y + 2$

EXERCISE 6 (h)

1. $a + 5$ 2. $x - 2$ 3. $x - 3$ 4. $7 - 5x$ 5. $Q = 2x + 3, R = -3$

6. $Q = x^2 + 4x + 4, R = 11$ 7. $Q = x^3 + 3x^2 + 4x + 12, R = 14$ 8. $x + 3$ 9. $2x + 5$

10. $2y^3 + 2y^2 + y + 1$ 11. $3x^3 + 2x^2 - 9x - \frac{1}{2}$ 12. Yes   13. Yes   14. No.

15. No   16. Yes   17. $Q = 3p^2 + p - \frac{1}{2}; R = 4\frac{1}{2}$ 18. $Q = x^2 - 5x + 29, R = -148$

19. $Q = 3x^2 + 2x - 1, R = 6$ 20. $Q = 3x^3 - 5x^2 + 2x + 4, R = -6x - 6$ 21. $14x - 10$ 22. $54x + \frac{15}{2}$

EXERCISE 6 (i)

1. (i) $x^2 + 4x + 4$ (ii) $9x^2 + 30x + 25$ (iii) $\frac{9}{16}x^4 + \frac{15}{2}x^2 + 25$

2. (i) $y^2 - 18y + 81$ (ii) $49t^2 - 7ut + \frac{1}{4}u^2$ (iii) $25x^4 - 40x^2y^2 + 16y^4$

3. (i) $p^2 + 10p + 25$ (ii) $4t^2 + 36t + 81$ (iii) $25c^2 + 20cd + 4d^2$

(iv) $81m^2 + \frac{9}{2}m + \frac{1}{16}$ (v) $9x^2 + 2 + \frac{1}{9x^2}$ (vi) $4y^4 + 20y^2z^2 + 25z^4$

(vii) $49x^6 + 2x^3y^3 + \frac{1}{49}y^6$ (viii) $\frac{1}{4}a^8 + \frac{1}{3}a^4b^7 + \frac{1}{9}b^{14}$

4. (i) $t^2 - 6t + 9$ (ii) $81t^2 - 198t + 121$ (iii) $49p^2 - 112pq + 64q^2$

(iv) $64m^2 - 8m + \frac{1}{4}$ (v) $144x^2 - \frac{24}{5} + \frac{1}{25x^2}$ (vi) $9m^6 - 42m^3n^4 + 49n^8$

(vii) $x^6 - 2 + \frac{1}{x^6}$ (viii) $\frac{1}{25}p^{10} - \frac{1}{5}p^5q^6 + \frac{1}{4}q^{12}$

5. (i) $a^2 + 16a + 64$ (ii) $x^2 + 2x + 1$ (iii) $d^2 - 12d + 36$

(iv) $49 - 14y + y^2$ (v) $a^4 + 2a^2b^2 + b^4$ (vi) $m^4 - 2m^2n^2 + n^4$

(vii) $m^2x^2 - 2mnxy + x^2y^2$ (viii) $4a^2x^2 + 36axy + 81y^2$ (ix) $a^6b^2 - 2a^3bxy^3 + x^2y^6$

(x) $0.09x^2 + 2.4x + 16$ (xi) $\frac{1}{16}x^6 + x^3 + 4$ (xii) $\frac{9}{25}a^2 - 12ab + 100b^2$

(xiii) $\frac{1}{9}b^4 - 2b^2c^2 + 9c^4$ (xiv) $4x^4 + \frac{4}{3} + \frac{1}{9x^4}$ (xv) $25m^6 - 2 + \frac{1}{25m^6}$

EXERCISE 6 (j)

1. 10404 2. 2809 3. 251001 4. 651249 5. 502681 6. 3481 7. 2304

8. 39601 9. 487204 10. 998001 11. 5929 12. 247009 13. 4 14. 16

15. 142 16. 23; 527 17. 51 18. 66; 4354 19. 5; 727 20. 49 21. 56

EXERCISE 6 (k)

1. (i) $x^2 - 4$ (ii) $d^2 - 64$ (iii) $49 - p^2$

(iv) $16a^2 - 9b^2$ (v) $25 - 81m^2$ (vi) $a^2b^2 - 81$

(vii) $x^4 - y^4$ (viii) $\frac{4}{25}a^2b^2 - c^2$ (ix) $\frac{4}{b^2} - \frac{25}{c^2}$

2. (i) $a^4 - 1$ (ii) $a^4 - x^4$ (iii) $x^4 - \frac{1}{x^4}$ (iv) $x^{12} - \frac{1}{x^{12}}$

3. (i) 396 (ii) 4899 (iii) 9999 (iv) 1537 (v) 1280

(vi) 2400 (vii) 480 (viii) 11400

4. (i) 103 (ii) 93 5. (i) 31600 (ii) 2.48 (iii) 500 (iv) 400

MENTAL MATHS – 5

1. $12a$ 2. $-21m$ 3. $11x - 7y$ 4. $-15abc$ 5. $3t + 8$ 6. $15a^5$ 7. $-88ab^2c$

8. $-3p^3q^3r^4$ 9. 0 10. x^{100} 11. $14a^2 + 21a$ 12. $10x^3 - 35x^2y^2$ 13. $-3x^3y + 3xy^3$

14. $x^2 + 11x + 30$ 15. $6m^2 - 5mn - 6n^2$ 16. $7x^2y$ 17. $\frac{7}{3}p^2 - 2p + 4$ 18. $3ypq$

19. (i) $x^2 + 6x + 9$ (ii) $4x^2 - 12xy + 9y^2$ 20. (i) $x^2 + 16x + 64$ (ii) $9a^2 + 30ab + 25b^2$

(iii) $4x^2 - 49$ (iv) $\frac{25}{81}x^2 - \frac{1}{4}y^2$ 21. 361 22. 2600 23. 199 24. 13.6

MULTIPLE CHOICE QUESTIONS – 5

1. (iv) 2. (iv) 3. (iii) 4. (iii) 5. (ii) 6. (iii)

7. (ii) 8. (iii) 9. (iii) 10. (ii)

7. Factorisation of Algebraic Expressions

7.1. Introduction

You know that two or more numbers that are multiplied to form a product are called factors. For example, since $15 = 3 \times 5$, therefore, 3 is a factor of 15 and also 5 is a factor of 15. In Algebra, since $a(b + c) = ab + ac$, therefore, the polynomial $ab + ac$ has the factors a and $b + c$. A factor such as a is a **common monomial factor** of the terms ab and ac. Look at these examples :

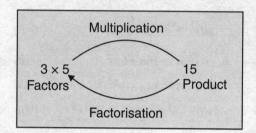

Finding products	Finding factors
$a(b + c) = ab + ac$	$ab + ac = a(b + c)$
$3(x + y) = 3x + 3y$	$3x + 3y = 3(x + y)$
$a(b + c + d) = ab + ac + ad$	$ab + ac + ad = a(b + c + d)$
$3x(4x^2 - 2x - 7) = 12x^3 - 6x^2 - 21x$	$12x^3 - 6x^2 - 21x = 3x(4x^2 - 2x - 7)$

In $3x + 3y$, 3 is the common monomial factor, and $x + y$ is the other factor. Notice that you usually do not factorise the number when you are factorising a polynomial. You do not need to write $10x + 10y$ as $2 \times 5(x + y)$.

7.2 Factorising a Given Algebraic Expression

Type 1. To factorise a polynomial whose terms have a common monomial factor.

Sample solutions :

Ex. 1. $7x - 7y = 7(x - y)$.   ⬡ Take out the common factor 7.

Ex. 2. $ac - bc + c = c(a - b + 1)$.   ⬡ Take out the common factor c.

Ex. 3. $6x^4 - 15x^3 + 3x^2 = 3x^2(2x^2 - 5x + 1)$.   ⬡ Take out the greatest common factor $3x^2$.

Ex 4. $4m^3n - 7m^2n^2 = m^2n(4m - 7n)$.   ⬡ Take out the greatest common factor m^2n.

EXERCISE 7 (a)

Factorise the following polynomials:

1. $3x - 12$
2. $80 + 16y$
3. $8x - 8y$
4. $7x + 14$
5. $a^2 + 7a$
6. $5y - 7y^2$
7. $8c^2 - 24c$
8. $5m^2 - 6m$
9. $12u - 20uv$
10. $10pq - 12p^2q$
11. $24d + 32d^3$
12. $30g + 54gh$
13. $28c^2d^2 - 21c^2d$
14. $36y^3z + 48y^2z^2$
15. $6p + 8p^2 - 4p^3$
16. $12a^3 - 15a^2 - 7a$
17. $15y^2z^3 - 20y^3z^4 + 35y^2z^2$
18. $14m^5n^4p^2 - 42m^7n^3p^7 - 70m^6n^4p^3$

Type 2. When the given algebraic expression contains common binomial factors.

Sample solutions :

Ex. 5. $b(b+d) - d(b+d) = (b+d)(b-d)$	The common binomial factor is $(b+d)$
Ex. 6. $y(y-3) + 7(y-3) = (y-3)(y+7)$	The common binomial factor is $(y-3)$
Ex. 7. $a(z^2+5) - (z^2+5) = a(z^2+5) - 1(z^2+5)$	$-(z^2+5)$ means $-1(z^2+5)$.
$= (z^2+5)(a-1)$	The common binomial factor is (z^2+5)

In working with common binomial factors, you should learn to recognize factors that are opposites of each other.

For example :

$$x - y = x + (-y) = -y + x = -(y-x).$$

$$\boxed{x - y = -(y-x)}$$

Ex. 8. $n(n-3) - 7(3-n)$	Notice that $n-3$ and $3-n$ are opposites.
$= n(n-3) - 7[-(n-3)]$ [Step 1]	After some practice you should be able
$= n(n-3) + 7(n-3)$ [Step 2]	to omit step 2 and write step 3 directly.
$= (n-3)(n+7).$ [Step 3]	

Ex. 9. $\dfrac{3b-3a}{7a-7b} = \dfrac{3(b-a)}{7(a-b)} = \dfrac{-3(a-b)}{7(a-b)} = -\dfrac{3}{7}$.

Ex. 10. $(x-2)^2 + 9(x-2) = (x-2)[(x-2)+9]$ $= (x-2)(x+7)$.

EXERCISE 7 (b)

Factorise the following polynomials:

1. $z(z-1) + 2(z-1)$	**2.** $6(3+x) + x(3+x)$	**3.** $2y(y+5) - 3(y+5)$	**4.** $5t(t-4) - 6(t-4)$
5. $5(2+b) - 6b(2+b)$	**6.** $x(x+11) + (x+11)$	**7.** $p(6-p) - (6-p)$	**8.** $d(d-5) + 7(5-d)$
9. $(x+2)^2 + 5(x+2)$	**10.** $(y-2)^2 - 3(y-2)$	**11.** $14(3y-5z)^3 + 7(3y-5z)^2$	
12. $(n-10)^2 + (10-n)$	**13.** $5x+10y - 7(x+2y)^2$	**14.** $(x+y)(3x-7) - (x+y)(2x-11)$	
15. $(3a-1)^2 - 6a + 2$	**16.** $x(x-2z) + y(x-2z) + (2z-x)$		

Type 3. By grouping suitable terms

Sometimes the terms of the given polynomial need to be arranged in suitable groups so that each group has a common factor.

Ex. 11. *Factorise :*

> By suitably rearranging the terms. To do so, you should work out mentally, what arrangement would give common binomial factor. Here we have shifted bc to a new position.

     (i) $a^2 + bc + ab + ac$ **(ii)** $p^2q - pr^2 - pq + r^2$

Sol.   (i) $a^2 + bc + ab + ac$ shift bc as shown.

     $= a^2 + ab + ac + bc = a(a+b) + c(a+b)$

     $= (a+b)(a+c).$

   (ii) $p^2q - pr^2 - pq + r^2$

> Here we have interchanged the positions of $-pq$ and $-pr^2$

     $= p^2q - pq - pr^2 + r^2 = pq(p-1) - r^2(p-1)$

     $= (p-1)(pq - r^2).$

EXERCISE 7 (c)

Factorise:

1. $ax^2 + by^2 + bx^2 + ay^2$
2. $a^2 + 2b + ab + 2a$
3. $px + qx + py + qy$
4. $x^3 + 3x^2 + 6x + 18$
5. $x^2 - ax - bx + ab$
6. $3ac + 2bc + 3ad + 2bd$
7. $8pr + 4qr + 6ps + 3qs$
8. $7ab + 9cb + 7ad + 9cd$
9. $3mn + 2pn + 3mq + 2pq$
10. $10pq - 3rq - 10ps + 3rs$
11. $ab^2 - bc^2 - ab + c^2$
12. $2b^2 + 8ab + 4ac + bc$
13. $6pm + 9mq + 8pn + 12qn$
14. $2axy^2 + 10x + 3ay^2 + 15$
15. $axy^2 + 3x + 2a^2y^2 + 6a$

7.3 Factorising Perfect Trinomial Squares

Method :

1. Determine whether the trinomial is a perfect square trinomial by the following rule :
   (a) Two terms must be perfect squares (usually the first and third terms) and must be preceded by plus signs.
   (b) The remaining term must be twice the product of the square roots of the perfect square terms.
2. If the trinomial is a perfect trinomial square, factorise as follows :
   (a) Find the square roots of the two perfect square terms.
   (b) Connect them with the sign of the remaining term.
   (c) Indicate that the binomial is to be used twice as a factor.
   Formulas : $a^2 + 2ab + b^2 = (a + b)^2$; $a^2 - 2ab + b^2 = (a - b)^2$

Sample solutions :

Ex. 1. $x^2 + 6x + 9 = x^2 + 2(3)x + 3^2 = (x + 3)(x + 3)$ or $(x + 3)^2$.

Ex. 2. $c^2 - 2cd + d^2 = (c - d)(c - d)$ or $(c - d)^2$.

Ex. 3. $4x^2 + 20xy + 25y^2 = (2x)^2 + 2(2x)(5y) + (5y)^2$
$= (2x + 5y)(2x + 5y)$ or $(2x + 5y)^2$.

Ex. 4. $49a^6 - 56a^3xy^2 + 16x^2y^4 = (7a^3)^2 - 2(7a^3)(4xy^2) + (4xy^2)^2$
$= (7a^3 - 4xy^2)(7a^3 - 4xy^2)$ or $(7a^3 - 4xy^2)^2$.

Ex. 5. $m^2 + 3m + \dfrac{9}{4} = m^2 + 2(m)\left(\dfrac{3}{2}\right) + \left(\dfrac{3}{2}\right)^2 = \left(m + \dfrac{3}{2}\right)\left(m + \dfrac{3}{2}\right)$ or $\left(m + \dfrac{3}{2}\right)^2$.

Remark. From the above, you can also find the **square root** of the given perfect trinomial square. Thus the square root of $x^2 + 6x + 9$ is $x + 3$, that of $c^2 - 2cd + d^2$ is $c - d$, that of $4x^2 + 20xy + 25y^2 = 2x + 5y$ and so on.

EXERCISE 7 (d)

A. Which are perfect trinomial squares ? Write Yes or No.

1. $a^2 + 10a + 16$
2. $b^2 + 14b - 49$
3. $x^2 - 5x + 4$
4. $x^2 + 10x + 25$
5. $c^2 - 2cd - d^2$
6. $81a^2 - 72ab + 16b^2$
7. $36d^2 + 13dx + x^2$
8. $4x^2 + 4x + 1$
9. $49m^2 + 140mn + 100n^2$
10. $16b^2 - 20by + 25y^2$
11. $25x^4 - 60x^2y^2 + 36y^4$

B. Fill in the missing term, making a perfect trinomial square :

12. $n^2 + ? + 49$
13. $x^2 - ? + 25$
14. $b^2 - ? + 9$
15. $? + 16x + 64$
16. $p^2 - 10pq + ?$
17. $? - 12x + 9$

C. Factorise the following trinomials :

18. $a^2 + 2a + 1$ **19.** $b^2 + 4b + 4$ **20.** $y^2 - 8y + 16$ **21.** $36 - 12r + r^2$

22. $81 + 18x + x^2$ **23.** $4c^2 + 4c + 1$ **24.** $9d^2 - 6d + 1$ **25.** $1 - 8ax + 16a^2x^2$

26. $16a^2 - 40ab + 25b^2$ **27.** $x^2 + 5x + \dfrac{25}{4}$ **28.** $49x^4 - 168x^2y^2 + 144y^4$

29. $a^2 + a + \dfrac{1}{4}$ **30.** $\dfrac{x^2}{4y^2} - \dfrac{2}{3} + \dfrac{4y^2}{9x^2}$ **31.** $\dfrac{x^2}{4y^2} - \dfrac{1}{3} + \dfrac{y^2}{9x^2}$

D. Find the square root of the following trinomials :

32. $9 + 6x + x^2$ **33.** $64 - 16y + y^2$ **34.** $144 + 24x + x^2$ **35.** $49y^2 - 56y + 16$

36. $64 - 176x + 121x^2$ **37.** $\dfrac{a^2}{b^2} + 2 + \dfrac{b^2}{a^2}$.

7.4 Factorising Difference of Two Squares

Formula: $a^2 - b^2 = (a+b)(a-b)$.

Method :

1. _Find the square roots of the two square terms._
2. _Write the sum of the two square roots as one of the factors._
3. _Write the difference of the two square roots as the other factor._

Caution: Two square terms with a plus sign between them (for example, $a^2 + b^2$) is the sum of two squares and cannot be factorised by the above method.

Ex. 1. _Factorise:_

(i) $x^2 - 16$ (ii) $9 - x^2$ (iii) $\dfrac{16}{81}m^2 - 121$ (iv) $64a^6 - 49b^2c^4$

(v) $49(2x + y)^2 - 64(x - 3y)^2$ (vi) $5 - 20x^2$

Type 1

Sol. (i) $x^2 - 16 = (x)^2 - 4^2 = (x + 4)(x - 4)$.

(ii) $9 - x^2 = (3)^2 - x^2 = (3 + x)(3 - x)$.

(iii) $\dfrac{16}{81}m^2 - 121 = \left(\dfrac{4}{9}m\right)^2 - (11)^2 = \left(\dfrac{4}{9}m + 11\right)\left(\dfrac{4}{9}m - 11\right)$.

(iv) $64a^6 - 49b^2c^4 = (8a^3)^2 - (7bc^2)^2 = (8a^3 + 7bc^2)(8a^3 - 7bc^2)$.

(v) $49(2x + y)^2 - 64(x - 3y)^2 = \left[7(2x + y)\right]^2 - \left[8(x - 3y)\right]^2$

$= (14x + 7y)^2 - (8x - 24y)^2$

$= (14x + 7y + 8x - 24y)(14x + 7y - 8x + 24y)$

(Note that because of the '–' sign before the bracket, –24y becomes + 24y).

$= (22x - 17y)(6x + 31y)$.

(vi) $5 - 20x^2 = 5(1 - 4x^2)$

$= 5\left[(1)^2 - (2x)^2\right]$

$= 5(1 + 2x)(1 - 2x)$.

> Always look for the common factor first. Here the common factor is 5

Type 2

Ex. 2. *Factorise:*

    (i) $b^4 - x^4$ **(ii)** $81x^4 - y^4$ **(iii)** $2x^4 - 32$.

Sol. (i) $b^4 - x^4 = (b^2)^2 - (x^2)^2$

$$= (b^2 + x^2)(b^2 - x^2) = (b^2 + x^2)(b + x)(b - x).$$

> **Caution:** Note that the expression in the second bracket *viz.* $b^2 - x^2$ is also a difference of two squares. Do not forget to factorise it.

(ii) $81x^4 - y^4 = (9x^2)^2 - (y^2)^2$

$$= (9x^2 + y^2)(9x^2 - y^2) = (9x^2 + y^2)\left[(3x)^2 - y^2\right]$$

$$= (9x^2 + y^2)(3x + y)(3x - y).$$

(iii) $2x^4 - 32 = 2(x^4 - 16) = 2\left[(x^2)^2 - 4^2\right]$

$$= 2(x^2 + 4)(x^2 - 4) = 2(x^2 + 4)(x + 2)(x - 2).$$

> First take out the common factor

Type 3

Ex. 3. *Factorise:*

    (i) $a^2 + 4b^2 - 4ab - 9c^2$ **(ii)** $16x^2 - 24yz - 9y^2 - 16z^2$

Sol. (i) $a^2 + 4b^2 - 4ab - 9c^2 = \left[a^2 - 2 \times 2a \times b + (2b)^2\right] - 9c^2$

$$= (a - 2b)^2 - (3c)^2 = (a - 2b + 3c)(a - 2b - 3c)$$

> You should be able to observe that the expression $a^2 + 4b^2 - 4ab$ is a perfect square trinomial

(ii) $16x^2 - 24yz - 9y^2 - 16z^2 = 16x^2 - (24yz + 9y^2 + 16z^2)$

$$= 16x^2 - \left[(3y)^2 + 2 \times 3y \times 4z + (4z)^2\right] = (4x)^2 - (3y + 4z)^2$$

$$= (4x + 3y + 4z)(4x - 3y - 4z).$$

EXERCISE 7 (e)

Factorise the following expressions :

1. $a^2 - 4$ **2.** $25 - x^2$ **3.** $9b^2 - 16$ **4.** $49p^2 - 16$ **5.** $a^2 - b^2$ **6.** $a^2x^2 - y^2$

7. $49c^2 - 25d^2$ **8.** $100 - r^2$ **9.** $49a^2 - 1$ **10.** $100b^2 - 81$ **11.** $x^2y^2 - 4$ **12.** $1 - d^2$

13. $b^4 - 100$ **14.** $25 - a^2x^2$ **15.** $144 - a^6$ **16.** $b^4 - a^2$ **17.** $a^2b^2 - y^2$ **18.** $\frac{1}{4}b^2 - 49$

19. $c^2 - 0 \cdot 36$ **20.** $x^2 - \frac{1}{9}$ **21.** $\frac{4}{25}m^2 - 64$ **22.** $\frac{x^2}{9} - \frac{y^2}{4}$ **23.** $\frac{36}{a^2} - \frac{25}{b^2}$ **24.** $x^2 - 0 \cdot 01$

25. $25(x + y)^2 - 36(x - 2y)^2$ **(Hint:** Give expression $= (5x + 5y)^2 - (6x - 12y)^2$)

26. $81 - (x - 7)^2$ **27.** $x^3 - x$ **28.** $18a^2x^2 - 32$ **29.** $3x^3y - 243xy^3$ **30.** $a^4 - 81$ **31.** $x^4 - y^4$

32. $a^4 - 16x^4$ **33.** $x^2 - y^2 + 2x + 1$ **34.** $x^2 + 4y^2 - z^2 - 4xy$ **35.** $100 - a^2 - b^2 - 2ab$

7.5 Factorising Trinomials of the Form x² + bx + c

Ex. 1. *Factorise :* $x^2 + 6x + 8$.

    Sol. First check to see if there is a common monomial factor. Since there is none, we can start factorising into the product of two binomials as follows :

First clue :	Since the product of the linear terms of the binomials must be x^2, therefore, the factors are of the form shown at the right.	$(x + ?) (x + ?)$
Second clue :	The product of the constant terms of the binomials must be 8. The factors of 8 are 1,2,4,8. Thus, the constant term should be 8×1 or 2×4. Of these, we choose that pair the sum of whose components gives the coefficient of the middle term 6. The sum of 2 and 4 is 6. Therefore, 2 and 4 are the second terms of binomials.	$(x \quad 2) (x \quad 4)$
Third clue :	The product of the constant terms of the binomials must be 8. Therefore, both constant terms must be positive numbers or both must be negative numbers. Hence, the only integral choices are 2, 4, or –2, –4. Since the middle term is $+6x$, we choose +2 and +4.	$(x + 2) (x + 4)$

Study the following also :   **Factors**

(i) $x^2 + 2x - 8$ $(x+4)(x-2)$

(ii) $x^2 - 2x - 8$ $(x-4)(x+2)$

In (i), since the product is negative, one constant term should be positive and the other negative.

Since the middle term is $+2x$, the greater constant term should be positive and the smaller negative. Therefore, we choose +4 and –2.

In (ii), since the middle term is $-2x$, the greater constant term should be negative, and the smaller positive. Therefore, we choose –4 and +2.

Ex. 2. *Factorise :* **(i)** $x^2 + 9x + 20$ **(ii)** $x^2 - 7x + 12$.

  Sol.   (i)   We have to find two numbers whose sum is +9 and the product is +20.

         These numbers are 5 and 4.

$$\text{Exp.} = x^2 + 9x + 20 = x^2 + 5x + 4x + 20$$
$$= x(x + 5) + 4(x + 5) = (x + 5) (x + 4)$$

    (ii)   We have to find two numbers whose product is 12 and the sum is –7. The numbers are –4 and –3.

$$\therefore \quad x^2 - 7x + 12 = x^2 - 4x - 3x + 12$$
$$= x(x - 4) - 3(x - 4) = (x - 4)(x - 3).$$

Ex. 3. *Factorise :* **(i)** $x^2 + 5x - 24$ **(ii)** $x^2 - 11x - 80$.

  Sol.   (i)   The two numbers, whose product is –24 and the sum is 5, are 8 and –3.

$$x^2 + 5x - 24 = x^2 + 8x - 3x - 24$$
$$= x(x + 8) - 3(x + 8)$$
$$= (x + 8)(x - 3).$$

> **Think !**
> Constant term is –24 which is negative. So one of the numbers will be –ve and another +ve. Since the coeff. of x is +5 which is +ve, therefore, the greater number will be +ve.

    (ii)   The two numbers whose product is –80 and the sum is –11, are –16 and +5.

$$\text{Exp.} = x^2 - 11x - 80 = x^2 - 16x + 5x - 80$$
$$= x(x - 16) + 5(x - 16) = (x - 16)(x + 5)$$

EXERCISE 7 (f)

Factorise :

1. $a^2 + 5a + 16$
2. $x^2 + 7x + 12$
3. $m^2 + 13m + 42$
4. $a^2 + 25a - 54$
5. $t^2 + 9t - 36$
6. $a^2 + 5a - 50$
7. $x^2 - 4x - 5$
8. $y^2 - 10y + 16$
9. $x^2 - 2x - 24$
10. $y^2 + 2y - 48$
11. $n^2 - 3n - 40$
12. $y^2 - 11y + 24$
13. $48 + 22x - x^2$
14. $c^2 - 18c + 65$
15. $x^2 - 29x + 204$
16. $p^2 - 5p - 176$
17. $n^2 - 19n - 92$
18. $j^2 - 11j - 102$
19. $2a^3 + 10a^2 - 28a$ **(Hint :** First take out the common factor $2a$.)
20. $12b + 15 - 3b^2$
21. $3c^5 - 18c^4 - 48c^3$
22. $-2y^3 + 22y^2 + 24y$
23. $b^2c^3 + 8bc^4 + 12c^5$
24. $a^4 - 5a^2 - 36$
25. $y^4 + 4y^2 - 32$

7.6 Factorising Trinomials of the Form ax² + bx + c

The difference in the two quadratic polynomials, $x^2 + bx + c$, considered so far and $ax^2 + bx + c$ which we will take up now, is that while in the first expression the coefficient of x^2 is 1, in the latter it is a. Now we will find two numbers such that

   (*i*)   Sum is equal to the coeffcient of x in the middle term.

  (*ii*)   Product is equal to $a\,c$, that is, equal to (coeff. of $x^2 \times$ constant term).

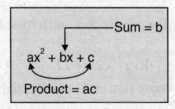

Ex. 1. *Factorise:* $2x^2 + 7x + 5$.

Sol. We have to find two numbers whose sum is 7 and the product is 2×5, that is, 10. The two numbers are 2 and 5.

$$\therefore \qquad \text{Given exp.} = 2x^2 + 7x + 5 = 2x^2 + 2x + 5x + 5$$
$$= 2x(x + 1) + 5(x + 1) = \textbf{(x + 1) (2x + 5)}.$$

Ex. 2. *Factorise :* $= 2x^2 + 9x - 5$

Sol.   Exp. $= 2x^2 + 9x - 5$

                    $= 2x^2 + 10x - x - 5$

                    $= 2x(x + 5) - 1(x + 5)$

                    $= \textbf{(x + 5) (2x - 1).}$

> **Think !**
> The two numbers whose sum is + 9 and the product $2 \times (-5)$ *i.e.,* –10, are 10 and –1

Ex. 3. *Factorise :* $12x^2 - x - 1$.

Sol.   Exp. $= 12x^2 - x - 1$

                    $= 12x^2 - 4x + 3x - 1$

                    $= 4x(3x - 1) + 1(3x - 1)$

                    $= \textbf{(3x - 1) (4x + 1).}$

> **Think !**
> The two numbers whose sum is –1 and the product is 12(–1), that is –12, are –4 and +3.

Ex. 4. *Factorise : $-5x^2 - x + 4$.*

Sol. Exp. $= -5x^2 - x + 4$.

$= -(5x^2 + x - 4)$

$= -(5x^2 + 5x - 4x - 4) = -[5x(x+1) - 4(x+1)]$

$= -(5x-4)(x+1)$.

> Change sign for the sake of convenience

Ex. 5. *Factorise : $12y^3 - 14y^2 - 10y$.*

Sol. Exp. $= 12y^3 - 14y^2 - 10y$.

$= 2y(6y^2 - 7y - 5)$

$= 2y(6y^2 - 10y + 3y - 5)$

$= 2y\{2y(3y-5) + 1(3y-5)\}$

$= 2y(3y-5)(2y+1)$.

> **Think !**
> $6 \times -5 = -30$
>
> | 2 | 30 |
> |---|----|
> | 3 | 15 |
> | | 5 |
>
> $-10 + 3 = -7$
> $-10 \times 3 = -30$

Ex. 6. *Factorise: $15x^4 + 3x^2 - 18$.*

Sol. Exp. $= 15x^4 + 3x^2 - 18 = 3(5x^4 + x^2 - 6)$

Take out the common factor 3

$= 3(5x^4 + 6x^2 - 5x^2 - 6)$

$= 3[x^2(5x^2 + 6) - 1(5x^2 + 6)]$

$= 3(5x^2 + 6)(x^2 - 1)$

can be factorised further

$= 3(5x^2 + 6)(x-1)(x+1)$.

EXERCISE 7 (g)

Factorise :

1. $4x^2 + 5x + 1$
2. $2x^2 + 11x + 14$
3. $2x^2 + 11x + 12$
4. $3x^2 + 13x + 4$
5. $2x^2 - 5x - 12$
6. $4x^2 + 8x - 5$
7. $13x^2 + 37x - 6$
8. $40n^2 + n - 6$
9. $4z^2 - 16z + 15$
10. $6 - 9c - 27c^2$
11. $1 - t - 6t^2$
12. $2a^2 + 7ab - 15b^2$
13. $4x^2 + 24x + 20$
14. $12a^2 + 2a - 4$
15. $12m^3 + 6m^2 - 6m$
16. $6x^5 - 22x^3 - 8x$
17. $6z^6 - 21z^4 - 12z^2$
18. $-12b^5 - b^3 + b$

LOOKING BACK

Summary of Key Facts

1. When an expression is the product of two or more expressions, then each of these expressions is called a **factor** of the given expression.

   e.g., (*i*) 5, x, y, $5x$, $5y$, xy are all factors of $5xy$.

   (*ii*) x and $(a+b)$ are factors of $x(a+b)$.

2. The process of writing a given algebraic expression as a product of two or more factors is called **factorisation**.

   e.g., factorising $x^2 + ax$ means writing it in the form $x(x+a)$.

3. The greatest common factor of two or more monomials is the product of the greatest common factors of the numerical coefficients and the common letters with smallest powers.

   e.g. greatest common factor of $16x^4y^9$ and $24x^7y^5$ is $8x^4y^5$.

4. A binomial may be factorised by taking out the greatest common factor of the terms of the binomial.

   e.g., $16x^4y^9 + 24x^7y^5 = 8x^4y^5(2y^4 + 3x^3)$.

5. When a binomial is a common factor, we factorise by writing the given expression as the product of this binomial and the quotient of the given expression by the binomial.

   e.g., $x(a+b) + y(a+b) = (a+b)(x+y)$.

6. If the given expression is the difference of two squares, we use the formula $a^2 - b^2 = (a+b)(a-b)$

   e.g., $16x^2 - 25y^2 = (4x)^2 - (5y)^2 = (4x+5y)(4x-5y)$.

7. If the given expression is a complete square, we use the following formulas:

   (i) $a^2 + 2ab + b^2 = (a+b)^2$ (ii) $a^2 - 2ab + b^2 = (a-b)^2$

   e.g., $4x^2 + 12xy + 9y^2 = (2x+3y)^2$, $64a^2 - 112ab + 49b^2 = (8a-7b)^2$.

MENTAL MATHS – 6

Factorise:

1. $x^2 + x$

2. $6x^2 + 12x$

3. $x^2y - yx^2$

4. $5x + 35$

5. $5(p+q) - 7q(p+q)$

6. $(x+3)y + (x+3)x$

7. $2p(y-x) + q(x-y)$

8. $9a^2 - 16b^2$

9. $100 - \dfrac{49}{16a^2}$

10. $3a^3 - 48a$

11. $9x^2 + 30x + 25$

12. $81m^2 - 18m + 1$

13. $x^2 + 16x + 63$

14. $x^2 - 3x - 40$

MULTIPLE CHOICE QUESTIONS – 6

1. $(r^2 - 3mn)(r^2 - 3mn)$ is equal to :

   (i) $r^2 - 9mn - 9m^2n^2$ (ii) $r^4 - 6mnr^2 + 9m^2n^2$ (iii) $r^4 + 6mn - 9m^2n^2$ (iv) $r^4 + 9mn + 9m^2n^2$

2. $(5m+4)(5m-4)(25m^2 + 16)$ is equal to :

   (i) $25m^2 - 256$ (ii) $625m^4 + 256$ (iii) $625m^4 - 256$ (iv) $625m^2 + 256$

3. If $x - \dfrac{1}{x} = 5$, then the value of $x^2 + \dfrac{1}{x^2}$ is :

   (i) 25   (ii) 27   (iii) 3   (iv) 23

4. The value of $\dfrac{12.4 \times 12.4 - 2.6 \times 2.6}{12.4 - 2.6}$ is equal to :

   (i) 9.8   (ii) 15   (iii) 322.4   (iv) 3.224

5. The value of $a^2 + b^2$ when $a - b = 5$ and $ab = 3$ is :

   (i) 19   (ii) 25   (iii) 31   (iv) 13

6. If one of the factors of the expression $x^2 - ax + 5x - 5a$ is $(x+5)$, the other factor is :

   (i) $(x-a)$ (ii) $(5-a)$ (iii) (x^2-5) (iv) $x+a$.

7. The factors of $x^2 + 9x - 36$ are :

   (i) $(x+12)$ and $(x+3)$ (ii) $(x-12)$ and $(x-3)$ (iii) $(x+12)$ and $(x-3)$ (iv) $(x-12)$ and $(x+3)$

8. $1 - (a-b)^2 = (1 + a - b) \times$?

   (*i*) $(1 - a - b)$ (*ii*) $(-1 + a - b)$ (*iii*) $(1 - a + b)$ (*iv*) $(1 + a + b)$

9. The factors of $2a^2 - 72b^2$ are :

   (*i*) $(2a - 6b)(a + 6b)$ (*ii*) $2(a - 6b)(a + 6b)$ (*iii*) $(2a - 9b)(a + 8b)$ (*iv*) $2(a + 4b)(a - 4b)$

10. The coefficient of mn, if $49m^2 + ?\ mn + 100\ n^2$ is a perfect square trinomial is :

   (*i*) 70   (*ii*) 140   (*iii*) 490   (*iv*) –70

ANSWERS

EXERCISE 7 (a)

1. $3(x-4)$ **2.** $16(5+y)$ **3.** $8(x-y)$ **4.** $7(x+2)$ **5.** $a(a+7)$ **6.** $y(5-7y)$

7. $8c(c-3)$ **8.** $m(5m-6)$ **9.** $4u(3-5v)$ **10.** $2pq(5-6p)$ **11.** $8d(3+4d^2)$ **12.** $6g(5+9h)$

13. $7c^2d(4d-3)$ **14.** $12y^2z(3y+4z)$ **15.** $2p(3+4p-2p^2)$ **16.** $a(12a^2-15a-7)$

17. $5y^2z^2(3z-4yz^2+7)$ **18.** $14m^5n^3p^2(n-3m^2p^5-5mnp)$

EXERCISE 7 (b)

1. $(z-1)(z+2)$ **2.** $(3+x)(6+x)$ **3.** $(y+5)(2y-3)$ **4.** $(t-4)(5t-6)$ **5.** $(2+b)(5-6b)$ **6.** $(x+11)(x+1)$

7. $(6-p)(p-1)$ **8.** $(d-5)(d+7)$ **9.** $(x+2)(x+7)$ **10.** $(y-2)(y-5)$ **11.** $7(3y-5z)^2(6y-10z+1)$

12. $(n-10)(n-11)$ **13.** $(x+2y)(5-7x-14y)$ **14.** $(x+y)(x+4)$

15. $(3a-1)(3a-3) = 3(3a-1)(a-1)$ **16.** $(x-2z)(x+y-1)$

EXERCISE 7 (c)

1. $(a+b)(x^2+y^2)$ **2.** $(a+2)(a+b)$ **3.** $(p+q)(x+y)$ **4.** $(x^2+6)(x+3)$ **5.** $(x-a)(x-b)$

6. $(3a+2b)(c+d)$ **7.** $(4r+3s)(2p+q)$ **8.** $(7a+9c)(b+d)$ **9.** $(3m+2p)(n+q)$ **10.** $(10p-3r)(q-s)$

11. $(ab-c^2)(b-1)$ **12.** $(2b+c)(b+4a)$ **13.** $(3m+4n)(2p+3q)$ **14.** $(2x+3)(ay^2+5)$ **15.** $(x+2a)(ay^2+3)$

EXERCISE 7 (d)

1. No   **2.** No   **3.** No   **4.** Yes   **5.** No   **6.** Yes

7. No   **8.** Yes   **9.** Yes   **10.** No   **11.** Yes   **12.** $14n$

13. $10x$ **14.** $6b$ **15.** x^2 **16.** $25q^2$ **17.** $4x^2$ **18.** $(a+1)^2$

19. $(b+2)^2$ **20.** $(y-4)^2$ **21.** $(6-r)^2$ **22.** $(9+x)^2$ **23.** $(2c+1)^2$ **24.** $(3d-1)^2$

25. $(1-4ax)^2$ **26.** $(4a-5b)^2$ **27.** $\left(x+\dfrac{5}{2}\right)^2$ **28.** $(7x^2-12y^2)^2$ **29.** $\left(a+\dfrac{1}{2}\right)^2$ **30.** $\left(\dfrac{x}{2y}-\dfrac{2y}{3x}\right)^2$

31. $\left(\dfrac{x}{2y}-\dfrac{y}{3x}\right)^2$ **32.** $(3+x)$ **33.** $(8-y)$ **34.** $(12+x)$ **35.** $(7y-4)$

36. $(8-11x)$ **37.** $\left(\dfrac{a}{b}+\dfrac{b}{a}\right)$

EXERCISE 7 (e)

1. $(a+2)(a-2)$ **2.** $(5+x)(5-x)$ **3.** $(3b+4)(3b-4)$ **4.** $(7p+4)(7p-4)$ **5.** $(a+b)(a-b)$

6. $(ax+y)(ax-y)$ **7.** $(7c+5d)(7c-5d)$ **8.** $(10+r)(10-r)$ **9.** $(7a+1)(7a-1)$ **10.** $(10b+9)(10b-9)$

11. $(xy+2)(xy-2)$ **12.** $(1+d)(1-d)$ **13.** $(b^2+10)(b^2-10)$ **14.** $(5+ax)(5-ax)$ **15.** $(12+a^3)(12-a^3)$

16. $(b^2+a)(b^2-a)$ **17.** $(ab+y)(ab-y)$ **18.** $\left(\dfrac{1}{2}b+7\right)\left(\dfrac{1}{2}b-7\right)$ **19.** $(c+0\cdot6)(c-0\cdot6)$ **20.** $\left(x+\dfrac{1}{3}\right)\left(x-\dfrac{1}{3}\right)$

21. $\left(\dfrac{2}{5}m+8\right)\left(\dfrac{2}{5}m-8\right)$ 22. $\left(\dfrac{x}{3}+\dfrac{y}{2}\right)\left(\dfrac{x}{3}-\dfrac{y}{2}\right)$ 23. $\left(\dfrac{6}{a}+\dfrac{5}{b}\right)\left(\dfrac{6}{a}-\dfrac{5}{b}\right)$ 24. $(x+0\cdot1)(x-0\cdot1)$ 25. $(11x-7y)(-x+17y)$

26. $(x+2)(-x+16)$ 27. $x(x+1)(x-1)$ 28. $2(3ax+4)(3ax-4)$ 29. $3xy(x+9y)(x-9y)$

30. $(a^2+9)(a+3)(a-3)$ 31. $(x^2+y^2)(x+y)(x-y)$ 32. $(a^2+4x^2)(a+2x)(a-2x)$

33. $(x+1+y)(x+1-y)$ 34. $(x-2y+z)(x-2y-z)$ 35. $(10-a-b)(10+a+b)$

EXERCISE 7 (f)

1. $(a+3)(a+2)$ 2. $(x+4)(x+3)$ 3. $(m+7)(m+6)$ 4. $(a+27)(a-2)$ 5. $(t+12)(t-3)$

6. $(a+10)(a-5)$ 7. $(x-5)(x+1)$ 8. $(y-8)(y-2)$ 9. $(x-6)(x+4)$ 10. $(y+8)(y-6)$

11. $(n-8)(n+5)$ 12. $(y-8)(y-3)$ 13. $(24-x)(2+x)$ 14. $(c-13)(c-5)$ 15. $(x-12)(x-17)$

16. $(p-16)(p+11)$ 17. $(n-23)(n+4)$ 18. $(j-17)(j+6)$ 19. $2a(a+7)(a-2)$ 20. $-3(b-5)(b+1)$

21. $3c^3(c-8)(c+2)$ 22. $-2y(y-12)(y+1)$ 23. $c^3(b+6c)(b+2c)$

24. $(a-3)(a+3)(a^2+4)$ 25. $(y-2)(y+2)(y^2+8)$

EXERCISE 7 (g)

1. $(4x+1)(x+1)$ 2. $(x+2)(2x+7)$ 3. $(2x+3)(x+4)$ 4. $(3x+1)(x+4)$ 5. $(2x+3)(x-4)$

6. $(2x+5)(2x-1)$ 7. $(13x-2)(x+3)$ 8. $(8n-3)(5n+2)$ 9. $(2z-5)(2z-3)$ 10. $3(1-3c)(2+3c)$

11. $(1+2t)(1-3t)$ 12. $(2a-3b)(a+5b)$ 13. $4(x+1)(x+5)$ 14. $2(2a-1)(3a+2)$ 15. $6m(2m-1)(m+1)$

16. $2x(x+2)(x-2)(3x^2+1)$ 17. $3z^2(z+2)(z-2)(2z^2+1)$ 18. $b(1-2b)(1-2b)(1+3b^2)$

MENTAL MATHS – 6

1. $x(x+1)$ 2. $6x(x+2)$ 3. $xy(x-y)$ 4. $5(x+7)$ 5. $(5-7q)(p+q)$

6. $(x+3)(y+x)$ 7. $(x-y)(-2p+q)$ 8. $(3a+4b)(3a-4b)$ 9. $\left(10+\dfrac{7}{4a}\right)\left(10-\dfrac{7}{4a}\right)$ 10. $3a(a+4)(a-4)$

11. $(3x+5)^2$ 12. $(9m-1)^2$ 13. $(x+9)(x+7)$ 14. $(x-8)(x+5)$

MULTIPLE CHOICE QUESTIONS – 6

1. (ii)   2. (iii)   3. (ii)   4. (ii)   5. (iii)
6. (i)   7. (iii)   8. (iii)   9. (ii)   10. (ii)

THINK ABOUT IT

1. A famous mathematician named Lagrange stated a theorem that all whole numbers could always be split into square numbers.

   Thus $24 = 16 + 4 + 4$; $35 = 25 + 9 + 1$

   Now try yourself

   Split the following numbers into square numbers.

   (i) 29   (ii) 37   (iii) 47   (iv) 52   (v) 59

2. Lagrange also stated that there are no numbers which need more than four square numbers. Try to contradict this statement if you can. A new theorem will then be named after you.

PUZZLE

What two perfect squares when subtracted equal another perfect square ?   (**Ans.** 25, 16)

8. Linear Equations

8.1 Introduction

$4x - 3$ and $2x + 5$ are *algebraic expressions*. x is called a *variable* as it can up take any value.

An algebraic expression becomes an equation when it *equals* something. For example $4x - 3 = 2x + 5$ is an equation. Unlike an algebraic identity, here x will take only one value which shall make the statement true. In this particular case, that value of x is 2. *Thus, that value of the variable which makes on equation true is called the solution to the equation.*

Methods of Solving a Linear Equation

A. An equation may be simplified and solved by :
- ■ *adding* the same number to **both** the sides.
- ■ *subtracting* the same number from **both** sides.
- ■ *multiplying both* sides by the same number.
- ■ *dividing both* sides by the same number.

Thus, we see that to keep an equation balanced, we have to do the same thing to both the sides.

B. The **rule of transposition** states that any term can be transposed from one side of an equation to the other by changing its sign. $(+ \text{ to } -, - \text{ to } +, \times \text{ to } \div, \div \text{ to } \times)$

For example : $\dfrac{5}{x} = x - 2$ can be solved by both the methods A and B as follows :

Method A	**Method B**	
$\dfrac{5x}{6} = x - 2$	$\dfrac{5x}{6} = x - 2$	
$\dfrac{5x}{6} \times 6 = 6 \times (x - 2)$	$\dfrac{5x}{6} - x = -2$	+x becomes −x
$5x = 6x - 12$	$\dfrac{5x - 6x}{6} = -2$	(LCM of LHS = 6)
$5x - 6x = 6x - 6x - 12$	$-\dfrac{x}{6} = -2$	$\dfrac{1}{6}$ becomes 6
$-x = -12$	$-x = -2 \times 6$	
$x = \mathbf{12}$	$-x = -12 \implies x = \mathbf{12}$	

Ex. 1. *Solve :* $8x - 11 - 5x + 3 = 2x + 4 - 3x$.

Sol. Transposing all the terms containing x to the left side and all the constant terms to the right we get,

$$8x - 5x - 2x + 3x = 4 + 11 - 3$$

> Signs of the terms are changed when taken from one side to the other.

or $\qquad\qquad 4x = 12 \qquad \therefore \qquad x = \dfrac{12}{4} = \mathbf{3.}$

113

Ex. 2. *Solve :* $\dfrac{3x}{4} + \dfrac{x}{6} = 22$

Sol. L.C.M of 4 and 6 = 12. Multiplying all the terms on both sides by 12, we get

$$12 \times \dfrac{3x}{4} + 12 \times \dfrac{x}{6} = 12 \times 22 \qquad \Rightarrow \qquad 9x + 2x = 264$$

$$\Rightarrow \qquad\qquad 11x = 264 \qquad \Rightarrow \qquad x = \dfrac{264}{11} = \textbf{24.}$$

Check : $\qquad$ L.H.S $= \dfrac{3 \times 24}{4} + \dfrac{24}{6} = 18 + 4 = 22 = $ RHS

Ex. 3. *Solve :* $\dfrac{x-3}{5} + \dfrac{x-4}{7} = 6 - \dfrac{2x-1}{35}.$

Sol. L.C.M. of 5, 7 and 35 = 35. Therefore, multiplying both sides of the equation by 35, we get,

$$35 \times \left(\dfrac{x-3}{5}\right) + 35 \times \left(\dfrac{x-4}{7}\right) = 35 \times 6 - 35 \times \left(\dfrac{2x-1}{35}\right)$$

$$\Rightarrow \qquad 7(x-3) + 5(x-4) = 210 - (2x-1)$$
$$\Rightarrow \qquad 7x - 21 + 5x - 20 = 210 - 2x + 1$$
$$\Rightarrow \qquad 7x + 5x - 21 - 20 = 210 + 1 - 2x$$
$$\Rightarrow \qquad\qquad 12x - 41 = 211 - 2x$$
$$\Rightarrow \qquad\qquad 12x + 2x = 211 + 41$$
$$\Rightarrow \qquad\qquad 14x = 252 \qquad \Rightarrow \qquad x = \dfrac{252}{14} = \textbf{18.}$$

Ex. 4. *Solve : 1.32y + 0.02y = 1.19 + y*

Sol. $1.32y + 0.02y = 1.19 + y$
$$\Rightarrow \qquad\qquad 1.34y = 1.19 + y$$
$$\Rightarrow \qquad\qquad 1.34y - y = 1.19$$
$$\Rightarrow \qquad\qquad 0.34y = 1.19 \qquad \Rightarrow \qquad y = \dfrac{1.19}{0.34} = \dfrac{119}{34} = \dfrac{7}{2}$$
$$\therefore \qquad\qquad y = \textbf{3}\dfrac{1}{2}.$$

Ex. 5. *Solve :* $\dfrac{3x+2}{4x+11} = \dfrac{4}{7}$

Sol. $\dfrac{3x+2}{4x+11} = \dfrac{4}{7}$ By cross-multiplication, we have

$$7(3x+2) = 4(4x+11)$$
$$\Rightarrow \qquad 21x + 14 = 16x + 44 \qquad \Rightarrow \qquad 21x - 16x = 44 - 14$$
$$\Rightarrow \qquad\qquad 5x = 30 \qquad\qquad \therefore \qquad x = \dfrac{30}{5} = \textbf{6}$$

$\dfrac{ax+b}{cx+d} \begin{matrix} = \\ \diagdown\diagup \end{matrix} \dfrac{p}{q}$

Ex. 6. *Solve :* $\dfrac{m-3}{m+4} = \dfrac{m+1}{m-2}.$

Sol. By cross-multiplication we have
$$(m-3)(m-2) = (m+1)(m+4)$$
$$\Rightarrow \qquad m^2 - 5m + 6 = m^2 + 5m + 4$$

$\dfrac{m-3}{m+4} \begin{matrix} \diagup \\ \diagdown \end{matrix} \dfrac{m+1}{m-2}$

$$\Rightarrow \qquad m^2 - 5m - m^2 - 5m = 4 - 6$$

$$\Rightarrow \qquad\qquad -10m = -2 \qquad \therefore \quad m = \frac{-2}{-10} = \frac{1}{5}.$$

Ex. 7. *Solve* : $\dfrac{x^2 - 9}{5 + x^2} = \dfrac{-5}{9}$ *for positive value of x.*

Sol. $\dfrac{x^2 - 9}{5 + x^2} = \dfrac{-5}{9}$

Cross - multipliying, we get

$$9(x^2 - 9) = -5(5 + x^2)$$

$$\Rightarrow \qquad 9x^2 - 81 = -25 - 5x^2 \Rightarrow 9x^2 + 5x^2 = -25 + 81$$

$$\Rightarrow \qquad\qquad 14x^2 = 56 \Rightarrow x^2 = \frac{56}{14} = 4 = (\pm 2)^2 \quad \therefore \quad \boldsymbol{x = 2} \quad \text{(Taking the positive value)}$$

Ex. 8. *Solve* : $\dfrac{(x + 2)(2x - 3) - 2x^2 + 6}{x - 5} = 2$.

Sol. $\qquad\qquad (x + 2)(2x - 3) = x(2x - 3) + 2(2x - 3)$

$$\qquad\qquad\qquad\qquad\qquad = 2x^2 - 3x + 4x - 6 = 2x^2 + x - 6 \qquad\qquad\qquad \dots (1)$$

The given equation is

$$\frac{(x + 2)(2x - 3) - 2x^2 + 6}{x - 5} = 2 \quad \Rightarrow \quad \frac{2x^2 + x - 6 - 2x^2 + 6}{x - 5} = 2$$

$$\Rightarrow \qquad\qquad\qquad \frac{x}{x - 5} = \frac{2}{1}$$

Cross multiplying, $1 \times x = 2(x - 5) \quad \Rightarrow \quad x = 2x - 10 \quad \Rightarrow \quad x - 2x = -10$

$$\Rightarrow \qquad\qquad\qquad -x = -10 \Rightarrow \boldsymbol{x = 10}.$$

EXERCISE 8 (a)

Solve the following equations and check your answer :

1. (*i*) $10p - (3p - 4) = 4(p + 1) + 9$ (*ii*) $7 + 2(a + 1) - 3a = 5a$ (*iii*) $4(x + 3) - 2(x - 1) = 3x + 3$

2. (*i*) $\dfrac{x}{2} = 8$ (*ii*) $\dfrac{x}{3} - 5 = 8$ (*iii*) $\dfrac{t + 8}{3} = t$

3. (*i*) $4y + \dfrac{y}{5} = 21$ (*ii*) $\dfrac{2m}{3} + \dfrac{3m}{4} = 17$ **4.** $\dfrac{2}{3}\left(x + \dfrac{3}{5}\right) = \dfrac{7}{2}$ **5.** $\dfrac{x + 3}{7} - \dfrac{2x - 5}{3} = \dfrac{3x - 5}{5} - 25$

6. $\dfrac{x + 3}{2} - \dfrac{3x + 1}{4} = \dfrac{2(x - 2)}{3} - 2$ **7.** $\dfrac{3x - 2}{10} - \dfrac{x + 3}{7} + \dfrac{4x - 7}{3} = x - 1$ **8.** $2.8v = 54 + v$

9. $0.26x + 0.09x = 8 - 0.45x$ **10.** $\dfrac{1}{6}(4y + 5) - \dfrac{2}{3}(2y + 7) = \dfrac{3}{2}$

Solve the following equations :

11. $\dfrac{3}{x + 1} = \dfrac{5}{2x}$ **12.** $\dfrac{6}{3m + 1} = \dfrac{9}{5m - 3}$ **13.** $\dfrac{2x + 3}{5} = \dfrac{4x + 9}{11}$

14. $\dfrac{9x-5}{7} = \dfrac{6x+2}{5}$

15. $\dfrac{5x-7}{3x} = 2$

16. $\dfrac{0.4z-3}{1.5z+9} = \dfrac{7}{5}$

17. $\dfrac{x-2}{x-4} = \dfrac{x+4}{x-2}$

18. $\dfrac{y-2}{y-5} = \dfrac{y+3}{y+5}$

19. $\dfrac{2y-4}{3y+2} = -\dfrac{2}{3}$ $\quad \left(\textbf{Hint:} \text{Write } -\dfrac{2}{3} \text{ as } \dfrac{-2}{3} \right)$

20. $\dfrac{\dfrac{x}{4} - \dfrac{3}{5}}{\dfrac{4}{3} - 7x} = -\dfrac{3}{20}$

21. $\dfrac{(2x+3) - (5x-7)}{6x+11} = \dfrac{-8}{3}$

22. $\dfrac{17(2-x) - 5(x+12)}{1-7x} = 8$

23. $\dfrac{(4+x)(5-x)}{(2+x)(7-x)} = 1$

24. $\dfrac{x^2 - (x+1)(x+2)}{5x+1} = 6$

25. **Solve and give the positive value of x which satisfies the given equation :**

$$\dfrac{y^2+4}{3y^2+7} = \dfrac{1}{2}.$$

8.2 Applications of Linear Equations to Practical Problems

You have already learnt in earlier classes how to solve some real life problems by converting them into linear equations in one variable. Here we will take up more problems of a slightly higher level.

Recall that to solve such problems we denote the unknown quantity by x and from the given relation, construct a linear equation in x.

8.3 Type 1. Problems on Numbers

Ex. 1. *Find three consecutive odd numbers whose sum is 45.*

Sol. Let the three consecutive odd numbers be $2x + 1$, $2x + 3$, $2x + 5$. Then

$$(2x + 1) + (2x + 3) + (2x + 5) = 45 \quad \Rightarrow \quad 6x + 9 = 45$$

$$\Rightarrow \quad 6x = 45 - 9 = 36 \quad \therefore \quad x = \frac{36}{6} = 6$$

So the required numbers are $2 \times 6 + 1$, $2 \times 6 + 3$, $2 \times 6 + 5$, *i.e.,* **13, 15 and 17.**

Check : $13 + 15 + 17 = 45$.

Ex. 2. *One number is 3 times another number. If 15 is added to both the numbers, then one of the new numbers becomes twice that of the other new number. Find the numbers.*

Sol. Let one number be x. Then the other number $= 3x$

By the given condition, one number $+15 = 2$ (other number $+15$)

i.e., $\quad 3x + 15 = 2(x + 15) \qquad \Rightarrow \qquad 3x + 15 = 2x + 30$

$\Rightarrow \quad 3x - 2x = 30 - 15 \qquad \Rightarrow \qquad x = 15.$

Hence, one number is **15** and the other number is $3 \times 15 = $ **45.**

Ex. 3. *Sum of the digits of a two-digit number is 9. The number obtained by interchanging the digits exceeds the given number by 27. Find the given number.*

Sol. Let the unit's digit be x; Then ten's digit $= (9 - x)$

Number formed by these digits $= 10 \times$ ten's digit $+$ unit's digit $= 10(9 - x) + x = 90 - 9x$

When the digits are interchanged, unit's digit becomes $9 - x$ and ten's digit becomes x.

$\therefore$ Number formed on interchanging the digits $= 10x + (9 - x) = 9x + 9$.

It is given that new number exceeds the given number by 27

i.e., new number – given number = 27

T	U	Number
$9 - x$	x	$10(9 - x) + x$
x	$9 - x$	$10x + (9 - x)$

i.e. $(9x + 9) - (90 - 9x) = 27$

$\Rightarrow \quad 9x + 9 - 90 + 9x = 27 \Rightarrow 18x - 81 = 27$

$\Rightarrow \quad 18x = 27 + 81 \Rightarrow 18x = 108 \quad \therefore \ x = \dfrac{108}{18} = 6.$

$\therefore$ Required number $= (90 - 9x) = 90 - 9 \times 6 = 90 - 54 = \textbf{36.}$

Check : Sum of the digits = 3 + 6 = 9

Number obtained on interchanging the digits = 63; We have, 63 – 36 = 27.

Ex. 4. *The denominator of a rational number is greater than its numerator by 8. If the numerator is increased by 17 and the denominator is decreased by 1, the number obtained is* $\dfrac{3}{2}$*. Find the rational number.*

Sol. Let the numerator be x then the denominator $= x + 8$

$\therefore$ Required rational number $= \dfrac{x}{x+8}$

New rational number $= \dfrac{\text{Numerator} + 17}{\text{Denominator} - 1} = \dfrac{x+17}{(x+8)-1} = \dfrac{x+17}{x+7}$

It is given that new rational number $= \dfrac{3}{2} \quad \therefore \ \dfrac{x+17}{x+7} = \dfrac{3}{2}$

$\Rightarrow \quad 2(x + 17) = 3(x + 7) \quad \Rightarrow \quad 2x + 34 = 3x + 21$

$\Rightarrow \quad 2x - 3x = 21 - 34 \quad \Rightarrow \quad -x = -13 \Rightarrow x = 13.$

$\therefore$ Reqd. rational number $= \dfrac{x}{x+8} = \dfrac{13}{13+8} = \dfrac{\textbf{13}}{\textbf{21}}.$

8.4 Type 2. Age Related Problems

Ex. 5. *Kiran is 24 years older than Rakesh. 10 years back Kiran's age was five times the age of Rakesh. Find their ages.*

Sol. Let Kiran's present age be x years.

Then Rakesh's present age $= (x - 24)$ years.

10 years ago, Kiran's age = (present age – 10) years = $(x - 10)$ years

Also, 10 years ago, Rakesh's age = $\{(x - 24) - 10\}$ years = $(x - 34)$ years

Given : 10 years ago, Kiran's age = 5 times Rakesh's age

$\therefore \quad x - 10 = 5(x - 34) \Rightarrow x - 5x = -170 + 10 \Rightarrow \quad -4x = -160 \quad \therefore x = \dfrac{-160}{-4} = 40.$

Therefore, Kiran's age is **40** years and Rakesh's age is (40 – 24) or **16 years.**

Ex. 6. *The ages of Ravi and Hema are in the ratio 5 : 7. Four years later, their ages will be in the ratio 3 : 4. Find their ages.*

Sol. Let Ravi's present age be $5x$ years and that of Hema be $7x$ years.

4 years later, Ravi's age = $(5x + 4)$ years, Hema's age = $(7x + 4)$ years.

By the given condition, $(5x + 4) : (7x + 4) = 3 : 4$

or $\dfrac{5x+4}{7x+4} = \dfrac{3}{4} \Rightarrow 4(5x + 4) = 3(7x + 4) \Rightarrow 20x + 16 = 21x + 12$

$\Rightarrow 20x - 21x = 12 - 16 \Rightarrow -x = -4 \Rightarrow x = 4.$

$\therefore$ Ravi's age = $5 \times 4 = $ **20 years**, Hema's age = $7 \times 4 = $ **28 years.**

8.5 Type 3. Problems on Mensuration

Ex. 7. *The width of Sudha's garden is $\dfrac{2}{3}$ of its length. If its perimeter is 40 m, find its dimensions.*

Sol.   Let the length of the garden be x m. Then, width = $\dfrac{2}{3} x$ m.

Perimeter = 2 (length + width) = $2\left(x + \dfrac{2}{3}x\right)$

$\therefore$ Equation is $2x + 2\left(\dfrac{2x}{3}\right) = 40 \Rightarrow 2x + \dfrac{4x}{3} = 40$ Given : Perimeter is 40 m.

$\Rightarrow 6x + 4x = 120 \Rightarrow 10x = 120 \therefore x = \dfrac{120}{10} = 12$ Clear off fractions.

$\therefore$ Length is **12 m** and width is $\dfrac{2}{3} \times 12 = $ **8 m.**

Ex. 8. *Each side of a triangle is increased by 10 cm. If the ratio of the perimeters of the new triangle and the given triangle is 5 : 4, find the perimeter of the given triangle.*

Sol.   Let sides of the given triangle be a, b, c. Then perimeter of the triangle = $a + b + c = x$ (say)

Perimeter of the new triangle = $(a + 10) + (b + 10) + (c + 10) = (a + b + c) + 30 = (x + 30)$.

By given condition, $(x + 30) : x = 5 : 4 \Rightarrow \dfrac{x+30}{x} = \dfrac{5}{4} \Rightarrow 4(x + 30) = 5x$

$\Rightarrow 4x + 120 = 5x \Rightarrow 4x - 5x = -120 \Rightarrow -x = -120 \Rightarrow x = 120.$

$\therefore$ Perimeter of the given triangle = $x = $ **120 cm.**

Ex. 9. *The perimeter of a rectangle is 240 cm. If its length is decreased by 10% and its breadth is increased by 20%, we get the same perimeter. Find the length and breadth of the rectangle.*

Sol.   Given perimeter = 240, *i.e.*, $2(l + b) = 240 \Rightarrow l + b = 120$ cm.   Perimeter = 2(length + breadth

Let length of the rectangle be x cm. Then, breadth of the rectangle = $(120 - x)$ cm

The length is decreased by 10%, so new length = $x - x \times \dfrac{10}{100} = x - \dfrac{x}{10} = \dfrac{9x}{10}$ cm.

Breadth is increased by 20%, so new breadth is

$(120 - x) + (120 - x) \times \dfrac{20}{100} = (120 - x) + (120 - x) \times \dfrac{1}{5}$

Short-cut		
Length	=	$\dfrac{90}{100}x$
Breadth	=	$\dfrac{120}{100}(120 - x)$

$= \dfrac{5(120 - x) + (120 - x)}{5} = \dfrac{600 - 5x + 120 - x}{5} = \dfrac{720 - 6x}{5}$ cm

By the condition, perimeter remains the same, *i.e.*, 240 cm

So, $2\left(\dfrac{9x}{10} + \dfrac{720 - 6x}{5}\right) = 240 \Rightarrow \dfrac{9x}{10} + \dfrac{720 - 6x}{5} = 120$

$\Rightarrow \qquad 9x + 1440 - 12x = 120 \times 10$

$\Rightarrow \quad 1440 - 3x = 1200 \Rightarrow -3x = 1200 - 1440 \Rightarrow -3x = -240 \Rightarrow x = \dfrac{-240}{-3} = 80.$

$\therefore \qquad$ Length of the rectangle $= x = $ **80 cm** and breadth $= 120 - x = 120 - 80 = $ **40 cm.**

8.6 Type 4. Problems on Speed, Time and Distance

Ex. 10. *A car travelling at 60 km/hr left Dehradun at 3 P.M. One hour later another car travelling at 80 km/hr started over the same road to overtake the first. How long must the second car travel ?*

Sol. Let the second car overtake the first, x hours after it started. First car travelled for $(x + 1)$ hours and distance covered by both the cars is the same.

Distance covered by 1st car in $(x + 1)$ hours $= 60(x + 1)$ km $\qquad \boxed{\text{Distance} = \text{Speed} \times \text{Time}}$

Distance covered by 2nd car in x hours $= 80x$ km

$\therefore \quad 60(x + 1) = 80x \Rightarrow 60x + 60 = 80x \Rightarrow 60 = 80x - 60x = 20x \therefore x = \dfrac{60}{20} = \mathbf{3}.$

Hence, the second car travelled for **3 hours.**

Ex. 11. *A motor boat covers a certain distance downstream in a river in five hours. It covers the same distance upstream in five hours and a half. Find the speed of the boat in still water.*

Sol. Let the speed of the boat $= x$ km/hr.

Then speed of the boat downstream $= (x + 1.5)$ km/hr and speed of the boat upstream
$\qquad = (x - 1.5)$ km/hr

Distance covered by the boat downstream in 5 hours $= (x + 1.5) \times 5 = (5x + 7.5)$ km

$\qquad\qquad\qquad\qquad\qquad\qquad\qquad\qquad\qquad \boxed{\text{Distance} = \text{Speed} \times \text{time}}$

Distance covered by the boat upstream in $5\dfrac{1}{2}$, *i.e.*, $\dfrac{11}{2}$ hours $= (x - 1.5) \times \dfrac{11}{2} = \dfrac{11x - 16.5}{2}$ km

By the given condition $5x + 7.5 = \dfrac{11x - 16.5}{2} \Rightarrow 2(5x + 7.5) = 11x - 16.5$

$\Rightarrow \quad 10x + 15 = 11x - 16.5 \Rightarrow 10x - 11x = -16.5 - 15 \Rightarrow -x = -31.5 \Rightarrow x = 31.5$

$\therefore \quad$ Speed of the boat $= x = $ **31.5 km/hr.**

8.7 Other Problems

Ex. 12. *Saurabh can finish a work in 18 hours while Vinod can complete the same work in 24 hours. How long will it take them together to complete this work if Saurabh is called away for 2 hours while Vinod continues with the work?*

Sol. Suppose Vinod continues with the work for x hours.

Then Saurabh is available to do the work for $(x - 2)$ hours.

$\therefore \quad$ Work done by Saurabh in 1 hr $= \dfrac{1}{18} \Rightarrow$ Work done by Saurabh in $(x - 2)$ hrs $= \dfrac{x - 2}{18}$

Similarly, work done by Vinod in x hrs. $= \dfrac{x}{24}$

Work done by them together $= \dfrac{x - 2}{18} + \dfrac{x}{24}$

Since the whole work which is completed can be taken as 1, therefore,

$\dfrac{x - 2}{18} + \dfrac{x}{24} = 1 \Rightarrow 72 \times \dfrac{x - 2}{18} + 72 \times \dfrac{x}{24} = 72 \times 1 \Rightarrow 4x - 8 + 3x = 72$ $\qquad \boxed{\begin{array}{l}\text{To clear off the fractions multiply} \\ \text{by the LCM of 18, 24 } i.e., 72\end{array}}$

$\Rightarrow 7x = 72 + 8 = 80 \therefore \quad x = \dfrac{80}{7} = 11\dfrac{3}{7}$ hours.

Hence, together, they can finish the work in $11\frac{3}{7}$ hours.

Ex.13. *Prema receives a certain amount of money on her retirement from her employer. She gives half of this money and an additional sum of Rs 10,000 to her daughter. She also gives one third of the money received and an additional sum of Rs 3000 to her son. If the daughter gets twice as much as the son, find the amount of money Prema received on her retirement.*

Sol. Let the amount of money received by Prema be Rs x.

Money given to her daughter $= \text{Rs} \left(\dfrac{x}{2} + 10000 \right) = \text{Rs} \left(\dfrac{x + 20000}{2} \right)$

Money given to her son $= \text{Rs} \left(\dfrac{x}{3} + 3000 \right) = \text{Rs} \left(\dfrac{x + 9000}{3} \right)$

By the given condition, daughter's share $=$ twice the son's share

$\therefore \quad \dfrac{x + 20000}{2} = 2\left(\dfrac{x + 9000}{3} \right) = \dfrac{2x + 18000}{3}$ | Multiplying both sides by L.C.M. of 2 and 3, *i.e.*, 6 |

$\Rightarrow 3(x + 20000) = 2(2x + 18000) \Rightarrow 3x + 60000 = 4x + 36000 \Rightarrow 3x - 4x = 36000 - 60000$

$\Rightarrow -x = -24000 \Rightarrow x = 24000.$

$\therefore$ Amount of money received by Prema $=$ **Rs 24000.**

EXERCISE 8 (b)

1. The greater of two numbers is 12 more than the smaller and the sum of the two numbers is 10. Find the numbers.

2. One number is 5 times another. If 18 is subtracted from the greater, the remainder will be 3 times the smaller. Find the numbers.

3. (*i*) Find three consecutive numbers whose sum is 108.

   (*ii*) Find three consecutive odd numbers whose sum is 93.

   (*iii*) Find three consecutive even numbers whose sum is 246.

   (*iv*) The sum of three consecutive multiples of 7 is 777. Find these multiples.

   (**Hint :** Let the numbers be $7x$, $7x + 7$ and $7x + 14$)

4. Divide 534 into three parts such that the second part will be 32 less than twice the first, and the third will be 18 more than the first.

5. Three times the smallest of three consecutive odd numbers decreased by 7 equals twice the largest one. Find the numbers.

6. One number is 7 more than another and its square is 77 more than the square of the smaller number. What are the numbers?

7. The square of the greater of two consecutive even numbers exceeds the square of the smaller by 36. Find the numbers.

8. The denominator of a fraction is 3 more than the numerator. If 5 is added to both parts, the resulting fraction is equivalent to $\frac{4}{5}$. Find the fraction.

9. The difference between two positive integers is 50 and the ratio of these integers is 1:3. Find these integers.

10. The sum of the digits of a two-digit number is 7. The number obtained by interchanging the digits exceeds the original number by 27. Find the number.

11. Sushma is now 15 years older than Vijay but in 3 more years she will be 8 times as old as Vijay was 3 years ago. How old are they now?

12. Mary is 3 times as old as Bhawna, and the sum of their ages 5 years from now will be twice Mary's present age. How old are they now?

13. Sanjay is now $\frac{1}{2}$ as old as his brother. In 6 more years he will be $\frac{3}{5}$ as old as his brother then. What is the present age of each boy?

14. (*a*) If the area is $3x$ cm^2, make an equation, and find x. (*b*) If the perimeter is 40 cm, make an equation, and find x.

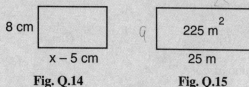

Fig. Q.14   Fig. Q.15

15. $4(x - 2)$ metres of rope is used to fence this rectangular enclosure. Find x.

16. Madhu's flower garden is now a square. If she enlarges it by increasing the width 1 metre and the length 3 metres, the area will be 19 sq metres more than the present area. What is the length of a side now?

17. The sides (other than hypotenuse) of a right triangle are in the ratio 3 : 4. A rectangle is described on its hypotenuse, the hypotenuse being the longer side of the rectangle. The breadth of the rectangle is four-fifth of its length. Find the shortest side of the right triangle, if the perimeter of the rectangle is 180 cm.

(**Hint :** Hypotenuse = $\sqrt{\text{sum of squares of sides}}$ = $\sqrt{(3x)^2 + (4x)^2}$ = $\sqrt{25x^2} = 5x$

∴ Breadth of the rectangle = $\frac{4}{5}(5x) = 4x$ Now, use perimeter of the rectangle = 2(length + breadth)

= $2(5x + 4x) = 180$ given).

18. Two cars leave Delhi at the same time, travelling in opposite directions. If the average speed of one car is 5 km/h more than that of the other and they are 425 km apart at the end of 5 hrs, what is the average speed of each?

19. Two automobiles start out at the same time from cities 595 km apart. If the rate of one is $\frac{8}{9}$ of the rate of the other and if they meet in 7 hours, what is the rate of each?

20. A motorboat goes downstream in a river and covers the distance between two coastal towns in five hours. It covers this distance upstream in six hours. If the speed of the stream is 2 km/h, find the speed of the boat in still water.

21. A steamer, going downstream in a river, covers the distance between two towns in 20 hours. Coming back upstream, it covers this distance in 25 hours. The speed of water is 4 km/h. Find the distance between the two towns.

(**Hint :** First find the speed of the steamer in still water.)

22. Ranjana's mother gave her Rs 245 for buying New Year cards. If she got some 10-rupee cards, $\frac{2}{3}$ as many 5 rupee cards, and $\frac{1}{5}$ as many 15-rupee cards, how many of each kind did she buy?

23. A painter can paint a building in 4 days and his apprentice can do it in 6 days. How long will it take them to paint this building if they work together on it except for 1 day when the painter is ill and the apprentice works alone?

24. The enrolment in a school this year is 552. This is an increase of 15% over last year's enrolment. How many were enrolled last year?

25. A fruit vendor buys some oranges at the rate of Rs 5 per orange. He also buys an equal number of bananas at the rate of Rs 2 per banana. He makes a 20% profit on oranges and a 15% profit on bananas. At the end of the day, all the fruit is sold out. His total profit is Rs 390. Find the number of oranges purchased.

MULTIPLE CHOICE QUESTIONS – 7

1. The solution of the equation $10 - 5(x + 2) = 7x$ is :

    (*i*) 5   (*ii*) –2   (*iii*) 0   (*iv*) 7

2. When $5 = \frac{2}{3}(2x - 1)$, the value of x is :

    (*i*) $\frac{7}{2}$ (*ii*) –1   (*iii*) $\frac{17}{4}$ (*iv*) 4

3. The root of the equation $0.3x + 5 = 0.7x - 3$ is :
    (i) 10   (ii) 3.2   (iii) 20   (iv) 1.5

4. If $x - \dfrac{(x-1)}{3} = \dfrac{x+1}{4}$, then the value of x is :

    (i) -5 (ii) $-\dfrac{1}{5}$ (iii) 1   (iv) $\dfrac{2}{5}$

5. If $\dfrac{3b}{10} - \dfrac{2b}{15} = \dfrac{2}{3}$, then the value of b is :
    (i) 4   (ii) -2 (iii) 3   (iv) 0

6. The three consecutive odd integers whose sum is 45 are :
    (i) 11, 13, 15   (ii) 13, 15, 17   (iii) 15, 17, 19   (iv) 17, 19, 23

7. The length of a rectangle is 7 times its width. If the perimeter of the rectangle is 208 cm, its length is :
    (i) 80 cm   (ii) 91 cm   (iii) 76 cm   (iv) 104 cm

8. A boy gets 3 marks for each correct sum and loses 2 marks for each incorrect sum. He does 24 sums and obtains 37 marks. The number of correct sums were :
    (i) 20   (ii) 17   (iii) 31   (iv) 19

9. When a certain number is added to the numerator and denominator of $\dfrac{9}{17}$, the new fraction is $\dfrac{5}{7}$. The number is :
    (i) 10   (ii) 9   (iii) 11   (iv) -1

10. Reema is one seventh as old as here cousin. In 8 years she will be one third as old as her cousin. Their present ages are :
    (i) 5 years, 35 years   (ii) 4 years, 28 years   (iii) 6 years, 42 years   (iv) 2 years, 14 years

ANSWERS

EXERCISE 8 (a)

1. (i) $p = 3$ (ii) $a = \dfrac{3}{2}$ (iii) $x = 11$ 2. (i) $x = 16$ (ii) $x = 39$ (iii) $t = 4$

3. (i) $y = 5$ (ii) $m = 12$ 4. $x = 4\dfrac{13}{20}$ 5. $x = 25$ 6. $x = 5$ 7. $x = 4$ 8. $v = 30$

9. $x = 10$ 10. $y = -8$ 11. $x = 5$ 12. $m = 9$ 13. $x = 6$ 14. $x = 13$ 15. $x = -7$

16. $z = -9.18$ 17. $x = 5$ 18. $y = -1$ 19. $y = \dfrac{2}{3}$ 20. $x = -\dfrac{1}{2}$ 21. $x = -\dfrac{118}{39}$ 22. $x = 1$

23. $x = \dfrac{3}{2}$ 24. $x = -\dfrac{8}{33}$ 25. $y = 1$

EXERCISE 8 (b)

1. $-1, 11$ 2. $9, 45$ 3. (i) 35, 36, 37   (ii) 29, 31, 33   (iii) 80, 82, 84   (iv) 252, 259, 266

4. 137, 242, 155   5. 15, 17, 19   6. 2, 9   7. 8, 10   8. $\dfrac{7}{10}$ 9. 25, 75   10. 25

11. 21 years, 6 years   12. 5 years, 15 years   13. 12 years, 24 years

14. (a) $x = 8$ (b) $x = 17$ 15. $x = 19$ 16. 4m   17. 30 cm.   18. 40 km/hr, 45 km/hr

19. 45 km/hr, 40 km/hr   20. 22 km/hr   21. 800 km

22. 15 of 10 rupees each, 10 of 5 rupees each, 3 of 15 rupees each   23. 3 days   24. 480   25. 300

MULTIPLE CHOICE QUESTIONS – 7

1. (iii)   2. (iii)   3. (iii)   4. (ii)   5. (i)   6. (ii)   7. (ii)

8. (ii)   9. (iii)   10. (ii)

UNIT III : RAIO AND PROPORTION

9. Percentage and its Application

9.1 Introduction

The word per cent is often heard about in our daily life in the form of reduction in prices during 'sales', examination result of a student, increase in wages and discounts etc.

The words '**per cent**', symbolically written as **%** means '**in every hundred**' or **per hundred**. Thus 40% means '40 in every hundred.'

9.2 Percentages, Fractions and Decimals

Percentages, Fractions and Decimals are linked to each other, 20% can be written as the fraction $\frac{20}{100}$ or as the decimal 0.2.

- *To change a percentage to a fraction, write it as a fraction with a denominator 100 and simplify if possible. To change it to a decimal, change the fraction so obtained to a decimal.*

Ex. $30\% = \dfrac{30}{100} = \dfrac{3}{10} = 0.3$ $225\% = \dfrac{225}{100} = \dfrac{9}{4} = 2.25$

              ↑   ↑   ↑   ↑

           Fraction   Decimal   Fraction   Decimal

- *To change fractions and decimals to percentages, multiply by 100.*

Ex. $0.64 = 0.64 \times 100\,\% = 64\%$, $\dfrac{3}{20} = \dfrac{3}{20} \times 100\% = 15\%$

- *To find a percentage of a quantity, change the percentage to a fraction or a decimal and multiply it by the quantity.*

$$25\% \text{ of Rs } 80 = \frac{25}{100} \times \text{Rs } 80 = \textbf{Rs } 20.$$

9.3 Percentage Increase and Decrease

- **To increase a quantity** by a percentage find the percentage of the quantity and add it to the original quantity.

Ex. 1. *Increase 320 by 20%.*

Sol.   20% of 320 $= \dfrac{20}{100} \times 320 = 64$

∴   Increased amount = Rs 320 + Rs 64 = **Rs 384.**

- **To decrease a quantity** by a percentage, find the percentage of the quantity and subtract it from the original quantity.

Ex. 2. *Decrease Rs 120 by $12\frac{1}{2}\%$.*

Sol. $12\frac{1}{2}\%$ of $120 =$ Rs $\frac{12.5}{100}$ of $120 =$ Rs $\frac{125}{10\times100}\times120 =$ Rs 15

∴ Decreased amount = Rs 120 – Rs 15 = **Rs 105.**

9.4 To Find one Quantity as a Percentage of the Other

Method   **1.** _Write the two quantities as a fraction._

             2. _Multiply by 100%_

Ex. 3. _Express 30 cm as a per cent of 2 m 40 cm._

Sol. 2 m 40 cm = 240 cm   ∴ Reqd. % = $\frac{30}{240}\times100\% =$ **12.5%.**

9.5 Percentage Change

$$\text{Percentage change} = \left(\frac{\text{Actual change (Increase or Decrease)}}{\text{Original quantity}}\times100\right)\%$$

$$\text{Percentage error} = \left(\frac{\text{error}}{\text{actual value}}\times100\right)\%$$

Ex. 4. _Rita's weight decreased from 80 kg to 60 kg. Find the percentage decrease._

Sol. Decrease in weight = (80 – 60) kg = 20 kg.

∴ % decrease = $\frac{20}{80}\times100\% =$ **25%.**

Ex. 5. _The distance between two places was 200 km. It was measured as 280km. Find the percentage error._

Sol. Error = 280 km – 200 km = 80 km.

∴   % error = $\frac{\text{error}}{\text{actual value}}\times100\% = \frac{80}{200}\times100 =$ **40%.**

9.6 Finding the Original Amount Before a Percentage Change

Ex. 6. _The cost of a train ticket from New Delhi to Dehradun has risen by 20% to Rs 600. What was the original price of the ticket?_

Sol. Let the original price be Rs x.

∴ Increase in price = 20% of Rs $x =$ Rs $\frac{20}{100}$ of $x =$ Rs $\frac{x}{5}$

∴ Increased price = original price + increase in price = Rs $x +$ Rs $\frac{x}{5} =$ Rs $\frac{6x}{5}$.

Given, new cost of the ticket = Rs 600.   ∴ $\frac{6x}{5} = 600 \Rightarrow x = \frac{600\times5}{6} =$ Rs 500

∴ Original price was **Rs 500.**

EXERCISE 9 (a)

1. **Write these percentages as fractions and decimals :**

     (_i_)   60%   (_ii_)   240%   (_iii_) $12\frac{1}{2}\%$ (_iv_) $55\frac{2}{3}\%$

2. **Write these numbers as percentages :**

     (_a_) $\frac{3}{4}$ (_b_) $\frac{21}{40}$ (_c_)   0.008   (_d_)   0.375   (_e_)   1.07

3. Express the following percentage as ratios:

   (a) 200%   (b) $6\frac{2}{3}\%$ (c) 75%   (d) $33\frac{1}{3}\%$

4. Express the following ratios as percentage:

   (a) 1 : 2   (b) 7 : 10   (c) 21 : 25   (d) 5 : 12

5. Evaluate :

   (i) 19% of Rs 4200   (ii) 75% of 440 kg   (iii) 30% of 20 g   (iv) 2.5% of 350 m

6. Express the first quantity as a percentage of the second :

   (i) 20 g of 4 kg   (ii) 200 ml of 5 litres   (iii) 48 cm of 1m   (iv) $\frac{2}{3}$ of $\frac{1}{2}$

7. (i) If 14% of a certain number is 63, find the number.

   (ii) If $12\frac{1}{2}\%$ of a certain amount is Rs 62.50, find the amount.

8. There were 4200 people at a concert and 1400 of these were female. What percentage were male?

9. The cost of a theatre ticket is increased by 40% for a special movie. What is the new price if the normal price was Rs 160.

10. A motorcycle originally cost Rs 40,000. Its value has decreased by 22%. What is its value now?

11. The price of a garment has been reduced by 15% in a sale to Rs 306. Find its original price.

12. A piece of elastic was stretched by 24% to a length of 31 cm. Find its unstretched original length.

9.7 Some More Solved Examples

Ex. 1. *In a class, 80 students passed and the rest failed. If 80% of the students failed, find the number of students in the class.*

Sol. 80% of the students failed ⇒ 20% of the students passed. Then

20% of total number of students in the class = 80 ⇒ $\frac{20}{100}$ × Total no. of students = 80

⇒   Total no. of students = $\frac{80 \times 100}{20}$ = **400.**

Hence the total number of students in the class is **400.**

Ex. 2. *Two candidates A and B contest an election. A gets 46% of the valid votes and is defeated by 1600 votes. Find the total number of valid votes cast in the election.*

Sol. A gets 46% of the valid votes ⇒ B gets (100 – 46)% = 54% of the valid votes.

   ∴   % difference between the votes = 54% – 46% = 8%.

   ∴   8% of valid votes = 1600 ⇒ $\frac{8}{100}$ × valid votes = 1600 ⇒ valid votes = $\frac{1600 \times 100}{8}$ = **20000.**

Hence the number of valid votes cast in the election were **20,000.**

Ex. 3. *Gun powder contains 75% nitre and 10% sulphur. The rest of its charcoal. Find the amount of charcoal in 9 kg of gun-powder.*

Sol. Amount of nitre in 9 kg of gun-powder

$$= 75\% \text{ of } 9 \text{ kg} = \frac{75}{100} \times 9 \text{ kg} = \frac{27}{4} \text{ kg} = \textbf{6.75 kg}$$

Amount of sulphur in 9 kg of gun-powder

$$= 10\% \text{ of } 9 \text{ kg} = \frac{10}{100} \times 9 \text{ kg} = \frac{9}{10} \text{ kg} = \textbf{0.9 kg}$$

Since the rest is charcoal, therefore,

Amount of charcoal in 9 kg of gun-powder

$$= 9 \text{ kg} - (6.75 + 0.90) \text{ kg} = 9 \text{ kg} - 7.65 \text{ kg} = 1.35 \text{ kg}$$

Alternatively :

Amount of charcoal $= 15\% \text{ of } 9 \text{ kg} = \frac{15}{100} \times 9 \text{ kg} = 1.35 \text{ kg}$

Ex. 4. *An alloy of tin and copper consists of 15 parts of tin and 105 parts of copper. Find the percentage of copper in the alloy.*

Sol. Since the alloy contains 15 parts of tin and 105 parts of copper

$$\therefore \quad \text{Percentage of tin} = \frac{15}{15+105} \times 100\% = \frac{15}{120} \times 100\% = \frac{25}{2}\% = \textbf{12.5\%}$$

$$\text{Percentage of copper} = \frac{105}{120} \times 100\% = \frac{175}{2}\% = \textbf{87.5\%}$$

Alternatively, Percentage of copper $= (100 - 12.5)\% = 87.5\%$

Ex. 5. *My income was increased by 10% and later decreased by 10%. What is the total change in per cent in my income.*

Sol. Let my income be Rs 100.

10% increase means that my income becomes Rs 110.

$$\text{Decreased income} = \text{Rs } 110 - \text{Rs } \frac{10}{100} \times 110 = \text{Rs } 110 - \text{Rs } 11 = \text{Rs } 99.$$

$$\therefore \quad \% \text{ change in income} = \frac{\text{change in income}}{\text{original income}} \times 100\% = \frac{\text{Rs } 100 - \text{Rs } 99}{\text{Rs } 100} \times 100\% = \textbf{1\%}.$$

Ex. 6. *In an examination, a candidate A scores 30% and fails by 40 marks while another candidate B scores 40% and gets 20 marks more than the minimum pass marks. Find the maximum marks and minimum pass marks.*

Sol. Let the maximum marks be x.

$$\therefore \quad \text{Pass marks for } A = 30\% \text{ of } x + 40 = \frac{30x}{100} + 40$$

$$\text{Pass marks for } B = 40\% \text{ of } x - 20 = \frac{40x}{100} - 20$$

$\because$ Pass marks for both the cases are same

$$\therefore \quad \frac{30x}{100} + 40 = \frac{40x}{100} - 20 \Rightarrow \frac{40x}{100} - \frac{30x}{100} = 40 + 20 \Rightarrow \frac{10x}{100} = 60 \Rightarrow x = 600$$

$$\therefore \quad \text{Maximum marks} = 600 \text{ and Pass marks} = \frac{30}{100} \times 600 + 40 = \textbf{220 marks.}$$

(We can find pass marks using any of the statements *i.e.* for A or for B.)

Ex. 7. *Raj has some apples. He sold 40% more than he ate. If he sold 70 apples, how many did he eat?*

Sol. Let x be the number of apples he ate.

$$\therefore \quad \text{He sold 40\% more than he ate means he sold } x + \frac{40}{100} x \text{ apples} = x + \frac{2}{5}x = \frac{7x}{5} \text{ apples.}$$

Given : Apples sold $= 70$ ∴ $\dfrac{7x}{5} = 70 \Rightarrow x = \dfrac{70 \times 5}{7} = 50$.

∴ Hence he ate **50 apples.**

Ex. 8. *A man gives 40% of his money to his children and 20% of the remaining to a trust. If he is still left with Rs 9600, what did he originally have?*

Sol. Let the original amount of money with him be Rs 100

∵ 40% of the original money is given to children,

∴ Remaining money $=$ Rs 100 – Rs 40 = Rs 60

Money given to trust $= 20\%$ of remaining = Rs $\dfrac{20}{100} \times 60 =$ Rs 12

∴ Remaining money $=$ Rs 60 – Rs 12 = Rs 48

It is given that remaining money = Rs 9600.

When remaining money is Rs 48, original money = Rs 100

When remaining money is Re 1, original money = Rs $\dfrac{100}{48}$

∴ When remaining money is Rs 9600, original money = Rs $\dfrac{9600 \times 100}{48}$ = **Rs 20,000**

∴ The man originally had Rs **20,000.**

EXERCISE 9 (b)

1. A man whose income is Rs 576 a year spends Rs 432 a year. What percentage of his income does he save ?

2. If 70% of the students in a school are boys and the number of girls is 540, find the number of boys in the school?

3. An alloy consists of 13 parts of copper to 7 parts of zinc and 5 parts of nickel. What is the percentage composition of the alloy?

4. The population of a town increases by 10% annually. If the present population is 22000, find its population a year ago.

5. Manoj's income increased by 20% and then decreased by 20%. What is the total percentage change in Manoj's income?

6. Sameer gets Rs 800 as his pocket money every month. If this is increased by 10%, how much will he get?

7. In an examination Piyush secured 490 marks. If he secured 70% marks, find the maximum marks.

8. Calculations show that an angle is $37\dfrac{1}{2}°$. The size obtained by drawing and measurement is 35°. Find the error percent.

9. Chalk contains 10% calcium, 3% carbon and 12% oxygen. Find the amount (in grams) of each of these compounds in 1 kg of chalk.

10. A candidate scored 25% marks in an examination and failed by 30 marks, while another candidate who scored 50% marks got 20 marks more than the minimum pass marks. Find the maximum marks and minimum pass marks.

11. There are 120 girls and 57 boys in a school. If 5% of the girls leave and no new pupils are admitted, what percentage of the whole school will be boys?

12. In an election, a candidate got 65% of the total valid votes. 8% of the total votes were declared invalid. If the total number of votes cast were 6,00,000, find the number of valid votes polled in favour of the candidate.

13. The sides of a rectangle are 20 cm and 15 cm. If each side of the rectangle is increased by 20%, find the percentage increase in the area.

14. In an examination 2500 students appeared out of which 1100 were girls. 50% of the boys and 40% of the girls passed the examination. What percentage of candidates failed in the examination?

15. An electric supply company raises its charges by 20% and a year later increases the new charges by 20%. If the total increase had been made all at once, to what percentage would it have been equivalent.

PROFIT AND LOSS

9.8 Introduction

In earlier classes, you have learnt about percentage and its application in problems related to profit and loss. In this chapter we will take up more problems on profit and loss and discount.

9.9 Quick Review

1. Cost price (C.P.) is the amount at which a shopkeeper buys his goods.
2. Selling price (S.P.) is the amount at which a shopkeeper sells his goods.
3. **Profit or gain = S.P. – C.P.**
   A loss is made when the selling price is less than the cost price.
   Loss = C.P. – S.P.
4. Profit or loss per cent is calculated on cost price and not on selling price.
5. $\text{Gain}\% = \left(\dfrac{\text{Gain} \times 100}{\text{C.P.}}\right)$, $\text{Loss}\% = \left(\dfrac{\text{Loss} \times 100}{\text{C.P.}}\right)$
6. $\text{S.P.} = \left(\dfrac{100 + \text{Gain}\%}{100}\right) \times \text{C.P.}$, $\text{S.P.} = \dfrac{100 - \text{Loss}\%}{100} \times \text{C.P.}$
7. $\text{C.P.} = \left(\dfrac{100}{100 + \text{Gain}\%}\right) \times \text{S.P.}$, $\text{C.P.} = \left(\dfrac{100}{100 - \text{Loss}\%}\right) \times \text{S.P.}$
8. If an article is sold at a gain of 10%, then S.P. = 110% of C.P.
   If an article is sold at a loss of 10%, then S.P. = 90% of C.P.
9. **Overheads :** If there are some additional expenses incurred on transportation, repair etc. of an article purchased, they are included in the cost price of the article and are called **overheads.**
10. If C.P. and S.P. are given for different number of articles, first find C.P. and S.P. of equal number of articles and then calculate profit and loss percentage.

9.10 Solved Examples

Ex. 1. *An article was bought for Rs 1500 and sold for 2000. Find the gain and gain %.*

Sol. C.P. = Rs 1500, S.P. = Rs 2000 ∵ C.P. < S.P. ∴ it is a gain

Gain = S.P. – C.P. = Rs (2000 – 1500) = **Rs 500**

$\text{Gain}\% = \dfrac{\text{Gain}}{\text{C.P.}} \times 100 = \dfrac{500}{1500} \times 100 = 33\dfrac{1}{3}\%$.

Ex. 2. *Asha bought a cycle for Rs 720 and sold it for Rs 698.40 find the loss%.*

Sol. C.P. = Rs 720, S.P. = Rs 698.40 ∵ C.P. > S.P. ∴ it is a loss

Loss = C.P. – S.P. = Rs (720 – 698.40) = Rs 21.60

∴ $\text{Loss}\% = \left(\dfrac{\text{Loss}}{\text{C.P.}} \times 100\right)\% = \dfrac{21.60}{720} \times 100 = \textbf{3\%}.$

Ex. 3. *A shopkeeper buys 300 bicycles at Rs 1500 per bicycle. He spends Rs 75 per bicycle on transportation. He also spends Rs 7500 on advertising. Then he sells all the bicycles at Rs 1700 per piece. Find his profit or loss. Also calculate it as a percentage.*

Sol. Cost price of 300 bicycles at Rs 1500 per piece = 300 × Rs 1500 = Rs 4,50,000

Total Amount spent on transportation of bicycles = $300 \times$ Rs 75 = Rs 22,500

Amount spent on advertising = Rs 7500

$\therefore$ Cost price of the 300 bicycles = Rs 4,50,000 + $\underbrace{\dfrac{\text{Rs } 22500 + \text{Rs } 7500}{}}_{\text{Overheads}}$ = Rs 4,80,000

Selling price of 300 bicycles at Rs 1700 per piece = $300 \times$ Rs 1700 = Rs 5,10,000.

$\because$ S.P. > C.P., it is a profit.

Profit = S.P. – C.P. = Rs 5,10,000 – Rs 4,80,000 = **Rs 30000**

Profit% = $\dfrac{\text{Profit}}{\text{C.P.}} \times 100 = \dfrac{30000}{4,80,000} \times 100 = \dfrac{25}{4}\% = 6\dfrac{1}{4}\%$.

Ex. 4. *If the C.P. of 10 articles is equal to the S.P. of 12 articles. Find the gain or loss %.*

Sol. Let the C.P. of 1 article = Re 1, $\therefore$ C.P. of 12 articles = Rs 12

S.P. of 12 articles = C.P. of 10 articles = Rs 10

$\because$ S.P. < C.P., it is a loss

Loss = C.P. – S.P. = Rs 12 – Rs 10 = Rs 2

$\therefore$ Loss % = $\left(\dfrac{\text{Loss}}{\text{C.P}} \times 100\right) = \dfrac{2}{12} \times 100 = 16\dfrac{1}{3}\%$.

Ex. 5. *If a person sells an article for Rs 400 gaining $\dfrac{1}{4}$ of its C.P., find the gain per cent.*

Sol. Let the C.P. of the article be Rs 100. Then Gain = $\dfrac{1}{4}$ of C.P. = Rs $\dfrac{1}{4} \times$ Rs 100 = Rs 25

$\therefore$ Gain % = $\dfrac{\text{Gain}}{\text{C.P}} \times 100 = \left(\dfrac{25}{100} \times 100\right)\% = \mathbf{25\%}.$

Ex. 6. *12 bananas are bought for Rs 10 and 10 bananas are sold for Rs 12. Find the gain % or loss %.*

Sol. Suppose number of bananas = 120   (LCM of 10 and 12 = 120)

C.P. of 12 bananas = Rs 10, $\therefore$ C.P. of 120 bananas = Rs $\dfrac{10}{12} \times 120$ = Rs 100

S.P. of 10 bananas = Rs 12, $\therefore$ S.P. of 120 bananas = Rs $\dfrac{12}{10} \times 120$ = Rs 144

$\because$ S.P. of 120 bananas > C.P. of 120 bananas, $\therefore$ it is a gain

Gain = S.P. – C.P. = Rs 144 – Rs 100 = Rs 44

$\therefore$ Gain % = $\left(\dfrac{\text{Gain}}{\text{C.P}} \times 100\right)\% = \left(\dfrac{44}{100} \times 100\right)\% = \mathbf{44\%}.$

Ex. 7. *Toffees are bought at the rate of 7 for a rupee and sold at the rate of 5 for a rupee. Find the gain per cent?*

Sol. (L.C.M of 7 and 5) = 35. Suppose there are 35 toffees which are bought at rate of 7 for a rupee and sold at the rate of 5 for rupee.

$\therefore$ C.P. of 35 toffees = Rs $\dfrac{35}{7}$ = Rs 5, S.P. of 35 toffees = Rs $\dfrac{35}{7}$ = Rs 7

$\because$ S.P. > C.P., it is a gain and Gain = S.P. – C.P. = Rs 2

$$\therefore \quad \text{Gain\%} = \left(\frac{\text{Gain}}{\text{C.P.}} \times 100\right)\% = \left(\frac{2}{5} \times 100\right)\% = \textbf{40\%}.$$

Ex. 8. *A television set was purchased for Rs 3200 and Rs 560 were spent on its repairs. Then it was sold at a gain of $12\frac{1}{2}\%$. How much did the seller receive?*

Sol. C.P. of the television set = Rs 3200 + Rs 560 (overheads) = Rs 3760.

Gain $= 12\frac{1}{2}\% = \frac{25}{2}\%$. $\quad \therefore$ If C.P. = Rs 100, then S.P. = Rs $\left(100 + \frac{25}{2}\right) =$ Rs $\frac{225}{2}$

If C.P. is Rs 100, then S.P. = Rs $\frac{225}{2}$

If C.P. is Re 1, then S.P = Rs $\frac{225}{2} \times \frac{1}{100}$

If C.P. is Rs 3760, then S.P. = Rs $\frac{225}{2} \times \frac{1}{100} \times 3760 =$ **Rs 4230.**

Alternative Method

$$\text{S.P.} = \frac{(100 + \text{Gain \%})}{100} \times \text{C.P.} = \text{Rs} \frac{\left(100 + \frac{25}{2}\right)}{100} \times 3760 = \frac{225}{200} \times 3760 = \textbf{Rs 4230.}$$

Ex. 9. *What is the cost price of an article which is sold at a loss of 25% for Rs 150?*

Sol. Let the C.P. Rs 100, Then S.P. = Rs 75.

When the S.P. is Rs 75, C.P. = Rs 100

$\therefore$ When the S.P. is Rs 150, C.P. = Rs $\frac{100}{75} \times 150 =$ **Rs 200.**

Alternative Method :

$$\text{C.P.} = \frac{100}{(100 - \text{Loss\%})} \times \text{S.P.}$$

$$= \text{Rs} \frac{100}{(100 - 25)} \times 150 = \text{Rs} \frac{100}{75} \times 150$$

$$= \textbf{Rs 200.}$$

Ex. 10. *By selling a washing machine for Rs 11400, a dealer loses 5%. For how much should he sell this machine to gain 5%?*

Sol. First we find the C.P. If the S.P. is Rs 95 then C.P. is Rs 100

$\therefore$ If the S.P. is Rs 11,400, then C.P. is Rs $\frac{100}{95} \times 11,400 =$ Rs 12000

Now, if the C.P. is Rs 100, then S.P. is Rs 105

$\therefore$ If the C.P. is Rs 12000, then S.P. is Rs $\frac{105}{100} \times 12,000 =$ Rs 12,600

Therefore, to gain 5% he should sell the machine for **Rs 12,600.**

Alternative Method

S.P. = Rs 11,400, Loss = 5%

$\therefore \quad$ C.P. $= \frac{100}{(100 - \text{loss\%})} \times \text{S.P.} = \text{Rs} \frac{100}{(100 - 5)} \times 11,400 = \text{Rs} \frac{100}{95} \times 11,400 = \textbf{Rs 12,000}$

Now, $\quad$ C.P. = Rs 12,000, Gain = 5%

$\therefore \quad$ S.P. $= \frac{(100 + \text{Gain\%})}{100} \times \text{C.P.} = \text{Rs.} \frac{(100 + 5)}{100} \times 12,000 = \text{Rs} \frac{105}{100} \times 12,000 = \textbf{Rs 12,600}$

Ex. 11. *A man sold two articles for Rs 2970 each, gaining 10% on one and losing 10% on the other. Find his gain (or) loss per cent on the whole transaction.*

Sol.

Ist article
S.P. = Rs 2970, Gain% = 10%
C.P. = $\dfrac{S.P \times 100}{100 + gain\%}$ = Rs $\left(\dfrac{2970 \times 100}{110}\right)$
= Rs 2700

IInd article
S.P. = Rs 2970, Loss % = 10%
C.P. = $\dfrac{S.P \times 100}{100 - loss\%}$ = Rs $\left(\dfrac{2970 \times 100}{90}\right)$
= Rs 3300

S.P. of both the articles = Rs (2 × 2970) = Rs 5940

C.P. of both the articles = Rs 2700 + Rs 3300 = Rs 6000

∵ C.P. > S.P., therefore it is a loss

$$\text{Loss} = \text{C.P.} - \text{S.P.} = \text{Rs } (6000 - 5940) = \text{Rs } 60$$

∴ $\quad$ Loss % $= \left(\dfrac{\text{Loss}}{\text{C.P.}} \times 100\right)\% = \left(\dfrac{60}{6000} \times 100\right)\% =$ **1%.**

∴ It is a **loss of 1%** on the **whole transaction**.

Ex. 12. *By selling 100 Diwali cards, a shopkeeper gains the S.P. of 40 cards. Find his gain per cent.*

Sol. Gain = (S.P. of 100 cards) – (C.P. of 100 cards)

$\Rightarrow$ S.P. of 40 cards = S.P. of 100 cards – C.P. of 100 cards.

$\Rightarrow$ S.P. of 60 cards = C.P. of 100 cards

Let C.P. of 1 card be Re 1, then S.P. of 60 cards = Rs 100

∴ $\quad$ Gain = S.P. of 40 cards = Rs $\dfrac{100}{60} \times 40$ = Rs $\dfrac{200}{3}$

This gain is on C.P. of 100 cards which is Rs 100 ∴ Gain% = $\dfrac{200}{3}\% =$ **$66\dfrac{2}{3}\%$** .

Ex. 13. *Prem sells an article to Dinesh at a gain of 20% and Dinesh sells it to Sudhir at a gain of 10% and Sudhir sells it to Prashant at a gain of $12\dfrac{1}{2}\%$. If Prashant pays Rs 14850, find the cost price of Prem.*

Sol. Let Prem's C.P. be Rs 100, then C.P. of Dinesh = Rs 120

C.P. of Sudhir = 110 % of Rs 120 = Rs $\dfrac{110}{100} \times 120$ = Rs 132

C.P. of Prashant = $112\dfrac{1}{2}\%$ of Rs 132 = Rs $\dfrac{225}{2 \times 100} \times 132$ = Rs $\dfrac{297}{2}$

When C.P. of Prashant is Rs $\dfrac{297}{2}$, C.P. of Prem = Rs 100

When C.P. of Prashant is Rs 14850, C.P. of Prem = Rs $100 \times \dfrac{2}{297} \times 14850$ = **Rs 10,000.**

Ex. 14. *A dinner set is sold at a gain of 16%. Had it been sold for Rs 200 more, the gain would have been 20%. Find the C.P. of the dinner set.*

Sol. Let C.P. of the dinner set = Rs 100

First gain = 16% $\quad$ ∴ First S.P. = Rs (100 + 16) = Rs 116

Second gain = 20% $\quad$ ∴ Second S.P. = Rs (100 + 20) = Rs120

Difference between the two S.P.'s = Rs 120 – Rs 116 = Rs 4

If the difference is Rs 4, then C.P. = Rs 100

If the difference is Re 1, then C.P. = Rs $\frac{100}{4}$

If the difference is Rs 200, then C.P. = Rs $\frac{100}{4} \times 200 =$ **Rs 5000.**

Hence C.P. of the dinner set = **Rs 5000.**

Ex. 15. *Irshad bought 100 hens for Rs 8000 and sold 20 of these at a gain of 5%. At what gain per cent must he sell the remaining hens so as to gain 20% on the whole?*

Sol. C.P. of 100 hens = Rs 8000,   Gain = 20%

S.P.. of 100 hens = $\frac{100 + \text{Profit}\%}{100} \times$ C.P. = Rs $\frac{100 + 20}{100} \times 8000 =$ Rs $\frac{120}{100} \times 8000 =$ Rs 9600

C.P. of 100 hens = Rs 8000

∴   C.P. of 20 hens = Rs $\frac{8000}{100} \times 20 =$ Rs 1600.

Gain = 5%   ∴ S.P. of 20 hens = $\frac{100 + 5}{100} \times 1600 =$ Rs $\frac{105}{100} \times 1600 =$ Rs 1680

∴   S.P. of 80 hens = S.P. of 100 hens – S.P. of 80 hens = Rs 9600 – Rs 1680 = Rs 7920.

C.P. of 80 hens = C.P. of 100 hens – C.P. of 20 hens = Rs 8000 – Rs 1600 = Rs 6400

∴   Gain = Rs 7920 – Rs 6400 = Rs 1520

∴   Gain % = $\frac{\text{Total gain}}{\text{C.P.}} \times 100 = \frac{1520}{6400} \times 100 = \frac{95}{4}\% = 23\frac{3}{4}\% =$ **23.75%.**

Hence, he should sell the remaining hens at a gain of **23.75%.**

Ex. 16. *A farmer sold two bullocks for Rs 18,000 each. On one he gained 20% and on the other he lost 20%. Find his loss or gain per cent on the whole transaction.*

Sol.   **First bullock**   **Second bullock**
        S.P. = Rs 18,000, Gain = 20%   S.P. = Rs 18,000, Loss = 20%

∴ C.P. = $\frac{100 \times \text{S.P.}}{(100 + \text{Gain}\%)}$ ∴ C.P. = $\frac{100 \times \text{S.P.}}{(100 - \text{Loss}\%)}$

= Rs $\frac{100 \times 18,000}{(100 + 20)} =$ Rs $\frac{100 \times 18,000}{120}$ = Rs $\frac{100 \times 18,000}{(100 - 20)} =$ Rs $\frac{100 \times 18,000}{80}$

= **Rs 15,000**   = **Rs 22,500**

Total C.P. = Rs 15,000 + Rs 22,500 = Rs 37,500

Total S.P. = 2 × Rs 18,000 = Rs 36,000

∴   C.P. > S.P. it is a loss

Loss = C.P. – S.P. = Rs 37,500 – Rs 36,000 = Rs 1500

Loss% = $\frac{\text{Loss}}{\text{C.P.}} \times 100 = \frac{1500}{37,500} \times 100 =$ **4%.**

Ex. 17. *Bhawna bought two fans for Rs 3605. She sold one at a profit of 15% and the other at a loss of 9%. If Bhawna obtained the same amount for each fan, find the cost price of each fan.*

Sol. Let C.P. of first fan = Rs x

Then C.P. of second fan = Rs $(3605 - x)$, profit = 15%

$\therefore$ S.P. of first fan $= \dfrac{100 + \text{Profit}\%}{100} \times \text{C.P.} = \text{Rs } \dfrac{100 + 15}{100} \times (x) = \text{Rs } \dfrac{115x}{100}$

For the sale of second fan, loss $= 9\%$

$\therefore$ S.P. of second fan $= \dfrac{100 - \text{Loss}\%}{100} \times \text{C.P.} = \text{Rs } \dfrac{100 - 9}{100} \times (3605 - x) = \text{Rs } \dfrac{91(3605 - x)}{100}$

By the given condition, S.P. of first fan $=$ S.P. of second fan

$\therefore \dfrac{115x}{100} = \dfrac{19(3605 - x)}{100} \Rightarrow 115x = 91(3605 - x)$

$\Rightarrow 115x = 91 \times 3605 - 91x \Rightarrow 115x + 91x = 91 \times 3605 \Rightarrow 206x = 91 \times 3605$

$\Rightarrow x = \dfrac{91 \times 3605}{206} = \dfrac{91 \times 35}{2} = \dfrac{3185}{2} = 1592.50$

$\therefore$ C.P. of first fan $= x = $ **Rs 1592.50**

and C.P. of second fan $=$ Rs 3605 $-$ Rs 1592.50 $=$ **Rs 2012.50.**

Ex. 18. *A man sells an article at 5% above its cost price. If he had bought it at 5% less than what he paid for it and sold it at Rs 2 less, he would have gained 10%. Find the cost price of the article.*

Sol. Let the C.P. of the article be Rs x. Profit is 5%

$\therefore \qquad$ S.P. $= \dfrac{100 + \text{Profit}\%}{100} \times \text{C.P.} = \text{Rs} \dfrac{100 + 5}{100} \times x = \text{Rs} \dfrac{105}{100} x = \text{Rs} \dfrac{21}{20} x$

If he buys the article at 5% less, then C.P. $= \text{Rs } x - \text{Rs } \dfrac{5x}{100} = \text{Rs } \dfrac{95}{100} x = \text{Rs } \dfrac{19}{20} x$

$\therefore \qquad$ New gain $= 10\% = \text{Rs } \dfrac{19x}{20} \times \dfrac{10}{100} = \text{Rs } \dfrac{19x}{200}$

$\therefore \qquad$ New S.P. $=$ C.P. $+$ Profit $= \text{Rs } \dfrac{19x}{20} + \text{Rs } \dfrac{19x}{200} = \text{Rs } \dfrac{190x + 19x}{200} = \text{Rs } \dfrac{209}{200} x$

It is given that old S.P. $-$ New S.P. $=$ Rs 2

$\therefore \qquad \dfrac{21}{20} x - \dfrac{209}{200} x = 2 \Rightarrow \dfrac{210 - 209}{200} x = 2 \Rightarrow \dfrac{x}{200} = 2 \Rightarrow x = 400.$

Hence the original C.P. of the article $=$ **Rs 400.**

EXERCISE 9 (c)

1. Ramesh bought a house for Rs 2,75,000. He spent Rs 25,000 on its repairs. Then he sold it for Rs 3,50,000. Find his gain per cent.

2. A man buys a T.V for Rs 6800. For how much should he sell it so as to (*i*) gain 10%, (*ii*) lose 5% on it ?

3. By selling a radio for Rs 528, Mohit gains 10%. Find his cost price.

4. A watch sold for Rs 448 gives a profit of only 12%. Find the profit % if the selling price had been Rs 512.

5. Prem sold a transistor to Sudhir at a gain of 10% and Sudhir sold it to Hari at a gain of 15%. Prem had bought it for Rs 500, what did it cost to Hari?

6. A manufacturer sells an article to a wholesaler at a profit of 18%, the wholesaler sells it to a retailer at a profit of 20%. The retailer sells it to a customer at a profit of 25%. If the customer pays Rs 30.09 for it, find the cost of the manufacturer.

7. A shopkeeper sold an article at a gain of 5%. If he had sold it for Rs 16.50 less, he would have lost 5%. Find the cost price of the article.

8. By selling a stool for Rs 67.50, a carpenter losses 10%. How much per cent would he gain or lose by selling it for Rs 82.50?

9. By selling a purse for Rs 250, Ranjana loses one-sixth of what it cost her. Find

   (*i*) the cost price of the purse   (*ii*) her loss percentage.

   (**Hint :** C.P. – S.P. = $\frac{1}{6}$ of C.P. $\Rightarrow (1 - \frac{1}{6})$ of C.P. = S.P. $\Rightarrow \frac{5}{6}$ of C.P. = Rs 250)

10. Anjali sells an almirah at 10% gain. If she had sold it for Rs 400 more, her gain would have been 18%. Find the cost price of the almirah.

11. If the cost price of 11 shirts is equal to the selling price of 10 shirts, find the percentage profit or loss.

12. Pens are bought at 12 for a rupee and sold at 9 for a rupee. Find the gain %.

13. By selling 100 mangoes, a fruit seller gains the S.P. of 20 mangoes. Find his gain%.

14. By selling 144 hens, Mala lost the S.P. of 6 hens. Find her loss%.

15. A shopkeeper sold two pairs of jeans for Rs 720 each, gaining 20% on one and losing 20% on the other. Find his gain or loss%.

16. John bought two horses at Rs 20,000 each. He sold one horse at 15% gain. But he had to sell the second horse at a loss. If he had suffered a loss of Rs 1800 on the whole transaction, find the selling price of the second horse.

17. A shopkeeper buys two T.V. sets of the same type. He sells one of them at a profit of 20% and the other at a loss of 5%. If the difference in selling prices is Rs 700, find the cost price of each T.V. set.

18. A publisher sells a book for Rs 168 at a profit of 20%. If his cost of production increases by 30%, what should be the increase in the price of the book so that his percentage profit remains the same?

19. The difference in prices when a commodity is sold at a profit of 4% and at a profit of 6% is Rs 3. Find the selling prices of the commodity in the two cases.

20. A man buys a plot of land at Rs 3,60,000. He sells one third of the plot at a loss of 20%. Again, he sells two - thirds of the plot left at a profit of 25%. At what price should he sell the remaining plot in order to get a profit of 10% on the whole?

21. A shopkeeper bought locks at the rate of 8 locks for Rs 34 and sold them at the rate of 12 locks for Rs 57. Calculate:

    (*i*) his gain per cent, and

    (*ii*) the number of locks he should sell to earn a profit of Rs 45.

22. Some toffees are bought at the rate of 11 for Rs 10 and the same number at the rate of 9 for Rs 10. If the whole lot is sold at one rupee per toffee, find the gain or loss per cent on the whole transaction.

    (**Hint :** Let the number of toffees bought be the LCM of 11 and 9)

23. Dinesh sold his motorcycle to Naveen at a loss of 28%. Naveen spent Rs 1680 on its repairs and sold the motorcycle to Saran for Rs 35,910 making a profit of 12.5%. Find the cost of the motor cycle for Dinesh.

24. Kamal bought paper sheets for Rs 7200 and spent Rs 200 on transport. Paying Rs 600, he had 330 boxes made, which he sold at Rs 28 each. Find his total profit and profit %.

25. The C.P. of two watches taken together is Rs 840. If by selling one at a profit of 16% and the other at a loss of 12%, there is no gain or loss in the whole transaction then find the C.P. of each watch.

DISCOUNT

9.11 Introduction and Definitions

Sometimes to increase the sale or dispose off the old stock, a dealer offers his goods at reduced prices. The reduction in price offered by the dealer is called **discount** .

- **Marked Price :** The printed price or the tagged price of an article is called the **marked price (M.P.).** It is also called the list price .

- **Discount :** The deduction allowed on the marked price is called **discount**. Discount is generally given as per cent of the marked price.

- **Net Price :** The selling price at which the article is sold to the customer after deducting the discount from the marked price is called the **net price.**

> Remember that discount is always calculated on the marked price of the article.

9.12 Formulas

(i)   S.P. = M.P. – Discount

(ii) Rate of discount = Discount% = $\dfrac{\text{Discount}}{\text{M.P.}} \times 100$

(iii) S.P. = M.P. $\times \left(\dfrac{100 - \text{Discount\%}}{100} \right)$ (iv) M.P. = $\dfrac{100 \times \text{S.P.}}{100 - \text{Discount\%}}$

Ex. 1. *Find the S.P. when M.P. = Rs 550 and discount = 10%.*

Sol. Discount = 10% on M.P. = Rs $\dfrac{10}{100} \times 550$ = Rs 55

∴ S.P. = M.P. – Discount = Rs 550 – Rs 55 = **Rs 495.**

Ex. 2. *Find the rate of discount when M.P. = Rs 600 and S.P. = Rs 510.*

Sol. M.P. = Rs 600, S.P. = Rs 510

∴ Discount = M.P. – S. P. = Rs 600 – Rs 510 = Rs 90

∴ Rate of discount, *i.e.,* discount% = $\dfrac{\text{Discount}}{\text{M.P.}} \times 100 = \dfrac{90}{600} \times 100\%$ = **15%.**

Ex. 3. *Find the M.P. When S.P. = Rs 9000 and discount = 10%*

Sol. S.P. = Rs 9000, discount = 10%

Let the M.P. be Rs 100. Since discount = 10%, So S.P. = Rs 90.

When S.P. is Rs 90, M.P. is Rs 100.

When S .P. is Re 1, M.P. is Rs $\dfrac{100}{90}$

When S.P. is Rs 9000, M.P. is Rs $\dfrac{100}{90} \times 9000$ = **Rs 10,000**

Aliter M.P. = $\dfrac{100 \times \text{S.P.}}{100 - \text{Discount\%}}$ = Rs $\dfrac{100 \times 9000}{100 - 10}$ = Rs $\dfrac{100 \times 9000}{90}$ = **Rs 10, 000.**

Ex. 4. *A dealer prices an article at 20% more than the cost price and allows a discount of 10% on it. Find the gain per cent.*

Sol. Let C.P. be Rs 100. Then marked price = Rs 120

Discount = 10%   ∴ S.P. = 90% of Rs 120 = Rs 108

∴ Gain = Rs 108 – Rs 100 = Rs 8 which is on Rs 100   ∴ Gain per cent = **8%.**

Ex. 5. *Shirish purchased a watch at 20% discount on its marked price but sold it at the marked price. Find the gain per cent of Shirish in this transaction.*

Sol. Let marked price be Rs 100. Discount = 20%.

So C.P. of watch for Shirish = Rs 100 – Rs 20 = Rs 80

Shirish sells the watch at marked price so S.P. for him = Rs 100

∴ Shirish's gain = S.P. – C.P. = Rs 100 – Rs 80 = Rs 20

This gain is on C.P. which is Rs 80. ∴ Gain% = $\frac{20}{80} \times 100$ = **25%.**

Ex. 6. _A garment dealer allows his customers 10 % discount on a marked price of the goods and still gets a profit of 25%. What is the cost price if a shirt of the marked price is Rs 1250._

Sol. M.P. = Rs 1250, Discount = 10%

When M.P. is Rs 100, S.P. is Rs 90

> **Think !**
> On a M. P. of Rs 100, discount = Rs 10 and so S.P. Rs 90.

When M.P. is Rs 1250, S.P. is Rs $\frac{90}{100} \times 1250$ = Rs 1125

Profit = 25%. So C.P. = $\frac{100}{100 + \text{Profit}} \times$ S.P. = Rs $\frac{100}{100 + 25} \times 1125$ = Rs $\frac{100}{125} \times 1125$

$$= \text{Rs}\,(100 \times 9) = \textbf{Rs 900.}$$

Ex. 7. _What price should Kiran mark on a sari which cost her Rs 3000 so as to gain 20% after allowing a discount of 10% ?_

Sol. C.P. = Rs 3000, Gain = 20%

∴ S.P. = $\frac{100 + \text{Gain\%}}{100} \times$ C.P. = Rs $\frac{100 + 20}{100} \times 3000$ = Rs $\frac{120}{100} \times 3000$ = Rs 3600

Discount = 10%. This mean for a M.P. of Rs 100, S.P. = Rs 90

When S.P. is Rs 90, M.P. is Rs 100

When S.P. is Rs 3600, M.P. is Rs. $\frac{100}{90} \times 3600$ = **Rs 4000.**

Hence, Kiran should mark a price of Rs 4000 on the sari.

Ex. 8. _A cycle merchant allows 25% discount on the marked price of the cycles and still makes a profit of 20%. If he gains Rs 360 over the sale of one cycle, find the marked price of the cycle._

Sol. Let the marked price of the cycle be Rs x

Then, discount = Rs $\left(\frac{25}{100} \times x \right)$ = Rs $\frac{x}{4}$

S.P. = M.P. – Discount = Rs $\left(x - \frac{x}{4} \right)$ = Rs $\frac{3x}{4}$, Profit = 20%

∴ C.P. = $\frac{100}{100 + \text{Profit \%}} \times$ S.P. = Rs $\frac{100}{100 + 20} \times \frac{3x}{4}$ = Rs $\frac{100}{120} \times \frac{3x}{4}$ = Rs $\frac{5x}{8}$

By the given condition, we get S.P. – C.P. = Profit

∴ $\frac{3x}{4} - \frac{5x}{8} = 360$ ⟹ $\frac{6x - 5x}{8} = 360$ ⟹ $\frac{x}{8} = 360$ ⟹ $x = 8 \times 360$ ⟹ $x = 2880$

Hence, marked price of the cycle = **Rs 2880.**

9.13 Successive Discounts

Ex. 9. _A car is marked at Rs 3,00,000. The dealer allows successive discounts of 6%, 4% and $2\frac{1}{2}$% on it. What is the net selling price?_

Sol. Marked price of the car = Rs 3,00,000

First discount = 6% of Rs 3,00,000 = Rs $\left(\dfrac{6}{100} \times 3,00,000\right)$ = Rs 18,000

Net price after first discount = Rs (3,00,000 – 18,000) = Rs 2,82,000

Second discount = 4% of Rs 2,82,000 = Rs $\left(\dfrac{4}{100} \times 2,82,000\right)$ = Rs 11,280

Net price after second discount = Rs (2,82,000 – 11,280) = Rs 2,70,720

Third discount = Rs $\left(\dfrac{2\frac{1}{2}}{100} \times 2,70,720\right)$ = Rs $\left(\dfrac{5}{200} \times 2,70,720\right)$ = Rs 6768

∴ Net selling price = Rs (2,70,720 – 6768) = **Rs 2,63,952.**

Ex. 10. *Find a single discount equivalent to two successive discounts of 20% and 5%.*

Sol. Let the marked price be Rs 100. First discount = Rs 20

∴ Net price after first discount = Rs (100 – 20) = Rs 80

Second discount = 5% of Rs 80 = Rs $\left(\dfrac{5}{100} \times 80\right)$ = Rs 4

∴ Net price after second discount = Rs (80 – 4) = Rs 76

∴ Total discount allowed = Rs (100 – 76) = Rs 24

Hence, the required single discount = **24%.**

EXERCISE 9 (d)

1. **Find the discount and the amount actually paid if**

   (*a*) A shirt having a price tag of Rs 600 is sold at 15% discount.

   (*b*) A vaccum cleaner with a marked price of Rs 6000 is sold at a discount of 5% on immediate cash payment.

2. Find the S.P. when M.P. = Rs 1500 and discount = 12%.

3. **Find the rate of discount when**

   (*i*) M.P. = Rs 300 and S.P. = Rs 240

   (*ii*) M.P. = Rs 2800 and S.P. = Rs 2100

4. **Find the M.P. when**

   (*i*) S.P. = Rs 1900 and discount = 5%

   (*ii*) S.P. = Rs 4200 and discount = 16%

5. A shopkeeper marks his goods 30% above the cost price and gives a discount of 15% on the marked price. What gain % does he make ?

6. A watch dealer pays 10% custom duty on a watch which costs Rs 500 abroad. For how should much he mark it, if he desires to make a profit of 20% after giving a discount of 25% to the buyer ?

7. A Shopkeeper allows a cash discount of 12.5% on a machine. A customer pays an amount of Rs 437.50 for a machine. At what price is the machine listed ?

8. A shopkeeper offers 10% off-season discount to the customers and still makes a profit of 26%. What is the cost price of a pair of shoes marked at Rs 1120 ?

9. Naseem runs a readymade garments shop. They mark the garments at such a price that even after allowing a discount of 12.5%, he makes a profit of 10%. Find the marked price of a suit which costs him Rs 1470.

10. A shopkeeper buys an article for Rs 400 and marks it for sale at a price that may give him 80% profit on his cost. He, however gives 15% discount on the marked price to his customer.

Calculate :

   (*i*) the marked price of the article,

   (*ii*) the discount in rupees given to the customer,

   (*iii*) the actual percentage profit made by the shopkeeper.

11. When a discount of 15% is allowed on the marked price of an article, it is sold for Rs 2975.

   (*i*) Calculate its marked price. Given that the marked price is 40% above the cost price of the article, calculate :

   (*ii*) its cost price

   (*iii*) the profit in Rs made by the sale of the article.

12. A shopkeeper allows a discount of 20% on the marked price of an article, and sells it for Rs 896.

   (*a*) Calculate the marked price of the article,

   (*b*) By selling the article at the discounted price if he still gains 12% on his cost price, what was the cost price ?

   (*c*) What would have been his profit percentage, if he had sold the article at the marked price ?

13. A firm dealing in furniture allows 4% discount on the marked prices of each item. What price must be marked on a dining table which costs Rs 4000 to assemble, so as to make a profit of 20%

14. A sells a car priced at Rs 36,000. He gives a discount of 8% on the first Rs 20, 000 and 5% on remaining Rs 16, 000. B also sells a car of the same make priced at Rs 36, 000. He gives a discount of 7% on the total price. Calculate the actual price charged by A and B for the cars.

15. A dealer of scientific instruments allows 20% discount on the marked price of the instruments and still makes a profit of 25%. If his gain over the sale of a instrument is Rs 150, find the marked price of the instruments.

16. A washing machine is marked at Rs 7500. The dealer allows successive discounts of 8%, 5% and 2% on it. What is the net selling price?

17. What single discount will be equivalent to two successive discounts of 8% and 5%?

18. After allowing two successive discounts of 15% and 5%, a fan is sold for Rs 2907. What is the marked price of the fan?

INCOME TAX

   Income Tax is a tax on the total income of a person. Every individual, whose annual income exceeds a specified limit is required to pay by law a part of his income to the Government. The rate of income tax and the law related to it vary from year to year..

Some Terms Related to Income Tax

   Assessee. *The person who pays income tax is called an assessee.*

   Financial Year (F.Y.) and Assessment Year (A.Y.). The income of a person earned during a year is assessed next year. For example, the income earned by a person during the year 2005–2006 will be assessed during the year 2006–2007. The year for which the income is taken into account is called the *financial year* and the year in which the income-tax is assessed and paid to the government is called the *assessment year.*

   A financial year begins on 1st April of a particular year and ends on 31st March in the next consecutive year. As the tax is paid in the year immediately following the financial year, the financial year may also be referred to as **previous year.** Thus, for the financial year, 1999–2000, the assessment year is 2000–2001 and for the financial year 2000–2001, the assessment year is 2001–2002.

   Income Tax Returns. Every assessee has to fill up a form stating therein, details of the total income during the financial year, and submit it to the income tax department. This form is called an *income tax return.*

The due date for submitting this form for salaried people is generally 30th June every year. Thus, an income tax return, showing the statement of income for the financial year 2007–2008 has to be filed on or before 30th June, 2008.

Income from Salaries. The income from salaries includes *Basic Pay : Dearness Allowance; City Compensatory Allowance; Interim Relief; House Rent Allowance (HRA)* with certain conditions; *Honorarium: Bonus: Overtime Allowance; Pension; Leave encashment during service period other than at the time of retirement and compensation; children's education allowance; Refund of tuition fees, etc.* The perks allowed by the employer to its employees have also become taxable as per conditions laid down by the government from time to time.

However, *Travel allowance; Conveyance allowance; Medical allowance; Leave travel concessions;* and *any payment from Provident Fund* are all free from income tax subject to some conditions. The *Gratuity* and the *Leave encashment* obtained at the time of retirement are also free from income tax subject to certain conditions.

Rule for House Rent Allowance (HRA)

(*i*) If a person does not live in his own house, then HRA is not included in his income.

(*ii*) If a person has self-occupied house, or lives in a rent free house, then HRA is included in his income.

Rules Effective from Assessment Year 2006–2007

Exemptions on Savings

Savings upto Rs 1 lakh in the following investments will be deducted before the computation of tax.	
(*i*) Contributory Provident Fund	(CPF)
(*ii*) General Provident Fund	(GPF)
(*iii*) Public Provident Fund	(PPF)
(*iv*) Life Insurance premium	(LIC)
(*v*) Unit Linked Insurance Plan	(ULIP)
(*vi*) National Savings Certificates	(NSC's)
(*vii*) National Saving Scheme	(NSS)
(*viii*) Equity Linked Savings Schemes	(ELSS)

Exemptions on Donations

An individual can donate at the most 10% of his/her income in a financial year for the purpose of tax relief. (Section 80 G)

DONATIONS	RATE OF RELIEF
(*i*) *Prime Minister's National Relief Fund*	*100%*
(*ii*) *National Defence Fund*	*100%*
(*iii*) *Donation to Medical Research Institute*	*100%*
(*iv*) *Charitable Trusts: Educational Institutions, Hospitals, Orphanages etc.*	*50%*

Remark. For certain funds such as National Defence Fund set up by the Central Government, there is no overall limit of contribution by an individual. It can be more than 10% of his/her income in a financial year.

Income Tax Slabs

(I) Rates of Income Tax for Male Persons

(Below 65 years)

TAXABLE INCOME	INCOME TAX
Up to Rs 1 Lakh	*Nil*
Rs 1 Lakh to Rs 1.5 Lakh	*10% of income exceeding Rs 1 Lakh*
Rs 1.5 Lakh to Rs 2.5 Lakh	*Rs 5,000 + 20% income exceeding Rs 1.5 Lakh*
More than Rs 2.5 Lakh	*Rs 25,000 + 30% of income exceeding Rs 2.5 lakh*

(II) Rates of Income Tax for Female Persons

(Below 65 years)

TAXABLE INCOME	INCOME TAX
Up to Rs 1.35 Lakh	*Nil*
Rs 1.35 Lakh to Rs 1.5 Lakh	*10% of income exceeding Rs 1.35 Lakh*
Rs 1.5 Lakh to Rs 2.5 Lakh	*Rs 1,500 + 20% of the income exceeding Rs 1.5 Lakh*
More than Rs 2.5 Lakh	*Rs 21,500 + 30% of income exceeding Rs 2.5 lakh*

(III) Rates of Income Tax for a Senior Citizen

(Age 65 year or More)

TAXABLE INCOME	INCOME TAX
Up to Rs 1.85 Lakh	*Nil*
Rs 1.85 Lakh to Rs 2.5 Lakh	*20% of income exceeding Rs 1.85 Lakh*
More than Rs 2.5 Lakh	*Rs 13,000 + 30% of income exceeding Rs 2.5 lakh*

(IV) Surcharge

For persons having taxable income exceeding Rs 10 Lakh, a surcharge of 10% is levied on the amount of tax payable.

(V) Education Cess

For every tax payer, an education cess of 2% is levied on the tax payable (including surcharge wherever applicable).

Computation of Income Tax (Steps)

Step 1. Find the total Gross Income.

Step 2. Subtract the savings from the total gross income, up to a maximum of Rs 1 Lakh.

Step 3. From the balance so obtained, subtract the amount of donations eligible for deduction under Section 80 G.

Step 4. The balance so obtained, to the nearest multiple of Rs 10 is the taxable income.

Step 5. Compute the tax payable on the taxable income according to the rules given above.

Step 6. Add a surcharge of 10% of the tax to the tax computed in (v) only if the taxable income calculated in (iv) exceeds Rs 10 Lakh.

Step 7. Calculate 2% of the total tax and add it to the total tax to get the net tax payable.

> **Note : 1.** The rebate and tax are always calculated to the nearest number of rupees.
> **2.** The taxable income is always taken to the nearest multiple of Rs 10.

Ex. 1. *Raghav's annual income during the financial year was Rs 2,38,000 as salary and allowances, excluding HRA for which he got full rebate. He contributed towards LIC premium and Provident Fund Rs 20,000. He purchased National Saving Certificates worth Rs 15,000. He contributed Rs 5000 to Unit Linked Insurance Plan (ULIP). He donated Rs 1500 to the Prime Minister's Relief Fund on which he got 100% rebate. Calculate his income tax.*

Sol. *Gross income* = Rs 2,38,000

(a) **Savings**

(i) LIC and PF	= Rs	20,000	Rs	2,38,000
(ii) NSC's	= Rs	15,000		– 40,000
(iii) ULIP	= Rs	5000	Rs	1,98,000
Total	Rs	40,000		

(b) **Donation**

100% of Rs 1500

= Rs 1500

Rs	1,98,000
	– 1,500
Taxble Income = Rs	1,96,500

(c) **Computation of Income Tax (For a man below 65 years)**

TAXABLE INCOME	INCOME TAX
Rs 1,96,500	Rs 5000 + 20% of income exceeding Rs 1.5 Lakh

$$= Rs\ 5000 + Rs\left[\frac{20}{100}\times(1,96,500-1,50,000)\right]$$

$$= Rs\ 5000 + Rs\left(\frac{20}{100}\times46500\right)$$

$$= Rs\ 5000 + Rs\ 9300 = Rs\ 14,300.00$$

Education Cess = 2% of Rs 14,300 = Rs 286.00

Net Tax payable = Rs 14,300 + Rs 286 = **Rs 14,586.00.**

Ex. 2. *Mrs Premvati is a Government employee. Her annual income is Rs 2,96,962. She contributes Rs 16,060 to her Provident Fund account. She pays Rs 18,036 as LIC insurance premium and deposits Rs 70,000 in Public Provident Fund. She donated Rs 8100 to a Charitable Trust (eligible for 50% exemption under Section 80 G). An amount of Rs 11,000 has been deducted by the government office as the tax deducted at source. What amount will be refunded by the income tax department to Mrs Premvati?*

Sol. *Gross income* = Rs 2,96,962

(a) **Savings**

(i) PF	= Rs	16,060		
(ii) LIC	= Rs	18,036	Rs	2,96,962
(iii) PPF	= Rs	70,000		– 1,00,000
Total	Rs	1,04,096	Rs	1,96,962

(*b*) **Donation**

50% of Rs 8100

    = Rs 4050

Rs	1,96,962	
	–	4050
Taxable Income Rs	1,92,912	

Taxable Income = Rs 1,92,912.00 = Rs 1,92,910 to the nearest multiples of Rs 10.

(*c*) **Computation of Income Tax (For a woman below 65 Years)**

TAXABLE INCOME   *INCOME TAX*

Rs 1,92,910   Rs 1500 + 20% of income exceeding Rs 1.5 Lakh

$$= \text{Rs } 1500 + \text{Rs} \left(\frac{20}{100} \times 42{,}910 \right)$$

$$= \text{Rs } (1500 + 8582) = \text{Rs } 10082.00$$

Education Cess = 2% of Rs 10,082 = Rs 201.64

    Net tax payable   = Rs (10,082 + 201.64) = Rs 10,283.64

                                 = **Rs 10,284**, to the nearest paisa.

             Refund   = Rs (11,000 – 10,284) = **Rs 716.**

Ex. 3. *Mr S.N. Gupta's annual income is Rs 18,57,609. He purchased National Savings Certificates worth Rs 5 Lakh. He deposited Rs 70,000 in Public Provident Fund. He donated Rs 3 Lakh to National Defence Fund, (eligible for 100% exemption). Calculate his income tax if he is 71 years old.*

Sol.   **Gross income** = Rs 1857609

(*a*) **Savings**

    (*i*) NSC's   = Rs 5,00,000

    (*ii*) PPF   = Rs   70,000

        Total   Rs 5,70,000

Rs	18,57,609	
	– 1,00,000	
Rs	17,57,609	

(*b*) **Donation**

100% of Rs 3 Lakh = Rs 3,00,000`

                        Taxable Income

Rs	17,57,609
	– 3,00,000
Rs	14,57,609 = Rs 14,57,610
	(to the nearest 10 rupees)

(*c*) **Computation of Tax (For a Senior Citizen)**

TAXABLE INCOME   *INCOME TAX*

Rs 14,57,610   Rs 13,000 + 30% of income exceeding Rs 2.5 Lakh

$$= \text{Rs } 13{,}000 + \text{Rs} \left(\frac{30}{100} \times 1{,}207{,}610 \right)$$

$$= \text{Rs } 13{,}000 + \text{Rs } 3{,}62{,}283 = \text{Rs } 3{,}75{,}283$$

         Surcharge = 10% of Rs 3,75,283 = Rs 37,528.30

         Total tax   = Rs (3,75,283 + 37,528.30 = Rs 4,12,811.30

   Education Cess = 2% of (Rs 4,12,811.30) = Rs 8256.23

  Net Tax payable = Rs (4,12,811.30 + 8256.23) = Rs 4,21,067.53 = **Rs 4,21,068** to the nearest rupee.

EXERCISE 9 (e)

1. Dr Ashish gets Rs 2,40,000 as his annual salary (excluding HRA). He contributes Rs 400 per month towards Provident Fund and Rs 16,000 as premium towards L.I.C. annually. Calculate the income tax that Dr. Ashish has to pay on his salary during the financial year.

2. Mr Naresh Mehta has total annual salary income of Rs 2,50,000 exclusive of HRA. He donated Rs 20,000 to Prime Minister Relief Fund which has 100% tax exemption. His total contribution of P.F. and L.I.C. premium for the financial year is Rs 64,000. Find the income tax liability of Mr Naresh for the financial year.

3. Miss Suneeta's monthly salary is Rs 22,000 (HRA not included). Her monthly contribution to G.P.F. is Rs 4000. She pays Rs 12,000 annually as L.I.C. premium and invests Rs 2000 in N.S.C. She donates Rs 10,000 towards Prime Minister's Relief Fund (100% tax exemption) and Rs 8000 to a charitable trust (50% tax exemption). Calculate the income tax liability of Miss Suneeta for the financial year.

4. Mr Singh, aged 69 years, gets a pension of Rs 18,750 per month. He has an annual income of Rs 2,28,500 from other sources. He contributes Rs 7500 per month towards PPF and pays Rs 2800 as L.I.C. premium quarterly. He donates Rs 6000 to National Defence Fund (eligible for 100% deduction) and Rs 2100 to a religious trust (eligible for 50% deduction). Calculate the income tax he has to pay in the financial year 2006–2007)

LOOKING BACK
Summary of Key Facts

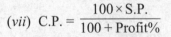

1. **In case of profit (if S.P. > C.P.)**

   (i) Profit = S.P. – C.P.

   (ii) S.P. = Profit + C.P.

   (iii) C.P. = S.P. – Profit

   (iv) Profit% = $\dfrac{\text{Profit}}{\text{C.P.}} \times 100$

   (v) Profit = $\dfrac{\text{C.P.} \times \text{Profit\%}}{100}$

   (vi) S.P. = C.P. $\times \left(\dfrac{100 + \text{Profit\%}}{100} \right)$

   (vii) C.P. = $\dfrac{100 \times \text{S.P.}}{100 + \text{Profit\%}}$

2. **In case of loss (if S.P. < C.P.)**

   (i) Loss = C.P. – S.P.

   (ii) S.P. = C.P. – Loss

   (iii) C.P. = Loss + S.P.

   (iv) Loss% = $\dfrac{\text{Loss}}{\text{C.P.}} \times 100$

   (v) Loss = $\dfrac{\text{C.P.} \times \text{Loss\%}}{100}$

   (vi) S.P. = C.P. $\times \dfrac{(100 - \text{Loss\%})}{100}$

   (vii) C.P. = $\dfrac{100 \times \text{S.P.}}{100 - \text{Loss\%}}$

3. (i) **Discount is usually expressed as a certain per cent of the M.P.**

   (ii) Discount = M.P. – S.P.

   (iii) Rate of Discount = Discount % = $\dfrac{\text{Discount}}{\text{M.P.}} \times 100$

   (iv) S.P. = M.P. $\times \dfrac{(100 - \text{Discount\%})}{100}$

   (v) M.P. = $\dfrac{100 \times \text{S.P.}}{100 - \text{Discount\%}}$

   (vi) Successive discounts are discounts in series that are allowed one after the other.

MENTAL MATHS – 7

1. Find 10% of 70?
2. What is the number whose 7% is 28.
3. Convert 35% into a simple fraction.
4. Write $\frac{2}{5}$ as a per cent.
5. Convert 9% into a decimal.
6. What percentage of 50 is 8?
7. 50% of a length is 30 cm. What is the whole length?
8. Sameer saves 15% of his monthly income of Rs 10,000. How much does he save every month?
9. An article was purchased for Rs 80 and sold for Rs 100. What is the gain?
10. A book was bought for Rs 60 and sold for Rs 50. What is the loss?
11. Suyash bought an article for Rs 800 and sold for Rs 1000. Find his gain per cent.
12. By selling a cycle for Rs 2000, a person gains $\frac{1}{5}$ th of the selling price. Find the cost price.
13. Find the C.P. when S.P. = Rs 850 and loss = 15%.
14. Find the C.P. when S.P. = Rs 2200 and gain = 10%.
15. Toffees are bought at the rate of 5 for a rupee and sold at 4 for a rupee. Find the gain per cent.
    (**Hint : Think mentally** C.P. of 20 toffees = ... S.P. of 20 toffees = ... etc.)
16. By selling 8 dozens of pencils, a shopkeeper gains the selling price of one dozen pencils. Find his gain per cent.
17. Find the S.P. when M.P. = Rs 500, discount = 20%.
18. Find the discount in per cent when M.P. = Rs 400 and S.P. = Rs 360.

MULTIPLE CHOICE QUESTIONS – 8

1. $45 \times ? = 25\%$ of 900
   (*i*) 16.20   (*ii*) 500   (*iii*) 4   (*iv*) 5
2. A number is increased by 20% and then again increased by 20%. The original number is increased by :
   (*i*) 20%   (*ii*) 30%   (*iii*) 40%   (*iv*) 44%
3. At an election involving 2 candidates, 68 votes were declared invalid. The winning candidate scores 52% and wins by 98 votes. The total number of votes polled is :
   (*i*) 2518   (*ii*) 2450   (*iii*) 2382   (*iv*) 2400
4. Vishal buys 11 candles for Rs 10 and sell them at 10 for Rs 11. Vishal's gain per cent is :
   (*i*) 21%   (*ii*) 15%   (*iii*) 10%   (*iv*) 0%
5. A man sells two horses for Rs 1475 each. The cost price of the first is equal to the selling price of the second. If the first is sold at 20% loss and the second at 25% gain, what is the total gain or loss (in rupees)?
   (*i*) Rs 80 gain   (*ii*) Rs 60 gain   (*iii*) Rs 60 loss   (*iv*) Neither gain nor loss
6. A sells a bicycle to B at a profit of 20% and B sells it to C at a profit of 25%. If C pays Rs 1500, what did A pay for it?
   (*i*) Rs 825   (*ii*) Rs 1000   (*iii*) Rs 1100   (*iv*) Rs 1125
7. A man sold an article at a loss of 20%. If he had sold it for Rs 12 more, he would have gained 10%. The cost price of the article is :
   (*i*) Rs 60   (*ii*) Rs 40   (*iii*) Rs 30   (*iv*) Rs 22
8. A man sells two watches at Rs 240 each. On one he gains 20% and one the other he loses 20%. What is the gain or loss per cent on the entire transaction?
   (*i*) 1% gain   (*ii*) 2% loss   (*iii*) 4% gain   (*iv*) 4% loss.
9. A sells a product having a printed price of Rs 2400 at a discount of 10% on the printed price. He earns a profit of 25% on this sale. What was the cost price at which A purchased the product.
   (*i*) Rs 1980   (*ii*) Rs 1728   (*iii*) Rs 2160   (*iv*) Rs 1800
10. The marked price of an article is 20% above the cost price. A discount of 10% is allowed to a customer. The profit per cent is :
    (*i*) 10%   (*ii*) 8%   (*iii*) 9%   (*iv*) 15%

ANSWERS

EXERCISE 9 (a)

1. (i) $\frac{3}{5}$; 0.6   (ii) $\frac{12}{5}$; 2.4   (iii) $\frac{1}{8}$; 0.125   (iv) $\frac{167}{300}$; 0.557 (approx)

2. (i) 75%   (ii) $52\frac{1}{2}$%   (iii) 0.8%   (iv) 37.5%   (v) 107%

3. (i) 2:1   (ii) 1:15   (iii) 3:4   (iv) 1:3   4. (i) 50%   (ii) 70%   (iii) 84%   (iv) $41\frac{2}{3}$%

5. (i) Rs 798   (ii) 330 kg   (iii) 6 gm   (iv) 8.75 m   6. (i) 0.5%   (ii) 4%   (iii) 48%   (iv) $133\frac{1}{3}$%

7. (i) 450   (ii) Rs 500   8. $66\frac{2}{3}$%   9. Rs 224   10. Rs 31,200   11. Rs 360   12. 25 cm.

EXERCISE 9 (b)

1. 25%   2. 1260   3. Copper 52%, Zinc 28%, Nickel 20%   4. 20,000   5. 4%

6. Rs 880   7. 700   8. $6\frac{2}{3}$%   9. Calcium 100 gm, Carbon 30 gm, Oxygen 120 gm

10. Maximum marks 200, Minimum 80   11. $33\frac{1}{3}$%   12. 3,58,800 votes   13. 44%

14. 54.4%   15. 44%.

EXERCISE 9 (c)

1. $16\frac{2}{3}$%   2. (i) Rs 7480   (ii) Rs 6460   3. Rs 480   4. 28%   5. Rs 632.50   6. Rs 17

7. Rs 165   8. Gain 10%   9. (i) Rs 300   (ii) $16\frac{2}{3}$%   10. Rs 5000   11. Profit 10%   12. $33\frac{1}{3}$%

13. 25%   14. 4%   15. 4%   16. Rs 15,200   17. Rs 2800   18. Rs 50.40

19. Rs 156, Rs 159   20. Rs 1,00,000   21. (i) $11\frac{13}{17}$%   (ii) 90   22. 1% loss   23. Rs 42,000

24. Rs 1240, 15.5%   25. Rs 360, Rs 480.

EXERCISE 9 (d)

1. (a) Rs 90, Rs 510   (b) Rs 300, Rs 5700   2. Rs 1320   3. (i) 20%   (ii) 25%

4. (i) Rs 2000   (ii) Rs 5000   5. 10.5%   6. Rs 880   7. Rs 500   8. Rs 800

9. Rs 1848   10. (i) Rs 720   (ii) Rs 108   (iii) 53%   11. (i) Rs 3500   (ii) Rs 2500   (iii) Rs 475

12. (i) Rs 1120   (ii) Rs 800   (iii) 40%   13. Rs 5000   14. Rs 33,600; Rs 33,480   15. Rs 937.50

16. Rs 6423.90   17. 12.6%   18. Rs 3600

EXERCISE 9 (e)

1. Rs 19,217   2. Rs 8364   3. Rs 9282   4. 47,051 (rounded off to nearest rupee)

MENTAL MATHS – 7

1. 7   2. 400   3. $\frac{7}{20}$ 4. 40%   5. 0.09   6. 16%   7. 60 cm

8. Rs 1500   9. Rs 20   10. Rs 10   11. 25%   12. Rs 1600   13. Rs 1000   14. Rs 2000

15. 25%   16. $14\frac{2}{7}$%   17. Rs 400   18. 10%

MULTIPLE CHOICE QUESTIONS – 8

1. (iv)   2. (iv)   3. (i)   4. (i)   5. (iv)   6. (ii)   7. (ii)

8. (iv)   9. (ii)   10. (ii)

10. Compound Interest

10.1 Introduction

First we give below some solved examples to revise simple interest which you have studied in class VII and which will you will be using while solving problems on compound interest.

10.2 Some Important Terms

1. **Principal (P)** : The money borrowed or lent.
2. **Interest (I)** : It is the additional money paid to the lender, for the use of the money borrowed.
3. **Rate (R)** : Interest for 1 year per Rs 100.
4. **Time (T)** : The time period for which the money is borrowed.
5. **Simple Interest or (S.I.)** : When the interest is paid to the lender regularly every year or every half year on the same principal (original money) we call the interest simple interest.
6. **Amount (A)** : Principal + Interest.

10.3 Formula Used for Simple Interest

(a) $S.I. = \dfrac{P \times R \times T}{100}$ $\qquad (b)$ $I = \dfrac{S.I. \times 100}{R \times T}$ $\qquad (c)$ $R = \dfrac{S.I. \times 100}{P \times T}$ $\qquad (d)$ $T = \dfrac{S.I. \times 100}{P \times R}$

(e) $A = P + S.I. = P + \dfrac{P \times R \times T}{100} = P\left(1 + \dfrac{R \times T}{100}\right)$

> **Note :**
> 1. (i) Rate 4% per annum means Rs 4 for every Rs 100 per year.
> (ii) Rate 1.5% per month means Rs 1.50 for every Rs 100 per month.
>   = Rs 1.5 × 12 = Rs 18 for every Rs 100 per year = 18% p.a.
> 2. (i) When time is given in days, we convert it to year by dividing it by 365.
> (ii) When time is given in months, we convert it to year by dividing it by 12.
> (iii) When dates are given, the day on which the sum is borrowed is not included but the day on which money is returned is included, while counting the number of days.

Ex. 1. *Find the simple interest and amount when, Principal = Rs 6250, Rate = 1% per month and Time = 73 days.*

Sol. $\qquad\qquad P$ = Rs 6250, $\quad R = 1\%$ per month = $(1 \times 12)\%$ p.a. = 12% p.a.

$$T = 73 \text{ days} = \frac{73}{365} \text{ year} = \frac{1}{5} \text{ year}$$

$$S.I. = \frac{P \times R \times T}{100} = \text{Rs } \frac{6250 \times 12 \times 1}{100 \times 5} = \textbf{Rs 150}$$

$\therefore \qquad$ Amount = P + S.I. = Rs 6250 + Rs 150 = **Rs 6400.**

Ex. 2. *The S.I. on a sum of money is $\frac{1}{9}$th of the principal and the number of years is equal to the rate per cent p.a. Find the rate %.*

Sol. Let the sum be Rs P. Then S.I. = Rs $\frac{P}{9}$

Given : Time = Rate

Then

$$\text{S.I.} = \frac{P \times R \times T}{100} \Rightarrow \frac{P}{9} = \frac{P \times x \times x}{100} \Rightarrow x^2 = \frac{100 \times P}{9 \times P} = \frac{100}{9}$$

$$\Rightarrow \qquad x = \sqrt{\frac{100}{9}} = \frac{10}{3} = 3\frac{1}{3}$$

$$\therefore \qquad \text{Rate \% p.a.} = 3\frac{1}{3}\%.$$

Ex. 3. *The simple interest on a certain sum for 5 years at 8% rate of interest p.a. is Rs 272 less than the simple interest on the same sum for 6 years at 12% per annum. Find the sum.*

Sol. Let the sum = Rs x

Ist Case	**IInd Case**
P = Rs x, R = 8% p.a., T = 5 years	P = Rs x, R = 12% p.a., T = 6 years
S.I. = Rs $\frac{P \times R \times T}{100}$ = Rs$\frac{x \times 8 \times 5}{100}$ = Rs$\frac{40x}{100}$	S.I. = Rs $\frac{P \times R \times T}{100}$ = Rs$\frac{x \times 12 \times 6}{100}$ = Rs$\frac{72x}{100}$

Given $\qquad \frac{72x}{100} - \frac{40x}{100} = 272 \Rightarrow \frac{32x}{100} = 272$

$$\Rightarrow \qquad x = \frac{272 \times 100}{32} = 850.$$

The required sum is **Rs 850**.

10.4 Compound Interest

You know how to calculate simple interest, but in normal business circles simple interest is very rarely used. Take for example a man who deposits Rs 1000 in a saving account at an interest rate of 10% per annum. At the end of one year he will get Rs 100 interest on his deposit. However, unless he takes out his Rs 100 in cash, it will be added to his original Rs 1000. Thus, if he leaves his money in his account, in the next year the bank will be paying him interest on his original Rs 1000 plus the Rs 100 interest, *i.e.,* Rs 1100. In the third year the interest will once again be added to the new principal of Rs 1100, and so on for as long as the money is left in the account.

This kind of interest is known as compound interest. Some banks and other institutions pay interest yearly, others every six or even three months.

Ex. 1. *Find the compound interest on Rs 8500 for 2 years at 8% per annum.*

Sol. **Step 1.** **Principal for the first year** = Rs 8500

Interest for the first year = Rs $\frac{8500 \times 8 \times 1}{100}$ = Rs 680

$I = \frac{P \times R \times T}{100}$.

$\therefore$ Amount at the end of first year = Rs 8500 + Rs 680 = Rs 9180

Step 2. Principal for the second year = Rs 9180

Interest for the second year = Rs $\frac{9180 \times 8 \times 1}{100}$ = Rs 734.40

∴ Amount at the end of second year = Rs 9180 + Rs 734.40 = Rs 9914.40.

∴ Compound interest after 2 years = Rs 9914.40 – Rs 8500 = Rs 1414.40.

Ex. 2. *Find the compound interest when principal*

= Rs 50000, rate = 10% p.a. and time = 2½ years. Find the amount payable at the end of 2½ years.

Sol. **Step 1. Principal for the first year principal** = Rs 50, 000, Rate = 10% *p.a.*

Interest for the first year = Rs $\dfrac{50000 \times 10 \times 1}{100}$ = Rs 5000

$$I = \frac{P \times R \times T}{100}$$

∴ Amount at the end of the first year = Rs (50000 + 5000) = **Rs 55000**

Step 2. ∴ **Principal for the second year = Rs 55000**

Interest for the second year = Rs $\dfrac{55000 \times 10 \times 1}{100}$ = Rs 5500

Amount at the end of second year = Rs (55000 + 5500) = **Rs 60500**

Step 3. ∴ **Principal for the remaining year = Rs 60500**

∴ Interest for the third year = Rs $\dfrac{60500 \times 10 \times 1}{100 \times 2}$ = Rs 3025

$$T = \frac{1}{2} \text{ year}$$

Amount at the end of third year = Rs (60500 + 3025) = **Rs 63525**

∴ Compound Interest = Rs 63525 – Rs 50000 = **Rs 13525.**

Let us also calculate the simple interest for the above example.

$$\text{S.I.} = \frac{P \times R \times T}{100} = \text{Rs} \frac{50000 \times 10 \times 5}{100 \times 2} = \text{Rs } 12500.$$

So what do you conclude?

EXERCISE 10 (a)

Find the compound interest on the following :

Principal	Rate% *p.a*	Number of years
1. Rs 10000	12%	2
2. Rs 5000	10%	2
3. Rs 625	16%	2
4. Rs 2000	20%	2
5. Rs 8000	15%	3

6. Find the amount and compound interest on a sum of Rs 15625 at 4% per annum for 3 years compounded annually.

7. To renovate his shop, Anurag obtained a loan of Rs 8000 from a bank. If the rate of interest at 5% per annum compounded annually, calculate the compound interest that Anurag will have to pay after 3 years.

8. A sum of Rs 9, 600 is invested for 3 years at 10% p.a. compound interest.

   (*i*) What is the sum due at the end of the first year ?

   (*ii*) What is the sum due at the end of the second year ?

   (*iii*) Find the compound interest earned in the first 2 years.

   (*iv*) Find the compound interest at the end of 3 years.

9. Shanker takes a loan of Rs 10,000 at a compound interest rate of 10% per annum (p.a.)

   (*i*) Find the compound interest after one year.

  (*ii*) Find the compound interest for 2 years.

 (*iii*) Find the sum of money required to clean the debt at the end of 2 years.

 (*iv*) Find the difference between the compound interest and the simple interest at the same rate for 2 years.

10.5 Compound Interest Formula

The arithmetic involved in working out compound interest can be quite complicated when the number of payments, or the length of time, or both are large.

However, just as there is a formula for calculating simple interest, there is a formula which can be used to work out compound interest also. Using this formula saves a great deal of time.

If the principal is Rs P, the period n years, and the rate $r\%$ p.a. then

$$\text{The amount after 1 year} = \text{P} + \text{S.I.} = P + \frac{P \times 1 \times r}{100} = P + \frac{Pr}{100} = P\left(1 + \frac{r}{100}\right)$$

Since the amount for the 1st year becomes the principal for the 2nd year.

$$\text{The amount after 2 years} = P\left(1 + \frac{r}{100}\right) + \frac{P\left(1 + \frac{r}{100}\right) \times 1 \times r}{100} = P\left(1 + \frac{r}{100}\right)\left(1 + \frac{r}{100}\right) = P\left(1 + \frac{r}{100}\right)^2$$

Similarly, the amount after 3 years $= P\left(1 + \frac{r}{100}\right)^3$. and so on.

Thus, the amount after n years $= P\left(1 + \frac{r}{100}\right)^n$

$$\boxed{A = P\left(1 + \frac{r}{100}\right)^n}$$

and

$$\boxed{\begin{aligned}\text{C.I.} = A - P &= P\left(1 + \frac{r}{100}\right)^n - P \\ &= P\left[\left(1 + \frac{r}{100}\right)^n - 1\right]\end{aligned}}$$

Type 1. *To find C.I. when interest is compounded annually.*

Ex. 1. *Find the amount and compound interest on Rs 5000 for 2 years at 10%, interest being payable yearly.*

Sol. Here, $\qquad P = \text{Rs } 5000, R = 10\%, n = 2 \text{ years}$

Using the formula A (Amount) $= P\left(1 + \frac{r}{100}\right)^n$, we have

$$A = \text{Rs } 5000\left(1 + \frac{10}{100}\right)^2 = \text{Rs } 5000 \times \frac{110}{100} \times \frac{110}{100} = \textbf{Rs 6050}$$

$\therefore$ Compound Interest $= A - P = \text{Rs } 6050 - \text{Rs } 5000 = \textbf{Rs 1050.}$

Ex. 2. *Find the compound interest on Rs 10752 at $12\frac{1}{2}\%$ p.a. for 3 years, interest being payable yearly.*

Sol. $\qquad P = \text{Rs } 10752, R = 12\frac{1}{2}\% = \frac{25}{2}\%, n = 3 \text{ years}$

$$\therefore \quad \text{Amount } (A) = P\left(1+\frac{r}{100}\right)^n$$

$$= \text{Rs } 10752\left(1+\frac{25}{2\times100}\right)^3 = \text{Rs } 10752\left(1+\frac{1}{8}\right)^3$$

$$= \text{Rs } 10752\left(\frac{9}{8}\right)^3 = \text{Rs } 10752\times\frac{9}{8}\times\frac{9}{8}\times\frac{9}{8} = \text{Rs } 15309$$

$$\therefore \text{ Compound Interest} = A - P = \text{Rs } 15309 - \text{Rs } 10752 = \textbf{Rs 4557.}$$

Type 2. *When the C.I. is compounded half-yearly.*

It is not necessary that the interest should be calculated yearly only. In some cases, the interest is **compounded semi-annually**, *i.e.,* the interest is calculated and added to the principal every six months (twice in a year). Also the interest can be compounded quarterly, *i.e.,* the interest is calculated and added to the principal every 3 months (four times in a year).

The time at the end of which the interest is calculated or compounded is called a **conversion period**.
Therefore,

Conversion periods are 2, when interest is compounded half-yearly.

Conversion periods are 4, when interest is compounded quarterly.

If the interest is paid half-yearly, then in the formula $A = P\left(1+\frac{r}{100}\right)^n$, for r we take $\frac{r}{2}$, because $r\%$ p.a.

means $\frac{r}{2}\%$ half-yearly, and for n we take $2n$, because n years is equal to $2n$ half-years.

$$\boxed{\therefore \quad A = P\left(1+\frac{r}{200}\right)^{2n}}$$

Ex. 3. *Find the amount of Rs 256 in one year at $12\frac{1}{2}\%$ per annum, when the interest is compounded half-yearly.*

Sol. $P = $ Rs 256, 1 year = 2 half years, $n = 2$,

$$\therefore \text{ Annual rate} = 12\frac{1}{2}\% = \frac{25}{2}\%, \quad \therefore \text{ Half-yearly rate} = \frac{1}{2}\left(\frac{25}{2}\%\right) = \frac{25}{4}\%$$

$$\text{Thus Amount } (A) = \left(1+\frac{r}{100}\right)^n = \text{Rs } 256\left(1+\frac{25/4}{100}\right)^2$$

$$= \text{Rs } 256\left(1+\frac{1}{16}\right)^2 = \text{Rs } 256 \times \frac{17}{16}\times\frac{17}{16} = \textbf{Rs 289.}$$

Ex. 4. *Sunil loaned Rs 8192 to Ravi to enable him to purchase a T.V. set. If Sunil charged interest at the rate of 12.5% per annum, compounded half-yearly, calculate the amount that Sunil will pay to Ravi after $1\frac{1}{2}$ years.*

Sol. $\text{Principal } (P) = \text{Rs } 8192, \text{ Rate } (r) = 12.5\% = \frac{25}{2}\%$ yearly $= \frac{1}{2}\left(\frac{25}{2}\right) = \frac{25}{4}\%$ half yearly,

$$\text{Time } (n) = 1\frac{1}{2} \text{ years} = \frac{3}{2} \text{ years} = \frac{3}{2}\times2 = 3 \text{ half years.}$$

$$\therefore \quad \text{Amount} (A) = P\left(1+\frac{r}{100}\right)^n = \text{Rs } 8192\left(1+\frac{25/4}{100}\right)^3$$

$$= \text{Rs } 8192\left(1+\frac{1}{16}\right)^3 = \text{Rs } 8192 \times \frac{17}{16}\times\frac{17}{16}\times\frac{17}{16} = \text{Rs } 9826.$$

Hence, amount paid by Sunil to Ravi after $1\frac{1}{2}$ years = **Rs 9826**.

Type 3. *When the rate of interest for successive years are different.*

If the rate of interest is different for every year say, r_1, r_2, r_3, for the first, second, third year, then the amount after 3 years is given by

$$\boxed{A = P\left(1+\frac{r_1}{100}\right)\left(1+\frac{r_2}{100}\right)\left(1+\frac{r_3}{100}\right)}$$

Ex. 5. *Find the compound interest on Rs 80,000 for 3 years if the rates for the 3 years are 4%, 5% and 10% respectively.*

Sol. Amount = Rs 80,000 $\left(1+\frac{4}{100}\right)\left(1+\frac{5}{100}\right)\left(1+\frac{10}{100}\right)$ = Rs 80,000 $\times \frac{104}{100}\times\frac{105}{100}\times\frac{110}{100}$ = Rs 96096

$\therefore$ Compound interest = Rs 96096 – Rs 80000 = **Rs 16096**.

EXERCISE 10 (b)

Calculate the amount and the compound interest by using the formula for compound interest.

	Principal	Rate of interest	Time (in years)
1.	Rs 625	4% p.a.	2
2.	Rs 8000	15% p.a.	3
3.	Rs 1000	10% p.a.	3
4.	Rs 2400	20% p.a.	3
5.	8000	10% half-yearly	$1\frac{1}{2}$
6.	Rs 700	20% half yearly.	$1\frac{1}{2}$
7.	Rs 64000	5% half yearly.	$1\frac{1}{2}$

8. Reena and Ruchira borrowed Rs 60000 and Rs 50000 respectively for a period of 3 years. Reena paid simple interest at the rate of 10% p.a., while Ruchira paid compound interest at the rate of 10% p.a. compounded annually. Who paid more interest and by how much?

9. Sangeeta lent Rs 40960 to Amar to purchase a shop at 12.5% per annum. If the interest is compounded semi-annually, find the interest paid by Amar after $1\frac{1}{2}$ years.

10. Sudhir lent Rs 2000 at compound interest at 10% payable yearly, while Prashant lent Rs 2000 at compound interest at 10% payable half-yearly. Find the difference in the interest received by Sudhir and Prashant at the end of one year.

11. Find the difference between the simple interest and compound interest on Rs 16000 for $1\frac{1}{2}$ years at 5% per annum, compound interest being reckoned half yearly.

12. How much will Rs 25000 amount to in 2 years at compound interest, if the rates for the successive years be 4 and 5 per cent per year?

13. Find the compound interest on Rs 3125 for 3 years if the rates of interest for the first, second and third year are respectively 4%, 5%, 6%.

14. Umesh set up a small factory by investing Rs 40,000. During the first three successive years his profits were 5%, 10% and 15% respectively. If each year the profit was on previous years' capital, calculate his total profit.

10.6 Growth and Decay

The formula $A = P\left(1 + \dfrac{r}{100}\right)^n$ is called the compound interest law, and applies to any quantity which increases or decreases so that the amount at the end of each period of constant lengths bears a constant ratio to the amount at the beginning of that period. This ratio is called the **growth factor,** if it is greater than 1, and the **decay factor,** if less than 1.

For example, if the population of a town increases steadily by 2% p.a. of the population at the beginning of each year, the yearly *growth factor* is $\left(1 + \dfrac{2}{100}\right)$, *i.e.,* 1.02, and the population after n year is $(1.02)^n$ times the population at the beginning of that period. If the population decreases by 2%, then the yearly *decay factor* is $\left(1 - \dfrac{2}{100}\right)$, *i.e.,* 0.98.

Ex. 1. *If the population of a town decreases 6.25% annually and the present population is 20480000, find its population after 3 years.*

Sol. Required population $= P\left(1 - \dfrac{d}{100}\right)^n$, Here $d = 6.25$

$\therefore$ Population after 3 years $= 20480000\left(1 - \dfrac{6.25}{100}\right)^3 = 20480000\left(1 - \dfrac{625}{10000}\right)^3$

$= 20480000\left(1 - \dfrac{1}{16}\right)^3 = 20480000 \times \dfrac{15}{16} \times \dfrac{15}{16} \times \dfrac{15}{16} = \textbf{16875000.}$

Ex. 2. *The Population of a certain city is 125000. If the annual birth rate is 3.3% and the annual death rate is 1.3% calculate the population after 3 years.*

Sol. Present population of the city $(P) = 125000$

Time $(n) = 3$ years, Rate of birth $(R_1) = 3.3\%$, Rate of death $(R_2) = 1.3\%$. So the net rate of increase $(R_1 - R_2) = 3.3 - 1.3 = 2\%$

$\therefore$ Population after 3 years $= 125000\left(1 + \dfrac{2}{100}\right)^3 = 125000 \times (1.02)^3$

$= 125000 \times 1.061208 = 132651 = \textbf{132651.}$

10.7 Appreciation and Depreciation

When the value of an article **increases** with the passage of time, the article is said to **appreciate.**

When the value of an article decreases with the passage of time, the article is said to **depreciate.**

For example, if a man buys a car and uses it for two years, it is obvious that the car will not be worth as much as a new one. The car will have **depreciated** in value.

On the other hand, if a man buys a piece of land, he will probably find that in a few years he will be able to get a better price for it than he paid in the first place. The value of the land will have appreciated. When things are difficult to obtain, they have a rarity value and appreciate.

Ex. 3. *The value of a residential flat constructed at a cost of Rs 100000 is appreciating at the rate of 10% per year annum. What will be its value 3 years after construction ?*

Sol. Present value of the flat (P) = Rs 100000, rate of appreciation = 10%, Time (n) = 3 years.

$$\therefore \text{ Value of the flat after 3 years } = 100000 \left(1 + \frac{10}{100}\right)^3$$

$$= 100000 \left(1 + \frac{1}{10}\right)^3 = 100000 \times \frac{11}{10} \times \frac{11}{10} \times \frac{11}{10} = \textbf{Rs 133100.}$$

Ex. 4. *Ramu purchased a boat for Rs 16000. If the cost of the boat is depreciating at the rate of 5% per annum, calculate its value after 2 years.*

Sol. Present value of the boat (P) = Rs 16000, Rate (r) of depreciation = – 5%

> **Note :** Negative sign of rate indicates the depreciation, time (n) = 2 years.

$$\therefore \text{ The value of the boat after 2 years}$$

$$= 16000 \times \left(1 - \frac{5}{100}\right)^2 = 16000 \left(1 - \frac{1}{20}\right)^2 = 16000 \times \frac{19}{20} \times \frac{19}{20} = \textbf{Rs 14440.}$$

EXERCISE 10 (c)

1. A district contains 64000 inhabitants. If the population increases at the rate of $2\frac{1}{2}$% per annum, find the number of inhabitants at the end of 3 years.

2. The Nagar Palika of a certain city started campaign to kill stray dogs which numbered 1250 in the city. As a result, the population of stray dogs started decreasing at the rate of 20% per month. Calculate the number of stray dogs in the city three months after the campaign started.

3. 8000 blood donors were registered with a charitable hospital. Some student organizations started mobilizing people for this noble cause. As a result, the number of donors registered, increased at the rate of 20% per half year. Find the total number of new registrants during $1\frac{1}{2}$ years.

4. The value of a residential flat constructed at a cost of Rs 100000 is depreciating at the rate of 10% per annum. What will be its value 3 years after construction.

5. The value of a machine depreciates each year by 10% of its value at the beginning of that year. Its value when new is Rs 750; find its value when it is 2 years old.

6. The national wealth of a country increases by 4% of its value at the beginning of every year. Find the national wealth of the country in 1985, if it was estimated at Rs 3.125×10^{12} in 1983.

7. The Industrial output of a scooter factory increases by 5% of what it had been in the beginning of every year. Find the production after 3 years if the factory turns out 80 000 scooters this year.

8. The price of a scooter depreciates by 2% of its value at the beginning of each year. Find the sale value of the scooter after 3 years, if its present sale value is Rs 12 000.

9. A machinery depreciates each year by 3% of its value at the beginning of each year. If its present value is Rs 94090, find its value two years back.

10. The population of Andhra Pradesh was 5.4×10^7 in 1988. If the population is growing at a constant rate of 2.4% per annum, find the population in 2008 A.D. [Given that $(1.024)^{20} = 1.60694$]

10.8 Inverse Problems on Compound Interest

(A) To find the principal

■ **Case 1.** *When amount, time and rate are given*

Ex. 1. *Find what sum will amount to Rs 55125 in two years at 5% per annum compound interest.*

Sol. $55\,125 = P\left(1+\dfrac{5}{100}\right)^2 = P \times \dfrac{105}{100} \times \dfrac{105}{100} \Rightarrow P = 55125 \times \dfrac{100}{105} \times \dfrac{100}{105} = 50\,000$

Hence, the required sum is **Rs 50 000.**

Ex. 2. *What sum will become Rs 4913 in $1\frac{1}{2}$ years if the rate of interest is $12\frac{1}{2}$% compounded half-yearly ?*

Sol. Amount $(A) = 4913$, rate $(r) = \dfrac{25}{2}\%$, $p.a. = \dfrac{25}{4}\%$ half-yearly, time $(t) = \dfrac{3}{2}$ years = 3 half years

∴ Using the formula, $A = P\left(1+\dfrac{r}{100}\right)^n$, We have

$$4913 = P\left(1+\dfrac{25/4}{100}\right)^3 = P\left(1+\dfrac{25}{400}\right)^3 = P\left(1+\dfrac{1}{16}\right)^3$$

$$4913 = P \times \dfrac{17}{16} \times \dfrac{17}{16} \times \dfrac{17}{16} \Rightarrow 4913 \times \dfrac{16}{17} \times \dfrac{16}{17} \times \dfrac{16}{17} = 4096$$

Hence, the required sum = **Rs 4096.**

- **Case 2.** *When the difference between compound interest and simple interest for a certain period is given.*

Ex. 3. *The difference between the simple and compound interest for a certain sum of money for 3 years at 5% per annum is Rs 61.00. Find the sum.*

Sol. Let the sum be Rs 100.

∴ S.I. on Rs 100 for 3 years @ 5% *p.a.* $= $ Rs $\dfrac{100 \times 3 \times 5}{100} = $ Rs 15

Amount at C.I. on Rs 100 for 3 years @ 5% *p.a.*

$$= \text{Rs } 100\left(1+\dfrac{5}{100}\right)^3 = \text{Rs } 100 \times \dfrac{105}{100} \times \dfrac{105}{100} \times \dfrac{105}{100} = \text{Rs } \dfrac{9261}{80}$$

∴ C.I. on Rs 100 for Rs 3 years $= $ Rs $\left(\dfrac{9261}{80} - 100\right) = $ Rs $\dfrac{1261}{80}$

Difference of C.I. and S.I. $= $ Rs $\dfrac{1261}{80} - $ Rs $15 = $ Rs $\dfrac{1261-1200}{80} = $ Rs $\dfrac{61}{80}$

If the difference is Re $\dfrac{61}{80}$, sum = Rs 100

∴ If the difference is Rs 61, sum $= 100 \times \dfrac{80}{61} \times 61 = $ **Rs 8000.**

(B) **To find the rate of interest**

Ex. 4. *Savita invested Rs 1 000 in a finance company and received Rs 1331 after 3 years, Find the rate of interest per cent per annum compounded annually.*

Sol. Principal $(P) = $ Rs 1 000, Amount $(A) = $ Rs 1331, Time $(n) = 3$ years

$$A = P\left(1+\dfrac{r}{100}\right)^n \quad \therefore \quad 1331 = 1000\left(1+\dfrac{r}{100}\right)^3 \therefore \left(1+\dfrac{r}{100}\right)^3 = \dfrac{1331}{1000} = \left(\dfrac{11}{10}\right)^3$$

$$\therefore \quad 1+\frac{r}{100}=\frac{11}{10} \Rightarrow \frac{r}{100}-1=\frac{1}{10} \therefore r=\frac{1}{10}\times100=10$$

Hence, the required rate of interest is **10% p.a.**

Ex. 5. *At what rate per cent compound interest, Rs 800 amounts to Rs 926.10 in $1\frac{1}{2}$ years, interest being compounded half yearly?*

Sol. Here, Principal (P) = Rs 800, Amount (A) = Rs 926.10, Rate = $r\%$ p.a. = $\frac{r}{2}$ per half year

Time $(n) = 1\frac{1}{2}$ years = 3 half years.

> **Note :** Interest is compounded half-yearly

$$A = P\left(1+\frac{r}{100}\right)^n \Rightarrow 926.10 = 800\left(1+\frac{r}{200}\right)^3$$

$$\Rightarrow \quad \frac{926.10}{800}=\left(1+\frac{r}{200}\right)^3 \Rightarrow \frac{9261}{8000}=\left(1+\frac{r}{200}\right)^3$$

$$\Rightarrow \quad \left(\frac{21}{20}\right)^3=\left(1+\frac{r}{200}\right)^3 \Rightarrow \frac{21}{20}=1+\frac{r}{200}$$

$$\Rightarrow \quad \frac{r}{200}=\frac{21}{20}-1 \Rightarrow \frac{r}{200}=\frac{1}{20} \Rightarrow r=\frac{200}{20}=10$$

$\therefore$ The required rate of interest is **10% p.a.**

(C) To find the time

Ex. 6. *The compound interest on Rs 30,000 at 7% per annum for a certain time is Rs 4347. Find the time period if the interest is compounded annually.*

Sol. Amount (A) = Rs 30 000 + Rs 4347 = Rs 34347, Principal (P) = Rs 30 000, rate (r) = 7%. Let the time be t years.

Then, $$A = P\left(1+\frac{1}{100}\right)^t \therefore 34347 = 30\,000\left(1+\frac{7}{100}\right)^t$$

$$= 30\,000 \times \left(\frac{107}{100}\right)^t \Rightarrow \left(\frac{107}{100}\right)^t=\frac{34347}{30000}=\frac{11449}{10000}=\left(\frac{107}{100}\right)^2 \therefore t=2$$

Hence, the required time is **2 years.**

Ex. 7. *In what time will Rs 64000 amount to Rs 68921 at 5% p.a., interest being compounded semi-annually?*

Sol. Principal (P) = Rs 64000, Amount (A) = Rs 68921, Rate (r) = 5% p.a. = $\frac{5}{2}$ per half year, Time = n.

$$A = P\left(1+\frac{r}{100}\right)^n \Rightarrow 68921 = 64000\left(1+\frac{5}{200}\right)^n$$

$$\Rightarrow \quad \frac{68921}{64000}=\left(1+\frac{1}{40}\right)^n \Rightarrow \frac{68921}{64000}=\left(\frac{41}{40}\right)^n$$

$$\Rightarrow \quad \left(\frac{41}{40}\right)^3=\left(\frac{41}{40}\right)^n \Rightarrow n=3$$

Here, time = 3 half years = $1\frac{1}{2}$ **years.**

1. What amount of money should Mohan invest in a bank in order to get Rs 1323 in 2 years at 5% compounded annually ?

2. Find the sum which amounts to Rs 1352 in 2 years at 4% compound interest.

3. A certain sum amounts to Rs 1331 in $1\frac{1}{2}$ years at 10% p.a. compound interest compounded yearly. Determine the sum.

4. On what sum of money does the difference between the simple interest and compound interest in 2 years at 5% per annum is Rs 15 ?

5. The difference between simple and compound interest on the same sum of money at $6\frac{2}{3}\%$ for 3 years is Rs 184. Determine the sum.

6. On what sum of money will the difference between the simple interest and the compound interest for 2 years at 5% per annum be equal to Rs 2050 ?

7. Find the rate per cent annum, if compounded yearly
   (i) Principal = Rs 196, Amount = Rs 225, time = 2 years.
   (ii) Principal = Rs 3136, Compound interest = Rs 345, Time = 2 years.

8. Rs 8000 became Rs 9261 in a certain interval of time at the rate of 5% per annum, C.I. Find the time.

9. In how many years will a sum of Rs 800 at 10% per annum compounded semi-annually become Rs 926.10?

10. Determine the rate of interest at which a sum of money will become $\frac{216}{125}$ times the original amount in $1\frac{1}{2}$ years, if the interest in compounded half-yearly.

LOOKING BACK
Summary of Key Facts

1. Simple Interest (S.I.) or simply $I = \frac{P \times R \times T}{100}$ where P = Principal, R = Rate of interest, T = Number of years.

2. In case of simple interest, the principal remains constant.

3. In case of compound interest, principal goes an changing periodically.

4. In case of compound interest, the principal for the second year is the sum of the principal for the first year and the simple interest for the first year. Similarly, the principal for the third year is the sum of the principal for the second year and the simple interest for the second year and so on.

5. The compound interest formula is $A = P \times \left(1 + \frac{r}{100}\right)^n$

   Where A = Amount, P = Principal, r = Rate of interest, n = number of years

6. Compound Interest= Amount – Principal = $A - P$.

7. If the interest is payable half-yearly, then for r we take $\frac{r}{2}$, as $r\%$ p.a. means $\frac{r}{2}\%$ half-yearly and for n we taken $2n$, because n year is equal to $2n$ half years. Then

$$A = P\left(1 + \frac{r/2}{100}\right)^n = P\left(1 + \frac{r}{200}\right)^{2n}.$$

MULTIPLE CHOICE QUESTIONS – 9

1. If the simple interest on a sum of money at 5% p.a. annum for 3 years is Rs 1200, the compound interest for the same sum for the same period at the same rate is :

   (*i*) Rs 1260   (*ii*) Rs 1261   (*iii*) Rs 1264   (*iv*) Rs 1265

2. If the difference between the compound interest and simple interest on a certain sum of money for 2 years at $12\frac{1}{2}\%$ per annum is Rs 150. The sum is :

   (*i*) Rs 9000   (*ii*) Rs 9200   (*iii*) Rs 9500   (*iv*) Rs 9600

3. On what sum of money will the simple interest for 3 years at 8% per annum be half of the compound interest on Rs 400 for 2 years at 10% per annum.

   (*i*) Rs 125   (*ii*) Rs 150   (*iii*) Rs 175   (*iv*) Rs 200

4. What is the principal amount which earns Rs 132 as compound interest for the second year at 10% per annum?

   (*i*) Rs 1000   (*ii*) Rs 1200   (*iii*) Rs 1320   (*iv*) Rs 1188

5. If the amount is $2\frac{1}{4}$ times the sum after 2 years at compound interest, the rate of interest per annum is :

   (*i*) 25%   (*ii*) 30%   (*iii*) 40%   (*iv*) 50%

6. The compound interest on Rs 4000 for 2 years compounded annually is Rs 410. The rate per cent per annum is :

   (*i*) 4%   (*ii*) 10%   (*iii*) 5%   (*iv*) 6%

7. The time in which Rs 1800 amounts to Rs 2178 at 10% per annum, compounded annually is :

   (*i*) 3 years   (*ii*) 2 years   (*iii*) 4 years   (*iv*) $1\frac{1}{2}$ years

8. The compound interest on a certain sum at 5% p.a. for 2 years is Rs 328. The simple interest on that sum at the same rate and for the same period will be :

   (*i*) Rs 320   (*ii*) Rs 322   (*iii*) Rs 325   (*iv*) Rs 326

9. Seema borrowed Rs 8000 at 12% simple interest for 3 years and lent it to Anjali for 3 years at 15% per annum compound interest, compounded annually. Seema's profit at the end of 3 years is :

   (*i*) Rs 1500   (*ii*) Rs 1301   (*iii*) Rs 1287   (*iv*) Rs 1783

10. The compound interest on Rs 16000 for $1\frac{1}{2}$ years at 10% per annum interest compounded half yearly is :

   (*i*) Rs 2500   (*ii*) Rs 2724   (*iii*) Rs 2522   (*iv*) Rs 18522

ANSWERS

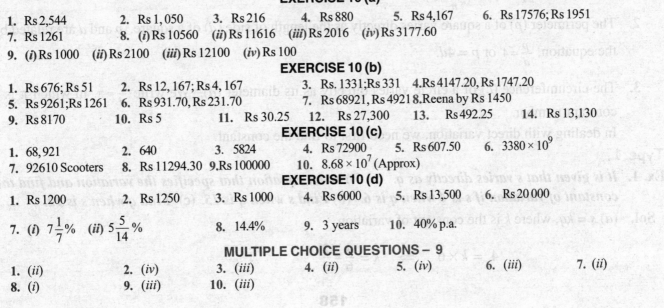

EXERCISE 10 (a)

1. Rs 2,544   **2.** Rs 1,050   **3.** Rs 216   **4.** Rs 880   **5.** Rs 4,167   **6.** Rs 17576; Rs 1951

7. Rs 1261   **8.** (*i*) Rs 10560   (*ii*) Rs 11616   (*iii*) Rs 2016   (*iv*) Rs 3177.60

9. (*i*) Rs 1000   (*ii*) Rs 2100   (*iii*) Rs 12100   (*iv*) Rs 100

EXERCISE 10 (b)

1. Rs 676; Rs 51   **2.** Rs 12,167; Rs 4,167   **3.** Rs. 1331; Rs 331   **4.** Rs 4147.20, Rs 1747.20

5. Rs 9261; Rs 1261   **6.** Rs 931.70, Rs 231.70   **7.** Rs 68921, Rs 4921 **8.** Reena by Rs 1450

9. Rs 8170   **10.** Rs 5   **11.** Rs 30.25   **12.** Rs 27,300   **13.** Rs 492.25   **14.** Rs 13,130

EXERCISE 10 (c)

1. 68,921   **2.** 640   **3.** 5824   **4.** Rs 72900   **5.** Rs 607.50   **6.** 3380×10^9

7. 92610 Scooters   **8.** Rs 11294.30 **9.** Rs 100000   **10.** 8.68×10^7 (Approx)

EXERCISE 10 (d)

1. Rs 1200   **2.** Rs 1250   **3.** Rs 1000   **4.** Rs 6000   **5.** Rs 13,500   **6.** Rs 20 000

7. (*i*) $7\frac{1}{7}\%$ (*ii*) $5\frac{5}{14}\%$ **8.** 14.4%   **9.** 3 years   **10.** 40% p.a.

MULTIPLE CHOICE QUESTIONS – 9

1. (*ii*)   **2.** (*iv*)   **3.** (*iii*)   **4.** (*ii*)   **5.** (*iv*)   **6.** (*iii*)   **7.** (*ii*)

8. (*i*)   **9.** (*iii*)   **10.** (*iii*)

11. Variation

11.1 Direct Variation

If a train travels uniformly at 72 km per hour, in 5 minutes it travels 6 km, in 10 minutes it travels 12 km, in 15 minutes it travels 18 km, and so on. When the time is doubled, the distance is doubled; when the time is tripled, the distance is tripled; when the time is halved, the distance is halved, and so on. We say that the distance is directly proportional to time, or that the distance varies directly as time.

If y km be the distance covered by a train in x minutes, then $y = \frac{6}{5}x$ or $\frac{y}{x} = \frac{6}{5}$, i.e., the ratio $\frac{y}{x}$ = constant.

> *One quantity varies directly as a second quantity if the ratio of the first to the second is constant. Let x and y be two variables, then y varies directly as x if the ratio $\frac{y}{x}$ equals a constant value k. We call k the constant of variation. In short, for the phrase "y varies directly as x", we write*
> $$y \propto x$$
> *The symbol $\propto$ means 'varies as'*
> *$y \propto x$ is replaced by the equation*
> $$y = kx$$
> *where k is any non-zero number. The constant k is called the **constant of variation**.*

For example :

1. If the cost of each pen is the same, say 5 rupees, the cost (c) of any number of pens (n) varies directly as the number of pens, then $\frac{c}{n} = 5$ or $c = 5n$.

2. The perimeter (p) of a square varies directly as the length of side (d) of a square. p and d are related by the equation, $\frac{p}{d} = 4$ or $p = 4d$.

3. The circumference (c) of a circle varies directly as its diameter (d). We write $\frac{c}{d} = \pi$, in which π is a constant number.

In dealing with direct variation, we need first to find the constant.

Type 1.

Ex. 1. *It is given that s varies directly as q. (a) Write an equation that specifies the variation and find the constant of variation if s is 4 when q is 6. (b) Find s when q is 15. (c) Find q when s is 12.*

Sol. (a) $s = kq$, where k is the constant of variation

$$4 = k \times 6 \quad \Rightarrow \quad k = \frac{4}{6} = \frac{2}{3}.$$

(b) $s = \frac{2}{3}q$ $\therefore$ $s = \frac{2}{3} \times 15 \Rightarrow s = 10$

(c) $s = \frac{2}{3}q$ $\therefore$ $12 = \frac{2}{3}q \Rightarrow q = 12 \times \frac{3}{2} = 18.$

Ex. 2. *In which of the following tables, x and y vary directly with each other ?*

(i)

x	2	5	6	8
y	6	15	18	24

(ii)

x	1.3	7	8.1	10
y	1.3	7	8.1	12

Sol. (i) On forming the ratio $\frac{x}{y}$ for corresponding values of x and y, we get $\frac{x}{y} = \frac{1}{3}$ in all cases. Therefore

x and y vary directly and the constant of variation is $\frac{1}{3}$.

(ii) The ratio $\frac{x}{y}$ is 1 for the first three values of x and y but it is not so when $x = 10$, $y = 12$. Therefore,

x and y do not vary directly.

Ex. 3. *Replace each star in the following table by a suitable number if x and y vary directly.*

x	3.6	5	9.5	17.1	*
y	*	10	*	*	11

Sol. As x and y vary directly, so $\frac{x}{y}$ is constant.

$\frac{x}{y} = \frac{5}{10} = \frac{1}{2}$ $\therefore$ The constant of variation 'k' = $\frac{1}{2}$.

Now, $\frac{3.6}{y} = k = \frac{1}{2} \Rightarrow y = 3.6 \times 2 = \mathbf{7.2.}$ $\frac{9.5}{y} = k = \frac{1}{2} \Rightarrow y = 9.5 \times 2 = \mathbf{19.}$

$\frac{17.1}{y} = k = \frac{1}{2} \Rightarrow y = 17.1 \times 2 = \mathbf{34.2.}$ $\frac{x}{11} = k = \frac{1}{2} \Rightarrow 2x = 11 \Rightarrow x = \frac{11}{2} = \mathbf{5.5.}$

11.2 Alternative Version of Direct Variation

The cost of different numbers of a certain book is given in the following table.

Number of books	1	2	6	8	15	40
Cost in rupees	10	20	60	80	150	400

> **Note that :**
> (i) The ratio of the number of books in the third column to the number of books in the fifth column is
> $\frac{6}{15} = \frac{2}{5}$. The ratio of the corresponding costs in the third column and fifth column is $\frac{\text{Rs } 60}{\text{Rs } 150} = \frac{2}{5}$, *i.e.,* it
> is the same.
> (ii) The cost increases when the number of books increases and decreases when the number of books
> decreases. In other words the two quantities change *in the same way.*
> For these reasons, we say that the cost of the books is *directly proportional* to the number of books or
> that the cost *varies directly* as the number.

Def. *A direct proportion* is indicated when two quantities are so related that (*i*) an increase in one causes a corresponding increase in the other or when a decrease in one causes a corresponding decrease in the other and (*ii*) they increase or decrease in the same ratio.

In the example discussed above, the proportion is ratio of 6 books to 15 books = ratio of cost of 6 books to cost of 15 books.

i.e., $\qquad\qquad$ 6 : 15 : : 60 : 150

We first write the ratio of the books and then the ratio of the costs in the *same order*.

Ex. 4. *If 15 books cost Rs 70, how much will 12 books cost ?*

Sol. 15 books cost Rs 70, 12 books cost ?

Ratio of no. of books = Ratio of their costs = *i.e.,* $\dfrac{15}{12} = \dfrac{70}{x}$

$\Rightarrow \qquad\qquad 15 \times x = 12 \times 70 \Rightarrow x = \dfrac{12 \times 70}{15} = 56$

∴ The cost of 12 books = **Rs 56.**

The following way of working out the solution is more convenient.

Let Rs x be the cost of 12 books. We construct the following table:

As it is a case of direct variation, so

$\dfrac{15}{70} = \dfrac{12}{x} \Rightarrow 15x = 12 \times 70 \Rightarrow x = \dfrac{12 \times 70}{15} = 56.$

Number of books	15	12
Cost in rupees	70	x

∴ The cost of 12 books is **Rs 56.**

Ex. 5. *If 20 men assemble 8 machines in a day, how many men are needed to assemble 12 machines in a day?*

Sol. Suppose the number of men needed to assemble 12 machines is x. More men will be required if we have more machines, so it is a case of direct variation. We construct the following table.

Number of machines	8	12
Number of men	20	x

$\dfrac{8}{20} = \dfrac{12}{x} \Rightarrow 8x = 20 \times 12 \Rightarrow x = \dfrac{20 \times 12}{8} = 30$

∴ The number of men required = **30.**

Ex. 6. *A machine takes 5 hours in cutting 120 tools. How many tools will it cut in 20 hours?*

Sol. Let the number of tools required be x. We have the following table:

Number of hours	5	20
Number of tools	120	x

As number of tools and number of hours taken in cutting tools vary directly, so

$\dfrac{5}{120} = \dfrac{20}{x} \Rightarrow 5x = 20 \times 120 \Rightarrow x = \dfrac{20 \times 120}{5} = 480$

Hence, the number of tools cut in 20 hours = **480.**

Ex. 7. *In a library 136 copies of a certain book require a shelf-length of 3.4 metres. How many copies of the same book would occupy a shelf-length of 5.1 metres?*

Sol. Let the required number of copies be x. Construct the following table:

Number of copies	136	x
Length in cm	3.4	5.1

Since the number of copies and length of shelf are in direct variation, therefore,

$$\frac{136}{3.4} = \frac{x}{5.1} \Rightarrow 3.4x = 136 \times 5.1 \Rightarrow x = \frac{136 \times 5.1}{3.4} = \frac{\overset{48}{\cancel{136}} \times 51}{\underset{1}{\cancel{34}} \cancel{2}} = 204$$

Hence the required number of copies = **204**.

Ex. 8. *11 men dig a trench* $6\frac{3}{4}$ *metres long in one day. How many men should be employed for digging a trench of the same type 27 metres long in one day?*

Sol. Let the number of men required be x. Then, we have the following table:

Number of men	11	x
Length of trench in metres	$6\frac{3}{4}$	27

Since the length of the trench dug and number of persons employed are in direct variation or proportion, so

$$\frac{11}{6\frac{3}{4}} = \frac{x}{27} \Rightarrow 6\frac{3}{4}x = 11 \times 27 \Rightarrow \frac{27}{4}x = 11 \times 27 \Rightarrow x = 11 \times 27 \times \frac{4}{27} = 44.$$

Hence the required number of persons = **44**.

EXERCISE 11 (a)

In which of the following, x and y vary directly with each other. For each direct variation, state the constant of variation.

1. $y = -8x$ **2.** $y = \frac{3}{4}x$ **3.** $xy = 5$ **4.** $y = \frac{3}{x}$ **5.** $y + 4x = 0$ **6.** $y - 3x = 1$

7.

x	1	2	3	4
y	−5	−10	−15	−20

8.

x	2	4	6	8
y	−1	2	−3	4

9.

x	−2	0	2	4
y	−4	0	4	8

10.

x	2	4	6	8
y	0	8	6	4

11. The height to which a balloon with hydrogen gas rises in the air varies directly as time. Given below are some observations about the time and the corresponding height of the balloon (in metres). Find the missing terms in the table.

Time (in minutes)	3	4	—	25	—
Height of the balloon (in metres)	—	48	84	—	1860

12. **Which of the following quantities vary directly with each other ?**

(*a*) Number of articles x and their price y.

(*b*) Weight of articles x and their cost y.

(*c*) Distance x and time y, speed remaining the same (Distance = Time × speed)

(d) Wages and hours of work.

(e) Speed and time (distance covered remaining the same).

(Answer carefully).

13. If d varies directly as t, and if $d = 4$ when $t = 9$, find d when $t = 21$.

14. If a varies directly as b, and if $a = 5$ when $b = 6$, find a when $b - 1 = 11$

15. The table shows the weights of various square pieces of tin cut from the same sheet :

Side of square in cm	l	1	2	2·5	4	10
Weight of piece in $grams$	w	0.4	1.6	2.5	6.4	40

  (i) What is the variation relation between w and l ?

  (ii) Write down the weights corresponding to $l = 20$, $l = \frac{1}{2}$.

  (iii) What formula connects w and l ?

16. If the thickness of 500 sheets of paper is 3·5 cm, what would be the thickness of 275 sheets of this paper?

17. The mass of a uniform copper bar varies directly as its length. If a bar 40 cm long has a mass of approximately 420 g, find the mass of a bar 136 cm long.

18. A fish with a mass of 3 kg causes a fishing pole to bend 9 cm. If the amount of bending varies directly as the mass, how much will the pole bend for a 2 kg fish ?

19. At a party, 8 bottles of soft drink are served for every batch of 5 children. How many bottles would be served if 40 children were present at the party ?

20. Harsh takes 150 steps in walking a distance of 125 metres. What distance would he cover in 360 steps ?

21. The second class railway fare for 240 km of journey is Rs 15·00. What would be the fare for a journey of 139.2 km? Assume that the fare varies directly as the length of the journey.

22. If the thickness of a pile of 12 cardboards is 35 mm, find the thickness of a pile of 294 cardboards.

23. The amount of extension in an elastic spring varies directly as the weight hung on it. If a weight of 150 g produces an extension of 2.9 cm, then what weight would produce an extension of 17.4 cm ?

24. Find the height of a pole which casts a shadow 20 m long at a time and place where the shadow of a stick 1 m long is 55 cm.

   [Let the height of the pole be x metres, then

   Ratio of heights = Ratio of lengths of shadows, i.e., $\dfrac{x}{1} = \dfrac{20}{0.55}$]

11.3 Inverse Variation

Study the following

   1. (i) The floor area of a rectangular passage is 60 m^2. The following table shows the relation between its length and breadth

Length (l) in $metres$	60	30	20	15	12	10
Breadth (b) in $metres$	1	2	3	4	5	6

This example illustrates inverse variation. When length is decreased, the breadth is increased in the same proportion. Thus if length is halved, i.e., it becomes 30 m, the breadth is doubled, i.e., it becomes 2 metres. Similarly, when length becomes 20 metres, i.e., one third, the breadth is trebled, i.e., it becomes 3 metres and so on. We say that *l varies inversely as b, i.e., $l \propto \dfrac{1}{b}$.*

   (ii) Do you see that the product lb remains constant. Here $lb = 60$.

2. The table at the right shows the time t, that it takes a car travelling at a speed of s km/h to cover a distance of 90 km. You can see that

s km/h	t (h)
45	2
50	1.8
60	1.5
75	1.2
90	1

$$s \propto \frac{1}{t} \Rightarrow st = \text{constant (Here } st = 90)$$

This relationship is an example of inverse variation.

3. The times taken by an aircraft to travel a certain distance at various speeds are as follows :

Speed in km/h	Times in hours	Speed in km/h	Times in hours
300	10	500	6
400	$7\frac{1}{2}$	600	5

Note that (i) If the ratio of the speeds is $\frac{300}{500} = \frac{3}{5}$; the ratio of the corresponding number of hours is $\frac{10}{6} = \frac{5}{3}$ and this is the multiplicative inverse of $\frac{3}{5}$.

(ii) The number of kilometres per hour is increased when the number of hours taken is decreased, and the number of kilometres per hour is decreased when the number of hours is increased. In other words, the two quantities change in *opposite ways*.

For these reasons, we say that the number of kilometres per hour is *inversely proportional* to the number of hours taken.

> **Def.** *An* **Inverse Variation or proportion** *is indicated when two quantities are so related that (i) an increase in one causes a corresponding decrease in the other, or vice versa, and (ii) the ratio of any two values of the one quantity is the inverse of the ratio of the corresponding values of the other.*

11.4 Alternative Version

The following are quantitative expressions in which the variables are inversely related.
(1) The greater the speed, the less the time.
(2) The slower the speed, the longer the time.
(3) The greater the volume, the less the density.
(4) The more men working, the shorter the time.
(5) The fewer men working, the longer the time.

> *Two quantities x and y are said to vary indirectly (inversely) if the product xy remains constant.*
> 'k' is called the **constant of variation** and it is always positive.
> **Rule.** If x and y vary inversely and y_1, y_2 are two values of y corresponding to the values x_1, x_2 of x respectively, then $x_1 y_1 = x_2 y_2$.

11.5 Solved Examples

Type 1.

Ex. 1. *Which of the following vary inversely as each other ?*

   (a) *The number of pencils x you can buy with Rs 12 and the cost y of the pencils (which you can assume to be a multiple of 25 paise in this case) ?*

(b) *The number x of men hired to construct a wall, if the time is y taken to finish the job.*

(c) *The length of a journey by bus and the price of the ticket.*

Sol. (a) Since on increasing the cost (y), the number of pencils (x) one can buy would decrease, therefore, x and y vary inversely.

(b) Since more persons are needed to finish the work in less time, therefore, x and y vary inversely.

(c) This is a case of direct variation, more the length of journey is, more will be the price of the ticket.

Type 2.

Ex. 2. *Look at the following tables. State in which of the cases do x and y vary inversely and in which vary directly.*

(i)

x	1	2	3	4	5	6
y	8	16	24	32	40	48

(ii)

x	1	2	3	4	6	12
y	48	24	16	12	8	4

(iii)

x	1	2	3	5	9
y	90	45	30	18	10

(iv)

x	72	9	24	36	288
y	1	8	3	2	0.25

Sol. (i) In all cases $\frac{x_1}{y_1} = \frac{x_2}{y_2} = \frac{1}{8}$, i.e., $\frac{x}{y}$ is constant for any two pairs of values for x and y. So this is a case of direct variation.

(ii) In all cases, the product xy is constant for any two pairs of values for x and y, $x_1 y_1 = 1 \times 48 = 48$, $x_2 y_2 = 2 \times 24 = 48$, $x_3 y_3 = 3 \times 16 = 48$, and so on. Also, $\frac{x_1}{y_1} = \frac{1}{48}, \frac{x_2}{y_2} = \frac{2}{24} = \frac{1}{12}$, so $\frac{x_1}{y_1} \neq \frac{x_2}{y_2}$.

Hence this is a case of inverse variation and not a case of direct variation.

(iii) In all cases, the product xy is constant for any two pairs of values for x and y.

Thus, $x_1 y_1 = 1 \times 90 = 90$, $x_2 y_2 = 2 \times 45 = 90$, $x_3 y_3 = 3 \times 30 = 90$

$x_4 y_4 = 5 \times 18 = 90$, $x_5 y_5 = 9 \times 10 = 90$. So this is a case of inverse variation.

(iv) In all cases, the product xy is constant for any two pairs of values for x and y.

Thus, $x_1 y_1 = 72 \times 1 = 72$, $x_2 y_2 = 9 \times 8 = 72$, and so on.

So this is a case of inverse variation.

Ex. 3. *Determine from the values of x and y given below whether they vary directly, inversely or in neither of these ways :*

	(i)	(ii)	(iii)	(iv)	(v)	(vi)	(vii)
x	5	10	15	20	25	30	35
y	1	2	10	15	20	25	30

If your answer is 'directly', think again. Is x/y the same for all pairs of values of x and y ?

Sol. Though y is increasing when x is increased, the ratio of corresponding values of x and y is not constant, which is clear from the following ratios.

(i) $\frac{x}{y} = \frac{5}{1} = 5$, (ii) $\frac{x}{y} = \frac{10}{2} = 5$, (iii) $\frac{x}{y} = \frac{15}{10} = \frac{3}{2}$, (iv) $\frac{x}{y} = \frac{20}{15} = \frac{4}{3}$,

(v) $\frac{x}{y} = \frac{25}{20} = \frac{5}{4}$, (vi) $\frac{x}{y} = \frac{30}{25} = \frac{6}{5}$ (vii) $\frac{x}{y} = \frac{35}{30} = \frac{7}{6}$

This shows that x and y do not vary directly. They do not vary inversely also because

(1) When one value increases, the other value also increases.

(2) The products of the corresponding values of x and y are not equal, *i.e.*,

$(5 \times 1) \neq (10 \times 2) \neq (15 \times 10) \neq (20 \times 15) \neq (25 \times 20) \neq (30 \times 25) \neq (35 \times 30)$

Hence the given values of 'x' and 'y' vary neither directly nor inversely.

Type 3.

Ex. 4. *If y varies inversely as x, and if y = 4 when x = 72, find the following.*

(a) *the constant of variation,* (b) *the value of y when x = 9.*

Sol. (*a*) Let $xy = k$, where k is the constant of variation.

since $y = 4$ when $x = 72$, $k = xy = 72 \times 4 = 288$.

$\therefore$ The constant of variation is **288**.

(*b*) Since $k = 288$ and $x = 9$,

$$y = \frac{k}{x} = \frac{288}{9} = 32$$

$\therefore$ When $x = 9$, the value of y is **32**.

Ex. 5. *It is known that for a given mass of gas, the volume V varies inversely as the pressure P. Fill in the missing entries in the following table.*

	(i)	(ii)	(iii)	(iv)	(v)	(vi)	(vii)
V (in cm³)	?	48	60	?	100	?	200
P (in atmosphere)	2	?	$\frac{3}{2}$	1	?	$\frac{1}{2}$	?

Sol. The volume (V) of the gas varies inversely as the pressure (P).

$\therefore \qquad\qquad PV = k$

$\therefore$ From (*iii*) $\frac{3}{2} \times 60 = k$, *i.e.* $k = 90$.

(*i*) For $P = 2$, $2 \times V = 90 \qquad \therefore \ P = \frac{90}{2} = 45$.

(*ii*) For $V = 48$; $P \times 48 = 90 \quad \therefore \ P = \frac{90}{48} = \frac{15}{8}$.

(*iv*) For $P = 1$, $1 \times V = 90 \qquad \therefore \ V = 90$,

(*v*) For $V = 100$, $P \times 100 = 90 \ \therefore P = \frac{90}{100} = \frac{9}{10}$ or $0 \cdot 9$

Similarly, calculate other entries.

V(in cm³)	45	48	60	90	100	180	200
P(in atmospheres)	2	$\frac{15}{8}$	$\frac{3}{2}$	1	$\frac{9}{10}$	$\frac{1}{2}$	$\frac{9}{20}$

EXERCISE 11 (b)

1. **In which of the following cases do x and y vary inversely as each other ?**

   (i) Time taken to travel a given distance if speed is constant.

   (ii) The time taken and distance travelled when the speed is constant.

   (iii) Amount available for purchase remaining constant, increase in cost and the number of articles that can be purchased.

   (iv) The number of people and the time taken to complete a work.

   (v) The length of a journey and the price of the ticket.

2. **State the relationship between the given variables as an equation, using k for the constant of variation.**

   (i) The volume V of a gas at a fixed temperature varies inversely as the pressure P.

   (ii) The current I in an electrical circuit of fixed voltage, varies inversely as the resistance R.

   (iii) The height h of a cylinder of fixed volume, varies inversely as the area A of the base.

   (iv) The frequency f of an electromagnetic wave is inversely proportional to the length l of the wave.

3. **Fill in the blanks in the following tables by determining first whether x and y vary directly or inversely :**

(a)

x	3	6	?	27	?
y	11	22	33	?	880

(b)

x	30	20	15	?	?
y	6	4	?	2	1

(c)

x	2	3	4	?	8
y	48	?	24	16	?

(d)

x	1	5	10	?	?
y	125	?	12.5	5	1

4. **It is given that 'u' varies inversely as 'v'. Complete the following table:**

u	30	3	10	?	15	?	0.2
v	5			25		0.5	

5. x and y vary inversely as each other. When $x = 10$, $y = 6$. Which of the following is not a possible pair of corresponding values of x and y.

   (i) 15 and 4   (ii) 20 and 3   (iii) 1.5 and 30   (iv) 0.6 and 100

6. (i) If y varies inversely as x, and if $y = 9$ when $x = 2$, find y when $x = 3$.

   (ii) If u is inversely proportional to v, and if $u = 12$ when $v = 3$, find u when $v = 9$.

   (iii) If c is inversely proportional to d, and if $c = 18$ when $d = \dfrac{2}{3}$, find d when $c = \dfrac{6}{7}$.

   (iv) If m is inversely proportional to n, and if $m = 0.02$ when $n = 5$, find m when $n = 0.2$.

7. If a varies as $b + 2$, and if $a = 8$ when $b = 1.5$, find a when $b = 3$.

8. If y is inversely proportional to x, how does y change when x is doubled ?

9. If x varies inversely as $y - 4$, and if $x = -5$ when $y = \dfrac{1}{2}$, find x when $y = -1$.

10. If a varies inversely as t^2, and if $a = 2$ when $t = 0.3$, write a formula for a in terms of t.

Ex. 6. *A shopkeeper has just enough money to buy 52 cycles worth Rs 525 each. If each cycle were to cost Rs 21 more than the amount he has, how many cycles would he be able to buy?*

Sol. Let the number of bicycles he is able to buy = x. We have the following table:

No. of cycles	52	x
Cost of a cycle (in rupees)	525	546

If the cost is more, the number of cycles bought are less, therefore, it is a case of inverse variation.

$$\therefore \ 52 \times 525 = x \times 546 \ \Rightarrow \ x = \frac{52 \times 525}{546} = 50$$

Hence, the number of cycles he would be able to buy = **50.**

Alternative method: Ratio of no. cycles = Inverse ratio of costs

$$\therefore \ 52 : x :: 546 : 525$$

$$\Rightarrow \ x \times 546 = 52 \times 525 \ \Rightarrow \ x = \frac{52 \times 525}{546} = 50$$

$$\boxed{\text{If } a : b :: c : d, \text{ then } ad = bc}$$

Remark. As done above, in inverse variation or proportion, we write the two ratios in the inverse order and not in the same order as we did in case of direct variation or proportion.

Ex. 7. *If 20 men consume a certain quantity of rice in 14 days, in how many days will 8 men consume the same quantity of rice?*

Sol. Let the required number of days = x. We construct the following table:

No. of men	20	8
No. of days	14	x

Less men, more days so it is a case of inverse variation.

$$\therefore \ 20 \times 14 = 8 \times x \ \Rightarrow \ x = \frac{20 \times 14}{8} = 35$$

Hence, 8 men will consume the rice in **35 days.**

Alternative method : Ratio of no. of men = Inverse ratio of days

$$20 : 8 :: \ x : 14 \ \Rightarrow \ 8 \times x = 20 \times 14 \Rightarrow x = \frac{20 \times 14}{8} = \textbf{35}.$$

Ex. 8. *Seema cycles to her school at an average speed of 12 km/h. It takes her 20 minutes to reach the school. If she wants to reach her school in 15 minutes, what should be her average speed?*

Sol. Let the required average speed of Seema be x km/h. Then, we have the following table:

Average speed	12 km/h	x
Time taken	20 min	15 min

As the speed of cycling increases, the time taken to reach the school decreases, so it is a case of inverse variation.

$$\therefore \ 12 \times 20 = x \times 15 \Rightarrow x = \frac{12 \times 20}{15} = 16$$

Hence, her average speed required is **16 km/h.**

Alternative method : Ratio of speeds = Inverse ratio of time.

$$\therefore \ 12 : x :: 15 : 20 \ \Rightarrow \ x \times 15 = 12 \times 20 \Rightarrow x = \frac{12 \times 20}{15} = \textbf{16}.$$

Ex. 9. *If 1800 persons can finish the construction of a building in 40 days, how many persons are needed to complete the construction of the building in 24 days?*

Sol. Let the number of persons needed be x. Then, we have the following table:

Number of persons	1800	x
Number of days	40	24

As the number of persons engaged in the construction of the building increases, the number of days for completion of construction decreases, so it is a case of inverse variation.

$\therefore 1800 \times 40 = x \times 24 \Rightarrow x = \dfrac{1800 \times 40}{24} = 3000$

Hence the number of persons needed is **3000.**

Alternative method : Ratio of number of persons = inverse ratio of number of days.

$\therefore 1800 : x :: 24 : 40 \Rightarrow 24x = 1800 \times 40 \Rightarrow x = \dfrac{1800 \times 40}{24} = \textbf{3000.}$

Ex. 10. *A fort had provisions for 150 men for 45 days. After 10 days 25 men left the fort. How long will the food last at the same rate ?*

Sol. The remaining food would last $(45 - 10)$ or 35 days for 150 men. But 25 men have left. Number of remaining men = $150 - 25 = 125$.

For 150 men, food lasts 35 days. Suppose for 125 men, food lasts x days

Less men, more days, so it is a case of inverse variation. We have the following table:

Number of persons	150	125
Number of days	35	x

$\therefore 150 \times 35 = 125 \times x \Rightarrow x = \dfrac{150 \times 35}{125} = 42$

Hence the food will last **42 days.**

Alternate method : Ratio of number of persons = Inverse ratio of number of days.

$\therefore 150 : 125 :: x : 35 \Rightarrow 125x = 150 \times 35 \Rightarrow x = \dfrac{150 \times 35}{125} = \textbf{42.}$

EXERCISE 11 (c)

1. Navin cycles to his school at an average speed of 12 km/hr. It takes him 20 minutes to reach the school. If he wants to reach his school in 15 minutes, what should be his average speed ?

2. The time needed to travel from one place to another is inversely proportional to the speed. A person travelling 72 km/h can go from Dehra Dun to Lucknow in 10 h. How fast must the person travel to make the trip in 9 h ?

3. 28 pumps can empty a reservoir in 18 hours. In how many hours can 42 such pumps do the same work?

4. A stock of foodgrains is enough for 400 persons for 9 days. How long will the same stock last for 300 persons?

5. A contractor who had a work force of 630 persons, undertook to complete a portion of a stadium in 14 months. He was asked to complete the job in 9 months. How many extra persons had he to employ?

6. 18 men can do a piece of work in 10 days. How many less men are required if the work is to be completed in 15 days?

7. Working 4 hours a day, Savita can type a manucript in 15 days. How many hours a day should she work so as to finish the work in 10 days?

8. A train moving at a speed of 60 km/h covers a certain distance in 7.5 hours. What should be the speed of the train to cover the same distance in 6 hours?

9. A garrison of 800 men had provisions for 39 days. However, a reinforcement of 500 men arrived. For how many days will the food last now?

10. A group of 210 men had provisions for 60 days. After 10 days, 60 men left. How long will the remaining food last?
    (**Hint :** The remaining food would have lasted 50 days for 210 men. Find out how long will the food last for 150 men).

11. A besieged town has provisions to last for 3 weeks. Its population is 22400. How many people must be sent away in order that the provisions may last for 7 weeks ?

12. A hostel had rations for 60 days for 500 students. After 12 days, 300 more students join the hostel. How long will the remaining rations last ?

13. The number of hours needed to clear the trees from some land is inversely proportional to the number of people who are working. If it would take 4 people 15 hours to do the job, how many people would be needed to complete the job in 6 hours ?

14. A pulley revolves at a speed that is inversely proportional to its diameter. A pulley with a diameter of 12 cm is belted to a pulley with a diameter of 8 cm. If the smaller pulley is revolving at a rate of 96 rpm (revolutions per minute), how fast is the larger pulley revolving ?

15. A man travels a certain distance by train in 4 hours and 12 minutes at the rate of 44·8 km per hour. How much time will it take to cover the same distance if the speed of the train is increased to 57.6 km per hour ?

16. The interest rate required to yield a given income is inversely proportional to the amount of money invested. Sameer receives income from Rs 16000 that he has invested at an annual interest rate of 8%. How much money should he invest to receive the same income if the annual interest rate increases to 10% ?

11.6 Compound Variation

There are many problems involving more than one variation in which more than two different types of quantities are used.

Ex. 1. *15 chests of tea, each chest containing 20 kg costs Rs 350. What will be the price at this rate of 12 chests each containing 25 kg.*

Sol. 15 chests each containing 20 kg cost Rs 350.

∴ 1 chest containing 20 kg costs Rs $\frac{350}{15}$ (less no. of chests, less cost)

∴ 1 chest containing 1 kg costs Rs $\left(\frac{350}{15\times20}\right)$ (less quantity, less cost)

∴ 12 chests containing 1 kg cost Rs $\left(\frac{350}{15\times20}\times12\right)$ (more no. of chests, more cost)

∴ 12 chests containing 25 kg cost Rs = $\left(\frac{350\times12\times25}{15\times20}\right)$ = **Rs 350.**   (more quantity, more cost)

Ex. 2. *25 horses eat 5 bags of corn in 12 days, how much will 10 horses eat in 18 days?*

Sol. In 12 days 25 horses eat 5 bags of corn

∴ In 1 day 25 horses eat $\frac{5}{12}$ bags of corn   (less days, less corn)

In 1 day 1 horse eats $\frac{5}{12\times25}$ bags of corn   (less no. of horses, less corn)

In 1 day 10 horses will eat $\frac{5}{12\times25}\times10$ bags   (more horses, more corn)

in 18 days 10 horses will eat $\frac{5\times10\times18}{12\times25}$ bags of corn = **3 bags.**   (more days, more corn)

EXERCISE 11 (d)

1. 4 men can make 4 cupboards in 4 days; how many cupboards can 14 men make in 14 days.

2. In a hostel it costs Rs 1800 to keep 50 children for 8 weeks. For what length of time did the cost of keeping 90 children amount to Rs 21060.

3. In how many days of working 8 hours each day, can 12 men do the same work as 10 men working 9 hours a day do in 16 days?

4. If 10 men, working 7 hours a day dig a trench 147 m long, how many men working 8 hours a day will dig a trench 168 m long (of the same breadth and depth as the first in the same number of days)?

5. Three pumps working 8 hours a day can empty a tank in 2 days. How many hours a day must 4 pumps work to empty the tank in 1 day?

6. If a man travels 65 km in 3 days by walking $7\frac{1}{2}$ hours a day, in how many days will he travel 156 km by walking 8 hours a day?

LOOKING BACK
Summary of Key Facts

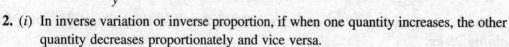

1. (i) Two quantities are in direct variation or direct proportion if with the increase in of the quantities, the other quantity also increases and vice versa.

   (ii) **Alternative version:** Two quantities x and y vary directly, if the ratio $\frac{x}{y}$ remains constant. If $\frac{x}{y} = k$ (a positive constant), then k is called the constant of variation.

2. (i) In inverse variation or inverse proportion, if when one quantity increases, the other quantity decreases proportionately and vice versa.

   (ii) **Alternative version :** Two quantities x and y vary indirectly (inversely) if the product xy remains constant. If $xy = k$ (a positive constant), k is called constant of variation.

MULTIPLE CHOICE QUESTIONS – 10

1. Deepak bought 12 oranges for Rs 7.20. Vimal bought x oranges more than Deepak's for Rs 9.60. The value of x is :
   (i) 2 (ii) 5 (iii) 4 (iv) 6

2. On a scale of map 0.7 cm represents 8.4 km. If the distance between two points on the map is 46.5 cm, the actual distance between the points is :
   (i) 56 km (ii) 55.80 km (iii) 62.80 km (iv) 72 km

3. If 20 men working together can finish a job in 20 days, then the number of days taken by 25 men of the same capacity to finish the job is :
   (i) 25 (ii) 20 (iii) 16 (iv) 12

4. In a factory, 600 men had provisions for 180 days. After 40 days, 100 men left the fort. The remaining food will last for :
   (i) 150 days (ii) 142 days (iii) 168 days (iv) 200 days

5. 14 pumps of equal capacity can fill a tank in 6 days. If the tank has to be filled in 4 days, the number of extra pumps needed is :
   (i) 7 (ii) 14 (iii) 21 (iv) 28

6. If 21 cows eat as much as 15 buffaloes, how many cows will eat as much as 105 buffaloes.
   (i) 75 (ii) 147 (iii) 63 (iv) 54

7. If 18 binders bind 900 books in 10 days, how many binders will be required to bind 660 books in 12 days?

    (*i*) 22   (*ii*) 14   (*iii*) 13   (*iv*) 11

8. If 16 men working 7 hours a day can plough a field in 48 days, in how many days will 14 men working 12 hours a day plough the same field.

    (*i*) 46   (*ii*) 35   (*iii*) 32   (*iv*) 30

ANSWERS

EXERCISE 11 (a)

1. Yes, $k = -8$ **2.** Yes, $k = \dfrac{3}{4}$ **3.** No.   **4.** No   **5.** Yes, $k = -4$ **6.** No   **7.** Yes, $k = -5$

8. No   **9.** Yes, $k = 2$ **10.** No   **11.** 36m; 7 min; 300 m; 155 min   **12.** All except (*e*)

13. $\dfrac{28}{3}$ **14.** 10   **15.** (*i*) $w \propto l^2$ (*ii*) 160, 0·1 g (*iii*) $w = 0·4l^2$ **16.** 1·925 cm   **17.** 1428 g

18. 6 cm   **19.** 64   **20.** 300 m   **21.** Rs 8.70   **22.** 857.5 cm   **23.** 900 g   **24.** $36\dfrac{4}{11}$ m

EXERCISE 11 (b)

1. (*i*), (*iii*) and (*iv*)   **2.** (*i*) $V = \dfrac{k}{P}$ (*ii*) $I = \dfrac{k}{R}$ (*iii*) $h = \dfrac{k}{A}$ (*iv*) $f = \dfrac{k}{l}$

3. (*a*) Direct 9, 99, 240   (*b*) Direct, 3, 10, 5   (*c*) Inverse, 32, 6, 12   (*d*) Inverse, 25, 25, 125   **4.** 50, 15, 6, 10, 300, 750

5. (*iii*)   **6.** (*i*) 6 (*ii*) 4 (*iii*) 14 (*iv*) 0.5   **7.** $5\dfrac{3}{5}$ **8.** *y* is halved   **9.** $-\dfrac{7}{2}$ **20.** $a = \dfrac{0.18}{t^2}$

EXERCISE 11 (c)

1. 16 km/h   **2.** 80 km/h   **3.** 12 hours   **4.** 12 days   **5.** 350 persons   **6.** 6 men   **7.** 6 hours

8. 75 km/h   **9.** 24 days   **10.** 70 days   **11.** 12800   **12.** 30 days   **13.** 10 people   **14.** 64 rpm

15. 3 h 16 min   **16.** Rs 12,800

EXERCISE 11 (d)

1. 49 cupboards   **2.** 52 weeks   **3.** 15 days   **4.** 10 men   **5.** 12 hours   **6.** $6\dfrac{3}{4}$ days

MULTIPLE CHOICE QUESTIONS – 10

1. (*iii*)   **2.** (*ii*)   **3.** (*iii*)   **4.** (*iii*)   **5.** (*i*)   **6.** (*ii*)

7. (*iv*)   **8.** (*iii*)

QUIZ

1. Who was the first mathematician to calculate the value of π.

    (*a*) Aristotle   (*b*) Euclid   (*c*) Aryabhata   (*d*) Archimedes.

2. The decimal point in the present form appeared for first time in a book by :

    (*a*) John Napier   (*b*) Simon Steven   (*c*) Al- kashi   (*d*) Auguste Conte

3. Who discovered negative numbers ?

    (*a*) Indians   (*b*) Greeks   (*c*) Arabs   (*d*) Egyptians

4. Under which Indian kings reign was Bhaskaras' Leelavati translated into Persian ?

ANSWERS

1. (*d*)   **2.** (*a*)   **3.** (*a*)   **4.** Akbar

12. Time and Work

12.1 Introduction

In solving problems on time and work, the following points should be remembered :

1. If a man finishes total work in d days, then in 1 day he does $\frac{1}{d}$ of the total work.

For example : If a man finishes work in 4 days, then in 1 day he does $\frac{1}{4}$ of the work.

2. Conversely, if the work in 1 day that a man does is given, then the total number of days taken to finish the work

$$= \frac{1}{\text{One day's work}}$$

For example : If a man does $\frac{1}{10}$ of the work in 1 day, then the total number of days required to finish the

work $= \frac{1}{\frac{1}{10}}$, i.e., $1 \div \frac{1}{10} = 1 \times \frac{10}{1} = 10$ days.

In other words, the total number of days is the reciprocal of the amount of work done in 1 day.

Ex. 1. *A can do a piece of work in 3 days, B can do it in 6 days. How long will A and B take to complete the work working together ?*

Sol. In 1 day A can do $\frac{1}{3}$ of the work.

In 1 day B can do $\frac{1}{6}$ of the work.

$\therefore$ A and B together can do $\left\{\frac{1}{3} + \frac{1}{6}\right\}$, i.e., $\frac{1}{2}$ of the work in 1 day.

$\therefore$ A and B together can do the whole work in $\left(1 \div \frac{1}{2}\right)$ days, i.e. in **2 days.**

$\left.\begin{array}{l} \frac{1}{3} + \frac{1}{6} = \frac{2+1}{6} \\[2mm] \quad\quad = \frac{3}{6} = \frac{1}{2} \end{array}\right.$

Ex. 2. *A and B together can do a piece of work in 8 days, but A alone can do it in 12 days. How many days would B alone take to do the same work ?*

Sol. In 1 day A and B together can do $\frac{1}{8}$ of the work.

In 1 day A alone can do $\frac{1}{12}$ of the work.

$\therefore$ In 1 day B alone can do $\left(\frac{1}{8} - \frac{1}{12}\right)$ of the work, i.e., $\frac{1}{24}$ of the work.

$\therefore$ B alone will take $\left(1 \div \frac{1}{24}\right)$, i.e., **24 days** to do the work.

Ex. 3. *A can do a piece of work in 12 days, and B can do the same work in 20 days. They work together for 3 days and then A goes away. In how many days will B finish the work ?*

Sol. In 1 day A and B together can do $\left(\dfrac{1}{12} + \dfrac{1}{20}\right)$ of the work,

$$\begin{aligned}\dfrac{1}{12} + \dfrac{1}{20} &= \dfrac{5+3}{60}\\ &= \dfrac{8}{60} = \dfrac{2}{15}\end{aligned}$$

i.e., $\dfrac{2}{15}$ of the work.

In 3 days A and B together can do $3 \times \dfrac{2}{15}$, *i.e.* $\dfrac{2}{5}$ of the work.

$\therefore$ Remaining work $= 1 - \dfrac{2}{5} = \dfrac{3}{5}$.

Since B can do $\dfrac{1}{20}$ of the work in 1 day, therefore the number of days he will take to finish $\dfrac{3}{5}$ of the work $=$

$\dfrac{3}{5} \div \dfrac{1}{20} = \dfrac{3}{5} \times \dfrac{20}{1} = \mathbf{12\ days}$.

Ex. 4. *Asheesh can paint the doll in 20 min. and his sister Chinki can do so in 25 min. They paint the doll together for 5 min. At this juncture they have a quarrel and Chinki withdraws. In how many minutes will Asheesh finish painting the remaining doll ?*

Sol. Asheesh can paint the doll in 20 min.

$\therefore$ Portion of the doll painted by Asheesh in 1 min. $= \dfrac{1}{20}$

Chinki can paint the doll in 25 min.

$\therefore$ Portion of the doll painted by Chinki in 1 min. $= \dfrac{1}{25}$

$\therefore$ Portion of the doll painted by Asheesh and Chinki together in 1 min

$$= \dfrac{1}{20} + \dfrac{1}{25} = \dfrac{5+4}{100} = \dfrac{9}{100}$$

$\therefore$ Portion of the doll painted by Asheesh and Chinki together in 5 min $= \dfrac{9}{100} \times 5 = \dfrac{9}{20}$

$\therefore$ Portion remaining unpainted $= 1 - \dfrac{9}{20} = \dfrac{11}{20}$

$\therefore$ Asheesh can paint the whole doll in 20 min.

$\therefore$ Asheesh can paint the remaining portion in $\dfrac{11}{20} \times 20$ min. $= \mathbf{11\ min.}$

Ex. 5. *A and B can do a piece of work in 10 days, B and C can do it in 15 days and A and C together can do it in 12 days. How long will they take to do it together and each separately ?*

Sol. $(A + B)$'s 1 day's work $= \dfrac{1}{10}$, $(B + C)$'s 1 day's work $= \dfrac{1}{15}$, $(A + C)$'s 1 day's work $= \dfrac{1}{12}$

Adding, we get, $2(A + B + C)$'s 1 day's work $= \dfrac{1}{10} + \dfrac{1}{15} + \dfrac{1}{12} = \dfrac{6+4+5}{60} = \dfrac{15}{60}$

$\therefore$ $(A + B + C)$'s 1 day's work $= \dfrac{1}{2} \times \dfrac{15}{60} = \dfrac{1}{8}$

$\therefore$ Together A, B and C can finish the work in 8 days.

A's 1 day's work $= (A + B + C)$'s 1 day's work $- (B + C)$'s 1 day's work

$$= \dfrac{1}{8} - \dfrac{1}{15} = \dfrac{15-8}{120} = \dfrac{7}{120}$$

$\therefore$ A alone takes $\dfrac{120}{7}$ days to complete the work.

B's 1 day's work = (A + B + C)'s 1 day's work – (A + C)'s 1 day's work

$$= \frac{1}{8} - \frac{1}{12} = \frac{3-2}{24} = \frac{1}{24}$$

∴ B alone takes **24 days** to complete the work.

C's 1 day's work = (A + B + C)'s 1 day's work – (A + B)'s 1 day's work

$$= \frac{1}{8} - \frac{1}{10} = \frac{5-4}{40} = \frac{1}{40}$$

∴ C alone takes **40 days** to complete the work.

EXERCISE 12 (a)

1. 6 men can complete the electric fitting in a building in 7 days. How many days will it take 21 men to do the job?

2. Shashi weaves 25 baskets in 35 days. In how many days will she weave 110 baskets ?

3. Working 8 hours a day Ashu can copy a book in 18 days. How many hours a day should he work so as to finish the work in 12 days ?

4. If 12 boys earn Rs 840 in 7 days, what will 15 boys earn in 6 days ?

5. If 9 girls can prepare 135 garlands in 3 hours, how many girls are needed to prepare 270 garlands in 1 hour ?

6. Two men can do a piece of work in 3 days and 6 days respectively. If they work together, in how many days will they finish the work ?

7. One man can do a piece of work in 3 hours ; another can do the same piece of work in 2 hours. How long will they take if they work together ?

8. A and B together can do a piece of work in 10 days, but A alone can do it in 15 days. How many days would B alone take to do the same work ?

9. Two motor-cycle mechanics, Vinod and Preetam, working together, can overhaul a motor-cycle in 3 days. Vinod working alone can do the job in 5 days. If Preetam works alone, how long will he take to do the same job ?

10. Two men can do a piece of work in 6 hours and 4 hours respectively. After the first has worked for 2 hours, he is joined by the other. By when should the work be completed ?

11. Three men, A, B and C, can do a piece of work in 9 hours, 18 hours and 12 hours, respectively. How long will they take if they work together ?

12. A, B and C can cultivate a field in 10, 12, and 15 days respectively. If they work together, in how many days will they finish the work and what fraction of the work will each of them do ?

13. A, B and C can do a piece of work in 10 days. A alone can do it in 40 days, and B alone can do it in 30 days. In how many days will C alone do the same work ?

14. A can do a piece of work in 3 days, B can do it in 9 days, and C in $4\frac{1}{2}$ days. How long will they take to do the work if all work together ?

15. A and B can do a given piece of work in 8 days; B and C can do the same work in 12 days and A, B, C complete it in 6 days. In how many days can A and C finish it ?

12.2 Problems on Pipes and Cisterns

A cistern or a water tank is connected with two types of pipes. One which fills it up is called an **inlet** and the other which empties it out is called an **outlet.**

(i) If a pipe fills a water tank in 10 hours, then in one hour it fills $\frac{1}{10}$ th part of it. In other words, we can say that the work done by the pipe in 1 hour is $\frac{1}{10}$.

(*ii*) Similarly, if an outlet empties a tank in $\frac{1}{8}$ hour, then in one hour it empties $\frac{1}{8}$ th part of the tank. We can say that the work done by the outlet in one hour is $\left(-\frac{1}{8}\right)$.

> **Remark.** The work done by the inlet is always positive whereas the work done by the outlet is always negative.

Ex. 1. *A cistern can be filled by one tap in 4 hours and another tap in 6 hours. How long will it take to fill the cistern if both taps are opened together?*

Sol. One tap fills the cistern in 4 hours. The other tap fills the cistern in 6 hours.

∴ Work done by one tap in 1 hour = $\frac{1}{4}$

Work done by the other tap in 1 hour = $\frac{1}{6}$

The work done by both taps in 1 hour = $\left(\frac{1}{4}+\frac{1}{6}\right)=\frac{3+2}{12}=\frac{5}{12}$

∴ Both the taps when opened together will fill the cistern in $\frac{12}{5}$ **hours.**

Ex. 2. *A water tank can be filled by a tap in 8 hours and emptied by an outlet pipe in 12 hours. How long will it take to fill the cistern if both the tap and the pipe are opened together?*

Sol. The time taken by the tap to fill the tank = 8 hours.

The time taken by the pipe to empty the tank = 12 hours.

(*i*) The work done by the tap in 1 hour = $\frac{1}{8}$

The work done by the pipe in 1 hour = $-\frac{1}{12}$

Thus, when opened together, the work done by the tap and the pipe

$=\frac{1}{8}+\left(-\frac{1}{12}\right)=\frac{1}{8}-\frac{1}{12}=\frac{3-2}{24}=\frac{1}{24}$

∴ When both are opened together, the tank can be filled in **24 hours.**

Ex. 3. *A pipe can fill a cistern in 3 hours. Due to a leak in the bottom it is filled in 4 hours. When the cistern is full, in how much time will it be emptied by the leak?*

Sol. When there is no leakage, the pipe can fill the cistern in 3 hours.

∴ The pipe fills $\frac{1}{3}$ rd part of the cistern in 1 hour. When there is leakage, the pipe can fill the cistern in 4 hours. Thus, in case of leakage, the pipe fills $\frac{1}{4}$ th part of the cistern in 1 hour.

i.e., In 1 hour due to leakage $\left(\frac{1}{3}-\frac{1}{4}\right)$th $=\frac{1}{12}$ th part of the cistern is emptied out. Hence, the cistern will be emptied by the leakage in **12 hours.**

Ex. 4. *A tank can be filled by two taps A and B in 12 hours and 16 hours respectively. The full tank can be emptied by a third tap in 8 hours. If all the taps be turned on at the same time, in how much time will the empty tank be filled up completely?*

Sol. Time taken by tap *A* to fill the tank = 12 hours

Time taken by tap *B* to fill the tank = 16 hours

Time taken by tap C to empty the tank = 8 hours

$\therefore$ Tap A fills $\frac{1}{12}$ th part of the tank in 1 hour, Tap B fills $\frac{1}{16}$ th part of the tank in 1 hour,

Tap C empties $\frac{1}{8}$ th part of the tank in 1 hour.

Thus, in 1 hour $\left(\frac{1}{12} + \frac{1}{16} - \frac{1}{8}\right)$ th, *i.e.*, $\frac{1}{48}$ th part of the tank is filled.

$$\boxed{\frac{1}{12} + \frac{1}{16} - \frac{1}{8} = \frac{4+3-6}{48} = \frac{1}{48}}$$

$\therefore$ If all the three pipes are opened together, the tank will be filled in **48 hours.**

EXERCISE 12 (b)

1. A cistern can be filled by one tap in 4 hours and by another in 3 hours. How long will it take to fill if both taps are opened together?

2. A cistern can be filled by one tap in $2\frac{1}{2}$ hours and by another in $3\frac{3}{4}$ hours. How long will the cistern take to fill, if they are opened together ?

3. A cistern can be filled by a tap in 4 hours and emptied by an outlet pipe in 6 hours. How long will it take to fill the cistern if both taps are opened together ?

4. One tap fills a bath in 12 min. and another tap fills it in 15 min. The waste-pipe can empty the bath in 10 min. In what time will the bath be filled if both taps are turned on and if the waste-pipe has been left open accidentally ?

5. A pipe can fill a cistern in 6 hours. Due to a leak in the bottom it is filled in 7 hours. When the cistern is full, in how much time will it be emptied by the leak?

6. A cistern has two inlets A and B which can fill it in 15 hours and 20 hours respectively. An outlet can empty the full cistern in 12 hours. If all the three pipes are opened together in the empty cistern, how much time will they take to fill the cistern completely?

LOOKING BACK
Summary of Key Facts

1. If a person can finish a piece of work in n days, then the work done by the person in
   1 day = $\frac{1}{n}$.

2. If a person completes $\frac{1}{n}$ th part of a work in 1 day, then the time taken by the person to finish the work is n days.

3. A cistern is fitted with two pipes—one pipe to fill it which is called an **inlet** and the other pipe to empty it which is called an **outlet.**

4. If an inlet fills a tank in n hours, then it will fill $\frac{1}{n}$ th part of the tank in 1 hour, *i.e.*, the work done by it in 1 hour is $\frac{1}{n}$.

5. If an outlet empties a full tank in m hours, then it will empty $\frac{1}{m}$ th part of the tank in 1 hour, *i.e.*, the work done by it in 1 hour is $-\frac{1}{m}$. (Note that the work done by the outlet is negative)

MULTIPLE CHOICE QUESTIONS – 11

1. *A* alone can do a piece of work in 6 days, while *B* alone can do it in 15 days. In how many days will *A* and *B* together do the same work?

   (*i*) 12 days   (*ii*) 10 days   (*iii*) $9\frac{1}{5}$ days   (*iv*) $4\frac{2}{7}$

2. *A* and *B* together can do a piece of work in 6 days and *A* alone can do it in 8 days. In how many days can *B* alone do it?

   (*i*) 12 days   (*ii*) 15 days   (*iii*) 14 days   (*iv*) 24 days

3. *A* can do a piece of work in 15 days and *B* alone can do it in 10 days. *B* works at it for 5 days and then leaves. *A* alone can finish the remaining work in:

   (*i*) $6\frac{1}{2}$ days   (*ii*) $7\frac{1}{2}$ days   (*iii*) 8 days   (*iv*) 9 days

4. *A* can do $\frac{2}{3}$ of a certain work in 12 days and *B* can do $\frac{1}{6}$ of the same work in 4 days. Both *A* and *B* together can complete the work in:

   (*i*) $7\frac{3}{4}$ days   (*ii*) $8\frac{1}{7}$ days   (*iii*) $10\frac{2}{7}$ days   (*iv*) $6\frac{4}{5}$ days.

5. *A*, *B* and *C* together can finish a piece of work in 4 days; *A* alone can do it in 12 days and *B* in 18 days, then *C* alone can do it in :

   (*i*) 21 days   (*ii*) 16 days   (*iii*) 14 days   (*iv*) 9 days

6. *A* and *B* can do a piece of work in 12 days; *B* and *C* can do it in 15 days; *A* and *C* can do it in 20 days. Who among these will take the least time, if put to do it alone?

   (*i*) *A*   (*ii*) *B*   (*iii*) *C*   (*iv*) Data inadequate

7. To fill a cistern, pipes *A*, *B* and *C* take 20 minutes, 15 minutes and 12 minutes, respectively. The time in minutes that the three pipes together will take to fill the cistern is :

   (*i*) 5   (*ii*) 10   (*iii*) 12   (*iv*) $15\frac{2}{3}$

8. Two pipes can fill a tank in 10 hours and 12 hours respectively while a third pipe empties the full tank in 20 hours. If all the three pipes are opened simultaneously, in how much time the tank will be filled?

   (*i*) 7 hours   (*ii*) 8 hours   (*iii*) 7 hours 30 minutes   (*iv*) 8 hours 30 minutes

ANSWERS

EXERCISE 12 (a)

1. 2 days   2. 154 days   3. 12 hours   4. Rs 900   5. 54 girls   6. 2 days   7. $1\frac{1}{5}$ hrs.

8. 30 days   9. $7\frac{1}{2}$ days   10. 1 hr 36 min. 11. 4 hrs   12. 4 days ; *A*, $\frac{2}{5}$; *B*, $\frac{1}{3}$; *C*, $\frac{4}{15}$ 13. 24 days

14. $1\frac{1}{2}$ days   15. 8 days   (**Hint :** 2(*A* + *B* + *C*)'s 1 days work = $\frac{1}{8} + \frac{1}{12} + \frac{1}{x}$ ⇒ $2 \times \frac{1}{6} = \frac{1}{8} + \frac{1}{12} + \frac{1}{x}$)

EXERCISE 12 (b)

1. $1\frac{5}{7}$ hours   2. 1 hr 30 min   3. 12 hours   4. 20 min   5. 42 hours   6. 30 hours

MULTIPLE CHOICE QUESTIONS – 11

1. (*iv*)   2. (*iv*)   3. (*ii*)   4. (*iii*)   5. (*iv*)   6. (*ii*)

7. (*i*)   8. (*iii*)

13. Quadrilaterals

13.1 Quadrilateral

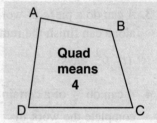

If *A*, *B*, *C* and *D* are co-planar points, such that (*i*) no three of them are collinear and (*ii*) the line segments *AB*, *BC*, *CD*, and *DA* do not intersect except at their end points, then the figure made up of the four line segments is called the **quadrilateral (abbreviation : quad).** The points *A*, *B*, *C* and *D* are called its **vertices**.

A quadrilateral is named by listing its vertices, starting at any vertex and reading clockwise or counter-clockwise. So *ABCD*, *BCDA*, *ADCB* and so forth, name the same figure.

13.2 Sides, Angles and Diagonals of a Quadrilateral

(*a*) The four line segments *AB*, *BC*, *CD* and *DA* are called its **sides;**

(*b*) The four angles ∠*DAB*, ∠*ABC*, ∠*BCD* and ∠*CDA* are called its **angles;** and

(*c*) A line segment joining two non-consecutive vertices is called a **diagonal**.

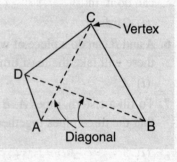

AC and *BD* are the two diagonals of the quad *ABCD*.

13.3 Adjacent Sides and Opposite Sides

(**1**) Two sides of a quadrilateral are said to be *adjacent sides* of the quadrilateral, if they have a common end point.

(**2**) Two sides of a quadrilateral are said to be *opposite sides* of the quadrilateral, if they are not adjacent sides.

Thus, in the quadrilateral *ABCD* shown here, *AB* and *AD* are a pair of adjacent sides. So also are the pairs of sides *AB*, *BC* and *BC*, *CD*. Again, in the same figure, *AB*, *DC* are a pair of opposite sides and *BC*, *AD* are the other pair of opposite sides.

13.4 Adjacent Angles and Opposite Angles

(**1**) Two angles of quadrilateral are said to be adjacent angles of the quadrilateral, if they have a side of the quadrilateral in common.

(**2**) Two angles of a quadrilateral are said to be opposite angles of the quadrilateral, if they are not adjacent angles.

Thus, in the figure ∠*A* and ∠*B* are a pair of adjacent angles of the quadrilateral *ABCD*. They have side *AB* in common. Similarly, ∠*B*, ∠*C*; ∠*C*, ∠*D*; and ∠*D*, ∠*A* are the other pairs of adjacent angles.

Again, in the same figure, ∠*A* and ∠*C* are a pair of opposite angles, so also are the pair of angles ∠*B* and ∠*D*.

EXERCISE 13 (a)

1. **Fill in the blanks:**

(*i*) A quadrilateral has .... sides and .... vertices.

(*ii*) A quadrilateral has .... angles and .... diagonals.

(*iii*) A diagonal of a quadrilateral is a line segment that joins two .... vertices of the quadrilateral.

(*iv*) The sum of the angles of a quadrilateral is .... right angles.

(*v*) The measure of each angle of a convex quadrilateral is .... 180°.

(*vi*) The measure of at least one angle of a concave quadrilateral is .... 180°.

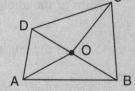

2. Take a point *O* inside a given quadrilateral *ABCD*. Join the point *O* to the vertices *A*, *B*, *C* and *D*. Into what figures will the quadrilateral be divided? Name the figures.

3. **In the adjoining figure, *ABCD* is a quadrilateral.**

(*i*) How many pairs of adjacent sides are there? Name them.

(*ii*) How many pairs of opposite sides are there? Name them.

(*iii*) How many pairs of adjacent angles are there? Name them.

(*iv*) How many pairs of opposite angles are there? Name them.

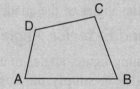

4. **Answer true or false:**

(*i*) No two vertices of a quadrilateral are collinear.

(*ii*) No three vertices of a quadrilateral are collinear.

(*iii*) All points on a quadrilateral belong to its interior.

(*iv*) A quadrilateral separates its interior from its exterior.

(*v*) A quadrilateral has only two pairs of adjacent sides.

13.5 Angle Sum Property of a Quadrilateral

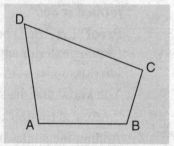

Activity. Draw any quadrilateral *ABCD*. Measure its angles and write the results as under:

$\angle ABC$ = ...°, $\angle BCD$ = ...°, $\angle CDA$ = ...°, $\angle DAB$ = ...°.

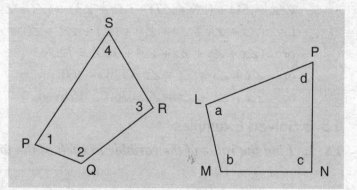

Now add and find the sum of these angles.

$\angle ABC + \angle BCD + \angle CDA + \angle DAB$ = ...°.

You will find that the sum is 360°. You can draw more quadrilaterals like *PQRS*, *LMNP* etc., measure their angles and add the measures. You will find that

$\angle 1 + \angle 2 + \angle 3 + \angle 4 = 360°$; $\angle a + \angle b + \angle c + \angle d = 360°$.

Hence, we conclude that

> **The sum of the angles of a quadrilateral is 360°.**

Proof: Without measuring, you could have found the sum as under :

Draw one of the diagonals, say *BD*.

The quadrilateral is divided into 2 triangles.

Sum of the angles of each triangle

$$= 2rt. \angle s \text{ or } 180°$$

Sum of the angles of 2 triangles

$$= 2 \times 2rt. \angle s = 4rt. \angle s$$

or $2 \times 180°$ or $360°$.

∴ Sum of the angles of the quadrilateral = 4 *rt.* $\angle s$ or $360°$.

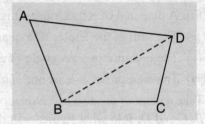

13.6 Interior and Exterior Angles of a Quadrilateral

In the adjoining figure, angles marked 1, 2, 3 and 4 are the interior angles or simply the angles of the quadrilateral *ABCD*.

If the sides of a quadrilateral are produced in an order, then angles marked *x*, *y*, *z* and *t* are called the exterior angles of the quadrilateral.

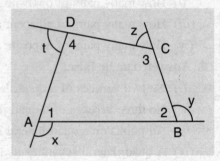

13.7 Exterior Angles Sum Property

If the sides of a quadrilateral are produced in an order, the sum of the four exterior angles so formed is 360°.

Proof: Let *ABCD* be quadrilateral whose sides are produced in an order forming exterior angles *x*, *y*, *z* and *t*. Angles marked 1, 2, 3 and 4 are the interior angles.

You know that the sum of the angles of a linear pair is 180°.

∴ $\angle x + \angle 1 = 180°; \angle y + \angle 2 = 180°; \angle z + \angle 3 = 180°; \angle t + \angle 4 = 180°$.

$\angle a + \angle b = 180°$
LINEAR PAIR

Adding the angles on both sides, we get,

$(\angle x + \angle 1) + (\angle y + \angle 2) + (\angle z + \angle 3) + (\angle t + \angle 4) = 180° + 180° + 180° + 180°$

i.e., $(\angle x + \angle y + \angle z + \angle t) + (\angle 1 + \angle 2 + \angle 3 + \angle 4) = 720°$

or $(\angle x + \angle y + \angle z + \angle t) + 360° = 720°$ (∵ Angle sum of a quad. = 360°)

or $\angle x + \angle y + \angle z + \angle t = 720° - 360°$

or $\angle x + \angle y + \angle z + \angle t = 360°$. **Proved.**

13.8 Solved Examples

Ex. 1. *Find the value of the variable in each of the following figures :*

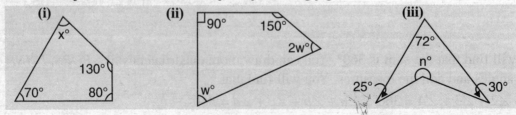

Sol. (i) ∵ The angle sum of a quadrilateral is 360°

$x + 130° + 70° + 80° = 360°$

$\Rightarrow x + 280° = 360° \Rightarrow x = 360° - 280° \Rightarrow x = \mathbf{80°}$.

(ii) From the figure, it follows :

$90° + 150° + 2w + w = 360°$ (The angle sum of a quadrilateral is 360°)

$\Rightarrow 240° + 3w = 360° \Rightarrow 3w = 360° - 240°$

$\Rightarrow 3w = 120° \Rightarrow w = \mathbf{40°}$.

(iii) From the given figure, it follows

$72° + 30° + n + 25° = 360°$ (The angle sum of a quadrilateral is 360°)

$\Rightarrow 127° + n = 360° \Rightarrow n = 360° - 127° \Rightarrow n = \mathbf{233°}$.

Ex. 2. *Two angles of a quadrilateral are of measure 50°, and the other two angles are equal. What is the measure of each of these two angles?*

Sol. Let the equal angles of the given quadrilateral be $x°$ each. The other two angles are 50° each.

By the angle sum property of a quadrilateral, we have

Sum of all the four angles = 360°

$\Rightarrow x + x + 50° + 50° = 360° \Rightarrow 2x + 100° = 360°$

$\Rightarrow 2x = 360° - 100° \Rightarrow 2x = 260° \Rightarrow x = \mathbf{130°}$.

Each of the equal angles is 130° each.

Ex. 3. *The angles of a quadrilateral are in the ratio 2 : 3 : 5 : 8. Find the measure of each of the four angles.*

Sol. The sum of the angles of a quadrilateral is 360°. Let the measures of the angles be $2x°$, $3x°$, $5x°$, and $8x°$. Then

$2x + 3x + 5x + 8x = 360° \Rightarrow 18x = 360° \Rightarrow x = \dfrac{360}{18} = 20°$

Hence, the measures of the four angles are 40°, 60°, 100° and 160°.

Alternatively, Sum of the ratios = 2 + 3 + 5 + 8 = 18

∴ The angles of the quad. are

$\dfrac{2}{18} \times 360°, \dfrac{3}{18} \times 360°, \dfrac{5}{18} \times 360°$ and $\dfrac{8}{18} \times 360°$,

i.e., 2 × 20°, 3 × 20°, 5 × 20°, 8 × 20°, i.e., 40°, 60°, 100° and 160°.

Ex. 4. *In the adjoining figure, the bisectors of ∠A and ∠B meet at a point P. If ∠C = 96°, and ∠D = 30°, find the measure of ∠APB.*

Sol. $\angle A + \angle B + \angle C + \angle D = 360°$ (Angle sum of a quad.)

∴ $\angle A + \angle B + 96° + 30° = 360° \Rightarrow \angle A + \angle B + 126° = 360°$

$\Rightarrow \angle A + \angle B = 360° - 126° = 234°$

$\Rightarrow \dfrac{1}{2}\angle A + \dfrac{1}{2}\angle B = \dfrac{1}{2} \times 234° = 117°$.

i.e., $\angle PAB + \angle PBA = 117°$

But in Δ PAB, $\angle APB + \angle PAB + \angle PBA = 180°$ (Angle sum of a Δ)

i.e., $\angle APB + 117° = 180° \Rightarrow \angle APB = 180° - 117° = \mathbf{63°}$.

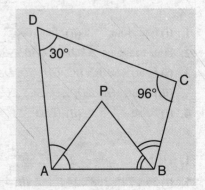

EXERCISE 13 (b)

1. The three angles of a quadrilateral are 65°, 55° and 130°. Find its fourth angle.

2. The two adjacent angles of a quadrilateral are 75° and 125°. The other two angles are equal. Find the measure of each of these equal angles.

3. In a quadrilateral $ABCD$, $\angle A = 150°$ and $\angle B = \angle C = \angle D$, find $\angle B$, $\angle C$ and $\angle D$.

4. In the adjoining figure, P is a point in the interior of $\angle AOB$ and $\angle AOB = 40°$. If $PM \perp OA$ and $PN \perp OB$, find the measure of $\angle MPN$.

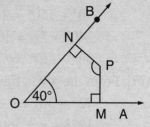

Fig. Q. 4

5. A quadrilateral has all four angles of the same measure, what is the measure of each angle?

6. Two angles of a quadrilateral measure 55° each. The third angle is 140°. What is the measure of the fourth angle ?

7. Find the measures of the four angles of a quadrilateral if: (*i*) they are in the ratio 1 : 2 : 3 : 4 (*ii*) they are in the ratio 3 : 5 : 7 : 9.

8. $ABCD$ is a quadrilateral. AO and BO are the angle bisectors of angle A and B which meet at O. If $\angle C = 70°$, $\angle D = 50°$, find $\angle AOB$.

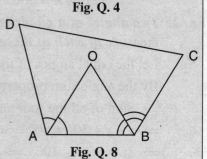

Fig. Q. 8

LOOKING BACK

(Summary of Key Points)

1. A quadrilateral is a plane figure bounded by four line segments such that
   (*a*) no two line segments cross each other, and
   (*b*) no two line segments are collinear.

2. The sum of the angles of a quadrilateral is 360°.

3. If the sides of a quadrilateral are produced in an order, the sum of the exterior angles so found is 360°, *i.e.*,
   $\angle a + \angle b + \angle c + \angle d = 360°$.

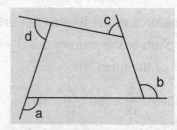

ANSWERS

EXERCISE 13 (a)

1. (*i*) four, four   (*ii*) four, two   (*iii*) opposite   (*iv*) four   (*v*) less than   (*vi*) more than

2. Four triangles, ΔAOD, ΔAOB, ΔBOC, ΔCOD.

3. (*i*) Four, AB, BC; BC, CD; CD, DA; DA, AB (*ii*) Two; AB, CD; AD, BC

   (*iii*) Four; $\angle A$, $\angle D$; $\angle D$, $\angle C$; $\angle C$, $\angle B$; $\angle B$, $\angle A$ (*iv*) Two; $\angle A$, $\angle C$; $\angle B$, $\angle D$

4. (*i*) False   (*ii*) True   (*iii*) False   (*iv*) True   (*v*) False

EXERCISE 13 (b)

1. 110°   2. 80°, 80°   3. 70°, 70°, 70°   4. 140°   5. 90°   6. 110°

7. (*i*) 36°, 72°, 108°, 144°   (*ii*) 45°, 75°, 105°, 135°   8. 60°

14. Parallelograms

14.1 Special Types of Quadrilaterals

There are various types of Quadrilaterals whose description is given below :

1. *A quadrilateral with both pairs of opposite sides parallel is a **parallelogram**.*

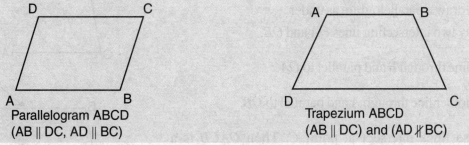

Parallelogram ABCD
(AB || DC, AD || BC)

Trapezium ABCD
(AB || DC) and (AD ∦ BC)

2. *A quadrilateral with exactly one pair of parallel sides is called a **trapezium**. An isosceles trapezium is a trapezium in which two non-parallel sides are equal.*

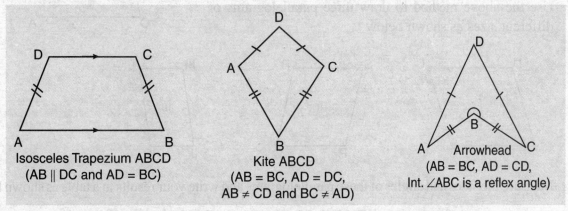

Isosceles Trapezium ABCD
(AB || DC and AD = BC)

Kite ABCD
(AB = BC, AD = DC,
AB ≠ CD and BC ≠ AD)

Arrowhead
(AB = BC, AD = CD,
Int. ∠ABC is a reflex angle)

3. *A **kite** is a quadrilateral in which two pairs of adjacent sides are equal.*
4. *A kite with one reflex angle is called an **arrowhead**.*
5. *A parallelogram in which all angles are right angles is called a **rectangle**.*
6. *A parallelogram whose all four sides are equal is called a **rhombus**.*
7. *A rectangle with all sides equal, or, a rhombus in which all angles are right angles is called a **square**.*

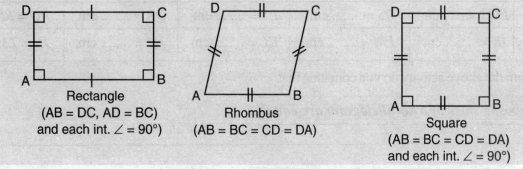

Rectangle
(AB = DC, AD = BC)
and each int. ∠ = 90°)

Rhombus
(AB = BC = CD = DA)

Square
(AB = BC = CD = DA)
and each int. ∠ = 90°)

183

This chart shows how special parallelograms are related.

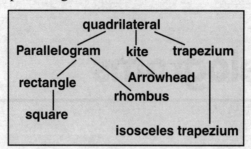

14.2 Properties of a Parallelogram

Activity 1

You can draw a parallelogram as under :

1. Draw any two intersecting lines *OA* and *OB*.

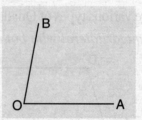

2. Draw a line through *B* and parallel to *OA*.

3. Draw another line through *A* and parallel to *OB*.

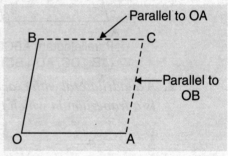

Let these lines intersect at point *C*. Then *OACB* is a parallelogram.

Use the above method to draw three parallelograms of different sizes as shown below :

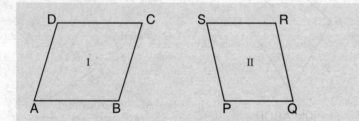

Measure the sides and angles of these parallelograms and write your results in a table as shown below.

Table I. Measurement of Sides

Parallelo-gram	First pair of opposite sides		Second pair of opposite sides		Do you observe that
I	*AB* = ... cm	*CD* = ... cm	*AD* = ... cm	*BC* = ... cm	*AB = CD, AD = BC*
II	*PQ* = ... cm	*RS* = ... cm	*PS* = ... cm	*QR* = ... cm	*PQ = RS, PS = QR*
III	*JK* = ... cm	*LM* = ... cm	*KL* = ... cm	*JM* = ... cm	*JK = LM, KL = JM*

From the above activity do you conclude that

Opposite sides of a parallelogram are equal?

Table II. Measurement of Angles

Parallelo-gram	First pair of opposite angles		Second pair of opposite angles		Do you observe that
I	∠A = ...°	∠C = ...°	∠B = ...°	∠D = ...°	∠A = ∠C, ∠B = ∠D
II	∠P = ...°	∠R = ...°	∠Q = ...°	∠S = ...°	∠P = ∠R, ∠Q = ∠S
III	∠J = ...°	∠L = ...°	∠K = ...°	∠M = ...°	∠J = ∠L, ∠K = ∠M

From the above activity do you conclude that

Opposite angles of a parallelogram are equal?

Activity 2

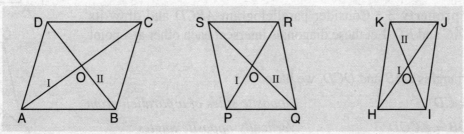

Draw three parallelograms and name them as shown. Draw their diagonals. Let the diagonals intersect at point *O*. Measure the two parts of each diagonal and note down your measurements in a table like the following:

Parallelogram	Measurements of the two parts into which each diagonal is divided		Do you observe that
	Diagonal I	**Diagonal II**	
ABCD	AO = ... cm, OC = ... cm	BO = ... cm, OD = ... cm	AO = OC, BO = OD
PQRS	PO = ... cm, OR = ... cm	QO = ... cm, OS = ... cm	PO = OR, QO = OS
HIJK	HO = ... cm, OJ = ... cm	IO = ... cm, OK = ... cm	HO = OJ, IO = OK

From the above activity do you conclude that

The diagonals of a parallelogram bisect one another?

Summary : *Properties of a Parallelogram.*
  1. *Each diagonal divides it into two congruent triangles.*
  2. *The opposite sides and angles of a parallelogram are equal.*
  3. *The diagonals of a parallelogram bisect each other.*

We can prove the above properties as under:

Proof : Consider a parallelogram *ABCD*. Draw its diagonal *AC*.
Then, in triangles *ABC* and *CDA*, we have

$\angle 1 = \angle 2$	Alternate angles, $AB \parallel DC$ and AC is the transversal
$\angle 3 = \angle 4$	Alternate angles, $AD \parallel BC$ and AC is the transversal
$AC = AC$	common
$\therefore \quad \triangle ABC \cong \triangle CDA$	ASA property of congruence of $\triangle s$.
$\Rightarrow \quad AB = CD$ and $BC = DA$	Corresponding parts of congruent triangles.

Also, $\angle B = \angle D$

Similarly, by drawing the diagonal BD, we can prove that

$$\triangle ABD \cong \triangle CDB \quad \Rightarrow \angle A = \angle C$$

Hence, properties 1 and 2 are proved.

To prove property 3 : Consider parallelogram $ABCD$ and draw its diagonals AC and BD. Let these diagonals intersect each other at a point O.

Then, in triangles OAB and OCD, we have

$AB = CD$	Opposite sides of a parallelogram
$\angle AOB = \angle COD$	Vertically opposite angles
$\angle OAB = \angle OCD$	Alternate angles; $AB \parallel DC$ and transversal AC cuts them.
$\therefore \quad \triangle OAB \cong \triangle OCD$	AAS property of congruence of triangles.
$\Rightarrow \quad OA = OC$ and $OB = OD$	Corresponding parts of congruent $\triangle s$

This proves the diagonal property of a parallelogram, _i.e._, the diagonals of a parallelogram bisect each other.

14.3 The Converse

The converse of the above properties is also true. Thus

A quadrilateral is a parallelogram,

    (i) _if its opposite sides are equal._   (ii) _if its opposite angles are equal._

    (iii) _if its diagonals bisect each other._   (iv) _if it has one pair of opposite sides parallel and equal._

14.4 Solved Examples

Ex. 1. _ABCD is a parallelogram : If_ $\angle A = 70°$_, calculate_ $\angle B$_,_ $\angle C$ _and_ $\angle D$_._

Sol. $\angle A + \angle B = 180°$ 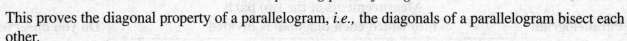 Co-interior angles, $AD \parallel BC$ and AB is a transversal

_i.e.,_ $70° + \angle B = 180°$

$\Rightarrow \angle B = 180° - 70° = 110°$

Also, $\angle C = \angle A = 70°$ Opposite angles of a Parallelogram

$\angle D = \angle B = 110°$ Opposite angles of a Parallelogram

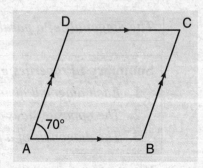

Ex. 2. _The adjacent angles of a parallelogram are as 2 : 3. Find the measures of all its angles._

Sol. Suppose $ABCD$ is a parallelogram and the two adjacent angles A and B are as $2 : 3$.

Suppose $\angle A = 2x$ and $\angle B = 3x$

Since ∠A and ∠B are a pair of adjacent interior angles and AD ∥ BC.

∴ ∠A + ∠B = 180° or 2x + 3x = 180°

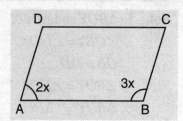

⇒ 5x = 180° ⇒ $x = \dfrac{180}{5} = 36°$

∴ ∠A = **72°** and ∠B = **108°**

Again, since opposite angles of a ∥gm are equal, ∴ ∠C = ∠A = 72° and ∠D = ∠B = 108°.

Ex. 3. *The ratio of of two sides of a ∥ gm is 3 : 5, and its perimeter is 48 cm. Find the sides of the ∥gm.*

Sol. Let the two sides of the ∥gm be 3x cm and 5x cm.

Since the opposite sides of a ∥gm are equal, therefore, the other two sides are 3x cm and 5x cm.

Now, perimeter of ∥gm = 48 cm

∴ 3x + 5x +3x + 5x = 48 or 16x = 48 ∴ $x = \dfrac{48}{16} = 3$

Hence the sides of the ∥gm are **9 cm, 15 cm, 9 cm** and **15 cm.**

Ex. 4. *The point of intersection of diagonals of a quadrilateral divides one diagonal in the ratio 2 : 3. Is it a ∥ gm? Why or why not?*

Sol. No, it is not a ∥gm, because in a ∥gm the diagonals of a ∥gm are bisected at their point of intersection.

Ex. 5. *In a parallelogram ABCD, diagonals AC and BD intersect at O and AC = 12.8 cm and BD = 7.6 cm. Find the measures of OC and OD.*

Sol. Given : AC = 12.8 cm, BD = 7.6 cm.

We know that the diagonals of a parallelogram bisect each other. Therefore,

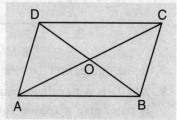

$AO = OC \Rightarrow OC = \dfrac{1}{2}AC = \dfrac{1}{2} \times 12.8$ cm = **6.4 cm.**

$BO = OD \Rightarrow OD = \dfrac{1}{2}BD = \dfrac{1}{2} \times 7.6$ cm = **3.8 cm.**

Ex. 6. *The perimeter of a parallelogram is 150 cm. One of its sides is greater than the other by 25 cm. Find the lengths of all the sides of the parallelogram.*

Sol. Let one side of the parallelogram = x cm. Then its other side = (x + 25) cm.

Since opposite sides of a parallelogram are equal, so its remaining two sides are x cm and (x + 25) cm.

∴ Perimeter of this parallelogram = x + (x + 25) + x + (x + 25) = (4x + 50)cm.

But perimeter = 150 cm (given) ∴ 4x + 50 = 150

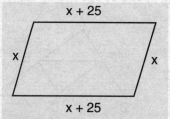

⇒ 4x = 150 – 50 = 100 ⇒ $x = \dfrac{100}{4} = 25$

∴ Lengths of all the sides of the parallelogram are

x, x + 25, x, x + 25 cm, *i.e.,* **25 cm, 50 cm, 25 cm, 50 cm.**

Ex. 7. *Diagonals of a ∥ gm ABCD intersect at O. XY contains O, and X, Y are points on opposite sides of the ∥ gm. Give reasons for each of the following statements.*

(i) OB = OD;   (ii) ∠OBY = ∠ODX   (iii) ∠BOY = ∠DOX;   (iv) ΔBOY ≅ ΔDOX.

Now, state if XY is bisected at O.

Sol. In $\triangle BOY$ and $\triangle DOX$

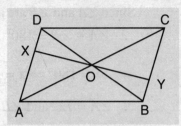

$\angle OBY = \angle ODX$ (Alt. $\angle s$, AD $\parallel$ BC)

$OB = OD$ (Diagonals of a $\parallel$ gm bisect each other)

$\angle BOY = \angle DOX$ (Vert. Opp. $\angle s$)

$\therefore \triangle BOY \cong \triangle DOX$ (ASA congruence condition)

$\therefore$ $OY = OX$. Hence, XY is bisected at the point O.

EXERCISE 14 (a)

1. The measure of one angle of a parallelogram is 80°. What are the measures of the remaining angles?

2. Two adjacent angles of a parallelogram are congruent. What is the measure of each?

3. Two adjacent sides of a parallelogram are 5 cm and 6 cm respectively. Find its perimeter.

4. Find each angle of a parallelogram if two consecutive angles are in the ratio 1 : 3.

5. The perimeter of a parallelogram is 180 cm. One of its sides is greater than the other by 30 cm. Find the length of the sides of the parallelogram.

6. Find the sizes of the angles of a parallelogram if one angle is 20° less than twice the smallest angle.

7. ABCD is a parallelogram. Find x, y and z.

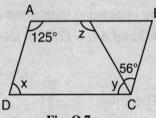

           Fig. Q.7

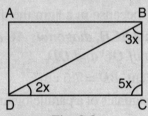

           Fig. Q.8

8. In the figure, find the four angles A, B, C and D of the parallelogram $ABCD$.

9. **ABCD is a parallelogram. CE bisects $\angle C$ and AF bisects $\angle A$. In each of the following, if the statement is true, give a reason for the same.**

    (i) $\angle A = \angle C$ (ii) $\angle FAB = \dfrac{1}{2} \angle A$ (iii) $\angle DCE = \dfrac{1}{2} \angle C$.

    (iv) $\angle FAB = \angle DCE$ (v) $\angle DCE = \angle CEB$ (vi) $\angle CEB = \angle FAB$

    (vii) $CE \parallel AF$ (viii) $AE \parallel FC$.

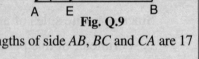

           Fig. Q.9

10. In a $\triangle ABC$, D, E, F are respectively, the mid-points of BC, CA and AB. If the lengths of side AB, BC and CA are 17 cm, 18 cm and 19 cm respectively, find the perimeter of $\triangle DEF$.

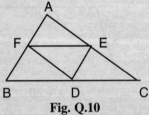

    Fig. Q.10

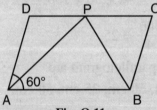

    Fig. Q.11

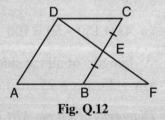

    Fig. Q.12

11. In the figure, ABCD is a parallelogram in which $\angle A = 60°$. If the bisectors of $\angle A$ and $\angle B$ meet at P, prove that $AD = DP$, $PC = BC$ and $DC = 2AD$.

12. In the figure, ABCD is a parallelogram and E is the mid-point of side BC. If DE and AB when produced meet at F, prove that $AF = 2AB$.

14.5 Properties of a Rectangle, Square and Rhombus

■ **The Diagonal Properties of a Rectangle**

A rectangle being a parallelogram has all the properties of a parallelogram and some more *i.e.*

1. *All angles of a rectangle are right angles,*

2. *The diagonals of the rectangle are equal.*

Activity 3

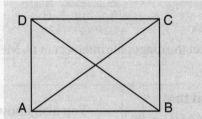 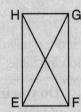 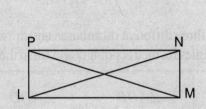

You already know how to draw a rectangle. Draw three rectangles as shown. Draw both their diagonals. Measure the two diagonals of each rectangle and write your measurements as under :

Rectangle $ABCD \rightarrow$ Diag. $AC =$ .... cm, Diag. $BD =$ .... cm

Rectangle $EFGH \rightarrow$ Diag. $EG =$ .... cm, Diag. $FH =$ .... cm

Rectangle $LMNP \rightarrow$ Diag. $LN =$ .... cm, Diag. $MP =$ .... cm

Do you find that
$AC = BD$
$FG = FH$
$LN = MP$

From the above activity do you conclude that

> *The diagonals of a rectangle are equal?*

The above property can be proved as under :

Given : $PQRS$ is a rectangle with diagonals PR and QS.

To prove : $PR = QS$.

Proof : In Δs PQS and PQR

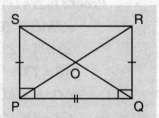

$$PS = QR \quad (Opposite\ sides\ of\ a\ rectangle)$$

$$\angle SPQ = \angle RQP \quad (each = 90°)$$

$$PQ = QP \quad (common)$$

$$\Delta PQS = \Delta PQR \quad (S.A.S)$$

$$\Rightarrow \quad QS = PR \quad (c.p.c.t.)$$

14.6 Diagonal Properties of a Rhombus

You know that a rhombus is a parallelogram with equal sides. So you can draw a rhombus in the same manner as you draw a parallelogram.

Since a rhombus is a parallelogram, the properties of a parallelogram hold good for a rhombus also. Thus, we have

1. *Opposite angles of a rhombus are equal.*

2. *Diagonals of a rhombus bisect each other.*

Activity 4

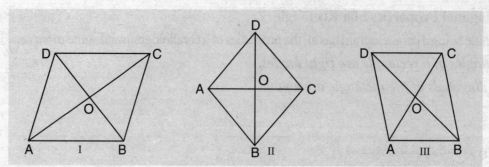

Draw three different rhombuses and draw their diagonals. Let the diagonals intersect at O. Measure two of the adjacent angles formed at point O and fill in the following table.

Rhombus	$\angle AOB$	$\angle AOD$	Do you find that $\angle AOB = \angle AOD = 90°$	You also know that
I	..........°	..........°	Yes/No	$\angle AOB = \angle COD$,
II	..........°	..........°	Yes/No	$\angle AOD = \angle BOC$
III	..........°	..........°	Yes/No	(Vertically opposite angles)

Does the above activity and the remarks made in the last column lead you to conclude that
$$\angle AOB = \angle AOD = \angle DOC = \angle COB = 90°$$

> **i.e., The diagonals of a rhombus bisect each other at right angles?**

- **Proof :** _To prove that the diagonals of a rhombus bisect each other at right angles._

  Given : A rhombus $ABCD$ with diagonal AC and BD intersecting at O.

  To prove : $OA = OC$; $OB = OD$; $\angle AOB = \angle COB = 90°$

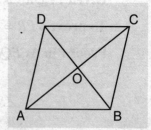

  Proof : In Δ's OAB and ODC

$\angle OAB = \angle OCD$	(AB ‖ CD, Alternate ∠s)
$\angle OBA = \angle ODC$	(AB ‖ CD, Alternate ∠s)
$AB = CD$	(Opp. sides of a rhombus)
$\Delta OAB \cong \Delta ODC$	(ASA)
$\Rightarrow \quad OA = OC, OB = OD$	(c.p.c.t)

  Again in Δ's OAB and OBC

$OA = OC$	(Proved)
$OB = OB$	(Common)
$AB = BC$	(Sides of a rhombus)
$\Delta OAB \cong \Delta OBC$	(S.S.S.)
$\Rightarrow \quad \angle AOB = \angle COB$	(c.p.c.t.)
But $\quad \angle AOB + \angle COB = 180°$	(Linear pair)
$\therefore \quad \angle AOB = \angle COB = 90°$	

■ *To prove that the diagonals of a rhombus bisect the interior angles.*

Proof : In Δ's *AOB* and *AOD*

	OB = *OD*	(*Diagonals of a rhombus bisect each other*)
	∠*AOB* = ∠*AOD*	(*Each = 90°, prove above*)
	AO is common	
∴	Δ*AOB* ≅ Δ*AOD*	(*SAS*)
⇒	∠*OAB* = ∠*OAD*	(*c.p.c.t*)

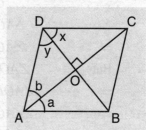

> **Summary :** *A rhombus has all the properties of a parallelogram and some more !*
>   1. *All the sides of a rhombus are equal.*
>   2. *The diagonals of a rhombus bisect the interior angles.*
>   3. *The diagonals of a rhombus bisect each other.*
>   4. *The diagonals of a rhombus cut at right angles.*

Thus, in rhombus *ABCD*, we have

(1) *AB* = *BC* = *CD* = *DA*   (2) ∠*a* = ∠*b*, ∠*x* = ∠*y*

(3) *AO* = *OC*, *BO* = *OD*,   (4) ∠*AOB* = ∠*AOD* = ∠*BOC* = ∠*COD* = 90°.

Maths Alert : The diagonals of a rhombus are not equal.

14.7 Properties of a Square

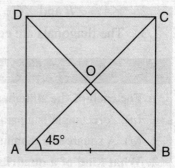

Since a square is a rectangle, it has all the properties of a rectangle, *viz.* its diagonals are equal.

Also, since a square is also a rhombus (it being a parallelogram whose sides are equal) it has all the properties of a rhombus, *viz.*, its diagonals bisect each other at right angles and also bisect the interior angles.

> **Summary :**
>   1. *All the sides of a square are equal.*
>   2. *The diagonals of a square are equal and bisect each other at right angles.*
>   3. *The angle which a diagonal makes with a side of the square is 45°.*

14.8 Properties of a Kite

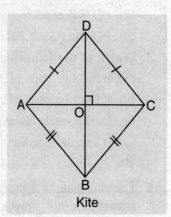

Kite

1. *The diagonal are perpendicular to each other, i.e., AC ⊥ BD.*
2. *Diagonal BD bisects ∠B as well as ∠D.*
3. ∠*A* = ∠*C*   4. *OA* = *OC*
5. Diagonal *BD* divides the kite into two congruent triangle, *i.e.,* Δ*ABD* ≅ Δ*DBC*.

Proof : (*i*) In Δ's *ABD* and *CBD*,

	AB = *BC*	(*Given*)
	AD = *CD*	(*Given*)

$$BD = BD \qquad (Common)$$
$$\therefore \qquad \Delta ABD \cong CBD \qquad (SSS)$$
$$\Rightarrow \qquad \angle ABD = \angle CBD \qquad \qquad \dots(1)$$
$$\text{and} \qquad \angle ADB = \angle CDB \qquad \qquad \dots(2) \ (c.p.c.t.)$$

i.e., diag. *BD* bisects $\angle ABC$ and $\angle ADC$.

(*ii*) In Δ's *AOD* and *COD*,

$$AD = CD \qquad (Given)$$
$$\angle ADO = \angle CDO \qquad (Property\ of\ kite,\ proved\ above)$$
$$OD = OD \qquad (Common)$$
$$\therefore \qquad \Delta AOD \cong \Delta COD \qquad (SAS)$$
$$\Rightarrow \qquad \angle AOD = \angle COD\ and\ AO = OC \qquad (c.p.c.t.)$$
$$\text{But} \qquad \angle AOD + \angle COD = 180° \qquad (Linear\ pair)$$
$$\Rightarrow \qquad \angle AOD + \angle AOD = 180° \qquad (\because \angle AOD = \angle COD,\ proved\ above)$$
$$\Rightarrow \qquad 2\angle AOD = 180° \qquad (Given)$$
$$\Rightarrow \qquad \angle AOD = \angle COD = 90° \qquad (Given)$$

14.9 Properties of an Isosceles Trapezium

The adjoining figure shows an isosceles trapezium in which $AB \parallel DC$ and $AD = BC$. It has the following properties.

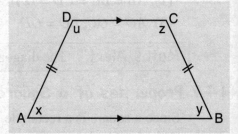

1. The co-interior angles x, u and y, z are supplementary, *i.e.,*
   $\angle A + \angle D = 180°$, $\angle B + \angle C = 180°$.
2. $\angle A = \angle B$ and $\angle C = \angle D$.
3. The diagonals are equal, *i.e.,* $AC = BD$.

EXERCISE 14 (b)

1. **For each of the statements given below, indicate if it is true (T) or false (F) :**
   (*a*) A rectangle is a parallelogram. (*b*) A square is a rectangle. (*c*) A parallelogram is a rhombus.
   (*d*) A square is a rhombus. (*e*) A rectangle is a square. (*f*) A square is a parallelogram.

2. **What kind of a quadrilateral is the following ?**
   (*a*) The diagonals cut each other perpendicularly at X such that $AX = XC$.
   (*b*) The diagonals and the sides form four congruent right-angled triangles.

3. **_PQRS_ is a quadrilateral. What kind of quadrilateral is it if**
   (*a*) *PQ* is parallel to *RS* and the diagonals are equal in length?
   (*b*) *PQ* and *RS* are parallel and $\angle P = \angle R$?

4. **Which of the following are true for a rhombus?**
   (*a*) It has two pairs of parallel sides.   (*b*) It has two pairs of congruent angles.
   (*c*) It has two pairs of congruent sides.   (*d*) Two of its angles are right angles.
   (*e*) Its diagonals bisect each other and are at right angles.   (*f*) Its diagonals are congruent and perpendicular.
   (*g*) It has all its sides of equal length.

5. The diagonals of a parallelogram are not perpendicular. Is it a rhombus? Why or why not?

6. The diagonals of a quadrilateral are perpendicular to each other. Is such a quadrilateral always a rhombus? If your answer is a 'no', draw a figure to justify your answer.

7. Which of the following are true for a rectangle?

(a) It has two pairs of congruent sides.

(b) It has all its sides of equal lengths.

(c) Its diagonals are congruent.

(d) Its diagonals bisect each other.

(e) Its diagonals are perpendicular.

(f) Its diagonals are perpendicular and bisect each other.

(g) Its diagonals are congruent and bisect each other.

(h) Its diagonals are congruent and perpendicular and bisect each other.

8. Repeat question 8 for a square, in place of a rectangle.

9. A window frame has one diagonal longer than the other. Is the window frame a rectangle? Why or why not?

10. What kind of quadrilateral are formed when the mid points of the sides of the following are joined?

(a) a rectangle,   (b) a rhombus,   (c) a kite,   (d) an isosceles trapezium.

11. *ABCD* is a rectangle, *EFGH* is a rhombus and *PQRS* is a square.

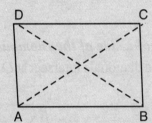 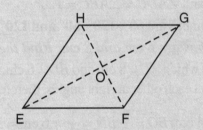 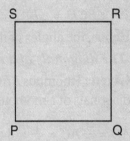

Complete the following :

(i) *FH* ⊥ ....

(ii) *GE* bisects ....

(iii) If ∠*FEH* = 130°, ∠*EHG*. = ...

(iv) If *AC* = 4, *BD* = ...

(v) If *PQ* = 4, *PS* = ...

(vi) If ∠*EHG* = 48°, ∠*HGF* = ...

(vii) If *HE* = 12, *GH* = ...

(viii) ∠*EOF* = ...

14.10 Solved Examples

Ex. 1. *ABCD is a rectangle with ∠BAC = 28°. Determine ∠DBC.*

Sol. $AO = \frac{1}{2} AC$ and $BO = \frac{1}{2} BD$ *(Diagonals of a rectangle bisect each other.)*

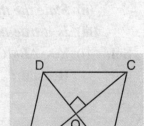

But *AC = BD*   *(Diagonals of a rectangle are equal.)*

∴ *AO = BO* ⇒ ∠*OBA* = ∠*OAB* = 28°   *(In a Δ, angles opposite equal sides are equal)*

Now, ∠*ABC* = 90°   *(angle of rectangle)*

∴ ∠*DBC* = 90° − ∠*OBA* = 90° − 28° = **62°.**

Ex. 2. *ABCD is a rhombus with ∠ABC = 126°. Determine ∠ACD.*

Sol. ∠*ABC* = ∠*ADC*   *(Opposite angles of a rhombus)*

∴ ∠*ADC* = 126°   (∠*ABC* = 126°, given)

∴ $∠ODC = \frac{1}{2} (∠ADC) = \frac{1}{2} × 126° = 63°$ *(Diagonals of a rhombus bisect interior angles)*

∴ In Δ*OCD*, ∠*OCD* + ∠*ODC* + ∠*DOC* = 180°   *(Angle sum of a Δ)*

But $\angle DOC = 90°$ (*Diagonals of a rhombus bisect at right angles*)

$\therefore$ $\angle OCD + 63° + 90° = 180°$

$\Rightarrow$ $\angle OCD = 180° - 63° - 90° = 180° - 153° = 27° \Rightarrow \angle ACD = \mathbf{27°}$.

Ex. 3. *One of the diagonals of a rhombus is congruent to one of its sides. Find the angles of the rhombus.*

Sol. Let *ABCD* be a rhombus in which diagonal

$BD = AB = AD$

$\therefore$ ΔABD is an equilateral triangle

$\therefore$ $\angle BAD = 60°$ (*each angle of an equilateral Δ is 60°*)

Also, $\angle BAD + \angle ABC = 180°$ (*adj. int. angles, AD || BC*)

$\therefore$ $\angle ABC = 180° - \angle BAD = 180° - 60° = 120°$

Since opposite angles of a rhombus are equal

$\therefore$ $\angle BCD = \angle BAD = 60°$ and $\angle ADC = \angle ABC = 120°$.

Hence, the angles of the rhombus are **60°, 120°, 60° and 120°**.

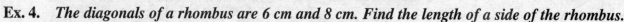

Ex. 4. *The diagonals of a rhombus are 6 cm and 8 cm. Find the length of a side of the rhombus.*

Sol. **Given :** Rhombus *ABCD* in which $AC = 8$ cm and $BD = 6$ cm. Let these diagonals intersect at *O*. Since the diagonals of a rhombus bisect each other at right angles, therefore

$AO = \frac{1}{2} AC = \frac{1}{2} \times 8$ cm $= 4$ cm, $BO = \frac{1}{2} BD = \frac{1}{2} \times 6$ cm $= 3$ cm,

$\angle AOB = 90°$

$\therefore$ In rt. $\angle d$ ΔAOB, by Pythogoras theorem, we have

$AB^2 = AO^2 + OB^2 = 4^2 + 3^2 = 16 + 9 = 25$

$\therefore$ $AB = \sqrt{25}$ cm $= 5$ cm. Hence, the length of each side of the rhombus is **5 cm**.

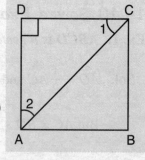

Ex. 5. *ABCD is a square. Determine $\angle DCA$.*

Sol. Since *ABCD* is a square, therefore, $AD = DC$ and $\angle ADC = 90°$

Now, in ΔADC, we have

$AD = DC \Rightarrow \angle 1 = \angle 2$ (*In a Δ, angles opposite equal sides are equal.*)

Also, $\angle 1 + \angle 2 + \angle ADC = 180°$ (*Angle sum of a Δ*)

or $\angle 1 + \angle 1 + 90° = 180°$ (∵ $\angle 2 = \angle 1$ and $\angle ADC = 90°$)

$\Rightarrow 2 \angle 1 = 180° - 90° = 90° \Rightarrow \angle 1 = \frac{90°}{2} = 45°$. *i.e,* $\angle ACD = \mathbf{45°}$.

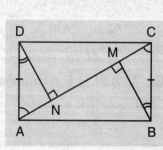

Ex. 6. *In the adjoining figure, ABCD is a rectangle. BM and DN are perpendiculars from B and D on AC.*

   (i) *Is $\Delta BMC \cong \Delta DNA$?*

   (ii) *State the three pairs of matching parts you used to answer* **(i)**.

   (iii) *Is it true that* **BM = DN***?*

Sol.   (*i*) Yes, $\Delta BMC \cong \Delta DNA$

        Reason : $\angle BCM = \angle DAN$ (*Alt. $\angle s$, AD || BC*)

                    $\angle BMC = \angle DNA$ (*each = 90°*)

                    $BC = AD$ (*opp. sides of rect.*)

        $\therefore$ $\Delta BMC \cong \Delta DNA$ (*AAS*)

  (*ii*) $\angle BCM = \angle DAN$, $BC = DA$ and $\angle BMC = \angle DNA$

  (*iii*) Yes, it is true that $BM = DN$. (*corresponding parts of congruent triangles*)

Ex. 7. *ABCD is a kite in which* $\angle OBC = 20°$ *and* $\angle OCD = 35°$, *find*

    (i) $\angle ABC$

    (ii) $\angle ADC$

    (iii) $\angle BAQ$

Sol. (*i*) Since diag. *BD* bisects $\angle ABC$, therefore,

$$\angle ABC = 2\angle OBC = 2 \times 20° = \mathbf{40°}.$$

(*ii*) $\angle DOC = 90°$ (*Diagonals of a kite intersect at right angles*)

$$\angle ODC = 180° - (\angle DOC + \angle OCD) = 180° - (90° + 35°)$$
$$= 180° - 125° = 55°.$$

As diag. *BD* bisects $\angle ADC$, so

$$\angle ADC = 2\angle ODC = 2 \times 55° = \mathbf{110°}.$$

(*iii*) In $\triangle OBC$, $\angle OCB = 180° - (\angle BOC + \angle OBC)$ (*Diagonals of a kite intersect at right angles*)

$$= 180° - (90° + 20°) = 180° - 110° = 70°$$

$\therefore$ $\angle BCD = \angle OCB + \angle OCD = 70° + 35° = 105°$

$\Rightarrow$ $\angle BAD = \mathbf{105°}.$ ($\because \angle BAD = \angle BCD$, Property of a kite)

EXERCISE 14 (c)

1. The diagonals of a rectangle *ABCD* intersect at *O*. If $\angle BOC = 44°$, find $\angle OAD$.

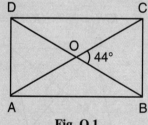 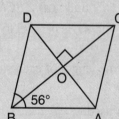 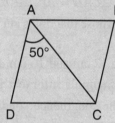 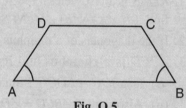

      Fig. Q.1   **Fig. Q.2**   **Fig. Q.3**   **Fig. Q.5**

2. *ABCD* is a rhombus with $\angle ABC = 56°$. Determine $\angle CAD$.

3. *ABCD* is a rhombus. If $\angle DAC = 50°$, find (*a*) $\angle ACD$ (*b*) $\angle CAB$ (*c*) $\angle ABC$.

4. (*i*) *ABCD* is a rhombus. $\angle BAC = 37°$. Draw a sketch and find the four angles of the rhombus.

    (*ii*) If an angle of a rhombus is 50°, find the size of the angles of one of the triangles which are formed by the diagonals.

5. *ABCD* is a trapezium in which *AB* ∥ *DC*. If $\angle A = \angle B = 40°$, what are the measures of the other two angles?

6. Calculate the angles marked with small letters in the following diagrams.

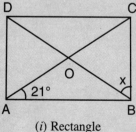 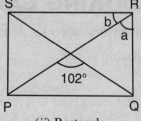 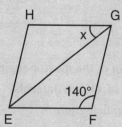

     (*i*) Rectangle   (*ii*) Rectangle   (*iii*) Rhombus

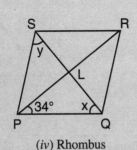

(iv) Rhombus

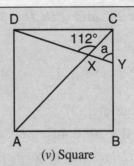

(v) Square

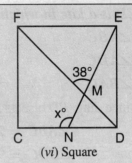

(vi) Square

7. *ABCD* is a kite. If ∠*BCD* = 40°, find (*a*) ∠*BDC* (*b*) ∠*ABC*.

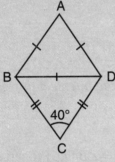

Fig. Q.7

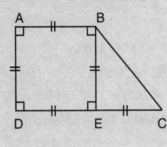

Fig. Q.8

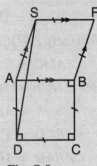

Fig. Q.9

8. *ABCD* is a trapezium and *ABED* is a square. If *BE* = *EC*, find (*a*) ∠*BAE* (*b*) ∠*ABC* (*c*) What shape is the figure *ABCE*?

9. *ABCD* is a square and *ABRS* is a rhombus. If ∠*SAD* = 120°, find (*a*) ∠*ASD* (*b*) ∠*SRB*.

10. *ABCD* is a kite and ∠*A* = ∠*C*. If ∠*CAD* = 70°, ∠*CBD* = 65°, find : (*a*) ∠*BCD* (*b*) ∠*ADC*.

11. *KLMN* is an isosceles trapezium whose diagonals cut at *X* and *KL* is parallel to *NM*. If ∠*KNL* = 25°, ∠*KMN* = 30°, find (*a*) ∠*KXN* (*b*) ∠*MLN*.

12. If the diagonals of a rhombus are 12 cm and 16 cm, find the length of each side.

13. *ABCD* is a rhombus and its diagonals intersect in *O*.

   (*i*) Is Δ*BOC* ≅ Δ*DOC* ? State the congruence condition used.

   (*ii*) Also state if ∠*BCO* = ∠*DCO*. Deduce that each diagonal of a rhombus bisects the angle through which it passes.

14. *AC* is the diagonal of a rectangle *ABCD*.

   (*i*) Is Δ*ACB* ≅ Δ*CAD* ?

   (*ii*) State the pairs of corresponding parts you use to answer (*i*).

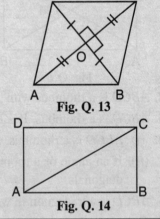

Fig. Q. 13

Fig. Q. 14

LOOKING BACK

Summary of Key Facts

1. The sum of the interior angles of a quadrilateral is 360°.

2. Types of Quadrilaterals.

   (*i*) Parallelogram   (*ii*) Trapezium   (*iii*) Rectangle

   (*iv*) Rhombus   (*v*) Square   (*vi*) Kite.

DEFINITIONS

3. (*i*) A quadrilateral with exactly one pair of parallel sides is called a **trapezium**.

(*ii*) A quadrilateral in which both pairs of opposite sides are parallel is called a **parallelogram**.

(*iii*) A parallelogram in which all the sides are equal is called a **rhombus**.

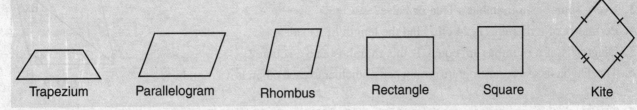

Trapezium   Parallelogram   Rhombus   Rectangle   Square   Kite

(*iv*) A parallelogram in which each angle is a right angle is called **rectangle**.

(*v*) A parallelogram in which all the sides are equal and each angle is equal to a right angle is called a **square**.

(*vi*) A quadrilateral which has two pairs of equal adjacent sides but unequal opposite sides is called a **kite**.

4. A quadrilateral is a parallelogram if

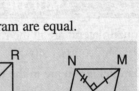

(*i*) its opposite sides are equal or

(*ii*) its opposite angles are equal or

(*iii*) its diagonals bisect each other or

(*iv*) it has one pair of opposite sides equal and parallel.

5. PROPERTIES : Opposite sides and opposite angles of a parallelogram are equal.

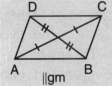

||gm   Rectangle   Square   Rhombus

6. The diagonals of a parallelogram bisect each other.

7. The diagonals of a rhombus bisect each other at right angles.

8. The diagonals of a rectangle are equal, *i.e.*, $AC = BD$

9. The diagonals of a square are equal and bisect each other at right angles ($PR = QS$ and $\angle POQ = 90°$)

10. The diagonals of a rhombus and a square bisect the internal angles.

11. Properties of an isosceles trapezium

- *Co-interior angles are supplementary.*
- *Angles of the same base are equal.*
- *Diagonals are equal.*

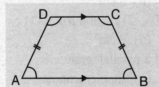

12. Properties of a kite.

1. The diagonals intersect at right angles

2. $OA = OC$

3. $\angle A = \angle C$

4. BD bisects $\angle B$ as well as $\angle D$.

5. BD divides the kite into two congruent triangles.

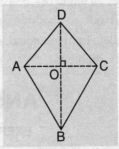

MENTAL MATHS – 8

1. One angle of a parallelogram is 60°. Find its opposite angle and the adjacent angle.

2. If one angle of a rhombus is 70°, find other angles.

3. Every square is a rhombus –True or False?

4. Perimeter of a rhombus is 24 cm. Find the length of its sides.

5. Diagonals of a rhombus are equal. Is this rhombus also a square?

6. The diagonals of a parallelogram are not perpendicular to each other. Is it a rhombus? Why?

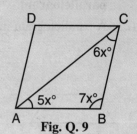
Fig. Q. 9

7. Two opposite angles of a parallelogram are $(3x - 2)°$ and $(50 - x)°$. Find the measure of each angle of the parallelogram

8. The perimeter of a parallelogram is 60 cm. If the smaller side is 12 cm long, find the measure of the longer side.

9. In the figure, find the four angles A, B, C, D of the parallelogram $ABCD$.

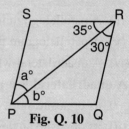
Fig. Q. 10

10. In the figure, find the value of a and b and measure of $\angle Q$ of the parallelogram $PQRS$.

MULTIPLE CHOICE QUESTIONS – 12

1. The angles of a quadrilateral are in the ratio 2 : 3 : 5 : 8. The smallest angle is :
   (i) 60°   (ii) 40°   (iii) 20°   (iv) 50°

2. Two sides of a parallelogram are in the ratio 5 : 4. If its perimeter is 54 cm, the length of the larger side is :
   (i) 9 cm   (ii) 11 cm   (iii) 12 cm   (iv) 15 cm

3. The length of a rectangle is 16 cm and each of its diagonal measures 20 cm. The breadth is :
   (i) 9 cm   (ii) 10 cm   (iii) 12 cm   (iv) 14 cm

4. A parallelogram whose diagonals are equal and bisect each other at right angles is a :
   (i) rhombus   (ii) square   (iii) trapezium   (iv) rectangle

5. A quadrilateral having exactly one pair of parallel sides is a :
   (i) square   (ii) rhombus   (iii) trapezium   (iv) rectangle

6. PQRS is a rhombus. Diagonals PR and QS bisect each other at point O such that PR = 6 cm and QS = 8 cm. Each side of the rhombus is :
   (i) 10 cm   (ii) 5 cm   (iii) 12 cm   (iv) 7 cm

7. In a square $ABCD$, $AC = (7x - 2)$ cm and $BD = (11x - 10$ cm). AC is :
   (i) 11 cm   (ii) 9 cm   (iii) 12 cm   (iv) 8 cm

8. Any two adjacent angles of a parallelogram are :
   (i) complementary   (ii) supplementary   (iii) equal   (iv) none of these

9. The diagonal of a square makes an angle of .... with each of its sides.
   (i) 90°   (ii) 60°   (iii) 45°   (iv) 75°

10. Two adjacent angles of a parallelogram are equal, its diagonals do not bisect each other at right angles. It is a :
    (i) square   (ii) rhombus   (iii) trapezium   (iv) rectangle

ANSWERS

EXERCISE 14 (a)

1. 100°, 80° and 100°   2. 90° each   3. 22 cm   4. 45°, 135°, 45°, 135°

5. 30 cm, 60 cm, 30 cm, 60 cm.   6. $66\frac{2}{3}°$, $113\frac{1}{3}°$, $66\frac{2}{3}°$, $113\frac{1}{3}°$ 7. $x = 55°, y = 69°, z = 111°$ 8. 90° each

9. (*i*) True, opposite angles of a ‖gm   (*ii*) True, *AF* bisects ∠*A* (given)

   (*iii*) True, *CE* bisects ∠*C* (given)   (*iv*) True, halves of opposite equal angles

    (*v*) True, Alternate angles   (*vi*) True, ∠*FAB* = ∠*DCE* and ∠*DCE* = ∠*CEB*

                                                             ∴ ∠*FAB* = ∠*CEB*

   (*vii*) True, corresponding angles *CEB* and *FAB* are equal.   (*viii*) True, *AB* ‖ *CD* ⇒ *AE* ‖ *FC*   10. 27 cm.

EXERCISE 14 (b)

1. (*a*) T   (*b*) T   (*c*) F   (*d*) T   (*e*) F   (*f*) T

2. (*a*) Kite   (*b*) Rhombus   3. (*a*) Isosceles trapezium   (*b*) Parallelogram.

4. (*a*) T   (*b*) T   (*c*) T   (*d*) F   (*e*) T   (*f*) F   (*g*) T

5. No   6. No, A kite also has this property

7. (*a*) T   (*b*) F   (*c*) T   (*d*) T   (*e*) F   (*f*) F   (*g*) T   (*h*) F

8. (*a*) T   (*b*) T   (*c*) T   (*d*) T   (*e*) T   (*f*) T   (*g*) T   (*h*) T

9. No.   10. (*a*) Rhombus   (*b*) Rectangle   (*c*) Rectangle   (*d*) Rhombus

11. (*i*) *EG*   (*ii*) *HF* at right angles   (*iii*) 50°   (*iv*) 4   (*v*) 4   (*vi*) 132°   (*vii*) 12   (*viii*) 90°

EXERCISE 14 (c)

1. 68°   2. 62°   3. 50°, 50°, 80°

4. (*i*) ∠*A* = 74°, ∠*B* = 106°, ∠*C* = 74°, ∠*D* = 106°   (*ii*) 25°, 65°, 90°   5. ∠*C* = ∠*D* = 140°

6. (*i*) 69° (**Hint :** Use the fact that diagonals of a rectangle being equal, Δ*AOB* is isosceles. Also, ∠*ABC* = 90°]

   (*ii*) *a* = 51°, *b* = 39°   (*iii*) 20°   (*iv*) *x* = *y* = 56°   (*v*) 67°   (*vi*) 83°

7. (*a*) 70°   (*b*) 130°   8. (*a*) 45°   (*b*) 135°   (*c*) parallelogram

9. 30°, 30°   10. 95°, 40°   11. 60°, 95°   12. 10 cm   14. (*i*) yes   (*ii*) *AB* = *CD*, *BC* = *DA*, *AC* = *CA*.

MENTAL MATHS – 8

1. 60°, 120°   2. 110°, 70°. 110°   3. True   4. 6 cm each   5. Yes   6. No

7. 37°, 143°, 37°, 143°   8. 18 cm   9. 70°, 110°, 70°, 110°   10. *a* = 30°, *b* = 35° ∠*Q* = 115°

MULTIPLE CHOICE QUESTIONS – 12

1. (*ii*)   2. (*iv*)   3. (*iii*)   4. (*ii*)   5. (*iii*)   6. (*ii*)   7. (*iii*)

8. (*ii*)   9. (*iii*)   10. (*iv*)

NUMBER FACTS

1. **The number 1000.** M is an abbreviation for the Roman word **mille,** meaning a thousand. It stood for 1000 in Roman numeration system. We have entered new millennium. A *millennium* is 1000 years and a millipede has 1000 legs as imagined by persons who named it so. A distance of one mile was originally 1000 paces- the Romans counted one pace as two steps.

2. **A prefix** is a word element you add on in front of a word to change its meaning. A prefix makes the differences between a **kilometre** and a centimetre since kilo means thousand and centi means1 **hundredth.**

    Prefixes given in the table can be used to build words to have very large and very small measurements.

    The following facts will give you an idea of very large and very small numbers.

1. A large power plant generates 300 megawatts of electricity. It is 30 crore watts (300, 000, 000 watts)

2. The nucleus of an atom is less than one picometre wide. (It means less than

    one trillionth $10^{-12} = \dfrac{1}{1,000,000,000,000}$ metre)

3. Pluto orbits at a distance of almost 6 terametres from the sun. It is equal to 6 trillion (6×10^{12}) metres.

4. Light can travel 30 centimetres in one nano second, i.e, one billionth second

    10^{-9} second $= \dfrac{1}{1,000,000,000}$ second

5. All the power plants in a developed country can generate 560 gigawatts (= 560 billion watts).

6. The speed of advanced computers is calculated in picoseconds, i.e., Trillionths of a second.

LARGE MEASUREMENTS		
Tera	**giga**	**mega**
1 trillion	1 billion	1million
SMALL MEASUREMENTS		
micro	**nano**	**pico**
1 millionth	1 billionth	1 trillionth

15. Construction of Quadrilaterals

15.1 Introduction

Quadrilaterals are constructed by splitting up the figure into two triangles, the construction of which you have already learnt. You know that a quadrilateral has ten parts in all, four sides, four angles and two diagonals. To construct a quadrilateral, we will need data about five specified parts out of ten.

You are *reminded to draw a rough free hand sketch* in every case before constructing the fair figure.

Case 1. **Construction of a quadrilateral when four sides and one diagonal are given.**

Ex. 1. *Construct a quadrilateral ABCD in which AB = 4.5 cm, BC = 4 cm, CD = 6.5 cm, DA = 3 cm and BD = 6.5 cm*

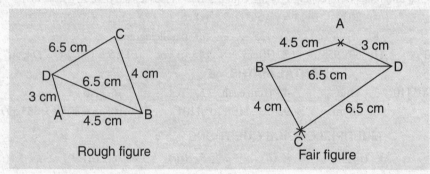

Rough figure   Fair figure

Sol. Draw a rough sketch of the quadrilateral *ABCD*, and write down its dimensions as shown. Clearly, we may divide it into two triangles *ABD* and *BCD*. It is convenient to draw the diagonal *BD* and construct the two triangles.

Steps of Construction :

1. Draw *BD* = 6.5 cm
2. With *B* as centre and *BA* = 4.5 cm as radius, draw an arc on any side of *BD*.
3. With *D* as centre and *DA* = 3 cm as radius, draw another arc to intersect the arc of step (2) at *A*.
4. With *B* as centre and *BC* = 4 cm as radius, draw an arc so that the arc and *A* are on opposite sides of *BD*.
5. With *D* as centre and *DC* = 6.5 cm as radius draw another arc to intersect the arc of step 4 at *C*.
6. Join *AB*, *BC*, *CD* and *AD*. Then *ABCD* is the required quadrilateral.

EXERCISE 15 (a)

Construct a quadrilateral :

1. *ABCD* in which *AB* = 3.6 cm, *BC* = 5.5 cm, *CD* = 4.9 cm, *DA* = 5.3 cm and *AC* = 7.2 cm.
2. *PQRS* in which *PQ* = 3.5 cm, *QR* = 5.5 cm, *QS* = 5.5 cm, *PS* = 4.5 cm, and *SR* = 4.5 cm.
3. *AB* = 6 cm, *BC* = 5 cm, *AD* = 4 cm, *CD* = 7 cm and *BD* = 6 cm.
4. Is it possible to construct a quadrilateral *ABCD* in which *AB* = 3 cm, *BC* = 4 cm, *CD* = 5.5 cm, *DA* = 6 cm and *BD* = 9 cm ? If not, give reason.

Case 2. **When three sides and two diagonals are given.**

Ex. 2. *Construct a quadrilateral ABCD in which BC = 4.2 cm, CA = 5.7 cm, AD = 4.7 cm, CD = 5.2 cm, and BD = 6.7 cm.*

Sol . We first draw a rough sketch and write the given dimension on it.

As is clear from the rough sketch, we can divide the quadrilateral into two triangles *DCA* and *DCB* with the three sides of each being known. So, to draw the required quadrilateral, we draw these two triangles.

Steps of Construction :

1. Draw *DC* = 5.2 cm.

2. With *D* as centre and radius 6.7 cm, draw an arc.

3. With *C* as centre and radius 4.2 cm, draw another arc intersecting the arc in (2) in *B*.

4. With *D* as centre and radius 4 .7 cm, draw an arc.

5. With *C* as centre and radius 5.8 cm, draw an arc intersecting the arc in (4) in *A*.

6. Join *CB*, *BA* and *AD*.

7. Then *ABCD* is the required quadrilateral.

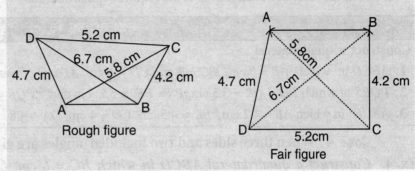

EXERCISE 15 (b)

Construct a quadrilateral :

1. *ABCD* in which *AB* = 4.5 cm, *BC* = 3.5 cm, *AD* = 3 cm, *AC* = 5 cm and *BD* = 4.5 cm.

2. *PQRS* in which *QR* = 7 cm, *PR* = *PS* = 5.5 cm, *RS* = 4.5 cm, and *QR* = 9.5 cm.

3. *ABCD* in which *AB* = 6.8 cm, *AD* = 5.8 cm, *AC* = 6.9 cm, *BD* = 7.3 cm and *BC* = 4.1 cm.

4. Is it possible to construct a quadrilateral *ABCD* in which *AD* = 3 cm, *CD* = 3 cm, *DA* = 7.5 cm, *AC* = 8 cm and *BD* = 4 cm? If not, give reason.

Case 3. **When four sides and one angle are given**

Ex. 3. *Construct a quadrilateral ABCD in which AB = 4 cm, BC = 3.5 cm, CD = 5 cm, AD = 5.5 cm and B = 75°.*

Sol.

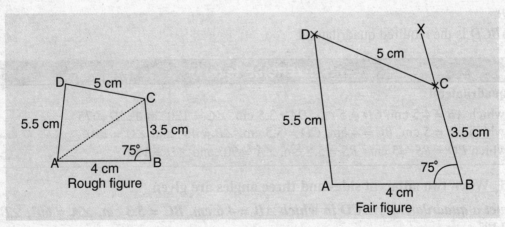

On drawing the rough sketch and writing its dimensions and angle, we see that it can be divided into two triangles *ABC* and *ACD*.

Steps of Construction :

1. Draw *AB* = 4 cm.

2. Make ∠*ABC* = 75° and cut off *BC* = 3.5 cm from *BX*.

3. Join *AC*.
4. With *A* as centre and 5.5 cm radius, draw an arc.
5. With *C* as centre and radius 5 cm, draw another arc intersecting the arc in (4) at point *D*.
6. Join *CD* and *AD*. Then *ABCD* is the required quadrilateral.

EXERCISE 15 (c)

Construct a quadrilateral

1. *ABCD* in which *AB* = 5 cm, *BC* = 4 cm, *CD* = 6 cm, *AD* = 7 cm, and ∠*B* = 80°
2. *PQRS* in which *PQ* = *QR* = 3.5 cm, *PS* = *RS* = 5.2 cm and ∠*PQR* =120°.
3. *ABCD* in which *AB* = 4.2 cm, *BC* = 4.5 cm, *CD* = 4 cm, *DA* = 4.8 cm, and ∠*A* = 72°

Case 4. When three sides and two included angles are given

Ex. 4. *Construct a quadrilateral ABCD in which BC = 6 cm, CD = 6 cm, DA = 4 cm, ∠C = 60° and ∠D = 75°.*

Sol.

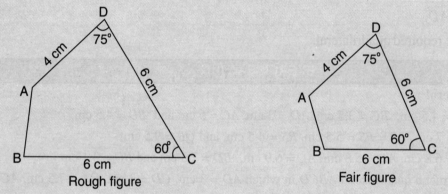

Rough figure   Fair figure

Steps of Construction :

1. Draw *BC* = 6 cm.
2. Construct ∠*BCD* = 60°and cut off *CD* = 6 cm.
3. Construct ∠*CDA* = 75°and cut off *DA* = 4 cm.
4. Join *AB*.
   Then *ABCD* is the required quadrilateral.

EXERCISE 15 (d)

Construct a quadrilateral

1. *ABCD* in which *AB* = 4.5 cm, *CD* = 5 cm, *DA* =3.5 cm, ∠*C* = 120° and ∠*D* = 75°.
2. *ABCD* in which *AB* = 5 cm, *BC* = 4 cm, *CD* = 5.5 cm, ∠*B* = 45° and ∠*C* = 150°.
3. *PQRS* in which *PQ* = *PS* =5 cm, *RS* = 5.5 cm, ∠*A* = 90°,and ∠*D* = 120°.

Case 5. When two adjacent sides and three angles are given

Ex. 5. *Construct a quadrilateral ABCD in which AB = 4.6 cm, BC = 5.3 cm, ∠A = 60°, ∠B = 100° and ∠C = 120°.*

Sol.   Steps of Construction :

1. Draw *AB* = 4.6 cm.
2. Draw *BC* = 5.3 cm making *ABC* = 100°.

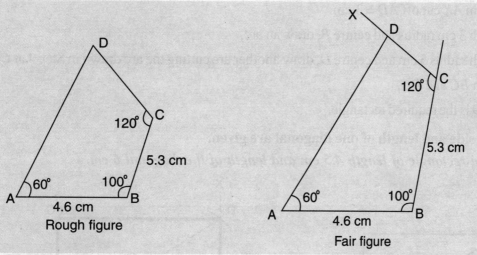

Rough figure

Fair figure

3. Draw *CX* making ∠*BCD* = 120° .
4. At *A* draw a line *AD* making ∠*BAD* = 60° and meeting *CX* at *D*.

   Then *ABCD* is the required quadrilateral.

EXERCISE 15 (e)

Draw a quadrilateral

1. *ABCD* in which *AB* = 5.8 cm, *BC* = 4.2 cm, ∠*A* = 70°, ∠*B* = 110° and ∠*C* = 105°.
2. *ABCD* in which *AB* = 6 cm, *BC* = 5 cm, ∠*A* = 55°, ∠*B* = 110° and ∠*D* = 90°.

   (**Hint** : ∠*C* = 360°– (∠*A* + ∠*B* + ∠*D*)

3. Is it possible to construct a quadrilateral *ABCD* in which *AB* = 5cm, *BC* = 7.5 cm, ∠*A* = 80°, ∠*B* = 140° and ∠*C* = 145°? If not, give reason.

   (**Hint** : ∠*A* + ∠*B* + ∠*C* = 365° > 360°. Here, it is not possible to construct a quadrilateral with the given data.)

CONSTRUCTION OF SPECIAL TYPES OF QUADRILATERALS

15.2 Construction of Rectangles

Case 1. Sides are given

Ex. 1. *Construct a rectangle of length 5 cm and breadth 3 cm.*

Sol.

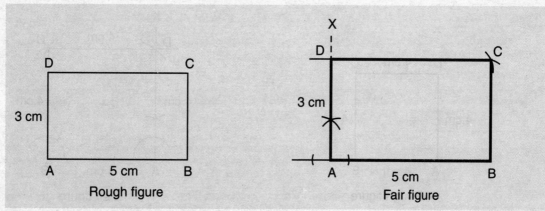

Rough figure

Fair figure

Step 1. Draw *AB* = 5 cm.

Step 2. At *A* draw *AX* ⊥ *AB*.

Step 3. From AX cut off $AD = 3$ cm.

Step 4. With 3 cm radius and centre B, draw an arc.

Step 5. With radius 5 cm and centre D, draw another arc cutting the arc drawn in Step 4 at C.

Step 6. Join BC and DC.

Then $ABCD$ is the required rectangle.

Case 2. **A side and length of one diagonal are given.**

Ex. 2. *Construct a rectangle of length 4.5 cm and length of the diagonal 6 cm.*

Sol.

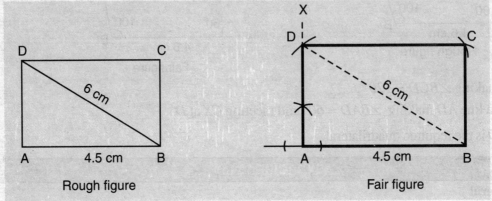

| Rough figure | Fair figure |

Step 1. Draw $AB = 4.5$ cm.

Step 2. At A draw $AX \perp AB$.

Step 3. With B as centre and radius 6 cm, draw an arc cutting AX at D.

Step 4. With B as centre and radius equal to AD, draw an arc. With D as centre and radius 4.5 cm draw an arc cutting the previous arc at C.

Step 5. Join BC and DC

Then $ABCD$ is the required rectangle.

15.3 Construction of Squares

Case 1. **One side given**

Ex. 3. *Construct a square of side 4 cm.*

Sol. You can construct a square of given side length in the same manner as you constructed a rectangle.

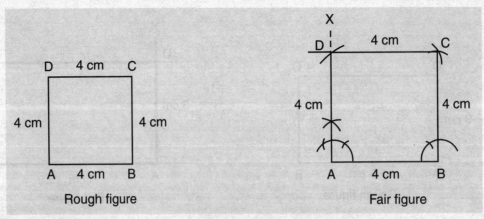

| Rough figure | Fair figure |

Step 1. Draw $AB = 4$ cm.

Step 2. At A, draw $AX \perp AB$.

Step 3. From *AX*, cut off *AD* = 4 cm.

Step 4. With *B* and *D* as centres and radii 4 cm each, draw two arcs cutting each other at *C*.

Step 5. Join *BC* and *DC*.

Then *ABCD* is the required square.

Case 2. A diagonal given

Ex. 4. *Construct a square whose one diagonal is 5 cm.*

Sol. *Use the fact that (i) the diagonals of a square are equal. (ii) They bisect each other at right angles.*

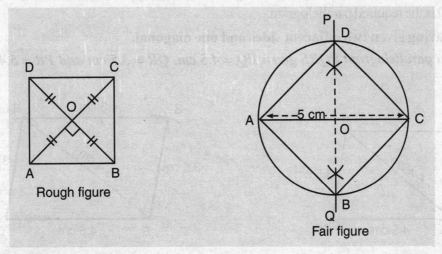

Rough figure

Fair figure

Step 1. Draw a diagonal *AC* = 5 cm.

Step 2. Draw *PQ* the perpendicular bisector of *AC*.

Step 3. Let *PQ* cut *AC* at *O*.

Step 4. With *O* as centre and *OA* radius draw a circle.

Let this circle cut *QP* at points *B* and *D*.

Step 5. Join *AB*, *BC*, *CD* and *DA*.

Then *ABCD* is the required square.

15.4 Parallelogram

Case 1. Having given adjacent sides and included angle.

Ex 5. *Construct a parallelogram ABCD in which AB = 4 cm, BC= 3 cm, ∠A = 60°.*

Sol. In constructing the parallelogram with the given measures, we will use the fact that the opposite sides of a parallelogram are equal.

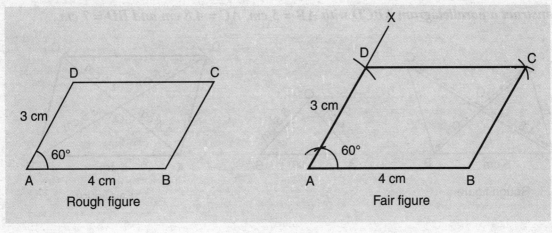

Rough figure

Fair figure

Step 1. Draw $AB = 4$ cm.

Step 2. Through A, draw AX making $\angle BAX = 60°$.

Step 3. From AX, cut off $AD = 3$ cm.

Step 4. With centre D and radius 4 cm, draw an arc.

Step 5. With B as centre and radius 3 cm, draw another arc cutting the arc drawn in Step 4.
Name the point as C.

Step 6. Join BC and DC.

Then $ABCD$ is the required parallelogram.

Case 2. **Having given two adjacent sides and one diagonal.**

Ex. 6. *Construct a parallelogram PQRS given PQ = 4.5 cm, QR = 3.5 cm and PR = 5.4 cm.*

Sol.

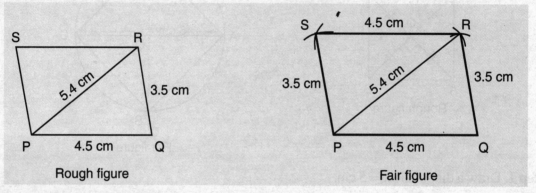

Rough figure   Fair figure

Step 1. Draw $PQ = 4.5$ cm.

Step 2. With Q as centre and radius 3.5 cm, draw an arc.

Step 3. With P as centre and radius 5.4 cm, draw another arc cutting the arc drawn in Step 2.
Name this point as R.

Step 4. Join QR and PR.

Step 5. With R and P as centres and radii 4.5 cm and 3.5 cm respectively, draw two arcs cutting each other.
Name this point as S.

Step 6. Join RS and PS.

Then $PQRS$ is the required parallelogram.

Case 3. **Having given one side and two diagonals.**

Ex. 7. *Construct a parallelogram ABCD with AB = 5 cm, AC = 4.8 cm and BD = 7 cm.*

Sol.

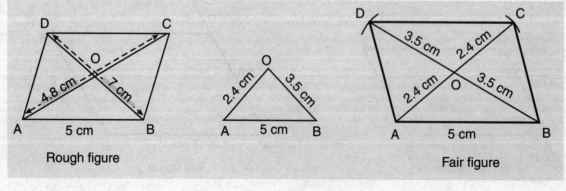

Rough figure   Fair figure

We will use the fact that the diagonals of a parallelogram bisect each other. Thus, $AO = \frac{1}{2}AC = \frac{1}{2} \times 4.8 = 2.4$ cm and $BO = \frac{1}{2}BD = \frac{1}{2} \times 7 = 3.5$ cm. We will, therefore, first construct $\triangle AOB$ with $AB = 5$ cm, $AO = 2.4$ cm and $BO = 3.5$ cm.

Step 1. Draw $AB = 5$ cm.

Step 2. With A as centre and radius 2.4 cm and with B as centre and radius 3.5 cm, draw arcs cutting each other at O.

Step 3. Join AO and BO.

Step 4. Produce AO to C such that $OC = 2.4$ cm.

Step 5. Produce BO to D such that $OD = 3.5$ cm.

Step 6. Join BC, CD and AD.

Then $ABCD$ is the required parallelogram.

Case 4. Height and two sides are given.

Ex.8. *Construct a ∥ gm ABCD so that AB = 4.5 cm, BC = 3.7 cm and height = 2.5 cm.*

Construction :

Step 1. Draw $AB = 4.5$ cm.

Step 2. Draw $XY \parallel AB$ at a height of 2.5 cm from AB.

Step 3. With centres A and B and radius 3.7 cm, draw arcs cutting XY at D and C respectively. Then $ABCD$ is the required parallelogram.

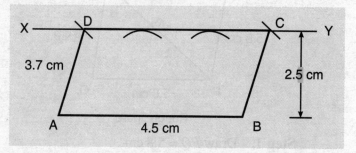

15.5 Rhombus

Recall that

The sides of a rhombus are equal. The construction of a rhombus is similar to that of a parallelogram. In case of parallelogram, the adjacent sides were given to be different. Here they are equal.

Case 1. Having given one side and an angle.

Ex. 9. *Construct a rhombus of side 6 cm and ∠A = 60°.*

Sol.

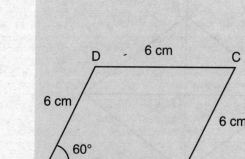

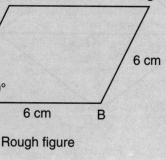

Rough figure

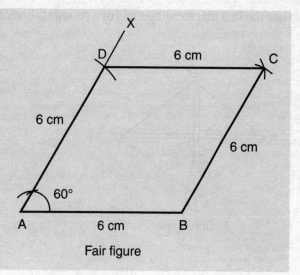

Fair figure

Step 1. Draw $AB = 6$ cm.

Step 2. At A, draw AX making $\angle A = 60°$.

Step 3. From AX, cut off $AD = 6$ cm.

Step 4. With D as centre and radius 6 cm and with B as centre and radius 6 cm, draw arcs cutting each other at C.

Step 5. Join BC and DC.

Then $ABCD$ is the required rhombus.

Case 2. **Having given one side and diagonal**

Ex. 10. *Construct a rhombus PQRS given PQ = 5.8 cm and PR = 7 cm.*

Sol.

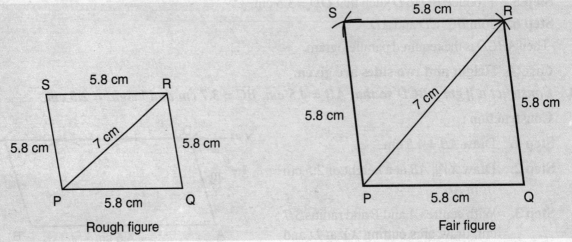

Rough figure   Fair figure

Step 1. Draw $PQ = 5.8$ cm.

Step 2. With P as centre and radius 7 cm and Q as centre and radius 5.8 cm, draw arcs cutting each other at R.

Step 3. With P as centre and radius 5.8 cm and R as centre and radius 5.8 cm, draw arcs cutting each other at S.

Step 4. Join PS and RS

Then $PQRS$ is the required rhombus.

Case 3. **Having given two diagonals.**

Ex. 11. *Construct a rhombus ABCD in which AC = 7 cm. and BD = 5 cm.*

Sol. We use the fact that the diagonals of a rhombus bisect each other at right angles.

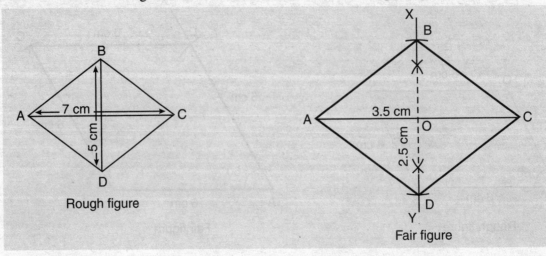

Rough figure   Fair figure

Step 1. Draw $AC = 7$ cm.

Step 2. Draw its right bisector XY cutting AC at O.

Step 3. With O as centre and radius $\frac{1}{2}BD = \frac{1}{2} \times 5 = 2.5$ cm, draw arcs on either side of XY cutting it at B and D.

Step 4. Join AB, CB, AD and CD.

Then $ABCD$ is the required rhombus.

15.6 Trapezium

Case 1. When its four sides are given and the parallel sides are indicated.

Ex. 12. *Construct a trapezium ABCD in which AB is parallel to DC and AB = 8 cm, BC = 4 cm, CD = 3.5 cm and DA = 4.2 cm.*

Sol.

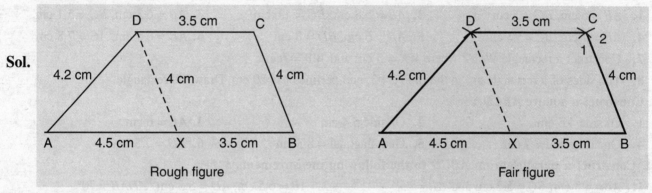

Rough figure   Fair figure

Steps of Construction

1. Draw $AB = 8$ cm, and cut off $AX = 4.5$ cm

2. Construct the $\triangle AXD$ such that $XD = 4$ cm and $AD = 4.2$ cm

3. With B as centre and radius equal to 4 cm, draw the arc 1. With D as centre and radius equal to 3.5 cm, draw the arc 2 cutting the arc 1 at C.

4. Join BC and DC.

Then $ABCD$ is the required trapezium.

Case 2. When one of the parallel sides, height and non-parallel sides are given.

Ex. 13. *Construct a trapezium ABCD when one of the parallel sides AB = 6 cm, height = 3.5 cm, BC = 4 cm and AD = 4.7 cm.*

Sol.

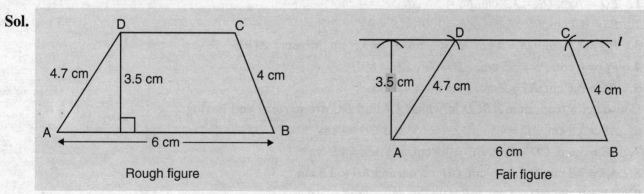

Rough figure   Fair figure

Steps of Construction

1. Draw a st. line $AB = 6$ cm.

2. Draw a line $l \parallel AB$ at a perp. distance of 3.5 cm.

3. With A and B as centres, in turn and radii of 4.7 cm and 4 cm respectively, draw arcs to cut l at D and C.

4. Join AD and BC.

Then $ABCD$ is the required trapezium.

> **Note :** If instead of the non-parallel sides, two diagonals are given, similar construction holds good.

EXERCISE 15 (f)

I. Construct a rectangle ABCD given

1. $AB = 6$ cm, $BC = 5$ cm
2. $AB = 5.8$ cm, $BC = 4.6$ cm
3. $AB = 6.3$ cm, $BC = 5.1$ cm
4. $AB = 7$ cm, $BC = 5.5$ cm
5. $AB = 6$ cm, $BD = 8$ cm
6. $AB = 6.4$ cm, $AC = 7.8$ cm
7. Construct a rectangle $WXYZ$ where $WX = 5$ cm and $WY = 7$ cm.
8. The sides of a rectangle are in the ratio 2 : 3, and perimeter is 20 cm. Draw the rectangle.

II. Construct a square ABCD :

1. Of side 4.5 cm
2. Of side 5.4 cm
3. $AB = 6$ cm
4. One diagonal = 7 cm
5. One diagonal = 8.3 cm
6. $BD = 7.5$ cm

III. Construct a parallelogram ABCD to the following measurements :

1. $AB = 6.5$ cm, $BC = 5.2$ cm and $\angle B = 45°$
2. $AB = 6.5$ cm, $AD = 5.5$ cm, $\angle DAB = 70°$
3. $AB = 7$ cm, $BC = 5.8$ cm, $\angle A = 120°$
4. $AB = 6.8$ cm, $AC = 8$ cm, $BD = 7.3$ cm
5. $AB = 7$ cm, $AC = 6$ cm, $BD = 9$ cm.
6. Construct a parallelogram $PQRS$ given $PQ = 8.2$ cm, $PR = 9.5$ cm, $QS = 10.8$ cm.

IV. Construct a rhombus ABCD given :

1. $AB = 6$ cm and $\angle A = 50°$
2. $AB = 7$ cm and $\angle A = 60°$
3. $AB = 7.4$ cm and $\angle B = 72°$
4. $AB = 6.5$ cm and $\angle B = 100°$
5. $AB = 6.8$ cm, $AC = 8$ cm
6. $AB = 7$ cm, $AC = 8.3$ cm
7. $AB = 6.3$ cm, $BD = 7.8$ cm
8. $AC = 6$ cm, $BD = 7$ cm
9. $AC = 7$ cm, $BD = 8.5$ cm
10. $AC = 5.8$ cm, $BD = 6.4$ cm

V. Construct the trapezium PQRS in which PQ is parallel to RS, from the given measurements without using set-squares and protractor as far as possible.

1. $PQ = 7$ cm, $QR = 4.5$ cm, $RS = 3.5$ cm, $SP = 4$ cm
2. $PS = 4.7$ cm, $RS = 8$ cm, $\angle P = 120°$, $\angle R = 45°$
3. $PQ = 7.5$ cm, $QR = 4$ cm, $RS = 3$ cm, $SP = 3.5$ cm. Measure $\angle QPS$.
4. $PQ = 6$ cm, $PS = 5.5$ cm, $\angle P = 60°$, $\angle Q = 80°$.
5. $PQ = 5.6$ cm, $RS = 9$ cm, $QR = PS = 4.8$ cm

Construct a trapezium ABCD in which AB and DC are parallel and having:

6. $AB = 5.5$ cm, $AD = 4.5$ cm, $\angle A = 65°$ and $CD = 4$ cm
7. $AB = 5$ cm, $CD = 7$ cm, $BC = 4.5$ cm, and $AD = 4.8$ cm
8. $AB = 7.2$ cm, $BC = 3.6$ cm, $CD = 5$ cm and $AD = 3.8$ cm
9. $AB = 9$ cm, $CD = 5$ cm, $\angle BAD = 70°$ and $\angle DBA = 50°$.
10. $AB = 6.5$ cm, $CD = 10$ cm, $\angle CAB = 45°$, $\angle CBA = 75°$.

ENRICHMENT

Fibonacci Numbers

The first ten Fibonacci numbers are 1, 1, 2, 3, 5, 8, 13, 21, 34, 55, 89, 144,...... Fibonacci numbers are generated by adding together the two previous numbers in the sequence $1 + 1 = 2$, $1 + 2 = 3$, $2 + 3 = 5$, $3 + 5 = 8$, $5 + 8 = 13$, and so on.

Fibonacci numbers are named after Leonardo Fibonacci of Pisa (1170 – 1250) who lived in 13th century Italy. He was nicknamed Fibonacci since he was the son (figlio) of Bonaccio. Can you name next five numbers in the Fibonacci sequence.

Fibonacci numbers have many interesting mathematical properties and can be found in many aspects of the living world, especially in the world of biology.

If you look at the picture of a pine cone you can see a pattern of spirals coming out from the centre. They go in two directions. There are 13 spirals going anti-clockwise and 8 going clockwise. Both 8 and 13 are Fibonacci numbers. If you count similar spiral patterns in other plants, such as sunflowers, you can count much larger Fibonacci numbers.

A very interesting fact is that the number of ancestors of a drone (a male bee) must in any generation be a Fibonacci number. A drone has a mother but no father, as the queen's unfertilised eggs hatch into drones. The queen's fertilised eggs produce either worker bees or queens.

16. Solid Shapes

16.1 Solids

Anything that occupies space and has three dimensions *viz.* length, breadth and height (depth) is called a solid or a **three-dimensional figure**.

Wherever you are, whether in your sweet home, your classroom, in a train or in an aeroplane, you come across various solid figures such as books, pencils, houses, bricks, refrigerators, footballs, cricket bats, tables etc.

16.2 Parts of a Solid

The adjoining figure shows a triangular prism. As can be seen from the markings in the figure,

1. **Face** is each flat surface of the solid.
2. **Vertex** is the point (corner) where three faces of a solid meet.
3. **Edge** is the line segment that is intersection of two faces.

Now based on the above definitions we will find out how many vertices, edges and faces each of the solids have.

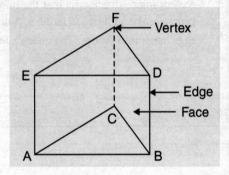

16.3 Various Types of Solids

I. Prisms : A prism is a solid formed by joining two congruent plane shapes together with straight lines. The two congruent shapes called the **bases** are parallel and determine the name of the prism.

For example : A rectangular prism is formed by joining two **identical rectangles** together with straight lines.

Solids	Rectangular prism (cuboid)	Square prism (cube)	Triangular prism	Pentagonal prism	Hexagonal prism
Vertices	8	8	6	10	12
Edges	12	12	8	15	18
Faces	6 (All rectangles)	6 (All squares)	5 [2 triangles 3 rectangles]	7 [2 pentagons 5 rectangles]	8 [2 hexagons 6 rectangles]

II. Pyramids : A pyramid is any three-dimensional solid where the upper surfaces are triangular and converge on one point. It has one base (usually a polygon). A pyramid is named according to the shape of its base.

For example : A pyramid with pentagonal base is a pentagonal pyramid.

Solids	Triangular pyramid	Rectangular pyramid	Pentagonal pyramid	Hexagonal pyramid
Vertices	4	5	6	7
Edges	6	8	10	12
Faces	4 (All triangles)	5 [4 Triangles 1 Rectangle]	6 [5 Triangles 1 Pentagon]	7 [6 Triangles 1 Hexagon]

III. Polyhedrons : A polyhedron is a geometric solid with faces and straight edges. A polyhedron may be classified according to the number of its faces, as shown below.

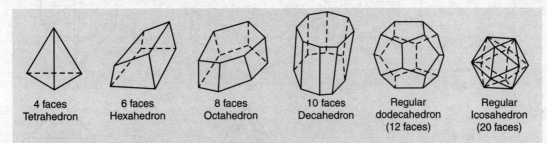

4 faces
Tetrahedron

6 faces
Hexahedron

8 faces
Octahedron

10 faces
Decahedron

Regular
dodecahedron
(12 faces)

Regular
Icosahedron
(20 faces)

Activity 1. Count the number of vertices and edges in each of these polyhedrons and fill the table given below :

	Tetrahedron	**Hexahedron**	**Octahedron**	**Decahedron**
Vertices				
Edges				

Regular Octahedron : A regular octahedron is a polyhedron composed of eight equilateral (congruent) triangles four of which meet at each vertex. It has 6 vertices, 12 edges and 8 triangular faces.

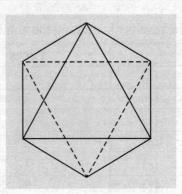

IV. Other Solids

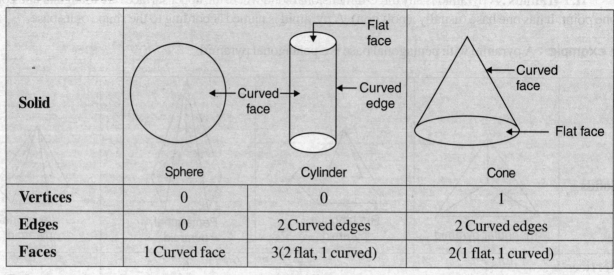

Solid	Sphere	Cylinder	Cone
Vertices	0	0	1
Edges	0	2 Curved edges	2 Curved edges
Faces	1 Curved face	3(2 flat, 1 curved)	2(1 flat, 1 curved)

16.4 Euler's Rule

As you have already studied, the following closed space figures have faces, vertices and edges. Is there some relationship among the number of faces, vertices and edges? Let us investigate.

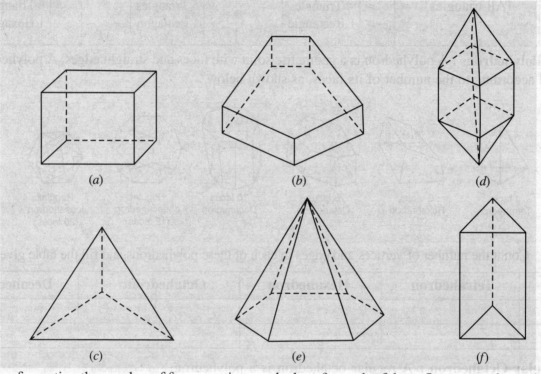

The results of counting the number of faces, vertices, and edges for each of these figures are shown in this table.

	Faces	Vertices	Edges
(a)	6	8	12
(b)	7	10	15
(c)	4	4	6
(d)	12	10	20
(e)	7	7	12
(f)	5	6	9

Clearly, the number of faces and the number of vertices are not always equal (although sometimes they are). As the number of faces increases, does the numbers of vertices increase ?

Number of faces	4	5	6	7	7	12
Number of vertices	4	6	8	7	10	10

Except for one case, you might have been tempted to accept that pattern, but the 6-sided figure has more vertices than one of the 7-sided figures!

In the cases pictured on the previous page, are there always more edges than either faces or vertices? Yes there are! Perhaps you are on the trail of something. Try adding the number of faces and the number of vertices. Could it be that these sums will equal the number of edges for the figure? No? Well, do not give up. You are very close to discovering a relationship that is generally true for closed space figures like these.

> **Generalization : Number of faces + Number of vertices = Number of edges + 2**
>
> **Leonarhd Euler** (1707–83) was a famous mathematician who discovered this rule called Euler's rule about solids (with straight edges only.) It is stated as
>
> $$F + V = E + 2$$

16.5 Nested Solids

Some of the solid figures that we observe in our everyday life are in fact made up of two or more solids. Some common examples are :

Rocket, tent, lipstick, hut, funnel, ice cream cone with a scoop of ice cream, etc.

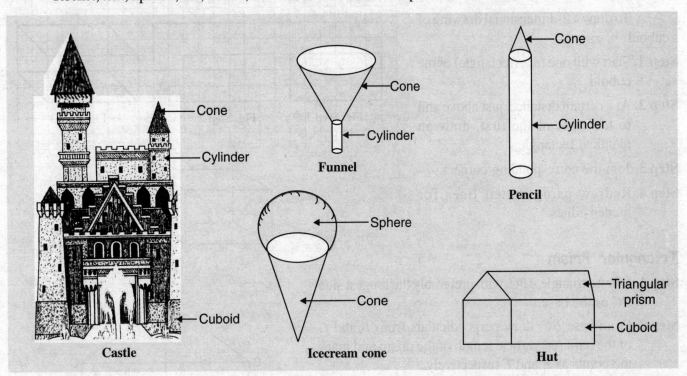

Castle   **Icecream cone**   **Hut**

Nets of Solids

A net of a solid is the outline of its faces joined together from which a model of the solid can be made.

Nets of some of the solid figures are shown on the next page.

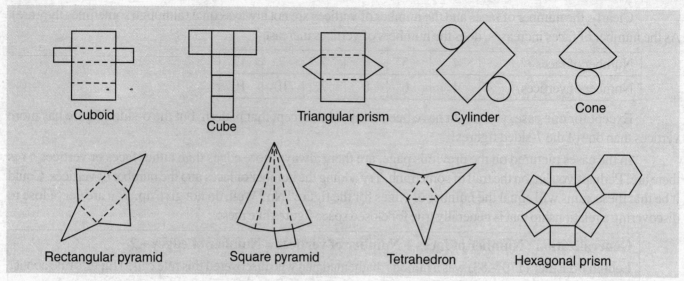

Cuboid   Cube   Triangular prism   Cylinder   Cone

Rectangular pyramid   Square pyramid   Tetrahedron   Hexagonal prism

16.6 Drawing Two-Dimensional (2-D) Representation of 3-D Objects

A 2-D (two-dimensional) figure has only two dimensions, *i.e.,* length and breadth. All plane figures, for example, square, rectangle, triangle, are all 2-dimensional figures.

The solid figures as cuboid, cube, triangular prism, square pyramid can all be represented by 2-D figures. Let us see how?

Cuboid

To draw a 2-dimensional drawing of a cuboid.

Step 1. Start with one face (rectangle) of the cuboid.

Step 2. At a certain distance, just above and to the right of the first, draw an identical rectangle.

Step 3. Join the corresponding corners.

Step 4. Redraw using dotted lines for hidden edges.

Fig. Step 1   Fig. Step 2   Fig. Step 3

Fig. Step 4

Triangular Prism

Step 1. Draw a triangle *ABC*, with preferably the longest side *BC* as the base.

Step 2. From base *BC,* draw perpendiculars from *B* and *C* of the required vertical length of the prism and mark the points as *E* and *F* respectively.

Step 3. From point *A* also drop a perpendicular of same length and mark the point as *D*.

Step 4. Join *A* to *D*, *E* to *D* and *F* to *D* with dotted lines for hidden edges.

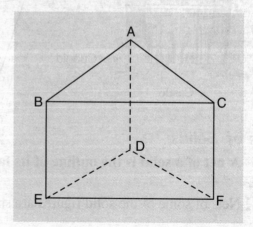

16.7 Square Pyramid

Suppose we have to draw a pyramid which has base length 4 cm and vertical height 3 cm.

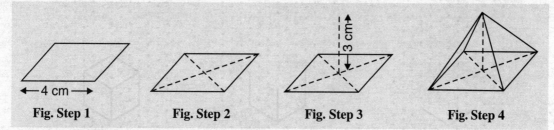

Fig. Step 1   Fig. Step 2   Fig. Step 3   Fig. Step 4

Step 1. Draw a rhombus of side length 4 cm.

Step 2. Draw the diagonals to locate the centre of the base. Use dotted lines.

Step 3. Draw the vertical height to scale. Use dotted lines.

Step 4. Draw the four slant edges by joining the vertices of the rhombus to the top point of the vertical height.

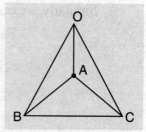

To draw a tetrahedron, *i.e.,* a triangular pyramid, draw the triangular base *ABC* of given dimensions, draw a vertical line *AO* from the vertex *A* and join the remaining vertices *B* and *C* to *O*.

Cylinder

To draw a cylinder.

Step 1. Draw an oval shape (ellipse) for the circular base.

Step 2. Draw two equal vertical lines to represent the height of the cylinder.

Step 3. Draw another ellipse for the top.

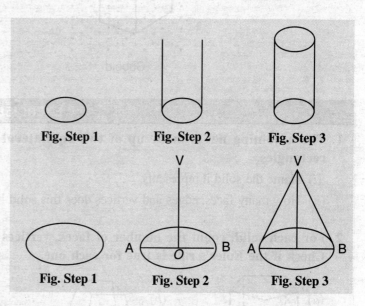

Fig. Step 1   Fig. Step 2   Fig. Step 3

Cone

To draw a cone.

Step 1. Draw an oval shape (ellipse) for the circular base.

Step 2. Draw a diameter *AB* and the *OV* a vertical line from the centre *O* representing the height.

Step 3. Join the ends *A* and *B* to *V*.

Fig. Step 1   Fig. Step 2   Fig. Step 3

We can use isometric paper to draw 3-D shapes as shown in the adjoining figure.

This 3 cm × 3 cm × 3 cm cube has been drawn using the dots as guides. The vertical lines are always vertical, but the horizontal lines are drawn at angles.

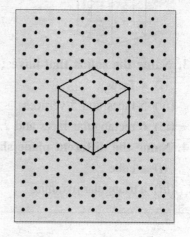

Following steps are involved in drawing a cube using an isometric paper.

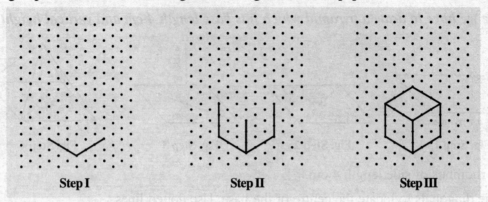

Step I   Step II   Step III

Similarly, we can see some other figures drawn on isometric paper.

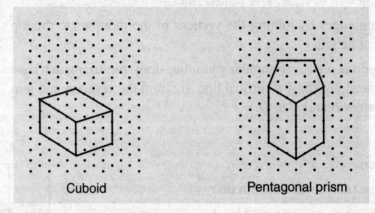

Cuboid   Pentagonal prism

EXERCISE 16

1. **The adjoining net is made up of two equilateral triangles and three rectangles.**

    (*i*) Name the solid it represents.

    (*ii*) How many faces, edges and vertices does this solid have?

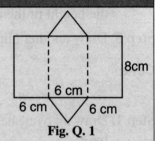

8cm

6 cm

6 cm   6 cm

Fig. Q. 1

2. **For each solid, count the number of faces, vertices and edges. Check if the Euler's rule is true for each one.**

    (*a*) 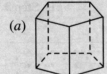   (*b*) 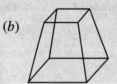   (*c*)   (*d*)

3. **Name the solids that have :**

    (*i*) 4 faces   (*ii*) 1 curved surface   (*iii*) 6 faces

    (*iv*) 5 faces and 5 vertices   (*v*) 8 triangular faces

    (*vi*) 6 rectangular faces and 2 hexagonal faces.

4. **Name the different plane shapes needed to draw the net of :**

    (*i*) a cube   (*ii*) a triangular prism

    (*iii*) a triangular pyramid   (*iv*) a cylinder

5. Given below is the net of an octahedron with numbers 0 to 7 on the faces. Enlarge these on a cardboard to make a model.

(*i*) How many faces, edges and vertices does this solid have?

(*ii*) Check whether Euler's rule is true for the octahedron or not.

6. Draw the 2-D representation of a

(*i*) cube

(*ii*) triangular prism

7. On an isometric dotted paper draw the following shapes :

(*i*) cube   (*ii*) cuboid   (*iii*) hexagonal prism   (*iv*) pentagonal prism

8. Name the solid that would be formed by each net :

(*i*)

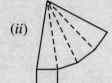

(*ii*)

(*iii*)

LOOKING BACK

Summary of Key Facts

1. Solids have 3-dimensions length, breadth and height and occupy space.

2. A solid has three parts : face, vertex and edge.

3. The main types of solids are :

     (*i*) Prisms   (*ii*) Pyramids   (*iii*) Polyhedrons

4. Euler's formula states that for every solid (with straight edges only) $F - E + V = 2$, where F, E and V denote the number of faces, edges and vertices respectively.

5. A solid composed of two or more solid figures is called a nested solid.

MULTIPLE CHOICE QUESTIONS – 13

1. The common name of a square prism is :

     (*i*) cuboid   (*ii*) cube   (*iii*) pyramid   (*iv*) polygon

2. A rectangular pyramid has _____ faces.

     (*i*) 6   (*ii*) 7   (*iii*) 5   (*iv*) 4

3. A pentagonal prism has _____ edges.

     (*i*) 10   (*ii*) 18   (*iii*) 12   (*iv*) 15

4. A solid figure with only one vertex is a :

     (*i*) square pyramid   (*ii*) tetrahedron   (*iii*) cone   (*iv*) cylinder

5. If the number of faces and vertices in a solid are 7 and 10 respectively, the number of edges are :

     (*i*) 17   (*ii*) 15   (*iii*) 19   (*iv*) 13

ANSWERS

EXERCISE 16

1. (*i*) Triangular Prism   (*ii*) Faces-5, Edges-9, Vertices-6
3. (*i*) Tetrahedron (*ii*) Cylinder   (*iii*) Cube, cuboid   (*iv*) Square pyramid and rectangular pyramid   (*v*) regular octahedron   (*vi*) hexagonal prism.
4. (*i*) Square   (*ii*) Triangle and rectangle   (*iii*) Triangle   (*iv*) Circle and rectangle
5. (*i*) Faces-8, Edges-12, Vertices-6
8. (*i*) Triangular pyramid   (*ii*) Square pyramid   (*iii*) Hexagonal pyramid.

MULTIPLE CHOICE QUESTIONS – 13

1. (*ii*)   2. (*iii*)   3. (*iv*)   4. (*iii*)   5. (*ii*)

17. Area of a Trapezium and a Polygon

17.1 Recall

You have learnt the following formulas in class VII.

(i)   Area of a rectangle = **length × breadth**

$$= l \times b \text{ sq units}$$

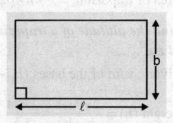

(ii)   Area of a square = **(side)²**

$$= a^2 \text{ sq units}$$

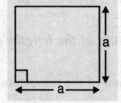

(iii)   Area of a parallelogram = **base × altitude**

$$= AB \times DE \text{ sq units} = BC \times DF \text{ sq units}$$

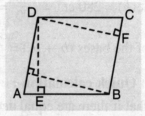

(iv)   Area of a triangle = $\dfrac{1}{2}$ × **base × altitude**

$$= \dfrac{1}{2} \times BC \times AD \text{ sq units}$$

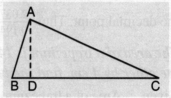

(v)   Area of a circle = **π × (radius)²**

$$= \pi r^2 \text{ sq units}$$

17.2 Area of a Trapezium

Area of trapezium $ABCD$ = area of $\triangle ABC$ + area of $\triangle ADC$

$$= \left(\dfrac{1}{2} BC \times AE\right) + \left(\dfrac{1}{2} AD \times FC\right)$$

But $AE = FC$

$\therefore$ Area of trapezium $ABCD = \dfrac{1}{2}(AD + BC)AE$

$$= \dfrac{1}{2} \text{ (sum of parallel sides)} \times \text{height}$$

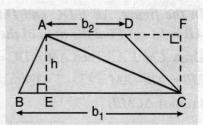

> Area of trapezium $= \frac{1}{2}$ (sum of parallel sides) × height
>
> $= \frac{1}{2} \times (b_1 + b_2) \times h$ where h is height and b_1, b_2 are the lengths of the parallel sides.

Ex. 1. *Find the area of a trapezium with base 12 cm and height 6 cm, if the side parallel to the given base is 7 cm long.*

Sol. Given Height (h) = 6 cm, Base b_1 = 12 cm, Base b_2 = 7 cm

Area of trapezium $= \frac{1}{2} \times h \times (b_1 + b_2) = \frac{1}{2} \times 6 \times (12 + 7)$ cm^2 $= (3 \times 19)$ cm^2 = **57 cm^2**.

Ex. 2. *Find the altitude of a trapezium, the sum of the lengths of whose bases is 8.5 cm and whose area is 34 cm^2.*

Sol. Given : sum of the bases $(b_1 + b_2)$ = 8.5 cm, Area = 34 cm^2

Height $(h) = \dfrac{2 \times \text{Area}}{b_1 + b_2} = \dfrac{2 \times 34}{8.5} = \dfrac{2 \times 34}{\frac{85}{10}} = \dfrac{2 \times 34 \times 10}{85}$ = **8 cm**.

Ex. 3. *Find the sum of the lengths of the bases of a trapezium whose area is 4.2 m^2 and whose height is 280 cm.*

Sol. Given : Area of the trapezium $= 4.2$ m^2,

Height $(h) = 280$ cm $= \dfrac{280}{100} = 2.8$ m

$\dfrac{4.2}{2.8} = \dfrac{\frac{42}{10}}{\frac{28}{10}} = \dfrac{42}{28}$

Sum of the bases $(b_1 + b_2) = \dfrac{2 \times \text{Area}}{h} = \dfrac{2 \times 4.2}{2.8} = \dfrac{2 \times 42}{28}$ = **3 m**.

- **Aid to Quick calculation :**

  Note that if there are equal decimal places in the numerator and denominator then you can just remove the decimal point. Thus $\dfrac{2.037}{0.194} = \dfrac{2037}{194}$. Here we have written $\dfrac{4.2}{2.8}$ as $\dfrac{42}{28}$.

Ex. 4. *The area of a trapezium is 143 cm^2 and its height is 11cm. If one of the parallel sides is longer than the other by 4 cm, find the two parallel sides.*

Sol. Given : Area of a trapezium = 143 cm^2, Height (h) = 11 cm.

Sum of the bases $(b_1 + b_2) = \dfrac{2 \times \text{Area}}{h} = \dfrac{2 \times 143}{11} = 2 \times 13$ = **26 cm**.

Let length of one base be x cm. Then the length of the other base is $(x + 4)$ cm.

∴ $x + (x + 4) = 26 \Rightarrow 2x = 26 - 4 \Rightarrow 2x = 22 \Rightarrow x = 11$

∴ one side = **11 cm** and the other side = 11 + 4 = **15 cm**.

Ex. 5. *In the figure, AB || DC and DA is perpendicular to AB. Further, DC = 7 cm, CB = 10 cm and AB = 13 cm Find the area of the quadrilateral ABCD.*

Sol. Draw $CM \perp AB$ Then $AM = DC = 7$ cm

$MB = AB - AM = 13 - 7 = 6$ cm

From rt $\triangle CMB$,

$CM = \sqrt{CB^2 - MB^2} = \sqrt{10^2 - 6^2} = \sqrt{100 - 36} = \sqrt{64}$ = 8 cm

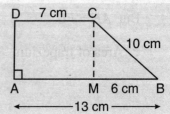

$\therefore$ Area of trapezium $ABCD = \frac{1}{2} \times$ height $\times$ sum of parallel sides

$$= \frac{1}{2} \times 8 \times (13 + 7) = \frac{1}{2} \times 8 \times 20 = \textbf{80 cm}^2.$$

Ex. 6. *The parallel sides DC and AB of a trapezium are 10 cm and 20 cm respectively. Its non-parallel sides are each equal to 13 cm. Find the area of the trapezium.*

Sol. Given $DC = 10$ cm, $AB = 20$ cm and $DA = CB = 13$ cm.

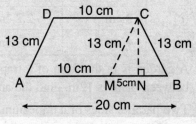

Through C, draw CM parallel to DA meeting AB at M.

Now, $AM = DC = 10$ cm, $MB = 20$ cm $– 10$ cm $= 10$ cm

Draw $CN \perp MB$

Since, ΔCMB is isosceles so CN bisects MB

$\therefore$ $MN = NB = 5$ cm

Now, from rt. ΔCMN, $CN = \sqrt{CM^2 - MN^2} = \sqrt{13^2 - 5^2} = \sqrt{169 - 25} = \sqrt{144} = 12$ cm

$\therefore$ Area of trapezium $ABCD = \frac{1}{2} \times$ height $\times$ (sum of the parallel sides)

$$= \frac{1}{2} \times 12 \times (10 + 20) \text{ cm}^2 = 6 \times 30 = \textbf{180 cm}^2.$$

Ex. 7. *The parallel sides of a trapezium are in the ratio 2 : 5 and the distance between the parallel sides is 10 cm. If the area of the trapezium is 350 cm^2, find the lengths of its parallel sides.*

Sol. Let the lengths of the parallel sides be $2x$ cm and $5x$ cm.

$\because$ Area of a trapezium $= \frac{1}{2}$ (sum of parallel sides) $\times$ height

$\therefore$ $350 = \frac{1}{2}(2x + 5x) \times 10 \Rightarrow 350 = 35x \Rightarrow x = \frac{350}{35} = 10$

$\therefore$ Lengths of parallel sides $= 2 \times 10$ cm and 5×10 cm

$$= \textbf{20 cm and 50 cm}.$$

Ex. 8. *Find the area of the field shown alongside. All dimensions are in metres.*

Sol. Area of field $ABCDE$ = Area of ΔAPB + Area of trap. $PBCR$

+ Area of ΔRCD + Area of ΔDQE

+ Area of ΔEQA

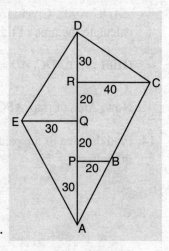

$\therefore$ Area of $\Delta APB = \frac{1}{2} AP \times PB = \frac{1}{2} \times 30 \times 20 = 300 \text{ m}^2.$

Area of trap. $PBCR = \frac{1}{2}(BP + RC) \times PR = \frac{1}{2}(20 + 40) \times 40 \text{ m}^2$

$$= 1200 \text{ m}^2.$$

Area of $\Delta RCD = \frac{1}{2} \times RC \times RD = \frac{1}{2} \times 40 \times 30 = 600 \text{ m}^2.$

Area of $\Delta DQE = \frac{1}{2} \times DQ \times EQ = \frac{1}{2} \times 50 \times 30 = 750 \text{ m}^2.$

Area of $\Delta EQA = \frac{1}{2} \times EQ \times AQ = \frac{1}{2} \times 30 \times 50 = 750 \text{ m}^2.$

Adding these, area of the field $= (300 + 1200 + 600 + 750 + 750) = \textbf{3600 m}^2.$

EXERCISE 17 (a)

1. Find the area of the following trapeziums:-

	Height	Parallel sides
(a)	7 cm	8 cm and 10 cm
(b)	15 cm	10 cm and 12 cm
(c)	2 cm	2.2 cm and 3.5 cm
(d)	4 cm	15 cm and 7.8 cm

2. A garden is in the form of a trapezium whose parallel sides are 40 m and 22 m and the perpendicular distance between them is 12m. Find the area of the garden.

3. Two parallel sides of a trapezium are 85 cm and 63 cm and its area is 2664 cm^2. Find its altitude.

4. Find the height of the trapezium, the sum of the lengths of whose bases is 50 cm, and whose area is 500 cm^2.

5. Find the sum of the lengths of the bases of a trapezium whose altitude is 17cm and whose area is 0.85 m^2.

6. The area of a trapezium is 210 cm^2 and its height is 14 cm. If one of the parallel sides is double that of the other, find the two parallel sides.

7. The area of a trapezium is 300 m^2. The perpendicular distance between the two parallel sides is 15 m. If the difference of the parallel sides is 16 m. Find the length of the parallel sides.

8. The lengths of the parallel sides of a trapezium are in the ratio 3 : 5 and the distance between them is 10 cm. If the area of trapezium is 120 cm^2. Find the lengths of its parallel sides.

9. Two parallel sides of an isosceles trapezium are 6 cm and 14 cm respectively. If the length of each non- parallel side is 5 cm, find the area of the trapezium.

10. ABCD is a trapezium of area 91 cm^2. CD is parallel to AB and CD is longer than AB by 8 cm. If the distance between AB and CD is 7cm, find AB and CD.

11. Find the cost of watering a trapezoidal field whose parallel sides are 10 m and 25 m respectively, the perpendicular distance between them is 15 cm and the rate of watering is Rs 4 per m^2.

12. The parallel sides of a trapezium are 25 cm and 13 cm, its non- parallel sides are equal, each being 10 cm. Find the area of the trapezium.

13. In the figure, AB and DC are parallel sides of a trapezium ABCD and ∠ADC = 90°. Given AB = 15 cm, CD = 40 cm and diagonal AC = 41 cm, calculate the area of trapezium ABCD.

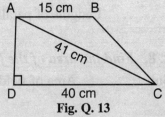
Fig. Q. 13

(**Hint :** In $\triangle ADC$, $AD = \sqrt{AC^2 - DC^2} = \sqrt{41^2 - 40^2} = 9$ cm

Now, Area of trap. $ABCD = \frac{1}{2} \times AD \times (AB + DC))$

14. Find the area of the pentagonal field shown alongside. All dimensions are in metres.

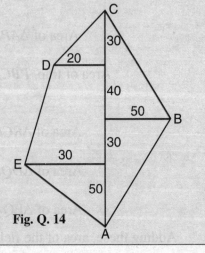
Fig. Q. 14

AREA OF A POLYGON

17.3 Definitions

Polygon : A *simple closed plane figure formed by line segments is called a* **polygon**. The *line segments* are called **sides** of the figure. Each end point of a side is called a vertex of the polygon.

Polygons are classified according to the number of sides they have

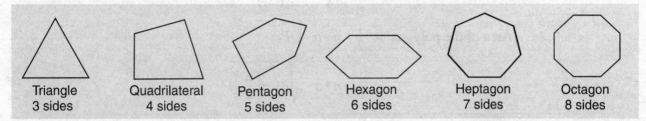

| Triangle | Quadrilateral | Pentagon | Hexagon | Heptagon | Octagon |
| 3 sides | 4 sides | 5 sides | 6 sides | 7 sides | 8 sides |

Regular Polygon : A regular polygon is a polygon with *all its sides and all its angles equal* (both equilateral and equiangular). An important property of a *regular polygon* is that it *fits exactly into a circle, i.e.,* we can draw a circle passing through each vertex of the polygon.

Central point of a Polygon : The inscribed and circumscribed circles of a polygon have the same centre, called the central point of the polygon.

In-radius : The length of perpendicular from the central point of a polygon upon any of its sides is the radius of the inscribed circle of the polygon. It is denoted by *r*. In the figure given here $OP = r$.

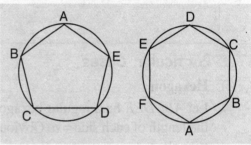

Circum-radius : The line segment joining the central point of a polygon to any vertex is the radius of the circumscribed circle of the polygon. It is denoted by **R**. In the figure given here $OA = R$.

17.4 Area of a Polygon of n-sides

To find the area of a polygon in terms of its side and radius of inscribed circle.

Let G, A, B, C be any four corners of a regular polygon of n sides. Let the bisectors of $\angle GAB$ and $\angle ABC$ meet in O. Then, O is the centre of the circle inscribed in the polygon. Let OP be drawn perpendicular from O to AB, then $OP = r$ (in radius).

Now, if we join the n-corners of the polygon to O, then we have

$$OG = OA = OB = OC \_ \_ \_ \_ \_ \_ = R \text{ (circum-radius)}$$

We will also get the polygon divided into n equal triangles like ΔAOB.

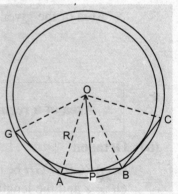

∴   Area of polygon = Area of $\Delta AOB \times$ Number of sides of the polygon.

$$= \frac{1}{2} \times OP \times AB \times n \text{ (each side} = a \text{ units)}$$

$$= \frac{1}{2} \cdot r.a.n = \frac{1}{2} n.a.r \text{ sq units.}$$

∵ Perimeter of a regular polygon of n sides each of length a units $= n \cdot a$

∴ Area of any regular polygon $= \frac{1}{2} \times$ Perimeter $\times$ in-radius

Also, $A = \frac{1}{2} nar \Rightarrow a = \frac{2A}{nr}$ and **Perimeter** $= na = \frac{2A}{r}$.

17.5 To find the area of the regular polygon in terms of the radius of the circumscribed circle

Given, **inradius** $= OP = r$ and **circumradius** $= OA = R$

From OAP, we have, $r = OP$

$$= \sqrt{(OA)^2 - (AP)^2} = \sqrt{(R)^2 - \left(\frac{a}{2}\right)^2}$$

$\therefore$ Area of the polygon $= \frac{1}{2} \cdot n \cdot a \cdot OP$

$$= \frac{1}{2} \cdot n \cdot a \cdot \sqrt{R^2 - \left(\frac{a}{2}\right)^2}$$

Hence, **Area of a regular polygon** $= \left(\frac{n}{2} \times a \times \sqrt{R^2 - \frac{a^2}{4}}\right)$ sq units

$$= \frac{1}{2} \times \textbf{Perimeter} \times \sqrt{(\textbf{Circumradius})^2 - \left(\frac{\textbf{Side}}{2}\right)^2}$$

17.6 Particular Cases

(i) Hexagon

Let $ABCDEF$ be a regular hexagon with OP as its inradius and the length of each side $= a$. Obviously, so, ΔOAB is an equilateral triangle

$\therefore$ $r = OP = $ Height of equilateral Δ

$$= \sqrt{a^2 - \left(\frac{a}{2}\right)^2} = \sqrt{a^2 - \frac{a^2}{4}} = \sqrt{\frac{3a^2}{4}} = \frac{\sqrt{3}a}{2}$$

$\therefore$ Area of the given hexagon

$$= 6\left(\frac{1}{2}AB \cdot OP\right) = 6\left(\frac{1}{2}ar\right) = \frac{1}{2} \times 6 \times a \times \frac{\sqrt{3}a}{2} = \frac{3\sqrt{3}}{2}a^2$$

$\therefore$ **Area of a regular hexagon** $= \dfrac{3\sqrt{3}}{2}$ sq units $= \dfrac{3\sqrt{3}}{2}$ (side)^2 sq units.

(ii) Octagon

Let $ABCDEFGH$ be the given octagon, O the in-centre, its radius $OP = r$ and the length of each side of the octagon $= a$. From the figure, we have

$$r = OP = OQ + OP = OQ + MB = \frac{1}{2}LM + \frac{BC}{\sqrt{2}},$$

(where BC is the diagonal of the square $MBNC$)

$\because$ $LM = CD = a$

$\therefore$ $r = \dfrac{a}{2} + \dfrac{a}{\sqrt{2}} = \dfrac{a}{2} + \dfrac{a\sqrt{2}}{2} = \dfrac{a(1+\sqrt{2})}{2}$

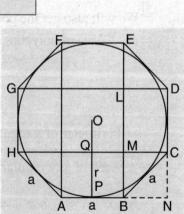

$\therefore$ Area of the regular octagon $= 8 \cdot$ (area of ΔOAB) $= 8\left(\frac{1}{2} AB \cdot OP\right) = 8\left(\frac{1}{2} \cdot a \cdot r\right)$

$$= 4a \cdot \frac{a(1+\sqrt{2})}{2} = 2(1+\sqrt{2})a^2 \text{ sq units.}$$

> Hence, **Area of a regular octagon** $= 2a^2(1+\sqrt{2})$ **sq units** $= 2(1+\sqrt{2})(\text{side})^2$ **sq units.**

17.7 Solved Examples

Ex. 1. *Find the area of a regular hexagon each of whose sides measures 5 cm.* $\left(\sqrt{3} = 1.732\right)$

Sol. Side of the given hexagon (a) = 5 cm

$$\text{Area of the hexagon} = \frac{3\sqrt{3}\,a^2}{2} \text{ cm}^2$$

$$= \frac{3 \times 1.732 \times 5 \times 5}{2} \text{ cm}^2 = \mathbf{64.95 \text{ cm}^2}$$

Ex. 2. *Find the area of a regular octagon each of whose sides measures 4 cm.*

Sol. Side of the given octagon (a) = 4 cm

$$\text{Area of the octagon} = 2(1+\sqrt{2})a^2 \text{ cm}^2 = 2(1+1.414) \times 4 \times 4 \text{ cm}^2$$

$$= 32 \times 2.414 \text{ cm}^2 = \mathbf{77.248 \text{ cm}^2.}$$

Ex. 3. *Find the area of a regular pentagon whose each side measures 6 cm and the radius of the inscribed circle is 4 cm.*

Sol. Here, $a = 6$ cm, $r = 4$ cm and $n = 5$

$$\therefore \quad \text{Area of the pentagon} = \frac{1}{2} \times n \times a \times r$$

$$= \frac{1}{2} \times 5 \times 6 \times 4 \text{ cm}^2 = \mathbf{60 \text{ cm}^2.}$$

Ex. 4. *Find the area of a regular polygon of 7 sides whose each side measures 4 cm and the circumradius is 3 cm.* $\left(\sqrt{5} = 2.236\right)$

Sol. Here $a = 4$ cm, $R = 3$ cm and $n = 7$

$$\text{Area of the polygon} = \frac{1}{2} \times n \times a \times \sqrt{R^2 - \frac{a^2}{4}} = \frac{1}{2} \times 7 \times 4 \times \sqrt{(3)^2 - \frac{16}{4}} \text{ cm}^2$$

$$= \frac{1}{2} \times 7 \times 4 \times \sqrt{9-4} \text{ cm}^2 = 14 \times \sqrt{5} \text{ cm}^2 = 14 \times 2.236 \text{ cm}^2 = \mathbf{31.304 \text{ cm}^2.}$$

EXERCISE 17 (b)

1. Find the area of a regular hexagon each of whose sides measures (*i*) 7 cm, (*ii*) 9 cm.

2. Find the area of a regular octagon each of whose sides measures (*i*) 8 cm, (*ii*) 5 cm.

3. Find the area of a regular pentagon whose each side measures 5 cm and the radius of inscribed circle is 4.5 cm.

4. Find the area of regular polygon of 7 sides whose each side measures 8 cm and the radius of the inscribed circle is 6 cm.

5. Find the area of a regular polygon of 9 sides whose each side measures 6 cm and the radius of the circumscribed circle is 4 cm.

6. Find the area of a regular pentagon whose each side measures 5 cm and the radius of the circumscribed circle is 3.5 cm.

LOOKING BACK
Summary of Key Facts

1. Area of a trapezium = $\frac{1}{2}$ × (Sum of lengths of parallel sides) × height.

2. Area of a regular polygon of n sides where each side = a cm and in-radius = r cm is given by :

$$A = \frac{1}{2} \times n \times a \times r \text{ sq units}$$

3. Area of a regular polygon of n sides where each side = a cm and circum-radius = R cm is given by :

$$A = \frac{1}{2} \times n \times a \times \sqrt{R^2 - \frac{a^2}{4}} \text{ sq units}.$$

4. Perimeter = $\frac{2A}{r}$; $a = \frac{2A}{nr}$.

5. Area of a hexagon = $\frac{3\sqrt{3}\,a^2}{2}$ sq units.

6. Area of an octagon = $2a^2\left(1+\sqrt{2}\right)$ sq units.

MULTIPLE CHOICE QUESTIONS – 14

1. The area of a trapezium whose parallel sides are 12 cm and 16 cm and with distance between than as 8 cm is :
   (i) 110 cm²   (ii) 112 cm²   (iii) 64 cm²   (iv) 76 cm²

2. The area of a trapezium is 243 cm². If the lengths of its parallel sides 15 cm and 12 cm, the distance between than is :
   (i) 10 cm   (ii) 14 cm   (iii) 18 cm   (iv) 22 cm

3. The area of a trapezium is 385 cm². Its parallel sides are in the ratio 3 : 4 and the perpendicular distance between them is 11 cm. Its longer side is :
   (i) 35 cm   (ii) 30 cm   (iii) 40 cm   (iv) 60 cm

4. The area of a regular hexagon each of whose sides measure 10 cm is :
   (i) 259.8 cm²   (ii) 326.4 cm²   (iii) 402.8 cm²   (iv) 300 cm²

5. The area of a regular octagon each of whose sides measure 7 cm is :
   (i) 246.88 cm²   (ii) 236.572 cm²   (iii) 364.48 cm²   (iv) 400 cm².

ANSWERS

EXERCISE 17 (a)

1. (a) 63 cm²   (b) 165 cm²   (c) 5.7 cm²   (d) 45.6 cm²   2. 372 cm²   3. 36 cm   4. 20 cm
5. 10 m   6. 10 cm, 20 cm   7. 28 m, 12 m   8. 9 cm, 15 cm   9. 30 cm²
10. AB = 9 cm, CD = 17 cm   11. Rs 1050   12. 152 cm²   13. 247.5 cm²   14. 6550 m²

EXERCISE 17 (b)

1. (i) 127.302 cm²   (ii) 210.438 cm²   2. (i) 308.992 cm²   (ii) 120.7 cm²   3. 56.25 cm²   4. 168 cm²
5. 71.435 cm²   6. 30.625 cm²

MULTIPLE CHOICE QUESTIONS – 14

1. (ii)   2. (iii)   3. (iii)   4. (i)   5. (ii)

Volume and Surface Area
18. of Solids

18.1 Surface Area of a Cuboid

The surface area of a cuboid is equal to the sum of the areas of the plane regions of its faces. Let us find the surface area of a cuboid which is 5 cm long, 3 cm wide, and 2 cm high. The six faces of the cuboid are shown in the following diagram:

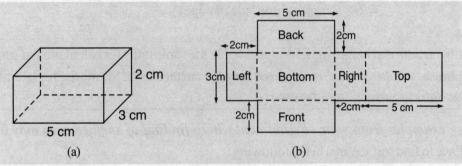

(a)   (b)

Area of the top = (5×3) cm^2 = 15 cm^2;   Area of bottom = (5×3) cm^2 = 15 cm^2

Area of front = (5×2) cm^2 = 10 cm^2;   Area of back = (5×2) cm^2 = 10 cm^2

Area of left face = (2×3) cm^2 = 6 cm^2;   Area of right face = (2×3) cm^2 = 6 cm^2

∴   Surface area = 15 + 15 + 10 + 10 + 6 + 6 = 62 cm^2

Note that

        Area of top and bottom = length × breadth

        Area of front and back = length × height

        Area of left and right faces = breadth × height

        Total Surface area = 2 (area of top) + 2 (area of front) + 2 (area of left face)

                = 2 (area of top + area of front + area of left face)

                = 2 (length × breadth + length × height + breadth × height)

If length, breadth and height be l, b and h respectively, then

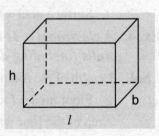

   Total surface area = $2 (l \times b + l \times h + b \times h)$

                    = **2 ($lb + lh + bh$) sq units**

If we exclude the bottom and top of the cuboid, then sum of the areas (called the **lateral surface area**) of the side faces is given by

   Lateral surface area of the cuboid = $2 (lh + bh)$ sq units

                       = **2 ($l + b$) h sq units**

                       = **perimeter of the base × height**

Note : The lateral surface area of a rectangular. From gives the area of its four walls.

18.2 Surface Area of a Cube

In the case of a cube, $l = b = h$

Therefore, surface area of a cube of side l units

$$= 2\,(l \times l + l \times l + l \times l) \text{ sq units}$$

$$= 6\,l^2 \text{ sq units}$$

Also, its lateral surface $= 2(l \times l + l \times l) = 4\,l^2$ **sq units.**

Remember :

Total Surface area of a cuboid

$$= (l \times b + b \times h + l \times h) \text{ sq units.}$$

$$= (length \times breadth + breadth \times height + length \times height) \text{ sq units.}$$

Total surface of a cube $= 6l^2$ sq units.

$$= 6 \times (\text{length of one side or edge})^2$$

Remarks.

1. Length, breadth and height must be expressed in the same units for calculation of surface area.

2. The phrase '*whole surface*' is also used for total surface area. Similarly, for lateral surface area, the phrase '*lateral surface*' may be used.

Ex. 1. *Give three examples from your environment where finding of surface area may be required.*

Sol. You will have to find surface area in the following :

(1) White washing of walls of a room, (2) Painting a box, (3) Preparing a cardboard box.

Ex. 2. *Find the area of the cardboard required to make a closed box of length 25 cm, breadth 0.5 m and height 15 cm.*

Sol. Length $(l) = 25$ cm, breadth $(b) = 0.5$ m $= 0.5 \times 100$ cm $= 50$ cm, height $= 15$ cm

$\therefore$ Surface area $= 2(lb + bh + hl)$

$$= 2\,[(25 \times 50) + (50 \times 15) + (15 \times 25)] \text{ cm}^2$$

$$= 2(1250 + 750 + 375) \text{ cm}^2 = 2(2375) \text{ cm}^2 = \textbf{4750 cm}^2.$$

Hence, 4750 cm^2 of cardboard is required.

Ex. 3. *Find the surface area of a cube whose edge is 11 cm.*

Sol. (*i*) Edge $= 11$ cm, surface area of a cube $= 6 \times (\text{side})^2$

$\therefore$ Surface area $= 6(11)^2 \text{ cm}^2 = 6 \times 121 \text{ cm}^2 = \textbf{726 cm}^2.$

Ex. 4. *A classroom is 11 m long, 8 m wide and 5 m high. Find the sum of the areas of its floor and the four walls (including doors, windows, etc.).*

Sol. Length of the room $(l) = 11$ m, Breadth of the room $(b) = 8$ m; Height of the room $(h) = 5$ m.

$\therefore$ Floor area $= l \times b = 11 \text{ m} \times 8 \text{ m} = 88 \text{ m}^2$

Area of the four walls $= 2h\,(l + b) = 2 \times 5 \times (11 + 8) \text{ m}^2 = 10 \times 19 \text{ m} = 190 \text{ m}^2$

$\therefore$ Area of the floor + Area of the four walls $= 88 \text{ m}^2 + 190 \text{ m}^2 = \textbf{278 m}^2.$

Ex. 5. *A room is 18 m long, 14 m wide, and 8 m high. Find the total surface area of the six faces of the room.*

Sol.   Total surface area $= 2(lb + bh + hl) = 2(18 \times 14 + 14 \times 8 + 8 \times 18) \text{ m}^2$

$$= 2(252 + 112 + 144)\text{m}^2 = 2 \times 508 \text{ m}^2 = \textbf{1016 m}^2.$$

Ex. 6. *A tank 12 m long, 8 m wide and 5 m deep is to be made. It is open at the top. Determine the cost of iron sheet, at the rate of Rs 3.50 per metre, if the sheet is 4 m wide.*

Sol. $l = 12$ m, $b = 8$ m, $h = 5$ m

Area of the iron sheet used in the tank

$$= \text{area of four walls} + \text{area of the base}$$

$$= 2(l+b)h + lb = 2(12+8)5 + 8 \times 12 = 296 \text{ m}^2$$

Width of the iron sheet = 4m. $\therefore$ Its length $\frac{296}{4} = 74$ m

$\therefore$ Cost of the iron sheet = Rs (74×3.50) = Rs $\left(74 \times \frac{35}{10}\right)$ = **Rs 259.**

Ex. 7. *Two cubes with 12 cm edge are joined end to end . Find the surface area of the resulting cuboid.*

Sol. For the resulting cuboid

$l = (12 + 12)$ cm $= 24$ cm, $b = 12$ cm, $h = 12$ cm

$\therefore$ Surface area of the resulting cuboid

$$= 2(lb + bh + hl) = 2(24 \times 12 + 12 \times 12 + 12 \times 24)$$

$$= 2(288 + 144 + 288) = 2 \times 720 = \textbf{1440 cm}^2.$$

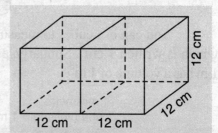

EXERCISE 18 (a)

1. Find the surface area of each of the cuboids whose dimensions are given below :

	(i)	(ii)	(iii)	(iv)	(v)	(vi)
l	5 cm	6 m	10 cm	4 cm	$5\frac{1}{2}$ cm	16 cm
b	4 cm	3 m	8 cm	1.7 cm	4 cm	8 cm
h	3 cm	2 m	5 cm	2.3 cm	$10\frac{1}{2}$ cm	6 cm

2. Find the surface area of the following cubes

(a) $l = 8$ cm   (b) $l = 12$ cm   (c) $l = \frac{1}{2}$ m   (d) $l = 5$ dm   (e) $l = 1.2$ m   (f) $l = 2.25$ m

3. The total surface area of a cube is 54 cm^2. What is the length of its sides?

4. Find the surface area of a wooden box which is in the shape of a cube, if the edge of the box is 27 cm.

5. Find the cost of painting the all round outer surface of a box with lid 60 cm long, 40 cm wide and 30 cm high at 50 p per 20 cm^2.

6. The dimensions of an oil tin are 26 cm × 26 cm × 45 cm. Find the area of the tin sheet required for making 20 such tins. If 1 sq m of the tin sheet costs Rs 10, find the cost of tin used for these 20 tins.

7. Find the area of the thin sheeting required for making an open cistern (*i.e.*, without a lid), 5 m long, 3 m wide, 4 m deep.

8. A swimming pool is 20 m in length, 15 m in breadth, and 4 m in depth. Find the cost of cementing its floor and walls at the rate of Rs 12 per square metre.

9. Two cubes, each of side 15 cm are joined end to end. Find the surface area of the resulting cuboid.

VOLUME

18.3 Introduction

The container is filled with water to the level of the spout. If a solid is put into the water, some water will flow out into the measuring beaker. The volume of this water will be equal to the volume of the solid.

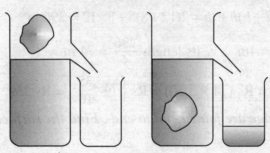

You can use cubes to measure volume. A cube with a side of 1 cm has a volume of 1 cubic centimetre which is written **1 cm³**. Similarly, a cube with a side of 1 mm has a volume of **1 mm³** and a cube with a side of 1 m has a volume of **1 m³**.

1 millimetre cube (volume = 1 mm³)	1 centimetre cube (volume = 1 cm³)	1 metre cube (volume = 1 m³)
The size of a grain of sand.	The size of a sugar cube or die.	The size of a large washing machine.

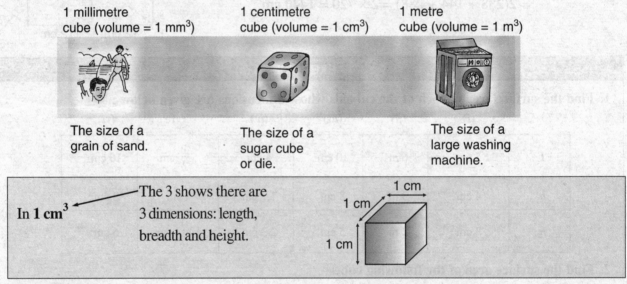

In **1 cm³** — The 3 shows there are 3 dimensions: length, breadth and height.

1 cm
1 cm
1 cm

When we say that the volume of a box measuring 30 cm by 20 cm by 40 cm is 24000 cm³, it means we can fit 24,000 centimetre cubes in the box. Its capacity is 24,000 cm³.

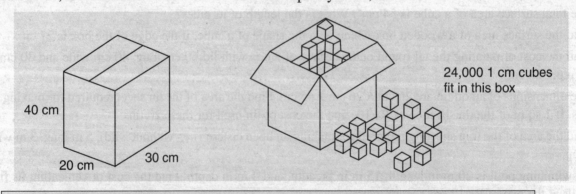

40 cm
20 cm
30 cm

24,000 1 cm cubes fit in this box

■ **The volume is the amount of space that a shape takes up in three dimensions.**

■ **The amount of space inside a hollow three dimensional shape is its capacity.**

18.4 Finding the Volume of a Cuboid
Activity

■ You can find the volume of a cuboid by counting cubes:

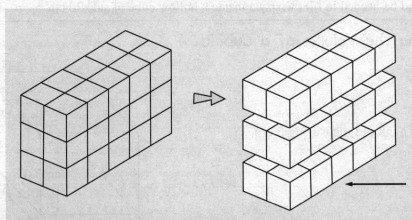

Count the cubes. There are 30, so the volume of the cuboid is 30 cm³.

Think
2 × 5 = 10 cubes in one layer. There are 3 such layers. So the total number of cubes is 30.

EXERCISE 18 (b)

These objects are made of centimetre cubes. Find the volume of each object.

1.

2.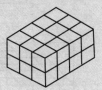

3.

4.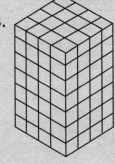

5.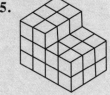

6.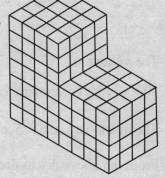

7. Draw a cube of side 8 cm. How many cubes of side 2 cm would be needed to fill the same space ?

Sol.

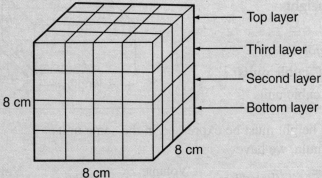

Top layer
Third layer
Second layer
Bottom layer

8 cm
8 cm
8 cm

2 cm
2 cm
2 cm

The bottom layer requires 4 × 4, *i.e.*, 16 cubes of side 2 cm, and there are four layers altogether.
Therefore **64 cubes** are required.

8. Draw a cube of side 6 cm. How many cubes of side 2 cm would be needed to fill the same space?

9. Draw a cuboid measuring 8 cm by 6 cm by 2 cm. How many cubes of side 2 cm would be needed to fill the same space?

10. How many cubes of side 5 cm would be needed to fill the space inside a hollow cube of side 20 cm ?

18.5 The Formula for Finding the Volume of a Cuboid
Activity

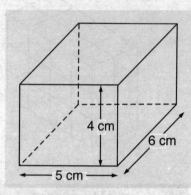

Let us work out the volume of a cuboid measuring 5 cm by 6 cm by 4 cm.

You can fit

| 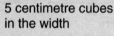 5 centimetre cubes in the width | 6 centimetre cubes in the length | 6 × 5 = 30 centimetre cubes in the base | 4 layers like the base |

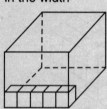 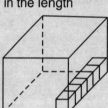 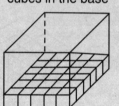

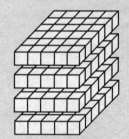

The volume is

30 × 4 = 120 centimetre cubes.

The quick way is: $6 \times 5 \times 4 = 120 \text{ cm}^3$.

From the above discussion, we arrive at the following result:

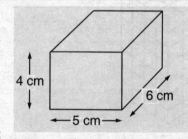

■ **For any cuboid :**
  Volume = length × breadth × height
  $= l \times b \times h$ ***cubic units.***
■ For a cube, since *l = b = h therefore,*
  Volume of a cube $= l \times l \times l = l^3$ **cubic units**
  $=$ (one edge)^3 cubic units

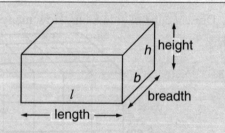

Remarks. **1.** Length, breadth and height must be expressed in the same units.

2. From the above formula, we have

$$\text{Length} = \frac{\text{Volume}}{\text{Breadth} \times \text{Height}}, \text{Breadth} = \frac{\text{Volume}}{\text{Length} \times \text{Height}}, \text{Height} = \frac{\text{Volume}}{\text{Length} \times \text{Breadth}}$$

3. One side or edge of a cube $= \sqrt[3]{\text{volume}}$, *i.e.,* cube root of volume.

Ex. 1. *Find the volume of a cuboid measuring 14 cm by 10 cm by 8 cm.*

Sol. Volume of a cuboid $= l \times b \times h$

$$= (14 \times 10 \times 8) \text{ cm}^3 = \textbf{1120 cm}^3.$$

Ex. 2. *Find the volume of a cube with the given side 6 cm.*

Sol. Volume of cube $= \text{side}^3 = 6^3 \text{ cm}^3 = \textbf{216 cm}^3.$

Ex. 3. *What will happen to volume of a cube if its each edge is* **(i)** *doubled?* **(ii)** *halved?* **(iii)** *tripled?*

Sol. Let x units be the edge of the cube.

(*i*) New length $= 2x$.

$\therefore$ New volume $= (2x)^3 = 8x^3$ cu units

$\therefore$ The number of times the volume is increased $= \dfrac{8x^3}{x^3} = \textbf{8 times}.$

(*ii*) New length $= \dfrac{x}{2}$

$\therefore$ New volume $= \left(\dfrac{x}{2}\right)^3 = \dfrac{x^3}{8}$ cu units

$\therefore$ The number of times the volume is decreased $= \dfrac{\frac{x^3}{8}}{x^3} = \dfrac{1}{8}$ times.

(*iii*) New length $= 3x$

$\therefore$ New volume $= (3x)^3 = \dfrac{27x^3}{x^3}$ cu units

$\therefore$ The number of times the volume is increased $= \dfrac{27x^3}{x^3} = \textbf{27 times}.$

Ex. 4. *Two cubes, each of side 6 cm, are joined end to end. Find the volume of the resulting cuboid.*

Sol. Side of a cube $= 6$ cm.

If *V* is the volume of the resulting cuboid after joining the two cubes, then

$$V = \left[(6)^3 + (6)^3\right] \text{cm}^3 = (216 + 216) \text{ cm}^3 = \textbf{432 cm}^3.$$

Ex. 5. *A beam 9 m long, 50 cm wide and 20 cm deep is made of wood which weighs 30 kg per m³; find the weight of the beam.*

Sol. $l = 9$ m, $b = 50$ cm $= \dfrac{50}{100} = \dfrac{1}{2}$ m, $h = \dfrac{20}{100} = \dfrac{1}{5}$ m

Volume of beam $= l \times b \times h = 9 \times \dfrac{1}{2} \times \dfrac{1}{5} = \dfrac{9}{10}$ m³

$\therefore$ Weight of the beam $= \dfrac{9}{10} \times 30$ kg $= \textbf{27 kg}.$

Ex. 6. *A carpenter makes a letter-box which has a volume of 13400 cm³. The base has an area of 670 cm², what is the height of the letter-box ?*

Sol. Volume $=$ Area $\times$ height

$\therefore$ Height of the letter-box $= \dfrac{\text{its volume}}{\text{its area}} = \dfrac{13400}{670}$ cm $= \textbf{20 cm}.$

Ex. 7. *Find the volume of wood required for making a closed box with external measurements 14 cm by 9.5 cm by 6 cm, and wood is 7.5 mm thick.*

Sol. External dimensions are 14 cm, 9.5 cm, and 6 cm. Thickness of wood = 7.5 mm. To get the internal dimensions, subtract double the thickness from each external dimension.

∴ Internal length = 14 cm – 15 mm = 14 cm – 1.5 cm = 12.5 cm

Internal breadth = 9.5 cm – 1.5 cm = 8 cm,

Internal height = 6 cm – 1.5 cm = 4.5 cm

External volume of the box = $(14 \times 9.5 \times 6)$ cm^3 = $14 \times \dfrac{\cancel{95}^{19}}{\cancel{10}_{\cancel{5}_1}} \times \cancel{6}^3$ = 798 cm^3

Internal volume of the box = $(12.5 \times 8 \times 4.5)$ cm^3 = $\dfrac{\cancel{125}^{25}}{\cancel{10}_2} \times \cancel{8}^{\cancel{4}^2} \times \dfrac{\cancel{45}^9}{\cancel{10}_{\cancel{5}_1}}$ cm^3 = 450 cm^3

∴ Volume of wood = External volume – Internal volume = 798 cm^3 – 450 cm^3 = **348 cm^3**.

EXERCISE 18 (c)

1. Work out the volume of each cuboid.

(a)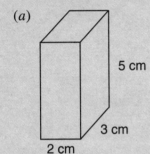

(b)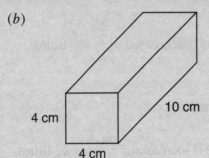

(c)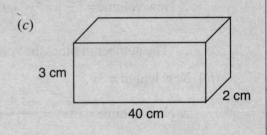

2. Find the volume of each of the following cuboids:

	Length	Breadth	Height		Length	Breadth	Height
(a)	5 cm	5 cm	4 cm	(d)	10 cm	8 cm	7 cm
(b)	45 mm	30 mm	10 mm	(e)	6.8 m	5 m	4 m
(c)	12 cm	1.2 cm	0.5 cm	(f)	1.2 m	0.9 m	0.7 m

3. Complete the table : Measurements are in cm.

	(i)	(ii)	(iii)	(iv)	(v)	(vi)	(vii)	(viii)
Length	4	2	7	12	16	?	40	60
Breadth	3	6	3	9	14	28	24	?
Height	5	8	4	12	18	24	?	5
Volume	?	?	?	?	?	26208	2400	5400

4. Find the volume of a cube with the given side:

(a) 3 cm (b) $\dfrac{1}{5}$ cm (c) 1.2 m (d) 2.5 m

5. Find each edge of the cubes whose volumes are:

(a) 216 m^3 (b) 512 cm^3 (c) 1728 cm^3 (d) 2197 m^3

6. Find the volume of air in a room measuring 4 m by 5 m which is 3 m high.

7. Which has the greater volume : a box that measures 10 cm by 6 cm by 4 cm or one that measures 6 cm by 6 cm by 7 cm ?

8. The bottom of a tank measures 25 m × 20 m. Find its depth if it contains 2000 m³ water.

9. Find the volume of a cube, one face of which has an area of 64 cm².

10. A heap of wood is a pile 5 dm wide, 9 dm long, and 3 dm high. What is the volume of the heap of wood ?

11. The volume of a soap cake is 160 cm³. Its length and width are 10 cm and 5 cm. Find its height.

12. A cuboidal vessel is 10 cm long and 8 cm wide. How high should it be made so that it may hold 480 cubic centimetres of a liquid ?

13. If 60 cm³ of a metal weighs 1 kg, find the weight of a block of the same metal of the size 20 cm by 12 cm by 5 cm.

14. In a shower, 5 cm of rain falls. Find the volume of water that falls on 2 hectares of land.

15. A river 2 metres deep and 45 metres wide is flowing at the rate of 3 km per hour. Find the amount of water that runs into the sea per minute.

16. A beam 9 m long, 50 cm wide, and 20 cm deep is made of wood which weighs 30 kg per m³, find the weight of the beam.

17. A wooden box (including the lid) has external dimensions of 40 cm by 34 cm by 30 cm. If the wood is 1 cm thick, how many cm³ of wood are there in it ?

18. The outer dimensions of a closed wooden box are 10 cm by 8 cm by 7 cm. Thickness of the wood is 1 cm. Find the total cost of wood required to make the box if 1 cm³ of wood costs Rs 2.00.

19. 500 men took dip in a tank which is 80 m long, 50 m broad. What is the rise in water level if the average displacement of water by a man is 4 m³ ?

   (**Hint :** Volume of water displaced by 500 men = (4 × 500) = 2000 m³

   Area of the tank = 80 × 50 = 4000 m². Let the rise in the level of water = h metres. Then 4000 × h = 2000)

18.6 Changing Units of Volume

Consider a cube of side 1 cm. If each edge is divided into 10 mm the cube can be divided into 10 layers, each layer with 10 × 10 cubes of side 1 mm,

i.e.,

$$\boxed{1 \text{ cm}^3 = (10 \times 10 \times 10) \text{ mm}^3 = 1000 \text{ mm}^3.}$$

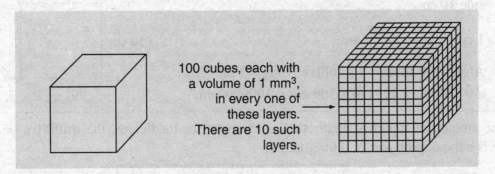

100 cubes, each with
a volume of 1 mm³,
in every one of
these layers.
There are 10 such
layers.

To convert cm³ to mm³, multiply by 1000,
To convert mm³ to cm³, divide by 1000.

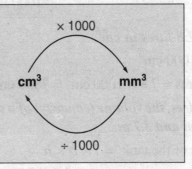

Similarly, since 1 m = 100 cm

$$1 \text{ cubic metre} = (100 \times 100 \times 100) \text{ cm}^3$$
$$1 \text{ m}^3 = 1000000 \text{ cm}^3$$

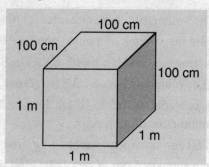

Ex. 1. *Convert (a) 3.5 cm^3 to mm^3 (b) 47 000 mm^3 to cm^3.*

Sol. (a) 3.5 cm^3 = (3.5 × 1000) mm^3 = **3500 mm^3**.

(b) 47000 mm^3 = (47000 ÷ 1000) cm^3 = **47 cm^3**.

Ex. 2. *Convert (a) 4.29 m^3 to cm^3 (b) 9500 cm^3 to m^3.*

Sol. (a) 4.29 m^3 = (4.29 × 1000000) cm^3 = **4290000 cm^3**.

(b) 9500 cm^3 = (9500 ÷ 1000000) m^3 = **0.0095 m^3**.

> In 9500, Count 6 places from the right and put decimal point.

18.7 Capacity

When you buy a bottle of milk or a can of oil you are not interested in the external measurements or volume of the container. What really concerns you is how much milk is inside the bottle, or how much oil is inside the can, *i.e.*, the *capacity* of the bottle or the container.

> **The volume of space inside a hollow object is called its capacity.**

The most common unit of capacity in the metric system is the **litre**. A litre is much larger than a cubic centimetre but much smaller than a cubic metre. The relationship between these quantities is :

1000 cm^3 = 1 litre (1 *l*)

i.e., a litre is the volume of a cube of side 10 cm.

$1 \text{ cm}^3 = \dfrac{1}{1000}$ litre = 1ml.

Also, **1000 litres = 1 kilolitre (1 *kl*) = 1 m^3**

Hence, 1 *kl* = **100 cm × 100 cm × 100 cm = 1000000 cm^3**.

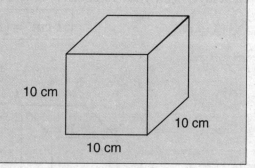

When the amount of liquid is small, such as dosages for medicines, the **millilitre** (*ml*) is used. A millilitre is a thousandth part of a litre, *i.e.*,

> 1000 m*l* = 1 litre or **1 m*l* = 1 cm^3**

Ex. 3. *Express 7.8 litres in cm^3.*

Sol. 1 litre = 1000 cm^3

∴ 7.8 litres = 7.8 × 1000 cm^3 = **7800 cm^3**.

Ex. 4. *Find in litres, the volume (capacity) of a storage tank whose length, breadth and depth are respectively 8 m, 5.5 m and 3.7 m.*

Sol. Volume of the tank = $l \times b \times h$

= (8 × 5.5 × 3.7) m^3 = 162.8 m^3

$$= 162.8 \times 100 \times 100 \times 100 \text{ cm}^3 = 162800000 \text{ cm}^3$$
$$= (162800000 \div 1000) \text{ litres} \quad \boxed{\because 1000 \text{ cm}^3 = 1 \text{ litre}}$$
$$= 162800 \text{ litres}$$

Hence, the capacity of the tank is **162800 litres**.

Ex. 5. *Capacity of a tank is 120 kl. If the length and breadth of the tank are respectively 6 m and 5 m, find its depth.*

Sol. Volume of the tank $= 120 \, kl = 120 \, m^3$ $\quad \boxed{\because 1 \, kl = 1 \, m^3}$

$$\therefore \text{ Depth} = \frac{\text{volume}}{\text{length} \times \text{breadth}} = \frac{120}{6 \times 5} \text{ m} = 4 \text{ m}$$

Thus, the depth of the tank is **4 m.**

18.8 Mixed Units

Before we can find the volume of a cuboid, *all* measurements must be expressed in the same unit.

Ex. 6. *Find the volume of a cuboid measuring 3m by 60 cm by 38 cm. Give your answer in (a) cm³ (b) m³.*

Sol. (a) All the measurements must be in centimetres so we first convert the 3m into centimetres.

Length of the cuboid $= 3\text{m} = (3 \times 100) \text{ cm} = 300 \text{ cm}$

Volume of cuboid $= l \times b \times h$
$$= (300 \times 60 \times 40) \text{ cm}^3 = \textbf{720000 cm}^3.$$

(b) We convert all the measurements to metres before finding the volume.

Breadth of cuboid $= 40 \text{ cm} = \dfrac{40}{100} \text{ m} = 0.4 \text{ m}$

Height of cuboid $= 38 \text{ cm} = \dfrac{38}{100} \text{ m} = 0.38 \text{ m}$

$\therefore$ Volume of cuboid $= l \times b \times h$

$$= (3 \times 0.4 \times 0.38) \text{ m}^3$$
$$= \textbf{0.456 m}^3.$$

$$\begin{array}{r} 3 \times 0.4 = 1\cdot 2 \\ 38 \\ \times 12 \\ \hline 456 \quad \therefore 1.2 \times 0.38 = 0.456 \end{array}$$

Put decimal point after 3 places in the product.

Ex. 7. *If the rainfall on a certain day was 5 cm, how many litres of water fell on 8 hectare field on that day?*

Sol. Height of water collected due to rainfall $= 5 \text{ cm}$

Area of the field $= 8 \text{ ha} = 80000 \text{ m}^2$ $\qquad\qquad$ $(1 \text{ ha} = 10000 \text{ m}^2)$

$$= 80000 \times 10000 \text{ cm}^2 = 800000000 \text{ cm}^2 \qquad (\because 1 \text{ m}^2 = 10000 \text{ cm}^2)$$

$\therefore$ Volume of water collected $= 5 \text{ cm} \times 800000000 \text{ cm}^2$

$$= 4000000000 \text{ cm}^3 = \frac{4000000000}{1000} \text{ litres} = 4000000 \text{ litres} = \frac{4000000}{1000} \, kl = \textbf{4000 kl.}$$

EXERCISE 18 (d)

1. Convert:

(a) 7 cm³ to mm³ $\qquad$ (b) 60000 mm³ to cm³ $\qquad$ (c) 8.59 cm³ to mm³ $\qquad$ (d) 5830 mm³ to cm³

(e) 4 m³ to cm³ $\qquad$ (f) 5000 cm³ to m³ $\qquad$ (g) 0.0086 m³ to cm³ $\qquad$ (h) 0.53 m³ to cm³.

2. **Find the volumes of the following cuboids, giving your answers in the units stated in brackets:**

	Length	Breadth	Height		Length	Breadth	Height
(a)	400 cm	100 cm	50 cm (**m³**)	(c)	0.5 cm	4 mm	2 mm (**mm³**)
(b)	6 cm	12 mm	8 mm (**cm³**)	(d)	1 m	40 cm	30 cm (**m³**)

3. (a) Work out in mm³, the volume of the cuboid shown here.

   (b) Express your answer to (a) in cm³.

   (c) Work out the volume of this cuboid in litres.

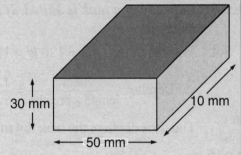

30 mm, 10 mm, 50 mm

4. **Express in cm³:**   (a) 36 litres   (b) 0.73 litre   (c) 0.0068 litre

5. **Express in litres:**   (a) 8000 cm³   (b) 2000 cm³   (c) 35 000 cm³

6. **Express in litres:**   (a) 4 m³   (b) 27 m³   (c) 3.8 cm³

7. A water storage tank is 4.8 m long, 5 m wide and $2\frac{1}{2}$ m deep. How many litres of water will it hold?

8. **Find (a) the volume of each of the following tanks and (b) the capacity of each tank in (i) litres (ii) kilolitres.**

   (i) Height = 2 m, length = 4 m, breadth = 3 m.

   (ii) Height = 3 m, length = 6 m, width = 4 m.

   (iii) Height = 1.6 m, length = 5 m, width = 3.5 m.

18.9 More Problems

Ex. 1. *A match-box measures 4 cm by 2.5 cm by 1.5 cm. What will be the volume of a packet containing 12 such match-boxes. How many such packets can be placed in a cardboard box of the size 60 cm by 30 cm by 24 cm ?*

Sol. Length of the match-box = 4 cm, breadth = 2.5 cm, height = 1.5 cm

∴ Volume of one match-box = $l \times b \times h$

$$= (4 \times 2.5 \times 1.5)\ cm^3 = 4 \times \frac{25}{10} \times \frac{15}{10}\ cm^3 = 15\ cm^3$$

∴ Volume of 12 match-boxes = $(12 \times 15)\ cm^3 = 180\ cm^3$

i.e., Volume of one packet = 180 cm³

Now, volume of the cardboard box = 60 cm × 30 cm × 24 cm

∴ Number of packets which the cardboard box can accommodate

$$= \frac{(60 \times 30 \times 24)}{180} = \mathbf{240}\ .$$

Ex. 2. *How many bricks, each 25 cm by 15 cm by 8 cm, are required for a wall 32 m long, 3 m high, 40 cm thick ?*

Sol. Length of the wall = 32 m = 3200 cm, length of one brick = 25 cm.

∴ Lengthwise, the number of bricks required = $\frac{3200}{25} = 128$

Similarly, heightwise, number of bricks required = $\frac{300}{15} = 20$

Thicknesswise, number of bricks required $= \dfrac{40}{8} = 5$

∴ The bricks can be arranged in 128 layers, each containing 20 rows of bricks with 5 bricks in each row.

∴ The number of bricks required $= 128 \times 20 \times 5 = 12800$.

> **Note :** It is being presumed that no bricks are broken. Assuming this, we can work out as follows :
> Volume of the wall $= (3200 \times 300 \times 40)\ \text{cm}^3$
> Volume of 1 brick $= (25 \times 15 \times 8)\ \text{cm}^3$
>
> ∴ The number of bricks required $= \dfrac{\text{Volume of the wall}}{\text{Volume of 1 brick}} = \dfrac{3200 \times 300 \times 40}{25 \times 15 \times 8} = \mathbf{12800}$.

Ex. 3. *A solid cube of edge 10 cm is melted and cast into a cuboid whose base measures 20 cm by 10 cm. Find the height of the cuboid.*

Sol. Volume of the cube $= \text{edge}^3 = 10^3\ \text{cm}^3 = 1000\ \text{cm}^3$ ...(1)

This is melted and cast into a cuboid. The volume of cuboid so made will be equal to the volume of the cube.

Let the height of the cuboid be h cm. Then volume of the cuboid

$$= (\text{area of the base}) \times \text{height} = (20 \times 10) \times h = 200\ h\ \text{cm}^3 \qquad \text{...(2)}$$

Equating (1) and (2), we have $200\ h = 1000$ or $h = \dfrac{1000}{200} = 5$

Thus, the height of the cuboid is **5 cm.**

Ex. 4. *A metal cube of edge 9 cm is melted and formed into three smaller cubes. If the edges of two smaller cubes are 1 cm and 6 cm, find the edge of the third smaller cube.*

Sol. Edge of the original cube $= 9$ cm

∴ Volume of the original cube $= 9^3 = 729\ \text{cm}^3$

Edges of two smaller cubes are 1 cm and 6 cm

∴ Sum of volumes of two smaller cubes $= (1)^3 + (6)^3 = 1 + 216 = 217\ \text{cm}^3$

∴ Volume of the third cube $= 729 - 217 = 512\ \text{cm}^3$

∴ Edge of the third cube $= \sqrt[3]{512} = \mathbf{8\ cm.}$

Ex. 5. *The dimensions of a field are 15 m by 12 m. A pit 8 m long, 2.5 m wide and 2 m deep is dug in one corner of the field and the earth removed is evenly spread over the remaining area of the field, calculate by how much is the level of the field raised.*

Sol. Dimensions of the pit are $l = 8$ m, $b = 2.5$ m, $h = 2$ m

Volume of the earth dug out $= 8 \times 2.5 \times 2\ \text{m} = 40\ \text{m}^3$

Area of the field $= 15\ \text{m} \times 12\ \text{m} = 180\ \text{m}^2$

Area of the pit $= 8\ \text{m} \times 2.5\ \text{m} = 20\ \text{m}^2$

∴ Area where earth is to be spread
$$= 180\ \text{m}^2 - 20\ \text{m}^2 = 160\ \text{m}^2$$

∴ Rise in the level of the field

$$= \dfrac{\text{Volume}}{\text{Area}} = \dfrac{40}{160}\ \text{m} = \dfrac{1}{4}\ \text{m} = \dfrac{1}{4} \times 100 = \mathbf{25\ cm.}$$

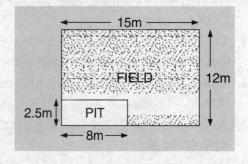

Ex. 6. *A godown measures 40 m × 25 m × 15 m. Find the maximum number of wooden crates each measuring 1.5 m × 1.25 m × 0.5 m that can be stored in the godown.*

Sol. Length of the godown = 40 m, Breadth = 25 m, Height = 15 m

∴ Volume of the godown = (40 × 25 × 15) m³

Volume of the wooden crate = (1.5 × 1.25 × 0.5) m³

If *n* is the number of crates, then number of crates that can be stored in the godown,

$$= \frac{\text{Volume of the godown}}{\text{Volume of one crate}}.$$

$$= \frac{40\times25\times15}{1.5\times1.25\times0.5} = \frac{40\times25\times15}{\frac{15}{10}\times\frac{125}{100}\times\frac{5}{10}} = \frac{40\times25\times15}{15\times125\times5}\times10\times100\times10 = \textbf{16000}.$$

Hence, the number of crates which can be stored in the godown = **16000.**

EXERCISE 18 (e)

1. A solid cube of edge 20 cm is melted and cast into a cuboid whose base measures 25 cm by 20 cm. Find the height of the cuboid.

2. A rectangular block of metal measuring 4 cm by 5 cm by 6 cm was melted down to make a block 8 cm long by 3 cm wide. How high was the block?

3. How many bricks, each of dimensions 25 cm×16 cm × 10 cm will be needed to build a wall 24 m long, 6 m high and 0.4 m thick.

4. Find the number of blocks 9 cm by 5 cm by 4 cm, contained in a crate measuring 27 cm by 15 cm by 8 cm.

5. The inside measurements of a cardboard box are $1\frac{1}{2}$ m by $\frac{3}{4}$ m by 60 cm. How many books, 20 cm by 10 cm by 7.5 cm each can be arranged in the box?

6. A class room is 12 m long, 5 m wide and 3 m high. How many pupils should it be used for if each pupil required 5m³ of air space?

7. How many lead cubes of side 2 cm could be made from a lead cube of side 8 cm?

8. How many wooden cubical blocks of edge 20 cm can be cut from a log of wood of size 8 m by 5 m by 80 cm, assuming there is no wastage.

9. How many wooden cubical blocks of edge 12 cm can be cut from another cubical block of wood of edge 3 m 60 cm ?

10. The capacity of a cuboidal tank is 5 kl of water. Find the breadth of the tank, if its length and depth are respectively 2.5 m and 10 m.

11. A cuboid of dimensions 10 cm by 2 cm by 2 cm is divided into 5 cubes of edge 2 cm. Find the ratio of the total surface area of the cuboid and that of the cubes.

12. A village, having a population of 4000 requires 150 litres water per head per day. It has a tank measuring 20 m by 15 m by 6 m. For how many days will the water of this tank last?

13. A pit 5m long and 3.5m wide is dug to a certain depth. If the volume of earth taken out of it is 14m³, what is the depth of the pit?

14. The dimensions of a field are 15 m by 12 m. A pit 7.5m long, 6m wide and 1.5 m deep is dug at one corner of the field. The earth removed is evenly spread over the remaining area of the field. Calculate the rise in the level of the field.

CYLINDER

18.10 Introduction

A solid like measuring jars, circular pillars, circular pipes etc., is called a cylinder. Cylinders have a **curved** (also called *lateral*) surface with congruent circular ends. The line joining the centres of the circular ends of a cylinder is called its axis. If it is perpendicular to the circular ends, then it is called a right circular cylinder. Here, by the word cylinder we will mean the right circular cylinder.

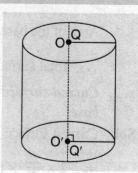

18.11 Area of Curved Surface of Cylinder

This cylinder has a circular base of radius r cm and a height of h cm. Its surface area is made up of the curved surface area plus the areas of the circular top and base.

If it is a paper cylinder and you cut it through the line AB, and spread this paper on a plane you will get a rectangle whose length will be equal to the circumference of the base of the cylinder, *i.e.*, $2\pi r$ and width equal to AB, *i.e.*, h

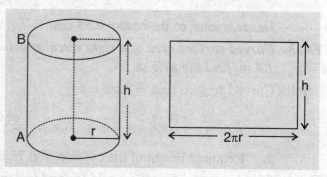

∴ **Area of the curved surface** = area of the rectangle = **$2\pi rh$.**

18.12 Total Surface Area of a Cylinder

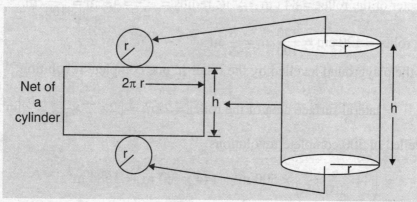

The total surface area of a cylinder is the sum of the *areas of its two bases* and its *curved surface.*

The area of the circular base and top are both equal to πr^2. So the combined area of the base and the top is $2\pi r^2$.

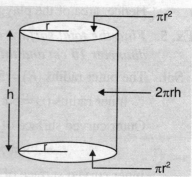

∴ *Total surface Area of a cylinder = $2\pi rh + 2\pi r^2$.*

Ex. 1. *The radius of a right circular cylinder is 7 cm and its height is 20 cm. Find its curved surface area and total surface area* $\left(\pi = \dfrac{22}{7}\right)$.

Sol. Given : radius (r) = 7 cm, height (h) = 20 cm.

Curved surface area $= 2\pi rh = 2 \times \dfrac{22}{7} \times 7 \times 20 \text{ cm}^2 = \textbf{880 cm}^2$.

Area of the base and the top $= 2\pi r^2 = 2 \times \dfrac{22}{7} \times 7 \times 7 \text{ cm}^2 = 308 \text{ cm}^2$

$\therefore$ Total surface area $= 2\pi rh + 2\pi r^2 = 880 \text{ cm}^2 + 308 \text{ cm}^2 = \textbf{1188 cm}^2$.

Ex. 2. *Curved surface area of a right circular cylinder of height 35 cm is 121 cm². Find the radius of the base.*

Sol. Curved surface area $= 2\pi rh = 121 \text{ cm}^2$

$\Rightarrow$ $2 \times \dfrac{22}{7} \times r \times 35 = 121 \Rightarrow r = \dfrac{7 \times 121}{2 \times 22 \times 35} = \dfrac{11}{20} = 0.55 \text{ cm}$

Hence, radius of the base $= \textbf{0.55 cm}$.

Ex. 3. *Curved surface area of a right circular cylinder is 6.6 m². If the radius of the base of the cylinder is 1.4 m, find the height.*

Sol. Curved surface area $= 2\pi rh = 6.6$

$\Rightarrow$ $2 \times \dfrac{22}{7} \times 1.4 \times h = 6.6 \Rightarrow h = \dfrac{7 \times 6.6}{2 \times 22 \times 1.4} = \dfrac{7 \times 66}{2 \times 22 \times 14} = \dfrac{3}{4} = 0.75$

$\therefore$ Required height of the cylinder $= \textbf{0.75 m}$.

Ex. 4. *The diameter of a roller is 84 cm and its length is 120 cm. It takes 500 complete revolutions to move once over to level playground. Find the area of the playground in m².*

Sol. *Given :* Diameter of the roller $= 84 \text{ cm} \Rightarrow$ its radius $= \dfrac{84}{2} = 42 \text{cm} = \dfrac{42}{100} \text{ m}$.

Length of the roller $= 120 \text{ cm} = \dfrac{120}{100} \text{ m} = \dfrac{6}{5} \text{ m}$

Now, area of the playground levelled by the roller in one complete revolution

$= \text{lateral surface area of the roller} = 2\pi rh = \left(2 \times \dfrac{22}{7} \times \dfrac{42}{100} \times \dfrac{6}{5}\right) \text{m}^2 = \left(44 \times \dfrac{6}{100} \times \dfrac{6}{5}\right) \text{m}^2$

$\therefore$ Area levelled in 500 complete revolutions

$= \left(44 \times \dfrac{6}{100} \times \dfrac{6}{5}\right) \times 500 \text{ m}^2 = (44 \times 36) \text{ m}^2 = 1584 \text{ m}^2$.

Hence, area of the playground $= \textbf{1584 m}^2$.

Ex. 5. *Find the total surface of a hollow cylinder open at both ends, if the length is 12 cm, the external diameter 10 cm and thickness 2 cm.*

Sol. The outer radius $(R) = 5 \text{ cm}$, Thickness $= 2 \text{ cm}$

$\therefore$ Inner radius $(r) = 5 \text{ cm} - 2 \text{ cm} = 3 \text{ cm}$

Outer curved surface of the cylinder $= 2\pi Rh$

$= 2 \times \pi \times 5 \times 12 = 120 \, \pi \text{ cm}^2$

Inner curved surface of the cylinder

$= 2\pi rh = 2 \times \pi \times 3 \times 12 = 72 \, \pi \text{ cm}^2$.

Both ends of the cylinder will be of the shape, as shown in Fig. *(ii)*.

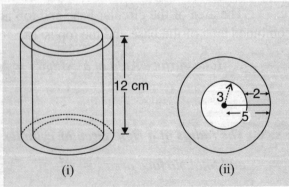

(i)   (ii)

∴ Area of one end of the cylinder $= \pi R^2 - \pi r^2$

$$= \pi \times 5^2 - \pi \times 3^2 = 25\pi - 9\pi = 16\pi \text{ cm}^2.$$

Area of both ends $= (2 \times 16\pi) \text{ cm}^2 = 32\pi \text{ cm}^2$

∴ Total surface of the cylinder = External curved surface + Internal curved surface + 2 (Area of the base of the ring)

$$120\pi + 72\pi + 32\pi = 224\pi \text{ cm}^2 = 224 \times \frac{22}{7} \text{ cm}^2 = \textbf{704 cm}^2.$$

Remark. It is advisable to put the value of π is the end in such calculations.

EXERCISE 18 (f)

1. Information about a few cylinders is given below. Copy and complete the table. $\left(\pi = \frac{22}{7}\right)$

	Radius (cm)	Height (cm)	Curved Surface	Area of the base	Whole surface
(a)	7	6			
(b)	14	10			
(c)	21	5			
(d)	$10\frac{1}{2}$	16			

2. Copy and complete the table. $\left(\pi = \frac{22}{7}\right)$

	(a)	(b)	(c)	(d)
Curved surface (cm²)	704	3960	1320	24200
Radius (cm)	?	15	?	35
Height (cm)	8	?	14	?

In the following problems, take $\pi = \frac{22}{7}$ if not mentioned otherwise.

3. The circumference of the base of a right circular cylinder is 220 cm. If the height of the cylinder is 2m, find the lateral surface area of the cylinder.

4. A closed circular cylinder has diameter 20 cm and height 30 cm. Find the total surface area of the cylinder. ($\pi = 3.14$)

5. The radius of the base of a closed right circular cylinder is 35 cm and its height is 0.5 m. Find the total surface area of the cylinder.

6. A cylindrical pillar is 1 m in diameter and 4.2 m in height. Find the cost of white washing the curved surface of the pillar at the rate of Rs 15 per m².

7. Find the height of the solid circular cylinder of total surface area is 660 cm² and radius is 5 cm.

(**Hint :** $2\pi r^2 + 2\pi rh = 660 \Rightarrow 2\pi r (r + h) = 660$

$\Rightarrow 2 \times \frac{22}{7} \times 5 \times (5 + h) = 660 \Rightarrow 5 + h = \frac{660 \times 7}{2 \times 22 \times 5} = 21]$

8. The inner diameter of a circular well is 4.2 m. It is 12 m deep. Find (*i*) its inner curved surface area (*ii*) the cost of plastering the inner curved surface at the rate of Rs 50 per m².

9. The outer diameter of a pipe is 1.4 m and it is 25 m long. Find (i) its outer curved surface area, (ii) the cost of painting the outer surface of the pipe at the rate of Rs 30 per m².

10. A cylindrical vessel open at the top has a base diameter 28 cm and height 10 cm. Find the cost of tin-plating the inner part at the rate of Rs 10 per 100 cm².

11. A metal pipe is 77 cm long, the inner diameter of the cross-section is 4 cm and the outer diameter is 4.8 cm. Find the (i) inner curved surface area (ii) outer curved surface area (iii) total surface area.

12. A hollow cylindrical pipe has inner circumference 44 dm and outer 45 dm. Find the cost of painting it from both sides (inside as well as outside) at Rs 2 per m² if length is 3.5m.

18.13 Volume of A Cylinder

Volume of a cylinder = (Area of the base) × height = $(\pi r^2) \times h$

∴ **Volume of a cylinder = $\pi r^2 h$**

18.14 Volume of the Material of a Hollow Cylinder

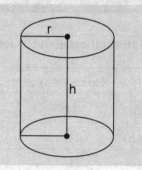

If the outer and inner radii of a hollow cylinder of height h are R and r respectively, then

Volume of the material composing the cylinder

= External volume – Internal volume

$$= \pi R^2 h - \pi r^2 h = \pi h (R^2 - r^2)$$

$$= \pi h (R + r)(R - r)$$

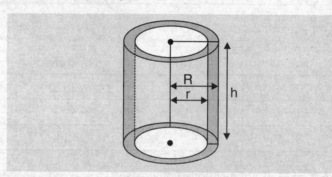

Ex. 1. *Find the volume of a cylinder which has a height of 21 cm and a base of radius 10 cm.*

Sol. Given : $r = 10$ cm, $h = 21$ cm

∴ Volume of the cylinder = $\pi r^2 h = \dfrac{22}{7} \times 10 \times 10 \times 21$ cm³ = **6,600 cm³**.

Ex. 2. *The circumference of the base of a cylindrical vessel is 176 cm and its height is 30 cm. How many litres of water can it hold?*

Sol. Given : Circumference of the base = $2\pi r$

∴ $2\pi r = 176 \Rightarrow 2 \times \dfrac{22}{7} \times r = 176 \Rightarrow r = \dfrac{7 \times 176}{2 \times 22} = 28$ cm

∴ Volume of the right circular cylinder = $\pi r^2 h$.

$$= \dfrac{22}{7} \times 28^2 \times 30 \text{ cm}^3 = \dfrac{22}{7} \times 28 \times 28 \times 30 \text{ cm}^3 = 73920 \text{ cm}^3$$

$$= \dfrac{73920}{1000} \, l = 73.92 \, l \qquad [\because 1 \text{ litre} = 1000 \text{ cm}^3]$$

Hence, it can hold **73.92 litres** of water.

Ex. 3. *The radius and height of a cylinder are in the ratio 5 : 7 and its volume is 550 cm³. Find its radius (use π = 22/7).*

Sol. Let the radius and height of the cylinder $5x$ and $7x$ respectively, then.

Volume of the cylinder $= \pi r^2 h \Rightarrow 550 = \frac{22}{7} \times 5x \times 5x \times 7x$

$\Rightarrow \quad 550 = \frac{22}{7} \times x^3 \times (5 \times 5 \times 7) \Rightarrow x^3 = \frac{550 \times 7}{22 \times 5 \times 5 \times 7} = 1 \Rightarrow x = 1$

Hence, radius of the cylinder $= 5 \times 1 = $ **5 cm.**

Ex. 4. *The area of the base of a right circular cylinder is 15400 cm² and its volume is 92400 cm³. Find the area of the curved surface.*

Sol. Volume of a cylinder $= \pi r^2 h = $ (Area of base) $\times$ height (h)

$\therefore \quad 92400 = 15400 \times h \Rightarrow h = \frac{92400}{15400} = 6$ cm

Now, area of base $= 15400$ cm² $\Rightarrow \pi r^2 = 15400 \Rightarrow \frac{22}{7} \times r^2 = 15400$

$\Rightarrow \frac{22}{7} \times r^2 = 15400 \Rightarrow r^2 = \frac{7 \times 15400}{22} = 4900 \Rightarrow r = \sqrt{4900} = 70$ cm

$\therefore$ Area of the curved surface $= 2\pi rh = 2 \times \frac{22}{7} \times 70 \times 6$ cm² $= $ **2640 cm².**

Ex. 5. *Two cylindrical cans have bases of the same size. The diameter of each is 14 cm. One of the cans is 10 cm high and the other is 20 cm high. Find the ratio of their volumes.*

Sol. Let the dimensions of the two cans be as under :

Can I : radius $= r_1 = 7$cm, height $h_1 = 10$ cm, volume V_1

Can II : radius $= r_2 = 7$cm, height $h_2 = 20$ cm, volume V_2

Then, $V_1 = \pi r_1^2 h_1 = \pi \times 7^2 \times 10$ cm³ $= 490\pi$ cm³

$\qquad V_2 = \pi r_2^2 h_2 = \pi \times 7^2 \times 20$ cm³ $= 980\pi$ cm³

$\therefore$ the ratio of their volumes $= \frac{V_1}{V_2} = \frac{490\pi}{980\pi} = \frac{1}{2}$

$\therefore$ Ratio of their volumes $= $ **1 : 2.**

Ex. 6. *A hollow cylindrical copper pipe is 21 dm long. Its outer and inner diameters are 10 cm and 6 cm respectively. Find the volume of the copper used in making the pipe.*

Sol. Length of the pipe $= 21$ dm $\Rightarrow h = 21 \times 10 = 210$ cm

Its outer diameter $= 10$ cm $\Rightarrow$ outer radius, $R = \frac{10}{2} = 5$ cm

Inner diameter $= 6$ cm $\Rightarrow$ Inner radius, $r = \frac{6}{2} = 3$ cm

$\therefore$ Volume of the copper used in making the pipe $= \pi R^2 h - \pi r^2 h$

$= \pi h (R^2 - r^2) = \frac{22}{7} \times 210 \times (5^2 - 3^2)$ cm³ $= \frac{22}{7} \times 210 \times (25 - 9)$ cm³

$= 660 \times 16$ cm³ $= 10560$ cm³

Hence, volume of the copper used in making the pipe $= $ **10,560 cm³.**

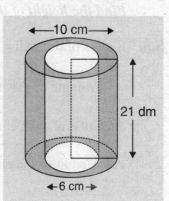

Ex. 7. *The inner and outer radii of the hollow cylinder are 15 cm and 20 cm respectively. The cylinder is melted and recast into a solid cylinder of the same length. Find the radius of the base of the new cylinder. (Take $\sqrt{7}$ = 2.65)*

Sol. The outer radius of the cylinder, $R = 20$ cm

The inner radius of the cylinder, $r = 15$ cm

Let height be h cm

Then, Volume of the hollow cylinder $= \pi h(R^2 - r^2) = \pi h(20^2 - 15^2)$ cm³

$$= \pi h(400 - 225) = 175\,\pi h \text{ cm}^3$$

After recasting, let the radius of the new solid cylinder $= r$

Its height is the same, *i.e.*, h.

$\therefore$ Volume of the new cylinder $= \pi r_1^2 h$

Volume of the new cylinder = Volume of the cylinder before melting

$\therefore \quad \pi r_1^2 h = 175\,\pi h \Rightarrow r_1^2 = 175 \Rightarrow r_1 = \sqrt{175} = \sqrt{5 \times 5 \times 7} = 5\sqrt{7}$

$$= 5 \times 2.65 = 13.25 = 13.3 \text{ cm} \quad \text{(approx)}$$

Hence, the required radius = **13.3 cm.**

Ex. 8. *The inner diameter of a wooden cylindrical pipe is 24 cm and its outer diameter is 28 cm. The length of pipe is 35 cm. Find the mass of the pipe, if 1 cm³ of wood weighs 3g.*

Sol. *Given :* outer diameter = 28 cm $\Rightarrow$ outer radius, $R = 14$ cm

Inner diameter = 24 cm $\Rightarrow$ inner radius, $r = 12$ cm

Length of pipe, $h = 35$ cm,

$\therefore$ Volume of the hollow cylinder $= \pi h(R^2 - r^2)$

$$= \frac{22}{7} \times 35 \times (14^2 - 12^2) = \frac{22}{7} \times 35 \times (196 - 144)$$

$$= \frac{22}{7} \times 35 \times 52 = 5720 \text{ cm}^3$$

1 cm³ of wood weights 3g

$\therefore$ Mass of the wood in the given pipe $= 5720 \times 3g = 17160$ g $= \dfrac{17160}{1000}$ kg = **17.16 kg.**

Ex. 9. *A well with 10 m inside diameter is dug 14 m deep. Earth taken out of it has been spread all-round to a width of 5 meters to form an embankment. Find the height of the embankment.*

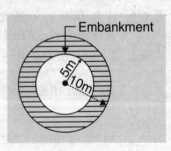

Sol. Radius of the well $= \left(\dfrac{1}{2} \times 10\right)$ m = 5 m, depth $(h) = 14$ m

$\therefore$ Volume of the earth dug out $= \pi r^2 h = \dfrac{22}{7} \times 5 \times 5 \times 14 = 1100$ m³

Area of embankment $= \pi R^2 - \pi r^2 = \pi \times 10^2 - \pi \times 5^2 = 75 \times \dfrac{22}{7}$ m².

$\therefore$ Height of the embankment $= \dfrac{\text{Volume of the earth dug out}}{\text{Area of the embankment}}$

$$= \dfrac{1100}{75 \times \frac{22}{7}} \text{ m} = \dfrac{1100 \times 7}{75 \times 22} = \dfrac{14}{3} = 4\dfrac{2}{3} \text{ m.}$$

EXERCISE 18 (g)

1. Copy and complete the table $\left(\pi = \dfrac{22}{7}\right)$.

	(a)	(b)	(c)	(d)
Radius of the circle (cm)	7	14	21	14
Height (cm)	8	16	40	8
Volume (cm³)	?	?	?	?

2. The volume of a cylinder is 660 cm³. Find its height if its radius is 5 cm.

3. The volume of a cylinder is 448 π cm³ and height 7cm. Find its lateral (curved) surface area and total surface area.

4. The volume of a right circular cylinder is 1100 cm³ and the radius of its base is 5 cm. Find its curved surface area. (π = 22/7)

5. A solid cylinder has total surface area of 462 sq cm. Its curved area is one third of its total surface area. Find the volume of the cylinder $\left(\text{Take } \pi = \dfrac{22}{7}\right)$.

6. If base radius of a right circular cylinder is halved, keeping the height same, find the ratio of the volume of the reduced cylinder to that of the original cylinder.

7. A cylindrical tank has a capacity of 6160 cu cm. Find its depth if its radius is 14 m. Calculate the cost of painting its curved outer surface at the rate of Rs 3 per square metre. $\left(\text{Take } \pi = \dfrac{22}{7}\right)$.

8. Into a circular drum of radius 4.2 m and height 3.5 m, how many full bags of wheat can be emptied, if the space required for the wheat in each bag is 2.1 cu. m $\left(\text{Take } \pi = \dfrac{22}{7}\right)$.

9. The circumference of the base of a cylindrical vessel is 132 cm and its height is 25 cm. How many litres of water can it hold ?

10. The diameter of a cylindrical tank is 28 m and depth 32 m. How many metric tonnes of water will it hold ? (one cubic metre of water weighs 1000 kg)

11. A hollow cylindrical tube open at both ends is made of iron 3 cm thick. If the external diameter be 56 cm and the length of the tube be 182 cm, find the number of cubic cm in it.

12. The thickness of a metallic tube is 1 cm and its outer radius is 11 cm. Find the mass of such a 1 metre long tube, if the density of the metal is 7.5 g per cm³.

13. What length of a solid cylinder 2 cm in diameter must be taken to recast into a hollow cylinder of length 16 cm, external diameter 20 cm and thickness 2.5 mm?

14. A well 14 m inside diameter is dug 15 m deep. Earth taken out is spread all around to a width of 7 m to form an embankment. Find the height of the embankment.

15. The rain falls 10 cm on a particular day. The rain water that falls on a roof 70 m long and 44 m wide was collected in a cylindrical tank of radius 14 m. Find
   (i) volume of the water that falls on the roof.
   (ii) rise of water level in the tank due to rain water.

   (**Hint :** Volume of rain water = $l \times b \times h = 70 \times 44 \times \dfrac{1}{10} = 308$ m³

   Let h m be the rise in water level. Then volume of the cylindrical column of water of height h = volume of rain water) i.e., $\pi \times 14^2 \times h = 308$.]

LOOKING BACK
Summary of Key Facts

1. A **solid** has three dimensions—length, breadth and height.

2. A **cuboid** is a solid having six rectangular faces. It has 12 edges and 8 vertices.

3. A cuboid in which length, breadth and height are all equal is called a **cube.** All the six faces of a cube are congruent squares.

4. With usual meaning for V, l, b, and h (volume, length, breadth and height respectively),

   (*i*) Surface area of a cuboid = $2(lb + bh + hl)$

   (*ii*) Surface area of a cube = $6l^2$

   (*iii*) Lateral surface of a cuboid = $2(l + b)h$

   (*iv*) Area of four walls of a room = $2(l + b)h$

   (*v*) Volume of a cuboid $(V) = l \times b \times h$

   (*vi*) Volume of a cube $(V) = l^3$.

5. **Standard units of volume**

   (*i*) $1\ cm^3 = 1000\ mm^3$ (*ii*) $1\ m^3 = 1{,}000{,}000\ cm^3$ (*iii*) $1\ cm^3 = 1\ ml$

   (*iv*) $1000\ cm^3 = 1l$ (1 litre)   (*v*) $1\ m^3 = 1000\ l = 1\ k\,l$

6. Each plane end of a right circular cylinder is called its base.

7. The line segment joining the centres of the two ends of a cylinder is called the axis of the cylinder

8. Lateral or Curved Surface Area of a right circular cylinder = $2\pi rh$ where r = radius of the base, h = height of the cylinder.

9. Total Surface Area of a right circular cylinder = $2\pi rh + 2\pi r^2 = 2\pi r(h + r)$.

10. Volume of a right circular cylinder is :

    $$V = (\text{Area of the base}) \times \text{height} = \pi r^2 h.$$

11. Total surface area of a hollow circular cylinder = $2\pi Rh + 2\pi rh + 2\pi(R^2 - r^2)$ where R is the external radius and r is the internal radius.

12. Volume of a hollow circular cylinder = $\pi R^2 h - \pi r^2 h = \pi h(R + r)(R - r)$.

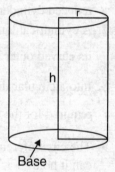

MENTAL MATHS – 9

Find the volume of a

1. Cuboid 5 cm by 4 cm by 3 cm.

2. Cube with edge $\sqrt[3]{8}$ cm.

3. Express 2 cm³ in mm³.

4. How many cubic centimetres make 1 litre?

5. The edge of a cube is $\sqrt{9}$ m. Find its surface area.

6. The volume of a cube is 64 cm³. Find its surface area.

7. The surface area of a cube is 54 cm². Find its volume

8. Find the edge of a cube whose volume is 125 cm³.

9. Find the height of a cuboid of volume 24m³ with length 4m and breadth 3m.

10. A cubical water tank is 4m long. Find its capacity in litres.

11. A tank is 2 m long, 1.5 m wide and 1m deep. Find the number of litres of water contained in it.

12. A cuboid of volume 135 cm³ is melted and cast into 5 equal cubes. Find the edge of one cube.

13. How many cubical blocks of edge 2 m can be cut from another cubical block of edge 6 m.
14. (*i*) 1 litre .... cm^3
    (*ii*) 1 m^3 = ... litres
    (*iii*) 1 litre = ... ml.

MULTIPLE CHOICE QUESTIONS – 15

1. The surface area of a cube is 486 cm^2. Its edge is
   (*i*) 8 cm   (*ii*) 9 cm   (*iii*) 6 cm   (*iv*) 7 cm

2. The number of coins 1.5 cm is diameter and 0.2 cm thick to be melted to form a right circular cylinder of height 10 cm and diameter 4.5 cm is
   (*i*) 540   (*ii*) 450   (*iii*) 380   (*iv*) 472

3. A cube of side 6 cm is cut into a number of cubes, each of side 2 cm. The number of cubes will be :
   (*i*) 6   (*ii*) 9   (*iii*) 12   (*iv*) 27

4. A beam 9 m long, 40 cm wide and 20 cm high is made up of iron which weighs 50 kg per cubic metre. The weight of the beam is :
   (*i*) 56 kg   (*ii*) 48 kg   (*iii*) 36 kg   (*iv*) 27 kg

5. The dimensions of a brick are 24 cm × 12 cm × 8 cm. How many bricks will be required to build a wall 24 m long, 8 m high and 60 cm thick, if 10% of the wall is filled with mortar?
   (*i*) 40000   (*ii*) 20000   (*iii*) 50000   (*iv*) 45000

6. The breadth of a room is twice its height and half its length. The volume of the room is 512 cm^3. The length of the room is :
   (*i*) 12 m   (*ii*) 16 m   (*iii*) 32 m   (*iv*) 20 m

7. If the diameter of a cylinder is 28 cm and its height is 20 cm, then total surface area is :
   (*i*) 2993 cm^2 (*ii*) 2992 cm^2 (*iii*) 2292 cm^2 (*iv*) 2229 cm^2

8. The curved surface area of a right circular cylinder of base radius r is obtained by multiplying its volume by :
   (*i*) $2r$ (*ii*) $\dfrac{2}{r}$ (*iii*) $2r^2$ (*iv*) $\dfrac{2}{r^2}$

9. The radii of two cylinders are in the ratio 2 : 3 and their heights are in the ratio 5 : 3. The ratio of their volumes is :
   (*i*) 4 : 9   (*ii*) 9 : 4   (*iii*) 20 : 27   (*iv*) 27 : 20

10. The radius of a wire is decreased to one-third and its volume remains the same. The new length is how many times the original length?
    (*i*) 1 time   (*ii*) 3 times   (*iii*) 6 times   (*iv*) 9 times

ANSWERS

EXERCISE 18 (a)

1. (*i*) 94 cm^2 (*ii*) 72 m^2 (*iii*) 340 cm^2 (*iv*) 39.82 cm^2 (*v*) 243.5 cm^2 (*vi*) 544 cm^2
2. (*a*) 384 cm^2 (*b*) 864 cm^2 (*c*) 1.5 m^2 (*d*) 150 dm^2 (*e*) 8.64 m^2 (*f*) 30.375 m^2 3. 3 cm
4. 4374 cm^2 5. Rs 270   6. 120640 cm^2; Rs 120.64   7. 79 m^2 8. Rs 6960   9. 2250 cm^2

EXERCISE 18 (b)

1. 16 cm^3 2. 24 cm^3 3. 36 cm^3 4. 112 cm^3 5. 30 cm^3 6. 176 cm^3
8. 9   9. 12   10. 64

EXERCISE 18 (c)

1. (*a*) 30 cm^3 (*b*) 160 cm   (*c*) 240 cm^3

2. (a) 100 cm^3 (b) 13500 mm^3 (c) 7.2 cm^3 (d) 560 cm^3 (e) 136 m^3 (f) 0.756 m^3

3. (i) 60 cm^3 (ii) 96 cm^3 (iii) 84 cm^3 (iv) 1296 cm^3 (v) 4032 cm^3 (vi) 39 cm (vii) 2.5 cm (viii) 18 cm

4. (a) 27 cm^3 (b) $\frac{1}{125} \text{ cm}^3$ (c) 1.728 m^3 (d) 15.625 m^3

5. (a) 6 m   (b) 8 cm   (c) 12 cm   (d) 13 m   6. 60 m^3 7. Second by 12 m^3

8. 4 m   9. 512 cm^3 10. 135 dm^3 11. 3.2 cm   12. 6 cm   13. 20 kg   14. 1000 m^3

15. 4500 m^3 16. 27 kg   17. 6752 cm^3 18. Rs. 640   19. 50 cm

EXERCISE 18 (d)

1. (a) 7000 mm^3 (b) 60 cm^3 (c) 8590 mm^3 (d) 5.83 cm^3 (e) $40,00,000 \text{ cm}^3$ (f) 0.005 m^3
(g) 8600 cm^3 (h) $5,30,000 \text{ cm}^3$ 2. (a) 2 m^3 (b) 5.76 cm^3 (c) 40 mm^3 (d) 0.12 m^3

3. (a) 15000 mm^3 (b) 15 cm^3 (c) $0.015 l$ 4. (a) 36000 cm^3 (b) 730 cm^3 (c) 6.8 cm^3

5. (a) $8 l$ (b) $2 l$ (c) $35 l$ 6. (a) $4000 l$ (b) $27000 l$ (c) $0.0038 l$ 7. $60,000 l$

8. (i) 24 m^3, $24000 l$, $24 kl$,   (ii) 72 m^3, $72000 l$, $72 kl$ (iii) 28 m^3, $28000 l$, $28 kl$

EXERCISE 18 (e)

1. 16 cm   2. 5 cm   3. 14,400   4. 18 blocks   5. 450 books   6. 36 pupils   7. 64 cubes

8. 4000 blocks   9. 27000 blocks 10. 20 cm   11. 11 : 15   12. 3 days   13. 80 cm   14. 50 cm

EXERCISE 18 (f)

1. (a) 264 cm^2, 154 cm^2, 572 cm^2 (b) 880 cm^2, 616 cm^2, 2112 cm^2 (c) 660 cm^2, 1386 cm^2, 3432 cm^2
(d) 1056 cm^2, 346.5 cm^2, 1749 cm^2 2. (a) 14 cm   (b) 42 cm   (c) 15 cm   (d) 110 cm

3. 4.4 m^2 4. 2512 cm^2 5. 18700 cm^2 6. Rs 198   7. 16 cm   8. 158.4 m^2, Rs 7920

9. Rs 110 m^2, Rs 3300   10. Rs 149.60   11. (i) 968 cm^2 (ii) 1161.6 cm^2 (iii) 2140.66 cm^2 12. Rs 62.30

EXERCISE 18 (g)

1. (a) 1232 cm^3 (b) 9856 cm^3 (c) 55440 cm^3 (d) 4928 cm^3 2. 8.4 cm   3. 352 cm^2, 754.28 cm^2

4. 440 cm^2 5. 539 cm^3 6. 1 : 4   7. 10 cm; Rs 2640   8. 92.4 bags   9. $34.65 l$

10. 19.712 metric tonnes   11. $90,948 \text{ cm}^3$ 12. 49.5 kg   13. 79 cm

14. 5m   15. (i) 308 m^3 (ii) 0.5 m

MENTAL MATHS – 9

1. 60 cm^3 2. 8 cm^3 3. 2000 mm^3 4. 1000 cm^3 5. 54 m^2 6. 96 m^2 7. 27 cm^3

8. 5 cm   9. 2 m   10. $64 kl$ 11. $3000 l$ 12. 3 cm   13. 27

14. (i) 1000   (ii) 1000   (iii) 1000

MULTIPLE CHOICE QUESTIONS – 15

1. (ii)   2. (ii)   3. (iv)   4. (iii)   5. (iv)   6. (ii)   7. (ii)

8. (ii)   9. (iii)   10. (iv)

THINK ABOUT IT

What is the Last Number ?

Suppose you were to start counting and did nothing but count, day and night, for the rest of your life, would you get to the last number ?

Mathematicians say that there is no last number. No matter how big a number you think of, there is always a number bigger than that.

This concept is called infinity and is written this way :

$$\infty$$

The largest number that has a name is a centillion. It is a 1 with 600 zeros after it.

UNIT VI : DATA HANDLING

19. Statistics

FREQUENCY DISTRIBUTION

19.1 Data

The test scores shown at the right are those obtained by 10 students in each of the two tests given in a mathematics course. These marks have been arranged in tables in such a way that whatever information we may wish to obtain about these tests may be got easily. We call such a collection of facts a **set of data**. Each member of a set of data is called a datum. (**Data** is plural of **datum**)

	Test 1	Test 2
Santosh	77	96
Negi	40	70
Aman	45	70
Amit	81	86
Rakesh	69	70
Sunil	81	91
Vinod	94	96
Anjali	51	70
Aditi	87	89
Renu	50	58

> *A collection of numerical facts about objects or events is called data.*
>
> *Statistics is the science of collecting, organising, and analyzing, sets of data in order to reveal information.*

19.2 Discrete and Continuous Data

There are two types of data

(i) Items which can be **counted** such as test marks, runs scored, words, and books. If the data have been counted then the values are **discrete**-they can be only whole numbers.

> *Discrete = Countable*
> *Continuous = measurable*

(ii) Data which are obtained from measurement. In such cases, there must have been some degree of approximation, depending on the accuracy of the measuring instrument whether it be a stop watch, a set of weighing scales or a ruler. Values so obtained are **continuous**-they can have any values (within a certain range).

Age, weight, height are some of the example of continuous data.

EXERCISE 19 (a)

1. The following is a listing of the names, heights, and weights of five boys in a eight-grade basket-ball team

   Devendra 167 cm, 66 kg;   Narendra 160 cm, 61 kg;   Sanjay 165 cm, 65 kg;   Piyush 175 cm, 68 kg
   Girish 155 cm, 60 kg

   Organise these data as follows :

   (a) Ascending order of heights   (b) Ascending order of weights,   (c) Alphabetical order.

2. **Some particulars of four pupils are shown below :**

   Pawan's height is 155 cm.   Hema's height is 140 cm.

   He is 12 years old.   She is 14 years old.

   He weighs 48 kg.   She weighs 45 kg.

   His hobby is stamp-collecting.   Her hobby is gardening.

Vivek's height is 145 cm.	Shyam's height is 158 cm.
He is 11 years old.	He is 13 years old.
He weighs 42 kg.	He weighs 46 kg.
His hobby is painting.	His hobby is photography.

Use the above data to complete the table below :

Name	Age	Height	Weight	Hobby
Pawan				
Hema				
Vivek				
Shyam				

19.3 Frequency

The marks scored by 35 students in a Mathematics test were as under :

60, 65, 100, 70, 85, 75, 95, 90, 65, 70, 80, 95, 70, 75, 75, 70, 80, 80,

70, 75, 85, 85, 70, 90, 75, 75, 80, 80, 85, 85, 90, 75, 75, 80, 80.

As in the above case, it often happens that some scores or measures occur more than once in a set of data. The number of times each score or measure occurs in the set is called its **Frequency**.

The score of 75 occurs 8 times in the set above, therefore its frequency is 8. What is the frequency of a score of 65? of 80 ? of 95 ?

It may be important to know the frequency of each score in a set. A convenient way to determine the frequency of each score by constructing a **frequency table** is shown at the right.

Such a table is called a **frequency distribution**. The column of tally marks is not necessary, but is a convenient way to determine the frequency of each score. How many students took the test? Notice that the sum of the frequencies is the same number as the number of members in the set of data.

We make bundles of tally marks by crossing the four tally marks by the fifth one.

Score (s)	Tally	Frequency (f)
60	I	1
65	II	2
70	ⅧI I	6
75	ⅧI III	8
80	ⅧI II	7
85	ⅧI	5
90	III	3
95	II	2
100	I	1

19.4 Range

The difference between the greatest and the least values of observations, in a set of data is called the *range* of the set of data. Thus the range of the set of data given above is $100 - 60 = 40$.

Relative frequency

The ratio of the frequency of each item to the total frequency is called the **relative frequency.**

$$\text{Relative frequency} = \frac{\text{frequency of item}}{\text{total of frequency}}$$

Ex. 1. *The scores (out of 100) obtained by 33 students in a Mathematics test are, 70, 49, 85, 59, 85, 49, 74, 84, 49, 67, 59, 67, 65, 72, 65, 67, 70, 67, 84, 67, 70, 72, 82, 72, 74, 70, 67, 67, 65, 59, 65, 70, 70.*

Prepare a frequency table for the above scores.

Sol. Arranging the data in ascending order, we have

49, 49, 49, 59, 59, 59, 65, 65, 65, 65, 67, 67, 67, 67, 67, 67, 67, 70, 70, 70, 70, 70, 70, 72, 72, 72, 74, 74, 82, 84, 84, 85, 85, counting how many times a particular score occurs, e.g., the score 49 occurs 3 times, we form the frequency table as under :

Score	49	59	65	67	70	72	74	82	84	85
Frequency	3	3	4	7	6	3	2	1	2	2

Remark : We can also use tally marks to count the various items in the given data.

Ex. 2. *Given below are the ages of 25 students of a class in a school. Prepare a frequency distribution.*

13, 15, 12, 13, 15, 16, 12, 15, 13, 16, 14, 12, 13, 15, 16, 12, 15, 16, 14, 12, 16, 13, 15, 14, 12

Sol. For counting, we use tally marks and prepare the frequency table as given below.

Age	Tally marks	Frequency
12	卌 I	6
13	卌	5
14	III	3
15	卌 I	6
16	卌	5
Total		25

We make bundles of 5 tally marks by crossing four tally marks by the fifth one

---

EXERCISE 19 (b)

1. Write true or false. Use the following frequency table.

Age	13	14	15	16	17	18	19
Frequency	3	2	7	2	3	2	1

  (*i*) The frequency of 19 is 1   (*ii*) The frequency of 14 is 3.   (*iii*) 17 has the lowest frequency

  (*iv*) 16 has a frequency of 2.   (*v*) 15 has the highest frequency   (*vi*) The frequency of 13 is 3.

2. Make a frequency distribution for the given data.

  15, 14, 11, 16, 12, 17, 15, 15, 18, 16, 13, 12, 14, 16, 15, 18, 16, 15, 14, 13.

3. A total of 20 patients admitted to a hospital have blood sugar levels as given below :

  67, 69, 74, 73, 70, 70, 71, 67, 73, 74, 73, 75, 69, 72, 70, 70, 72, 70, 73, 74. Make a frequency table.

4. The marks obtained by 30 students of a class in a test out of 10 marks are as follows :

  4, 6, 5, 1, 5, 4, 3, 6, 8, 10, 7, 1, 8, 5, 4, 9, 7, 10, 3, 2, 4, 5, 3, 6, 7, 8, 4, 10, 3, 9.

  Make a frequency distribution table for the above data. Use the table to find :

  (*i*) The number of students passed, if the minimum pass marks are 40%.

  (*ii*) How many students failed ?

  (*iii*) How many students secured the highest marks?

  (*iv*) How many students secured more than 60% marks?

  (**Hint :** Pass marks = 40% of 10 = 4, 60% of 10 = 6).

5. The weight (in kg) of 30 students of a class are 50, 49, 45, 49, 49, 50, 50, 54, 55, 44, 44, 42, 44, 56, 57, 49, 49, 42, 41, 50, 50, 50, 57, 45, 45, 45, 50, 54, 43 and 49.

  Prepare a frequency table for the above data and answer the following questions :

  (*i*) What is the least weight ?

  (*ii*) Find the number of students having the least weight in the above data.

  (*iii*) Find the number of students having the maximum weight in the above data.

  (*iv*) Which weight do the maximum number of students have ?

6. The value of π upto 50 decimal places is given below :

3.1415926535 8979323846 2643383279 50288841971 6939937510

Write the frequencies of the following digits in the decimal part of the above number.

(*i*) 2   (*ii*) 3   (*iii*) 5   (*iv*) 6   (*v*) 9   (*vi*) 1

GROUPED FREQUENCY DISTRIBUTION

19.5 Introduction

So far we have seen an ungrouped frequency distribution. If the data extends over a wide range, such tables become lengthy and unwieldy. In such, cases, statisticians usually condense the data into more usable form, *i.e*, in groups or classes. **For example,** consider the following ungrouped marks out of 50 awarded to 30 students.

3, 5, 8, 15, 25, 30, 16, 7, 35, 40, 49, 40, 30, 15, 14, 21, 23, 22, 25, 27, 29, 32, 15, 1, 9, 11, 14, 42, 43, 8.

Let us arrange them in the following array, *i.e.*, in ascending order

1, 3, 5, 7, 8, 8, 9, 11, 14, 14, 15, 15, 15, 16, 21, 22, 23, 25, 25, 27, 29, 30, 30, 32, 35, 40, 40, 42, 43, 49.

> **Note :** Arrangement in ascending or descending order is called an **array**

We can classify these marks into groups or classes as shown in the table given below.

Marks	No. of students	Marks	No. of students
0-5	2	25–30	4
5-10	5	30–35	3
10-15	3	35–40	1
15-20	4	40–45	4
20-25	3	45–50	1

The groups 0-5, 5-10 etc. are called the **class intervals.**

Each class interval is bounded by two figures which are called the class limits. The **class limits** of the **first class**, for example, are the numbers 0 and 5 and those of the second class are 5 and 10. The larger of these numbers namely 5 is called the **upper limit**, and the smaller number 0 is the **lower limit.** Similarly, the upper and the lower limits of the second class are 10 and 5 respectively, and so on.

It may be noted that :

(*i*) the upper limit of one class coincides with the lower limit of the next class, and

(*ii*) **the class 0 and 5 means 0 and less than 5 ; 5 –10 means 5 and less than 10,** and so on. Here the upper limit 5 belongs to the next class 5–10 and not to the class 0–5. Similar is the case in other classes.

> **Maths Alert :** marks '5' are included in the class interval 5–10 and not 0–5. Similarly, marks '15' are counted in the class interval 15–20 and not 10–15 and so on.

19.6 Types of Frequency Distributions

The frequency distribution of the form 0–10, 10–20, 10–30, ... in which the upper limit of one class interval is the same as the lower limit of the next larger class interval is called an **exclusive** distribution. There is another type of frequency distribution of the form 1–9, 10–19, 20–29, ... in which the upper limit of one class does not coincide with the lower limit of the next larger class interval. Such a frequency distribution is called an **inclusive** distribution. In this type of distribution **both the lower and upper limits of a class belong to that class only**, *i.e.*, both 1 and 5 belong to the class 1–5. [Refer Q. 4, Exercise 19(*c*)]

19.7 Class Size, Class - Mark and Class Frequency

1. The difference between the upper and the lower class limits is called the **size** or **width** of the class interval. For example, in the table, the size of the class interval 0 – 5 is 5 – 0 = 5, of 5 – 10 is 10 – 5 = 5, of 10 – 15 is 15 – 10 = 5, and so on.

2. The mid-value of a class-interval is called its **class mark**. Thus, the class mark of the class interval 10 – 15 is

$$\frac{10+15}{2} = \frac{25}{2} = \textbf{12.5}$$

3. The frequency of a class interval is called its **class frequency**. Thus, the class frequency of the class interval 0 – 5 is 2, of 5 –10 is 5, of 10 –15 is 3 and so on.

Ex. 1. *In an examination 40 boys secured the following marks :*

8, 11, 20, 37, 40, 15, 29, 31, 27, 8, 7, 13, 29, 25, 42, 37, 30, 10, 9, 27, 18, 25, 9, 2, 17, 47, 32, 11, 29, 6, 15, 41, 37, 10, 40, 21, 39, 13, 15, 3.

Represent the data by a frequency table.

Sol. Arranging the given marks in ascending order, we have

2, 3, 6, 7, 8, 8, 9, 9, 10, 10, 11, 11, 11, 13, 13, 15, 15, 15, 18, 20, 21, 25, 25, 27, 27, 29, 29, 29, 30, 31, 32, 37, 37, 37, 39, 40, 40, 41, 42, 47.

Here the maximum marks secured = 47,

The minimum marks secured = 2 ∴ Range = 47 – 2 = **45**

Classes	Tally	Frequency (f)
0–10	჻	8
10–20	჻	11
20–30	჻	9
30–40	჻	7
40–50	჻	5
Total		40

Suppose we want to form 5 classes, then the class interval should be $\frac{45}{5}$, *i.e.* 9 or roughly 10 as we prefer 5 or 10 or 20, etc. Therefore the class intervals are 0–10, 10–20, 20–30, 30–40, 40–50.

The frequency distribution is as given in the table.

Ex. 2. *Construct a frequency distribution table for the following data of the maximum temperature (in °C) using equal class intervals-one of them being 28 – 30 (30 not included).*

32.5, 30.3, 33.8, 31.0, 28.0, 33.9, 33.3, 32.4, 30.4, 32.6, 34.7, 34.9, 31.6, 35.2, 35.3, 35.5, 36.4, 35.6, 37.0, 34.3, 32.0, 34.0, 34.4, 36.0, 37.3, 38.0, 36.9, 37.0, 36.3, 38.0, 36.7.

Sol. Arranging the given data in ascending order, we have

28.0, 30.3, 30.4, 31.0, 31.6, 32.0, 32.4, 32.5, 32.6, 33.3, 33.8, 33.9, 34.0, 34.3, 34.4, 34.7, 34.9, 35.2, 35.3, 35.5, 35.6, 36.0, 36.3, 36.4, 36.7, 36.9, 37.0, 37.0, 37.3, 38.0, 38.0.

The highest temperature = 38.0°C,

The lowest temperature = 28.0°C

Range = 38.0°C – 28.0°C = 10°C

Size of the class interval = 2

∴ No. of class intervals = $\frac{10}{2} + 1 = 6$

Temperature (in °C)	Tally	Frequency (f)
28–30	჻	1
30–32	჻	4
32–34	჻	7
34–36	჻	9
36–38	჻	8
38–40	჻	2
Total	Σf	31

Note : The given data are continuous data

∴ The class intervals covering the given data are 28–30, 30–32, 32–34, 34–36, 36–38, and 38–40.

1. Fill in the blanks:

   (*i*) The difference between the maximum and the minimum observations in a data is called the .... of the data.

   (*ii*) The number of observations in a particular class interval is called the .... of the class interval.

2. Fill in the blanks:

   (*i*) lower limit of the class interval 26—33 is ....

   (*ii*) upper limit of the class interval 21—25 is ....

   (*iii*) The range of the data 5, 8, 15, 21, 7, 10, is ....

   (*iv*) The range of the data 15, 13, 14, 17, 19, 16, 14, 15 is

3. Fill in the blanks in the following table :

Weights in kg	10–20	20–30	30–40	40–50	50–60
Class marks					

Sol. (Hint : Class mark for 1st class interval = $\frac{10+20}{2} = \frac{30}{2}$ = 15. Similarly, the class marks of other class intervals are obtained)

4. For each set of data, make up a tally table, using the groupings suggested and complete the frequency column.

   (*a*) The number of tomatoes picked from tomato plants.

   18, 31, 25, 16, 21, 20, 34, 7   Suggested grouping

   19, 18, 24, 26, 30, 21, 26, 18   0—4, 5—9, 10—14, 15—19, ...

   28, 31, 11, 25, 33, 23, 17, 24

   (*b*) The number of books on 18 of the shelves in a college library.

   35, 42, 43, 31, 27, 39, 30, 45, 37   Suggested grouping

   33, 36, 26, 30, 29, 38, 36, 34, 43   21—25, 26—30, 31—35, 36—40, ...

5. The following are the monthly rents (in rupees) of 30 shops:

   42, 49, 37, 82, 37, 75, 62, 54, 79, 84, 75, 63, 44, 74, 36, 69, 54, 48, 74, 39, 48, 45, 61, 71, 47, 38, 80, 51, 31, 43

   Using the class intervals of equal width in which one class interval being 40–50 (excluding 50), construct a frequency table for the above data.

6. Construct a frequency table for the following marks obtained by 45 students using equal class intervals, one of them being 16–24 (24 not included).

   12, 35, 6, 10, 8, 24, 37, 32, 61, 52, 63, 7, 41, 48, 15, 16, 25, 29, 62, 40, 33, 46, 18, 20, 34, 28, 24, 56, 55, 12, 50, 56, 48, 47, 38, 26, 60, 42, 39, 40, 43, 25, 13, 46, 20.

7. The following list shows the weights in kg of the 22 boys students in a class.

37.48	61.93	58.72	49.78	51.70	68.10
49.87	38.75	69.10	65.39	36.49	65.62
54.63	46.17	48.80	57.35	62.25	
38.50	62.82	59.73	56.60	50.15	

   (Hint : Since observations like 37.48, 62.25, 59.73, do not fit in any intervals, the class intervals have to overlap in such a way that all values fit in. You may take the intervals as 35–40, 40–45, 45–50, ... 65–70.)

LOOKING BACK
Summary of Key Facts

1. Observations gathered initially are called **raw data**.

2. The difference between the highest and the lowest values of the observations in the given data is called the **range**.

3. In given data, the number of times a particular observation occurs is called its **frequency**.

4. A table showing the frequencies of various observations of the given data is called a frequency distribution table or simply a **frequency table**.

5. When the number of observations is large, we make use of tally marks to count the frequencies.

6. Tallies are usually marked in bunches of five to make the counting easier.

Tally mark

7. When the list of observations is large, the data are organised into groups like 0–5, 5–10, ... These are called **classes** or **class intervals**. The data so organised is called **grouped data** or a **grouped frequency distribution**. (**'Data is plural of 'datum'**)

8. The lower value of a class interval is called its lower class limit and the upper value of a class interval is called its upper class limit.

Upper class limit
5-10, 10-15, 15-20,
Lower class limit

9. The mid-value of a class interval is called its **class mark**. Thus, class mark of the class interval is $\frac{5+10}{2} = 7.5$.

10. The frequency of a class interval is called its **class frequency**.

ANSWERS

EXERCISE 19 (a)

1. (*a*) 155, 160, 165, 167, 175,   (*b*) 60, 61, 65, 66, 68
   (*c*) Devendra, Girish, Narendra, Piyush, Sanjay

2.

Name	Age	Height	Weight	Hobby
Pawan	12 yrs.	155 cm	48 kg	Stamp-collecting
Hema	14 yrs.	140 cm	45 kg	Gardening
Vivek	11 yrs.	145 cm	42 kg	Painting
Shyam	13 yrs.	158 cm	46 kg	Photography

EXERCISE 19 (b)

1. (*i*) T   (*ii*) F   (*iii*) F   (*iv*) T   (*v*) T   (*vi*) T
4. (*i*) 23   (*ii*) 7   (*iii*) 3   (*iv*) 11
5. (*i*) 41 kg   (*ii*) 1   (*iii*) 2   (*iv*) 50 kg
6. (*i*) 5   (*ii*) 8   (*iii*) 5   (*iv*) 3   (*v*) 8   (*vi*) 5

EXERCISE 19 (c)

1. (*i*) range   (*ii*) frequency
2. (*i*) 26   (*ii*) 25   (*iii*) 16   (*iv*) 6

3.

Weight in kg	10–20	20–30	30–40	40–50	50–60
Class marks	15	25	35	45	55

4. (a)

Tomatoes picked from Tomato plants	Tally	Frequency
5–9	I	1
10–14	I	1
15–19	卌 I	6
20–24	卌 I	6
25–29	卌	5
30–34	卌	5

(b)

Books on the shelves in a college library	Tally	Frequency
26–30	卌	5
31–35	IIII	4
36–40	卌	5
41–45	IIII	4

5.

Monthly rent (in rupees) :	30–40	40–50	50–60	60–70	70–80	80–90
f :	6	8	3	4	6	3

6.

Marks :	0–8	8–16	16–24	24–32	32–40	40–48	48–56	56–64
Number of Students (f) :	2	6	4	7	7	8	5	6

7.

Weight (in kg) :	35–40	40–45	45–50	50–55	55–60	60–65	65–70
f :	4	0	4	3	4	3	4

20. Graphical Representation of Data

20.1 Introduction

The two forms which are generally used for presenting data are :

(*i*) Tables   (*ii*) Graphs

We have dealt with the preparation of frequency distribution tables in the last chapter. Here we shall review the bar graphs for representing data pictorially which you have already studied in class VII and introduce you to two more types of graphs, *i.e.,* Histograms and Pie Charts.

20.2 Bar Graph

A bar graph is a pictorial representation of the numerical data by a number of bars of uniform width (with different heights), erected horizontally or vertically with equal spacing between them.

The examples given below will help you to revise the concept of bar graphs and the method of drawing them.

Ex. 1. *The following table shows the number of books of different subjects in a library.*

Subject	Physics	Chemistry	Biology	History	Geography	English	Maths	Computer
No. of Books	100	125	75	75	50	200	250	175

Draw a bar graph to represent the above data.

Sol. Take the subjects along the *x*-axis and the number of books along the *y*-axis. Construct the bars of same width, with same distance between them.

Take the scale as 25 books = 5 small divisions or $\frac{1}{2}$ cm.

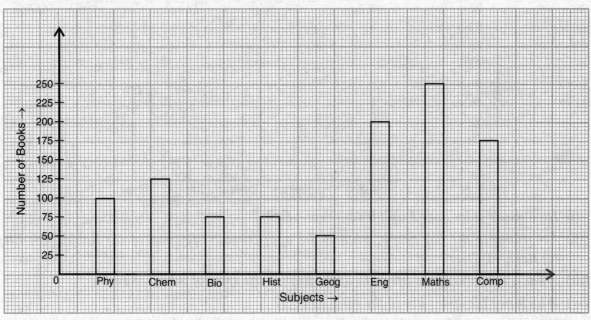

Ex. 2. *The following table shows the expenditure pattern of a family :*

Items	Food	Clothing	Rent	Education	Miscellaneous
Expenditure (in Rs)	3500	2000	1500	2500	1000

Draw a bar graph to represent the above data.

Sol. Take items along the *x*-axis and expenditure along the *y*-axis. Here we take the scale as 1 cm = Rs 1000 or 10 small divisions = Rs 1000.

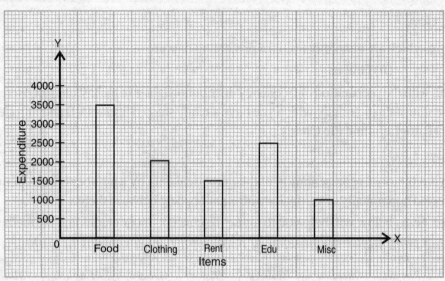

20.3 Interpreting a Bar Graph

Ex. 3. *Given below is a bar graph showing the approximate life spans of some animals. Read the bar graph and answer the questions that follow :*

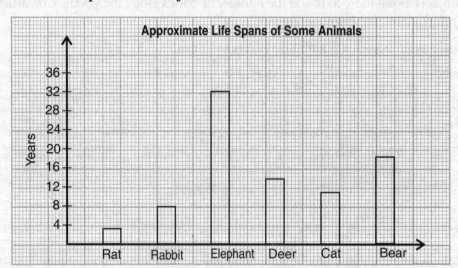

   (i) *How many years does 1 unit length represent?*

  (ii) *According to the bar graph, what is the approximate life span of* **(a)** *Rabbit,* **(b)** *Elephant,* **(c)** *Bear,* **(d)** *Deer?*

 (iii) *What is the ratio of the life span of the bear to life span of the elephant?*

 (iv) *Which two life spans are in the ratio of 4 : 1?*

  (v) *The elephant's life span is how many years longer than the deer's?*

Sol. (*i*) 1 unit length = 4 years

(*ii*) (*a*) Rabbit → 8 years, (*b*) Elephant → 32 years, (*c*) Bear → 18 years, and (*d*) Deer → 14 years.

(*iii*) Ratio of Bear's life span to Elephant's life span = $18 : 32 = \dfrac{18}{32} = \dfrac{9}{16} = \mathbf{9 : 16}$.

(*iv*) Elephant's and Rabbit's life spans are in the ratio 4 : 1.

(*v*) Elephant's life span is (32–14) years = 18 years longer than that of deer's life span.

Ex. 4. *The double bar graph shows the average monthly temperatures of two cities over a 3 month period.*

Read the graph carefully and answer the questions given below :

(i) *What does each 1 cm block on the vertical axis represent?*

(ii) *What was the average monthly temperature in Nainital in (a) March, (b) April, and (c) May.*

(iii) *What was the average monthly temperature in Delhi over the whole 3 month period.*

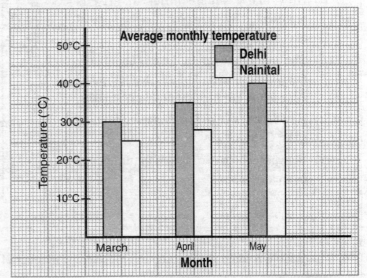

(iv) *In which month was the difference between the temperatures of Delhi and Nainital maximum and how much was the difference?*

Sol. (*i*) 1 cm block on the vertical axis = 10°C.

(*ii*) The average monthly temperature in Nainital in the month of

(*a*) March was 24°C   (*b*) April was 28°C   (*c*) May was 30°C

(*iii*) Average monthly temperature in Delhi over the whole 3 months

$$= \frac{\text{Av. Monthly temp. of (March + April + May)}}{3}$$

$$= \frac{30°\text{C} + 35°\text{C} + 40°\text{C}}{3} = \left(\frac{105}{3}\right)°\text{C} = \mathbf{35°C}$$

(*iv*) The difference between the average monthly temperatures of Delhi and Nainital was maximum in the month of May and is equal to (40°C–30°C) = **10°C**.

EXERCISE 20 (a)

1. The following table shows the number of students in a school playing five different games.

Games	Football	Hockey	Cricket	Tennis	Squash
Number of students	200	175	250	75	50

Present this information on a bar graph.

2. The following table shows how a student spends his pocket money during the course of a month.

Item	Food	Entertainment	Other expenditure	Savings
Expenditure	40%	25%	20%	15%

If the pocket money in Rs 1000, represent the above information on a table showing expenditure in rupees. Then draw a bar graph showing the expenditure.

3. Given alongside is a graph showing the areas (in thousand square miles) of the five Great Lakes.

Read the bar graph carefully and answer the questions given below :

(*i*) How many square miles of area is represented by 1 cm block on the vertical axis?

(*ii*) The area of the largest lake is about how many times the area of the smallest lake? Also name the smallest and largest lakes.

(*iii*) How much is Lake Erie larger in area than Lake Ontario?

(*iv*) Between which two lakes is the difference in area the least?

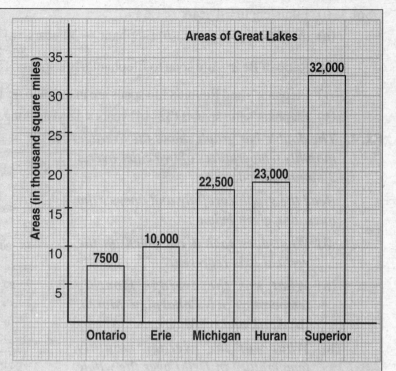

4. This double column graph compares the average number of hours an electrical appliance is used on weekdays and weekends.

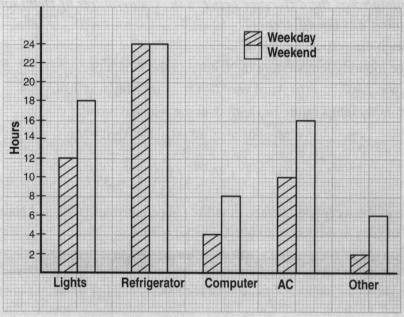

Read the graph and answer the following questions :

(*i*) Which appliance has got the maximum usage?

(*ii*) Which appliance is used twice as many hours on the weekend as it is used on weekdays?

(*iii*) What is the average number of hours an AC is used on weekend?

(*iv*) Which appliances are each used for 6 more hours on a day on weekends than on a weekday?

HISTOGRAMS

20.4 Introduction

You have learnt what we mean by a frequency distribution and how to make a frequency distribution table from the given data. You have also learnt how to draw bar graphs. Now, we will tell you about another kind of graph which can be used to display a given data. This is called a histogram. A histogram is very similar to a bar chart. However, unlike a bar graph, **the bars of a histogram are always vertical and there are no gaps between the bars**. Also, the data must be grouped into class intervals of equal width.

This table shows how long an audience's applause lasted for 67 jokes told by a comedian.

Duration of applause in seconds	Frequency
0 to less than 5	6
5 to less than 10	10
10 to less than 15	17
15 to less than 20	14
20 to less than 25	8
25 to less than 30	12

We convert the given table as under :

Duration of applause in seconds	Frequency
0–5	6
5–10	10
10–15	17
15–20	14
20–25	8
25–30	12

The data can be displayed in a histogram like this :

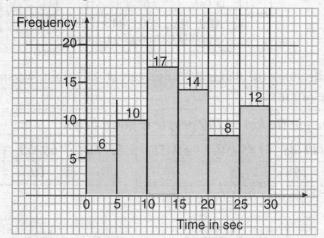

20.5 Drawing a Histogram

Method.   1.   On the horizontal axis, mark off the class intervals on a uniform scale.

2.   On the vertical axis mark off the frequencies, also on a uniform scale.

3.   Construct rectangles with class intervals as bases and the corresponding frequencies as heights.

Note. 1 : In a histogram the areas of the rectangles are proportional to the frequencies they represent.

In this case all the class intervals are the same (5 seconds) so the rectangles all have the same width and the height of each rectangle is proportional to its area and to the frequency.

Note. 2 : It should not be assumed that scale for both the axes is the same. We can have different scales for the two axes.

> **Note. 3** : You should not confuse a histogram with a bar chart. In a bar chart, the height of each bar matters and not its width. It is therefore one-dimensional. In a histogram, the height as well as the width of each bar (rectangle) matter. It is, therefore, two-dimensional.

Ex. 1. *Draw a histogram to represent the following data of the earnings of workers :*

Monthly earnings (in rupees)	Number of workers	Monthly earnings (in rupees)	Number of workers
80–120	4	200–240	8
120–160	7	240–280	5
160–200	13	280–320	2

Sol.

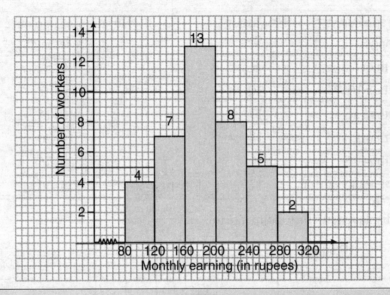

> **Note** : When the scale along the *x*-axis does not start at the origin, we show it by a kink (break or a zig-zag curve near the origin).

Ex. 2. *The distribution of weight (in kg) of 100 people is given below :*

Weight (in kg)	40–45	45–50	50–55	55–60	60–65	65–70	70–75
Frequency	10	25	27	16	10	7	5

Draw a histogram to represent the above data.

Sol.

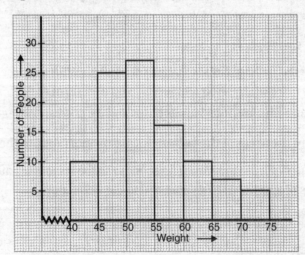

20.6 Interpreting Histograms

Ex. 1. *Prepare a grouped frequency for the histogram given here.*

Sol.

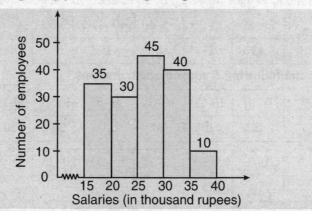

Salary (in thousand rupees)	15–20	20–25	25–30	30–35	35–40
No. of employees	35	30	45	40	10

Ex. 2. *Study the histogram and answer the questions given below :*
  (i) *What information is depicted by the histogram?*
  (ii) *What is the number of teachers in the oldest age group in the school?*
  (iii) *What is the number of teachers in the youngest age group in the school ?*
  (iv) *In which age group, the number of teachers is the least ?*
  (v) *In which age group, the number of teachers is the maximum ?*
  (vi) *What is the class size of each class interval ?*
  (vii) *What are the class marks of all the class intervals ?*
  (viii) *How many teachers are below 30 years in age ?*

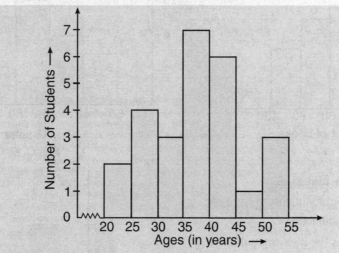

Sol. (*i*) It depicts the age of 26 teachers of a school.
  (*ii*) Number of teachers in the oldest age group = 3
  (*iii*) Number of teachers in the youngest age group = 2.
  (*iv*) Age group in which the number of teachers is the least = 45 – 50.
  (*v*) Age group in which the number of teachers is the maximum = 35 – 40.
  (*vi*) Class size of each interval = 5.
  (*vii*) Class marks of all the class intervals are 22.5, 27.5, 32.5, 37.5, 42.5, 47.5, 52.5.
  (*viii*) Number of teachers below 30 years in age = 6

EXERCISE 20 (b)

1. Represent the following distribution of ages (in years) of 35 teachers in a school by means of a histogram.

Age (in years) :	25–30	30–35	35–40	40–45	45–50
Number of Teachers :	12	11	8	1	3

Draw histograms for the following frequency distributions.

2.

Size :	0–10	10–20	20–30	30–40	40–50	50–60
Frequency :	5	10	20	25	20	10

3.

Class interval :	0–5	5–10	10–15	15–20	20–25
Frequency :	10	25	9	20	5

4.

Marks :	0–10	10–20	20–30	30–40	40–50
No. of Students :	5	9	14	7	5

5. Complete : In the histogram below— people were surveyed,— and of them own between 20 and 60 books.

6. Complete : In the histogram shown below—students received grades between 70 and 100, and .... students in all took the test.

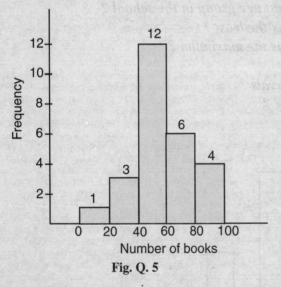

Fig. Q. 5

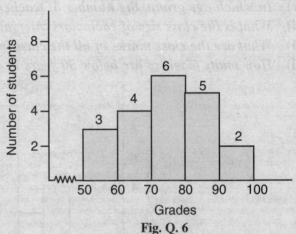

Fig. Q. 6

7. **For the histogram shown alongside :**

  (a) What is the total number of students over whom our study has been conducted?

  (b) Which time interval has the maximum number of students studying?

  (c) Which time interval has the minimum number of students studying?

  (d) How many times is the number of students in the time interval 3hrs–6hrs greater than the number of students in the time interval 9hrs–12hrs?

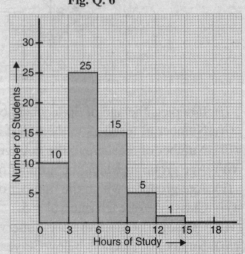

8. **For the histogram given alongside answer the questions that follow :**

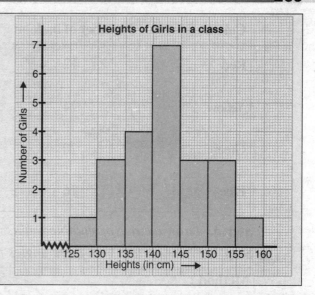

(a) What is the total number of girls in the class?

(b) Which group contains the maximum number of girls?

(c) Which groups have the minimum number of girls and how many?

(d) How many girls have a height of 145 cm or more?

PIE CHARTS

20.7 Introduction

A pie chart is a way of showing how something is shared or divided.

This pie chart shows how 36 pupils usually come to school :

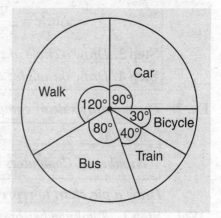

The number of the pupils is 36 and the whole group of 36 pupils is represented by the complete angle 360°. The angles at the centre are in proportion to each category. Thus, the angle of 120° at the centre corresponds to the walkgroup.

Since angle of 360° at the centre corresponds to the whole group of 36 pupils

∴ 1° corresponds to $\dfrac{36}{360}$ of the whole group.

∴ 120° corresponds to $\dfrac{36}{360} \times 120$, *i.e.,* 12 pupils. So, 12 pupils walk to school.

Similarly, number of pupils coming by car $= \dfrac{36}{360} \times 90 = 9$ and so on.

20.8 Drawing Pie Charts

Ex. 1. *A box of 72 coloured balloons contains the following numbers of balloons of each column. Draw a pie chart to show this information.*

Colour	Red	Yellow	Green	Blue
Number of balloons	12	24	20	16

Sol. **Step 1.** *Work out the total number of balloons :* 12 + 24 + 20 + 16 = 72

Step 2. *Work out the angle for each colour.*

It is easiest to put the information in a table.

Colour	Number of balloons	Angle
Red	12	$\frac{12}{72}\times360° = 60°$
Yellow	24	$\frac{24}{72}\times360° = 120°$
Green	20	$\frac{20}{72}\times360° = 100°$
Blue	16	$\frac{16}{72}\times360° = 80°$

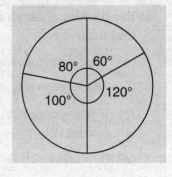

Step 3. *Draw a circle of suitable radius.*

Step 4. *Draw sectors with these angles to complete the pie chart.*

Method :

Step 1. *Find the total of all the components.*

Step 2. *Find the angles corresponding to different components by using the following formula.*

$$\text{Angle} = \frac{\text{Value of one component}}{\text{Total of all the components}}\times360°$$

Step 3. *Draw a circle of suitable radius.*

Step 4. *Draw the angles calculated in step 2 at the centre of the circle.*

Ex. 2. *The monthly sale of computers by a shopkeeper is as shown in the following table.*

Months	July	August	September	October	November
Number of Computers sold	*12*	*18*	*28*	*42*	*44*

Draw a pie chart to represent the data.

Sol. **Step 1.** *Total number of computers = 12 + 18 + 28 + 42 + 44 = 144*

Step 2. *Now work out the angle for sale in each month.*

Step 3. *Draw a circle of suitable radius.*

Step 4. *Draw the angles calculated in step 2.*

We obtain the pie chart required as shown.

Month	Number of computers sold	Angle
July	12	$\frac{12}{144}\times360° = 30°$
August	18	$\frac{18}{144}\times360° = 45°$
September	28	$\frac{28}{144}\times360° = 70°$
October	42	$\frac{42}{144}\times360° = 105°$
November	44	$\frac{44}{144}\times360° = 110°$

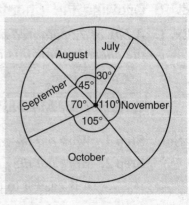

Ex. 3. *The way Mr. Sharma spends his allowance is given below. Draw the pie chart.*

Item	Per cent
Lunch	*25%*
Hobby	*20%*
Recreation	*40%*
Saving	*15%*
Total	**100%**

Represent the above information by a pie chart.

Sol.

Item	Per cent	Fractional part	Central angle
Lunch	25%	$\dfrac{25}{100} = \dfrac{1}{4}$	$\dfrac{1}{4} \times 360° = 90°$
Hobby	20%	$\dfrac{20}{100} = \dfrac{1}{5}$	$\dfrac{1}{5} \times 360° = 72°$
Recreation	40%	$\dfrac{40}{100} = \dfrac{2}{5}$	$\dfrac{2}{5} \times 360° = 144°$
Saving	15%	$\dfrac{15}{100} = \dfrac{3}{20}$	$\dfrac{3}{20} \times 360° = 54°$

Draw a circle of any convenient size.

Divide it into sectors of angles, 90°, 72°, 144°, and 54°.

You obtain the required pie chart.

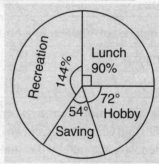

20.9 Reading Pie Charts

Ex. 4. *The pie chart drawn here represents the amount spent on different sports by a school in a year. If the money spent on football is Rs 9,000, answer the following questions :*

  (i) *What is the total amount spent on sports?*

 (ii) *How much amount is spent on hockey?*

(iii) *What is the amount spent on cricket?*

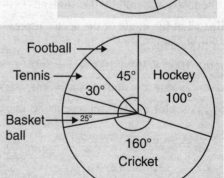

Sol.

Sports	Football	Hockey	Cricket	Basketball	Tennis
Amount spent	Rs 9,000				
Angle of sectors	45°	100°	160°	25°	30°

The pie chart shows that a sector of 45° represents an expense of Rs 9000

Therefore, a sector of 1° will represent an expense of Rs $\dfrac{9000}{45}$, *i.e.,* Rs 200.

(*i*) The total expense corresponds to a complete angle of 360° which will represent an expense of Rs (200 × 360) = **Rs 72000.**

(*ii*) A sector of 100° for hockey will represent an expense of Rs (200 × 100) = Rs 20,000

Hence, amount spent on hockey = **Rs 20,000**

(*iii*) Similarly, amount spent on cricket = Rs (200 × 160) = **Rs 32,000**

EXERCISE 20 (c)

Draw pie charts to represent the following information, first working out the angles.

1. The number of books lent out by a school library each day is shown in the following table.

Day	Mon	Tues	Wed	Thurs	Fri
Number of books lent	10	25	33	16	6

2. On a cornflakes packet the composition of 120 g of cornflakes is given in grams as follows :

Protein	Fat	Carbohydrates	Other ingredients
101	1	10	8

3. A large flower arrangement contained 15 dark red, 8 pale pink roses, 8 white roses and 14 deep pink roses.

4. A student secured marks in different subjects as shown in the following table.

Subjects	English	Computer	Science	Mathematics
Marks	35	40	45	60

5. The number of students in a hostel speaking different languages is given below. Present the data in a pie chart.

Language	Hindi	English	Marathi	Tamil	Bengali	Total
Number of students	40	10	8	8	4	72

6. A pie diagram of the marks secured by a student in Maths, English, Physics and Chemistry is shown here. Read the graph and find the marks in chemistry secured by the student.

[**Hint :** Let the angle of the sector representing the marks in chemistry be x in degrees.

Then, $100° + 75° + 100° + x = 360°$,

$\Rightarrow$ $275° + x = 360° \Rightarrow x = 360° - 275° = 85°$

Now, A sector of 100° represents 80 marks (Maths)

$\therefore$ A sector of 1° represents $\dfrac{80}{100}$ marks

$\therefore$ A sector of 85° represents $\dfrac{80}{100} \times 85 = 68$ marks

Hence, marks obtained in chemistry = **68.**]

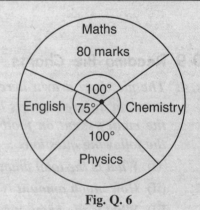

Fig. Q. 6

7. A pie chart representing the population of four cities is shown here. Read the pie chart and find the population of the city *D*.

(**Hint :** Similar to Q. 6)

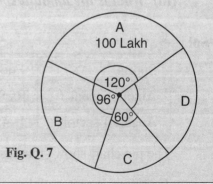

Fig. Q. 7

LOOKING BACK

Summary of Key Facts

1. A **histogram** is a graphical representation of grouped data in which class intervals are taken along the horizontal axis and frequencies along the vertical axis. For each class, a rectangle is constructed with class interval as the base and the height is proportional to the corresponding frequency.

2. A **pie chart** is a graphical representation of the given numerical data in the form of sectors of a circle.

3. Central angle for a sector $= \left(\dfrac{\text{Value of the component}}{\text{Total value}} \times 360 \right)^{\circ}$.

MULTIPLE CHOICE QUESTIONS – 16

A. Questions 1 and 4 are based on the graph given below which shows the number of deaths from road accidents occurred during rainy season of 2005.

Deaths from Road Accidents during Rainy Season 2005

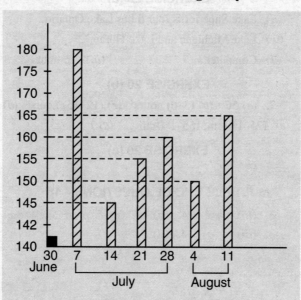

1. Between which two consecutive weeks was the rise in the number of deaths greatest?

  (*i*) 30 June–7 July   (*ii*) 14 July–21 July

  (*iii*) 4 August–11 August   (*iv*) 21 July–28 July

2. In how many weeks were there more than 150 deaths?

  (*i*) 1   (*ii*) 2   (*iii*) 3   (*iv*) 4

3. In how many weeks were there less than 150 deaths?

  (*i*) 0   (*ii*) 1   (*iii*) 2   (*iv*) 3

4. Between which two consecutive weeks was the fall in the number of deaths greatest?

  (*i*) 30 June–7 July   (*ii*) 7 July–14 July

  (*iii*) 28 July–4 August   (*iv*) None of these

B. The pie-graph drawn here shows the spendings of a school on various sports during a particular year. Study the graph and answer the questions that follow:

1. The ratio of the total amount spent on football to that spent on hockey is :
   (i) 1 : 15   (ii) 1 : 1
   (iii) 15 : 1   (iv) 3 : 20

2. If the total amount spent on sports during the year was Rs 1,20,000, the amount spent on basketball was :
   (i) Rs 9,500   (ii) Rs 10,000   (iii) Rs 12,000   (iv) Rs 15,000

3. Graph shows that the most popular game of the country is :
   (i) Hockey   (ii) Football   (iii) Cricket   (iv) Tennis

4. Out of the following, the country spent the same amount on :
   (i) Hockey and Tennis   (ii) Golf and Basketball   (iii) Cricket and Football   (iv) Hockey and Golf.

ANSWERS

EXERCISE 20 (a)

3. (i) 5000 sq. miles   (ii) Lake Superior is four times Lake Ontario
   (iii) 2500 sq. miles   (iv) Lake Michigan and Lake Huran.
4. (i) Refrigerator   (ii) Computer   (iii) 16 hours   (iv) Lights and AC.

EXERCISE 20 (b)

5. 26; 15   6. 13; 20   7. (a) 56 (b) (3–6) hours (c) (12–15) hours (d) 5
8. (a) 22   (b) 140–145 cm   (c) 125–130 cm; 155–160 cm   (d) 7

EXERCISE 20 (c)

7. 70 lakh.

MULTIPLE CHOICE QUESTIONS – 16

A. 1. (i)   2. (iv)   3. (iii)   4. (ii)
B. 1. (ii)   2. (iv)   3. (iii)   4. (ii)

21. Probability

21.1 Introduction

If we are to go to North Pole or Mount Everest, we are sure to find snow there. Similarly, if we travel down to a seashore, what are we sure to find there? Yes, sand of course!

On the other hand, there are some events about which we are not sure or certain like the following :

- Will rains be good this year?
- Will I get good marks in my next Maths test?
- Will I be able to get home on time to attend the party?
- Who will be the next World Cup Cricket Champions?

Also, if we toss a coin we cannot say for certain whether the head will show up or the tail will show up.

The outcomes of such actions, as tossing a coin, throwing up a die, or drawing a card from a well-shuffled pack of cards all depend on **CHANCE.**

Chance plays an important part in life and many important decisions depend on the result of such actions. Thus in a cricket match which team will have the right to decide whether to bat or field first is decided by the toss of a coin. Quality of goods purchased, for example, sweets, are determined by checking a sample, like tasting a single piece. Gamblers always depend on chance and make or ruin fortunes.

In fact, the theory of probability was first applied to gambling.

Activity

The spinners as shown may be drawn on the blackboard and the students made to answer the related questions.

Which spinner from each pair would you choose so that you are more likely to get a 1

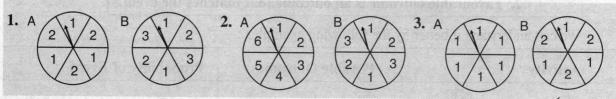

(Ans : A)

Which spinner in each pair would you use to get a 3? If you think the chances of getting a 3 are the same, write *Either.*

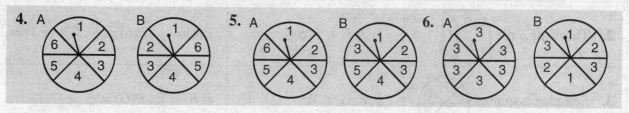

Choose the spinner that answer the questions :

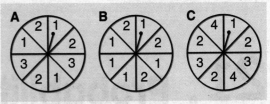

1. On which spinner is the probability of getting a 1 less than the probability of getting a 2?

2. On which spinner is the probability of getting a 1 equal to the probability of getting a 2?

3. On which spinner is the probability of getting a 1 equal to the probability of getting a 2?

4. Which spinner would you use if you wanted a 1? a 2? a 3?

21.2 The Probability Scale

Mathematically, an event that will not happen has a probability zero. An event that is sure to occur will have a probability 1.

If a die is rolled, the probability of getting 1, 2, 3, 4, 5 or 6 is 1 as one of the numbers is certain to show up.

However, the probability of getting a 7 is zero as this is **impossible**.

This shows that all probabilities must have a value greater than or equal to 0 and less than or equal to 1.

This can be shown on a **probability scale.**

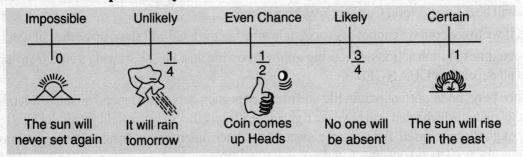

Impossible	Unlikely	Even Chance	Likely	Certain
0	$\frac{1}{4}$	$\frac{1}{2}$	$\frac{3}{4}$	1
The sun will never set again	It will rain tomorrow	Coin comes up Heads	No one will be absent	The sun will rise in the east

Probability is a way of measuring the chance of an event occurring.

We calculate the probability $P(E)$ of the occurrence of an event E by the formula :

$$P(E) = \frac{\text{Number of favourable outcomes}}{\text{Total number of possible outcomes}}$$

where,
1. **Outcome is the result of an experiment.**
2. **Favourable outcome is an outcome that matches the event.**

We can understand it better by the following examples :

Activity	Possible Outcomes	Probability of Event
1. Flipping a coin	Head, Tail	$P(\text{Head}) = \frac{1}{2},\ P(\text{Tail}) = \frac{1}{2}$
2. Throwing a die	1, 2, 3, 4, 5, 6	$P(4) = \frac{1}{6},\ P(6) = \frac{1}{6},\ P(1 \text{ or } 3) = \frac{2}{6} = \frac{1}{3}$
3. Spinning a spinner	B, R, G, Y, W	$P(B) = \frac{1}{5},\ P(G) = \frac{1}{5}$

> **Note :** **1.** The probabilities of all possible outcomes of an event add up to 1.
> **2.** P(event not happening) = 1 − P(event happening)

Ex. 1. *A spinner having the numbers 2, 3, 4, 5, 6, 7 is spun. What is the probability of getting :*

(i) *a 4 ?*   **(ii)** *a prime number ?*   **(iii)** *an even number ?*

Sol. Probability of an event = $\dfrac{\text{Number of favourable outcomes}}{\text{Total number of possible outcomes}}$

(*i*) Total number of possible outcomes = 6 (2, 3, 4, 5, 6, 7)

Chance of getting a 4 = 1

∴ $P(4) = \dfrac{1}{4}$

(*ii*) The prime numbers are 2, 3, 5, 7

∴   Number of favourable outcomes = 4

Total number of possible outcomes = 6

∴ $P(\text{Prime number}) = \dfrac{4}{6} = \dfrac{2}{3}$.

(*iii*) The even numbers are 2, 4, 6

∴   Number of favourable outcomes = 3

Total number of possible outcomes = 6

∴ $P(\text{even number}) = \dfrac{3}{6} = \dfrac{1}{2}$

Ex. 2. *Instead of numbers, the letters in the word CHANCE were stuck on a die. Find the probability of rolling :*

(i) *letter H*   **(ii)** *a vowel*   **(iii)** *a consonant*   **(iv)** *any letter except E.*

Sol. A die has six faces and the letters *C, H, A, N, C, E* are stuck on one face each.

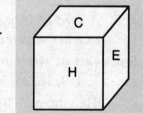

Total number of possible outcomes are **6**(*C, H, A, N, C, E*)

Also, Probability of an event = $\dfrac{\text{Number of favourable outcomes}}{\text{Total number of possible outcomes}}$

(*i*) The letter *H* appears on one face

∴   Number of favourable outcomes = 1

Total number of possible outcomes = 6

$P(\text{letter } H) = \dfrac{1}{6}$.

(*ii*) The vowels in the word CHANCE are *A* and *E*.

∴   Number of favourable outcomes = 2

Total number of possible outcomes = 6

∴ $P(a \text{ vowel}) = \dfrac{2}{6} = \dfrac{1}{3}$.

(iii) The consonants in the word CHANCE are C, H, N, C.

∴ Number of favourable outcomes = 4

Total number of possible outcomes = 6

∴ P(a consonant) $= \frac{4}{6} = \frac{2}{3}$.

(iv) The letters **except** E are C, H, A, N, C.

∴ Number of favourable outcomes = 5

Total number of possible outcomes = 6

∴ P(except E) $= \frac{5}{6}$.

Ex. 3. *A die is tossed once. What is the probability of the number "7" coming up? What is the probability of a number "less than 7" coming up?*

Sol. Since no face of the die is marked with the number 7,

$$P(\text{number '7'}) = \frac{0}{6} = 0 \qquad \boxed{\text{(The event is impossible)}}$$

Now, since the face of a die is marked with either of the numbers (1 to 6) so there are 6 favourable cases

∴ P(number less than 7) $= \frac{6}{6} = 1$ $\qquad \boxed{\text{(A sure event)}}$

Ex. 4. *A die is rolled. If the outcome is an odd number, what is the probability that it is a prime number?*

Sol. It is given that the outcome is an odd number which is a prime number.

The odd numbers are 1 or 3 or 5. Out of these 3 and 5 are prime numbers.

∴ Number of favourable cases = 2

Total number of possible cases = 6

∴ Probability of getting an odd number which is a prime number $= \frac{2}{6} = \frac{1}{3}$.

Ex. 5. *A card is drawn from a pack of 100 cards numbered 1 to 100. Find the probability of drawing a number which is a square.*

Sol. Out of the numbers 1 to 100, square numbers are
1, 4, 9, 16, 25, 36, 49, 64, 81, 100.

Thus there are 10 square numbers.

Total number of possible events = 100

The number of favourable events = 10

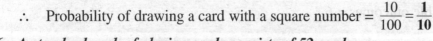

∴ Probability of drawing a card with a square number $= \frac{10}{100} = \frac{1}{10}$.

Ex. 6. *A standard pack of playing cards consists of 52 cards.*

   (i) *How many red cards are there? Find the probability of drawing a red card from the well-shuffled pack of cards?*

   (ii) *How many hearts are there? Find the probability of drawing a heart.*

  (iii) *What is the probability of drawing a queen?*

  (iv) *What is the probability of drawing a black jack?*

Sol. Total number of possible outcomes = 52 (as there are 52 cards)

(i) Number of red cards = 26

Number of favourable outcomes = 26

Total number of possible outcomes = 52

$$P(\text{red card}) = \frac{26}{52} = \frac{1}{2}.$$

(ii) Number of hearts = 13

∴ Number of favourable outcomes = 13

Total number of possible outcomes = 52

$$P(\text{a heart}) = \frac{13}{52} = \frac{1}{4}.$$

(iii) Number of favourable outcomes = 4   (∵ there are 4 queens)

Total number of possible outcomes = 52

$$\therefore \quad P(\text{a queen}) = \frac{4}{52} = \frac{1}{13}.$$

(iv) There are two black Jacks (One club + one spade)

Number of favourable outcomes = 2

Total number of possible outcomes = 52

$$\therefore \quad P(\text{black Jack}) = \frac{2}{52} = \frac{1}{26}.$$

EXERCISE 21

1. A die is rolled once. What is the probability of rolling :

(a) 3   (b) 7

(c) an even number   (d) a prime number ?

2. Ramesh chooses a date at random in April for a party. Calculate the probability that he chooses

(a) a Saturday

(b) a Sunday

(c) a Saturday or a Sunday

3. A normal die is rolled. Calculate the probability that the number on the uppermost face when it stops rolling will be

(a) 5   (b) not 5   (c) an odd number

(d) a prime number   (e) a 3 or a 4   (f) a 1 or a 2 or a 3 or a 4.

(g) an even prime number

4. A card is chosen at random from an ordinary deck of playing cards. What is the probability that

(a) a diamond is chosen ?

(b) a queen is chosen ?

(c) a black 4 is chosen ?

(d) a 7 of hearts is chosen ?

5. Nine playing cards are numbered 2 to 10. A card is selected from them at random. Calculate the probability that the card will be :

(a) an odd number   (b) a multiple of 4.

6. This spinner is spun. What is the probability of getting

(a) a 1?

(b) not a 1?

(c) an odd number?

(d) not an odd number?

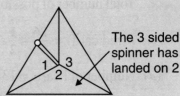

The 3 sided spinner has landed on 2

7. In a game at a fete a pointer is spun. You win the amount of money written in the sector where the pointer stops. Each sector is equally likely. Work out the probability that you win :

(a) no money

(b) Rs 2

(c) Rs 6

(d) Rs 10

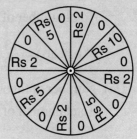

8. A spinner is made from a regular octagon. It is labelled with three *As*, two *Bs* and three *Cs*. Each of the sides is equally likely to be resting on the table when it stops spinning. Calculate :

(a) P(A resting on the table)

(b) P(B resting on the table)

(c) P(not C resting on the table)

9. A pair of die is thrown. Find the probability of getting a sum of 10 or more, if 5 appears an the first die.

(**Hint :** Favourable cases are (5, 5) and (5, 6)

10. A spinner is marked with numbers from 1 to 10. What is the probability of :

(a) getting an odd number?

(b) getting a prime number?

(c) not getting a multiple of 2?

11. In a scrabble game, there are small tiles with letters on them that are used to form words. The adjoining table shows the number of tiles for each letter. **What is the probability of selecting :**

(a) *O* from the full set?

(b) Consonant from the full set?

(c) *A, M* or *J* from the full set?

(d) Vowel from the full set?

Letter Distribution		
A–9	J–1	S–4
B–2	K–1	T–6
C–2	L–4	U–4
D–4	M–2	V–2
E–12	N–6	W–2
F–2	O–8	X–1
G–3	P–2	Y–2
H–2	Q–1	Z–1
I–9	R–6	Blank–2

12. A survey of 500 families shows the following results :

Number of girls in the family	1	2	3	0
Number of families	400	50	5	45

Out of these, one is chosen at random. Find the probability that the chosen family has 2 girls.

21.3 Estimating Probability by Experiments

Experimental Probability is found by collecting a large set of results by performing an experiment again and again.

Ananya tossed a coin 10 times and found that out of the 10 trials, she got a head in 3 outcomes only. This shows that :

$$\text{Probability of tossing a head} = \frac{\text{Number of favourable outcomes}}{\text{Number of trials}} = \frac{3}{10}$$

She repeated this experiment of 10 trials again and the probability of tossing a head came out to be $\frac{7}{10}$.

The probability thus calculated is the **experimental probability**. It is calculated by dividing the number of times the event occurs by the total number of trials.

We know that the probability of tossing a head when a coin is tossed $= \frac{1}{2}$ or in this case $\frac{5}{10}$. This is called **theoretical probability** which is found by saying that all the events are equally likely.

Comparing the probability calculated by experiment and the theoretical probability, we see that there is a big difference between them.

The number of trials in the experiment were increased to 1000 times and Ananya found that she got 515 heads and 485 tails this time. This, as you can see, is much closer to the theoretical probability which in this case would be $\frac{500}{1000}$. If we repeat this many times, the average number of heads (or tails) would be close to 500.

Thus we can see that the accuracy in calculating probability increases if there is increase in the number of trials.

Activity 1

(a) Toss a coin 40 times and record the results in a table, using tally marks.

(b) Calculate the experimental probabilities for your experiment.

(c) What is the theoretical probability of getting a head on a single toss?

(d) How many of your 40 trials give you heads as a result?

(e) Were your experimental probabilities close to the theoretical probabilities?

(f) Increase the number of trials to 60 and see what the change is.

Outcomes	Heads	Tails
Tally Marks		
Total		

Activity 2

Spin a spinner with six colours 100 times. Tally the colours that appear on the table below :

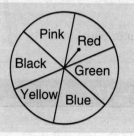

Colour	Tally	Total
Red		
Green		
Blue		
Yellow		
Black		
Pink		

(*a*) Calculate the experimental probability for each colour in your experiment by using

$$P(E) = \frac{\text{Number of favourable outcomes}}{\text{Number of trials}}$$

(*b*) What is the theoretical probability of getting any one of the given colours?

(*c*) How many of your 100 trials get you blue?

(*d*) Compare your experimental probabilities with the theoretical probabilities.

Activity 3

Form a group of 5 friends and each of you roll a die 40 times. Tally the numbers that appear on the tables, as is given below :

Number	Tally	Total
1		
2		
3		
4		
5		
6		

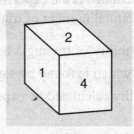

Now add up the frequencies of getting each number for the 200 trials (40 × 5).

(*a*) Calculate the experimental probability for each number.

(*b*) What is the theoretical probability for each number?

(*c*) For the number 4, calculate the experimental probability in case of (*i*) your 40 trials, (*ii*) 200 trials.

Which is much closer to the theoretical probability?

From the above experiments we can infer that,

> The more the number of trials are in a probability experiment, the closer the experimental probability would agree with the theoretical probability.

LOOKING BACK
Summary of Key Facts

1. Probability is a way of describing the chance of an event happening.

2. Probability of the occurrence of an event E : $P(E) = \dfrac{\text{Number of favourable outcomes}}{\text{Total number of possible outcomes}}$

3. The probabilities of all possible outcomes of an event add up to 1.

4. $P(\text{event not happening}) = 1 - P(\text{event happening})$.

5. All probabilities must have a value greater than or equal to 0 and less than or equal to 1.

MULTIPLE CHOICE QUESTIONS – 17

1. Flying to moon in a jet plane _____ event.

   (*i*) almost an impossible   (*ii*) not likely   (*iii*) likely   (*iv*) certain

2. If a dice is rolled once, the probability of rolling a 4 is :

(i) $\frac{1}{2}$ (ii) $\frac{1}{6}$ (iii) $\frac{1}{3}$ (iv) $\frac{1}{4}$

3. A bag contains 4 red marbles, 7 blue marbles and 4 blue marbles. The probabilities of selecting a red marble is :

(i) $\frac{4}{11}$ (ii) $\frac{4}{15}$ (iii) $\frac{7}{15}$ (iv) $\frac{7}{11}$

4. Out of 17 boys and 13 girls of a class, one student is to be selected. The probability of selecting a girl is :

(i) $\frac{17}{30}$ (ii) $\frac{13}{30}$ (iii) $\frac{15}{30}$ (iv) $\frac{13}{17}$

5. Six cards with numbers 10, 9, 8, 7, 6 and 5 are randomly placed face-down on a table. Ankita removed two cards– 8 and 10. The probability that the next one turned up is 9 is :

(i) $\frac{1}{6}$ (ii) $\frac{1}{2}$ (iii) $\frac{1}{4}$ (iv) $\frac{2}{9}$

6. In a game of chance the probability of winning is $\frac{1}{3}$. What is the probability of losing?

(i) 1 (ii) 0 (iii) $\frac{3}{4}$ (iv) $\frac{2}{3}$

7. From a standard pack of 52 playing cards, a card is selected at random. The probability that it is a black king is :

(i) $\frac{1}{13}$ (ii) $\frac{1}{26}$ (iii) $\frac{1}{2}$ (iv) $\frac{3}{4}$

ANSWERS

EXERCISE 21

1. (a) $\frac{1}{6}$ (b) $\frac{0}{6} = 0$ (c) $\frac{3}{6}$, *i.e.*, $\frac{1}{2}$ (d) $\frac{1}{2}$ 2. (a) $\frac{4}{30} = \frac{2}{15}$ (b) $\frac{4}{30} = \frac{2}{15}$ (c) $\frac{8}{30} = \frac{4}{15}$

3. (a) $\frac{1}{6}$ (b) $\frac{5}{6}$ (c) $\frac{3}{6} = \frac{1}{2}$ (d) $\frac{3}{6} = \frac{1}{2}$ (e) $\frac{2}{6} = \frac{1}{3}$ (f) $\frac{4}{6} = \frac{2}{3}$ (g) $\frac{1}{6}$

4. (a) $\frac{13}{52} = \frac{1}{4}$ (b) $\frac{4}{52} = \frac{1}{13}$ (c) $\frac{2}{52} = \frac{1}{26}$ (d) $\frac{1}{52}$ 5. (a) $\frac{4}{9}$ (b) $\frac{2}{9}$

6. (a) $\frac{1}{3}$ (b) $\frac{2}{3}$ (c) $\frac{2}{3}$ (d) $\frac{1}{3}$ 7. (a) $\frac{8}{16} = \frac{1}{2}$ (b) $\frac{4}{16} = \frac{1}{4}$ (c) 0 (d) $\frac{1}{16}$

8. (a) $\frac{3}{8}$ (b) $\frac{2}{8} = \frac{1}{4}$ (c) $\frac{5}{8}$ 9. $\frac{2}{36}$ or $\frac{1}{18}$ 10. (a) $\frac{5}{10} = \frac{1}{2}$ (b) $\frac{4}{10} = \frac{2}{5}$ (c) $\frac{5}{10} = \frac{1}{2}$

11. (a) $\frac{8}{100} = \frac{2}{25}$ (b) $\frac{56}{100} = \frac{28}{50}$ (c) $\frac{12}{100} = \frac{3}{25}$ (d) $\frac{42}{100} = \frac{21}{50}$ 12. $\frac{50}{100} = \frac{1}{2}$

MULTIPLE CHOICE QUESTIONS – 17

1. (i) 2. (ii) 3. (iii) 4. (ii) 5. (iii) 6. (iv) 7. (i)

22. Graphs

22.1 Introduction

Visualise the diagram at the right as that of a class room. The picture shows desks lined up in 5 rows, with 7 desks in a row. The teacher asked the students in row number 3 to stand . All the seven students sitting in that row would stand up but if the teacher wants only a particular boy to stand up, then he can say let the boy in the 3rd row and seat 4 stand up. Then only Ankur sitting over there will stand up.

Ankur's location can be given by the number (3, 4). Similarly, the positions of all the seats in the classroom can be indicated by assigning each location a pair of numbers. Thus the position of seat marked F will be indicated by the number (2, 1). Note that the number (1, 2) will not indicate F. It will indicate the desk at P. Thus the order in which the numbers are written is important. Such pairs are called *ordered pairs.*

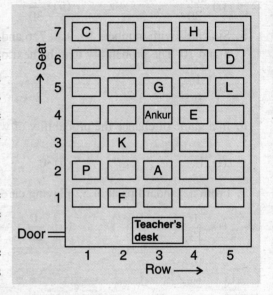

> **Ordered pair of numbers is needed to locate each student.**

EXERCISE 22 (a)

Oral

1. **Which labelled desk is named by**
   (*a*) row 3, seat 2?   (*b*) row 2, seat 3?   (*c*) row 1, seat 7?   (*d*) row 5, seat 6?
2. **Give the row number and seat for**   :   (*a*) E   (*b*) F   (*c*) G   (*d*) H   (*e*) L.
3. **Which desk matches :** (1, 7)? (5, 5)? (2, 1)? (3, 5)? (4, 7)? (5, 6)?

22.2 Coordinate Axes

The example of the classroom suggests a way of fixing the position of a point in a plane using two number lines.

It is done by selecting the *axes of reference* which are formed by combining the two number scales at right angles to each other so that their zero points coincide. The horizontal number scale is called the **x-axis** and the vertical

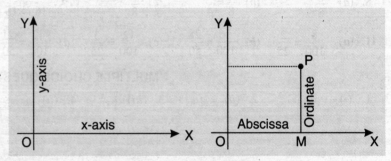

number scale the **y-axis.** The point where the two scales cross each other is called the **origin.** The two together are called the *rectangular axes* (so called because they are at right angles to each other.)

284

22.3 Coordinates-Definition and Notation

The position of each point of the planes is determined with reference to the rectangular axes by means of a pair of numbers called *coordinates* which are the distances of the point from the axes. The distance *OM* of the point *P* from the *y-axis* is called *x-coordinate* or **abscissa** and the distance *PM* of the point *P* from the *x-* axis is called the *y-coordinate* or ***ordinate***.

> **Note 1 :** In stating the coordinates of a point, the abscissa precedes the ordinate. The two are separated by a comma and enclosed in a bracket. Thus a point whose abscissa is *x* and whose ordinate is *y* is designated by the notation (*x, y*).

> **Note 2 :** The coordinates of the origin obviously are (0, 0). The coordinates of any point on the *x-axis* would be (*x*, 0) and the coordinates of any point on the *y-axis* would be (*0, y*).

22.4 Convention of Signs

1. For distances along the *x-axis,* positive values are measured to the right of the origin and negative values to its left.

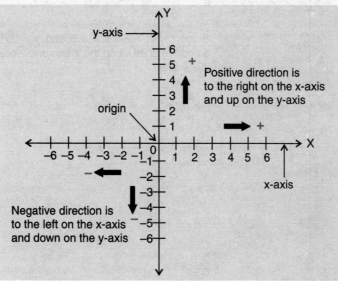

2. For distances along the *y-axis*, positive values are measured upward and negative values downward from the origin.

22.5 Quadrants

The coordinate axes separate the plane into four regions, called *quadrants*. By custom, the quadrants are numbered I, II, III and IV in the counter-clockwise direction as shown in the figure given below.

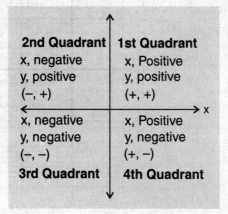

22.6 Points on the Axes

(a) *Any point on the x-axis*

The ordinate of every point on *x*-axis is zero. So the coordinates of any point on the *x*-axis are of the form $(x, 0)$

For example : Each of the points $(3, 0)$, $(-4, 0)$, $(7, 0)$, $(-8, 0)$ lies on the *x*-axis

(b) *Any point on the y-axis*

The abscissa of every point on *y*-axis is zero so the coordinates of any point on the *y*-axis are of the form $(0, y)$

For example : Each of the points $(0, 2)$, $(0, 6)$, $(0, -1)$, $(0, -4)$ lies on the *y*-axis

Ex. 1. *Graph (2, 5) and (5, 2).*

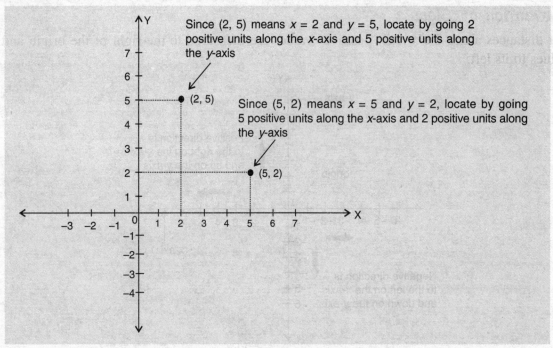

Since (2, 5) means x = 2 and y = 5, locate by going 2 positive units along the x-axis and 5 positive units along the y-axis

Since (5, 2) means x = 5 and y = 2, locate by going 5 positive units along the x-axis and 2 positive units along the y-axis

Ex. 2. *What are the coordinates of each point shown in the graph ?*

Sol.

Point	Coordinates	Point	Coordinates
A	(4, 3)	J	(2, –2)
B	(–4, 3)	K	$\left(-2\frac{1}{2}, -1\frac{1}{2}\right)$
C	(–4, –3)	M	(0, –4)
D	(4, –3)	O	(0, 0)
E	(4, 0)	P	(2, 0)
F	(–4, 0)	Q	(–1,0)
G	(0, 3)	R	(0, 4)
H	(0, –3)		

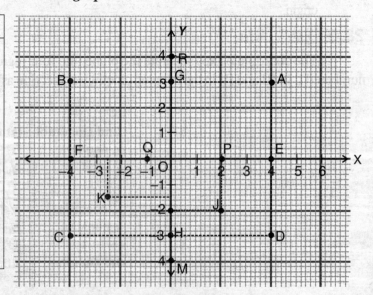

Scale : 1 unit = 5 small squares

Ex. 3. *State the quadrants in which the following points lie.*

    (i) *A (3, 5)*   **(ii)** *B(– 4, –7),*   **(iii)** *C (5, –1),*   **(iv)** *D (–6, 8)*

Sol.   *(i)* Since both *x* and *y* are positive (+, +), the point *A* lies in the first quadrant.

     (ii) Since both *x* and *y* are negative (–, –) , the point *B* lies in the third quadrant .

    (iii) Since *x* is positive and *y* negative (+, –), the point *C* lies in the fourth quadrant.

    (iv) Since *x* is negative and *y* positive (–, +), the point *D* lies in the second quadrant.

EXERCISE 22 (b)

1. Plot the following points using the same pair of axes and the same scale for each one.

(i) (0, 18)	*(ii)* (2, 9)	*(iii)* (5, 8)	*(iv)* (7, 0)	*(v)* (5, – 8)
(vi) (10, – 16)	*(vii)* (8, – 14)	*(viii)* (3, – 11)	*(ix)* (– 5, 6)	*(x)* (– 15, 4)
(xi) (– 20, 8)	*(xii)* (–9, 5)	*(xiii)* (–5, 8)	*(xiv)* (0, 7)	*(xv)* (– 8, – 15)
(xvi) (– 12, – 7)	*(xvii)* (– 10,– 11)	*(xviii)* (– 8, 0)	*(xix)* (– 4, 15)	*(xx)* (7, – 6)

2. Given the following ordered pairs of numbers, write the number of the quadrant in which you find the point represented by each of these ordered pairs.

	Ordered Pair	*Quadrant*		*Ordered Pair*	*Quadrant*
(a)	(2, 4)	_____	*(b)*	(3,– 5)	_____
(c)	(– 1, 6)	_____	*(d)*	(– 4, – 4)	_____
(e)	(7, – 2)	_____	*(f)*	(– 5, – 3)	_____
(g)	(6, 1)	_____	*(h)*	(– 3, 5)	_____

3. Look at the map of the Zoo. What can be found at :

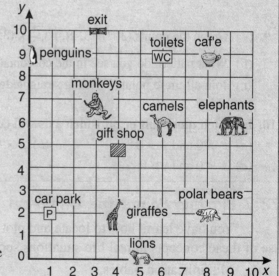

  (a) (8, 2)

  (b) (5, 0)

  (c) (8, 9)

  (d) (4, 5)

  (e) (4, 2)

  (f) (1, 2) ?

4. What are the coordinates of :

  (a) the exit   *(b)* the camels

  (c) the elephants   *(d)* the monkeys

  (e) the penguins ?

5. A new enclosure is placed half-way between the giraffes and the polar bears. What are the coordinates of the new enclosure ?

6. In which quadrant does the point lie if

  (a) both numbers of the ordered pair are positive?

  (b) both numbers of the ordered pair are negative?

  (c) the *x*-coordinate of an ordered pair is negative and the *y*-coordinate is positive?

  (d) the *x*-coordinate of an ordered pair is positive and the *y*-coordinate is negative?

7. *(a)* Plot the points (– 5, 4), (– 8, 4), (– 2.5, 4), (0, 4), (3.5, 4), (6, 4).

  (b) What do you observe about the ordinates of all six points ?

  (c) Join all these points by using straightedge. What do you observe ? The line so obtained is parallel to which axis ?

8. The radar screen shows aircraft positions. Write down the coordinates of the aircraft in various positions *A*, *B*, *C*, *D*, *E*, *F* and *G*.

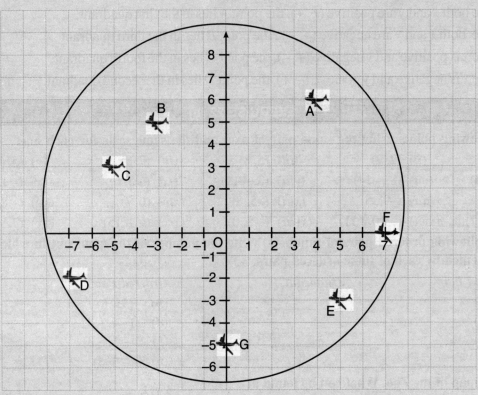

9. (*a*) Graph the points (3, 7), (3, 2), $\left(3, \frac{1}{2}\right)$, (3, 0), (3, – 2), (3, – 8).

   (*b*) What pattern do you see in the coordinates of these six points ?

   (*c*) Join all these points by using straightedge. What do you observe ? The line so obtained is parallel to which axis ?

10. **In which quadrant or on which axis will (*x*, *y*) be graphed if :**

   (*a*) *x* > 0 and *y* > 0 ?   (*b*) *x* < 0 and *y* < 0 ?   (*c*) *x* > 0 and *y* < 0 ?

   (*d*) *x* < 0 and *y* > 0 ?

22.7 Plotting Points for Different Kind of Situations

You have learnt how to locate and plot a point in the Cartesian plane. Now you will learn how to make use of these concepts in real life situations such as :

   1. Multiplication Tables   2. Perimeter of a square vs side of the square

   3. Area of the square vs side of the square   4. Simple interest accrued vs number of years etc.

I. Multiplication Table of 6

The general relation representing the table is *y* = 6*x*, where *y* represents the product and *x* takes up the values as 1, 2, 3, 4 etc. The table of values given below gives the corresponding values of *y*, for different values of *x*.

x	2	3	6	8
y	12	18	36	48